COAL MINING GEOLOGY

The Science of Geology is not, however, recommended only by the sublimity of the facts which it brings under our observation, but it is of the greatest utility to mankind in a civilized state; affording him the means of more readily procuring many of those substances, without which polished society could not exist.

Westgarth Forster,
1821

COAL MINING GEOLOGY

IAIN A. WILLIAMSON

Senior Lecturer in Geology
Wigan and District Mining and Technical College

London OXFORD UNIVERSITY PRESS

NEW YORK · TORONTO

1967

Oxford University Press, Ely House, London W.1

GLASGOW NEW YORK TORONTO MELBOURNE WELLINGTON
CAPE TOWN SALISBURY IBADAN NAIROBI LUSAKA ADDIS ABABA
BOMBAY CALCUTTA MADRAS KARACHI LAHORE DACCA
KUALA LUMPUR HONG KONG

PRINTED IN GREAT BRITAIN BY
HAZELL WATSON AND VINEY LTD
AYLESBURY, BUCKS

CONTENTS

Part Two: Advanced Aspects

PREFACE

In this book I have attempted to provide a review of those aspects of geology of practical importance and interest to those engaged in the coal mining industry. The book is primarily planned for the requirements of students reading for degrees and diplomas in mining engineering and mining surveying. However, it is also hoped that practising members of the mining fraternity, together with the more specialized geology student, will also find some appeal in this aspect of applied geology.

A textbook of this sort is only one of the aids available to the student. It is important that whenever possible he should consult the primary information sources in the form of specialist books and periodicals. With this in mind, I have included often fairly lengthy reference lists at the end of each chapter. In some cases only the latest reference to a particular aspect has been given, in which case the publication referred to itself contains a worthwhile bibliography listing earlier literature on the subject.

Finally, it is hoped that the book will appeal not only to British students, but also to a wider range of readers in other English-speaking countries. In this respect care has been taken to internationalize the text and to include examples of geological phenomena from a variety of different countries.

Wigan, Lancashire   I. A. W.
February 1966

LIST OF PLATES

ACKNOWLEDGEMENTS

In the compilation of material for this book numerous geologists, mining engineers and mining surveyors have been approached for information which has been readily supplied in the form of personal communications and offprints of many of the papers referred to in the text. Furthermore, others have engaged in often lengthy and, perhaps to them, tedious personal discussions concerning certain parts of the book. In all these respects the author is especially grateful to the following: D. ANDERSON, A. ARCHER, S. A. BILLINGHURST, MAVIS A. BUTTERWORTH, M. A. CALVER, J. CHALARD, A. M. CLARKE, M. P. COLEMAN, R. M. C. EAGAR, J. R. EARP, R. E. ELLIOTT, D. H. PARKER, R. H. PRICE, S. N. SARKAR, A. H. V. SMITH and T. J. WILLIAMS.

Again, the writing of a textbook of this type is only possible with the aid of an efficient library service. In this respect the library staff, notably K. B. SWALLOW and JANE WILLIAMS, of the Wigan Mining College have considerably eased the burden upon the author's shoulders.

The many fossil illustrations of Chapters 12, 14 and 15 have been admirably executed by KEITH PERCIVAL, to whom grateful thanks are due.

Many national and industrial organizations have generously contributed information unobtainable elsewhere. Of these the writer records his especial thanks to the Bord na Mòna, British Coal Utilisation Research Association, Department of Scientific and Industrial Research of New Zealand, Indian Standards Institution, National Coal Board, State Electricity Commission of Victoria and the U.S. Bureau of Mines.

For permission to use copyright material in the form of tables, photographic plates and line diagrams, the author is under obligation to the following: Aerofilms Limited (Plate 9), American Society for Testing Materials (Table 49), British Coal Utilisation Research Association (Fig. 19.9), British Standards Institution (Fig. 18.5), Commonwealth Trans-Antarctic Expedition (Plate 2b), The Controller of H.M. Stationary Office (Plates 4b, 11c & 13), Council of the Institution of Mining Engineers (Tables 10 & 11, Figs 17.11 & 19.1), Council of the Leeds Geological Association (Figs 8.33 & 10.2), Councils of the Manchester Geological Association and Liverpool Geological Society (Fig. 14.11). The Director of the Geological Survey of Canada (Figs 17.1 & 17.2), The Director of the Geological Survey of Nigeria (Fig. 16.2), Department of Scientific and Industrial Research of New Zealand (Fig. 19.5), International Committee for Coal Petrology and the Centre National de la Recherche Scientifique (Plate 10), National Coal Board (Tables 43 & 50, Figs 19.6 & 19.7), Society of Economic Palaeontologists and Mineralogists (Plates 15b & 15c), Vickers Instruments Ltd (Plate 1).

Lastly, but certainly not least of all, I place on record the constant help and encouragement of my wife PATRICIA who, besides assisting in the preparation of the typescript, has for several years borne with great understanding and tolerance my obsession with mining geology.

I. A. W.

Part One
Elementary Aspects

1

GEOLOGY, THE STUDY OF THE EARTH

INTRODUCTION

Geology is a modern science which was commenced as a serious study only in the late eighteenth century by a number of European scientists. Previously, various scholars, from the Greek philosophers of classical time, had correctly interpreted the occasional geological problem, but there was no concerted study and the work was little heeded, if indeed known at all by others. Leonardo da Vinci, famous for his portrait of Mona Lisa, would, if denied his artistic achievements, still have universal acclaim as one of the foremost late fifteenth century natural scientists. His notebooks contain much of geological importance, and he had for instance correctly interpreted the significance of marine fossil shells in the hills around Parma and Verona as evidence of the former existence of a sea in that area (Stebbing, 1943, pp. 49–52). For over another 200 years, however, similar remains were still to be treated as 'sports', curiosities, or the work of the Devil who placed such material in unlikely places 'to delude and deceive mankind'!

Miners, by nature of their occupation, have always been keenly aware of geological problems, though until the beginning of the present century their solution of such problems has been largely an unconscious utilization of the geological method. Nevertheless a few historic works survive in which geology is considered as a vital adjunct to mining. Foremost of these early writers was George Bauer, writing in the mid-sixteenth century under the pseudonym of Agricola, whose researches in mining and geology culminated in 1556 in the publication of *De Re Metallica*. Concerned with metal mining, Agricola's work was to serve as the major source of information to the early mining engineer. Over a century later, in 1672, George Sinclar, a Scottish physicist, proved the essential synclinal structure of the Midlothian Coalfield and was clearly familiar with *dip*, *strike*, *dykes* and other terms still in everyday geological use (Briggs, 1925). Other similar pioneers observed and theorized at about this time but were in the nature of lone voices crying out in the wilderness.

It was in the late eighteenth century that geo-logical research was stimulated by the first sparks of the industrial revolution. The outstanding workers were Abraham Gottlob Werner at the Freiberg Mining College in Germany and James Hutton in Edinburgh. Werner, a gifted teacher, explained all rocks and minerals as the deposits of a once universal ocean, and hence he and his many followers were soon branded as 'Neptunists'. Hutton led an opposite school, the 'Plutonists', who attributed the igneous rocks to subterranean effusions of molten or semi-molten rock. He also correctly interpreted the geological record as being 'a succession of events in which we see neither the beginning nor the end'. As is often characteristic of the development of a science, there was fierce argument between the two schools of thought but, as with many an early scientific controversy, the differences of opinion led to further researches and so commenced the long chain of geological observation and reasoning which leads us to the present (Moore, 1957). Though preceded by several Continental workers, the self-taught land surveyor and civil engineer, William (Strata) Smith (Sheppard, 1917; Cox, 1942) is famous for the preparation of one of the earliest geological maps. Published in 1815, Smith's map of England and Wales, on the scale of 5 miles to 1 in, correctly shows the positions of most of the major groups of strata and indicates an acute perception of fundamental knowledge. By this time the science had become firmly established.

A warning

It will soon, if it has not already, become apparent to the reader that geology, like any specialized subject, has its own technical language. Many students are often at first antagonized by being suddenly confronted with a totally unfamiliar mass of strange-sounding, often long and seemingly unpronounceable words. The mine manager who once remarked, 'I don't care if you call it *Carbonicola os-lancis*, what I know is that when we find them oval b . . . . . s in the roof then the seam's the Trencherbone', is still with us today.

If geology is to be fully utilized in mining, with consequent benefit to the industry, there is a need for a precise definition and understanding of geological terminology. Otherwise geological publications and reports would consist of an endless succession of definitive sentences and one would become bogged down in a swamp of description. For instance, a dislocation or fault penetrated by a cross-measures drivage may be described as 'hading 30 degrees south' or alternatively as being 'inclined 30 degrees from the vertical in a southerly direction'. Furthermore, the use of standard geological terms is to be preferred to the often local and inexact nomenclature to be seen on many old shaft sections and unfortunately still used at the present day. The terms 'blaes', 'bass' and 'bind' may be understood by the Fife, Lancashire and Staffordshire miners respectively, but the newcomer to the area may rightly be excused for not knowing that all three names are applied to the rock geologically defined as shale.

So the reader has been warned: geological terminology *is* complicated; there is no short cut to its mastery. However, it is the writer's belief that geology will prove an interesting study and therefore the work involved will not appear onerous. Let us hope he is right!

THE SCOPE OF GEOLOGY

Geology may itself be simply defined as the science of the Earth: it strives to obtain the answers to questions as to the composition, history and development of matter on the planet. A simple way to understand its implications is to consider its major branches (Table 1).

Mineralogy

Obviously mineralogy is the study of minerals. But what is a mineral? A mineral is a naturally occurring solid chemical compound or element. Thus, pyrite, a combination of iron and sulphur (FeS_2) is often found in coal as a brassy-yellow deposit. Another mineral sometimes found in coal is anker-

ite, that white or yellowish 'spar' deposited along the cleat of certain seams. Three major mineral groups may be distinguished, rock-forming, ore and gangue minerals. The former are chiefly found as constituents of rocks. Ores are of economic value, such as galena, the principal source of lead, and generally occur in association with minerals of lesser value commonly called gangue minerals.

Petrology

Petrology is concerned with the examination, occurrence and origin of rocks. A rock is predominantly composed of crystals and fragments of minerals and/or pre-existing rocks. An immense number of rock varieties occur in nature but each major type can be accurately defined on the basis of its constituents and structure.

Rocks may be classified into three principal groups as determined by their mode of origin: *igneous*, *sedimentary* and *metamorphic*. The former originate by crystallization from a previously molten or semi-molten fluid having a source deep in the Earth's crust or, in certain cases, in a sub-crustal zone. The most obvious group is the *extrusive rocks* which flow from volcanic fissures and vents over parts of the Earth's surface. The heat loss from these rocks is relatively rapid so they are characterized by a fine-grained texture. Though no such rocks are now being erupted in Britain, in the geological past many areas, such as the Inner Hebrides, the English Lake District and Snowdonia, were the sites of active volcanoes. It is these hard volcanic rocks which have resisted erosion and so now form some of the more rugged and mountainous scenery of Britain. Other igneous rocks are intruded into the Earth's crust without reaching the surface. Such intrusions are of many forms and variable size. Since the *intrusive rocks* cool more slowly than the volcanic lavas, being protected by a blanket of overlying rocks, their constituent minerals crystallize more slowly and hence form large crystals.

TABLE 1

The Major Divisions of Geology

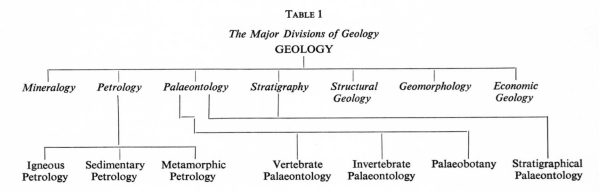

GEOLOGY						
Mineralogy	*Petrology*	*Palaeontology*	*Stratigraphy*	*Structural Geology*	*Geomorphology*	*Economic Geology*
	Igneous Petrology	Sedimentary Petrology	Metamorphic Petrology	Vertebrate Palaeontology	Invertebrate Palaeontology	Palaeobotany	Stratigraphical Palaeontology

Sedimentary rocks are the commonest of all types and occur as a thick mantle over large parts of the Earth's crust. Principally they result from the accumulation of sediment in ancient seas, lakes and deserts. They may contain fragments of pre-existing rocks and minerals derived by the erosion of a former land mass. Alternatively, they may accumulate as chemical precipitates and organic material. As distinct from most forms of igneous and metamorphic rocks they are frequently bedded or layered and, excepting the oldest sediments, may contain fossil remains. The bulk of the rocks associated with coal deposits are of this type.

Metamorphic rocks are altered sedimentary or igneous material. The alteration or metamorphism is caused by the action of heat or pressure or both, often at considerable depths in the Earth's crust. A simple example is the alteration of coal to a natural coke or cinder by the thermal effects of an adjacent igneous intrusion. In the extreme case of ultra-metamorphism, the rocks may become a liquid which, on cooling and solidification, forms an igneous rock. Thus we have the petrologic cycle (Fig. 1.1), an ever open field for geological discussion and argument! Truly 'we see neither the beginning nor the end.'

Palaeontology

In the roof of many coal seams there may be perfectly preserved impressions of plant leaves, the decay of which contributed to the formation of the coal. Above other seams 'mussels' may be found, the remains of a variety of shell fish which formerly lived in the Coal Measure swamps. Such remains and traces of past life are termed *fossils* and are considered in palaeontology. Naturally, such a vast field of inquiry, embracing the whole range of former life on our planet, is itself divided into specialized fields. Vertebrate palaeontology, concerning the study of backboned animals, is from a practical viewpoint of little use in mining geology but of great importance in evolutionary studies, for man himself is a vertebrate. Invertebrate palaeontology deals with more lowly animals which are nevertheless of extreme importance in the elucidation of stratigraphy. The fossil plants, so important in the formation of coal, are studied in palaeobotany.

Stratigraphy

Stratigraphy may be defined as the study of the structural history of the Earth. As historians divide

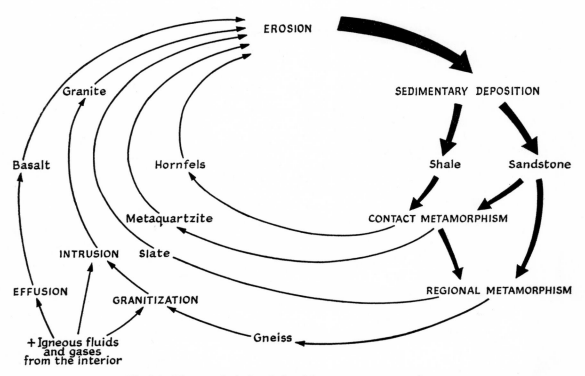

Fig. 1.1   The petrological cycle involving some common rock types.

recent time into periods named in Britain after the reigning monarch, so geologists separate much greater lengths of the Earth's history into a group of major units. The resulting succession is termed the stratigraphical or geological column (Table 2). A *period* is a length of time; the term *system* embraces the rocks of that period. Much greater divisions of time characterized by marked differences in life are termed *eras*. At first the names of the periods will appear unfamiliar and quite probably meaningless. Each name was chosen for a good reason; for instance, the Carboniferous System was so called after the coal deposits characteristic of the system in many parts of the world. Again, the Triassic System in continental Europe may easily be divided into three major units, and the succeeding Jurassic System is well exposed in the Jura mountains of France and Switzerland.

Apart from the Pre-Cambrian, in which fossils are extremely rare, each system is primarily defined by the nature of its fossils, so that *stratigraphical*

palaeontology is an important merger between the two subsciences. On the one hand, facts concerning the succession of life are of great importance in evolutionary studies and on the other furnish evidence which indicates the relative age of beds. Each system is characterized by a particular fossil assemblage and can be subdivided into a large number of minor units. Thus the spirally coiled shell of *Gastrioceras listeri* is a diagnostic Carboniferous fossil, and its discovery in a rock succession indicates that the horizon is of Upper Carboniferous age and, more particularly, is one of the lowest beds of the Coal Measures. The fossil ranges through only a few hundred feet of Carboniferous strata out of a maximum thickness of over 20000 ft for the whole system. Moreover, the predominance of *Gastrioceras listeri* in a fossiliferous roof can be used to correlate the underlying seam over many British coalfields, since the form occurs in abundance only in one thin band.

The discovery of radioactivity in the last years of

TABLE 2

Stratigraphical Column showing the Eras, Periods and Approximate Ages

Era	Period	Approximate dates in years
CAINOZOIC (Kainos = recent, Zoe = life)	Pleistocene	1 000 000
	Tertiary	
		70 000 000
MESOZOIC (Meso = middle)	Cretaceous	135 000 000
	Jurassic	180 000 000
	New Red Sandstone { Triassic	225 000 000
	Permian	270 000 000
	Carboniferous	350 000 000
PALAEOZOIC (Palaios = ancient)	Devonian or Old Red Sandstone	400 000 000
	Silurian	440 000 000
	Ordovician	500 000 000
	Cambrian	600 000 000
PRE-CAMBRIAN		Duration about 4 000 000 000

the nineteenth century led to a chain-reaction of important discoveries of consequence to many sciences. Geology has particularly benefited in the field of stratigraphy, for now we have a method for the absolute dating of systems, based on the decay rates of certain radioactive minerals. Radiogeology is of great importance in the study of sparsely fossiliferous or unfossiliferous groups such as the Pre-Cambrian, a vast assemblage of rocks representing at least 4000 million years of the Earth's history. In the near future we can expect this colossal group to be divided into many new periods based upon radiogeological datings.

Structural geology

The Earth is fundamentally a structure composed of three principal layers, an outer crust, thickest under the continents, a mantle and a deep-seated core. Structural geology concerns the study of these layers and, with regard to mining, more particularly the detailed structures of the crust. Because of differential pressures, the crustal rocks have in the geological past been tilted, folded and dislocated. Consequently, most coalfield areas, whilst consisting of stratified sedimentary rocks originally deposited as flat layers, are structurally complex. The seams are often inclined and may be dislocated or faulted. Where the strata have been so affected, an accurate prediction of their position underground is a primary requirement of the mining industry. Many mistakes involving expense in life and money have been made owing to a lack of knowledge of the detailed geological structure of a mining area.

Geomorphology

Geomorphology, or the 'study of scenery' is basically concerned with the origin and development of land forms arising from processes of erosion and deposition. Regarding economic considerations, the mining engineer is little concerned with the shapes of mountains, but his work may be affected by the materials eroded from such places. In lowland areas, where most major coalfields are situated, the consolidated rocks are often overlaid by a cover of *drift* or *superficial deposits* derived from recent erosion of the land surface. Since unconsolidated material is often waterlogged, special precautions against flooding and subsidence have to be taken in shallow mining beneath such deposits, and it is imperative that the mining engineer be acquainted with their characteristics.

Economic geology

Economic geology is concerned with all aspects of geological knowledge in the material improvement

of the world. It is therefore concerned with mineral resources, water supply, civil engineering, land utilization and even such matters as the choice of wartime landing beaches. Our present civilization is dependent on the applications of economic geology. Industry constantly needs raw materials from the earth, and civil engineering works require detailed site investigations of the geology; water consumption is rising, and therefore underground sources must be discovered. Such a list is seemingly endless.

Fundamentally economic geology is based on the preparation of the geological map or plan, upon which most geological information may be represented. The map should be the key to the economic geology of an area. It is therefore not surprising that there is frequently a correlation between a country's prosperity and the proportion of its area geologically surveyed.

PRACTICAL WORK

The study of geology is essentially practical and to understand fully the many aspects and applications of the science the student must come to grips with the raw materials on which all geological knowledge is founded. A balanced programme of practical work is of fundamental importance in any geological course and only through such studies will the subject become alive and interesting. In the solution of practical problems the student will benefit far more from practical studies than from any amount of book work. It is therefore hoped that practical studies will accompany the study of this book, for mere reading and thinking are insufficient.

Geological practical work is broadly of two types, laboratory and field studies. In the former, the examination of the common rocks, minerals and fossils will be recorded in laboratory notebooks. In this way the student will learn to observe often microscopic detail and, moreover, will understand the value of accurate description and reasoning. Associated with such work on the materials of geology, the student should also consider structural and stratigraphical map problems. He should work on underground structures as applied to mining and will certainly find that stratigraphy may most easily be learnt by an examination of published geological maps.

Most laboratory work is, however, only an aid to the science, whereas the fundamentals, the very roots of geology, are out in the field. In the open countryside the outcrops, the small undulations in the fields and other such subtle indications, reveal to the trained eye the many complexities of the general outcrop pattern ultimately shown on the geological map. Besides field work being such an aid to the under-

standing of map work, the study of a particular
system or feature in the field is the easiest aid to the
memory of the student. For field work, which may
be either underground or in more idyllic settings, gives
him the opportunity to see for himself at first hand
and not merely become acquainted through second-
hand knowledge.

Go out into the field, observe and collect. Back in
the laboratory identify and, in the study, theorize.
Then go back into the field and check. Good hammering!

REFERENCES

BRIGGS, H. (1925) Sinclar's treatise of coal-mining, 1672,
Trans. Instn Min. Engrs **69**, 132–42.

COX, L. R. (1942) New light on William Smith and his
work, *Proc. Yorks. geol. Soc.* **25**, 1–99.

MOORE, R. (1959) *The Earth We Live On*, London,
Readers Union Ed.

SHEPPARD, T. (1917) William Smith: his maps and
memoirs, *Proc. Yorks. geol. Soc.* **19**, 75–253.

STEBBING, W. P. D. (1943) Some early references to
geology from the sixteenth century onwards, *Proc.
geol. Ass.* **54**, 49–63.

2

MINERALOGY

DIAGNOSTIC PHYSICAL PROPERTIES OF MINERALS

The determination of the common minerals may be made with a series of simple tests based upon their physical properties. Rarer minerals and exceedingly small particles may require chemical analysis and even the application of X ray crystallography beyond the scope of the non-specialist. Fortunately most important minerals can be relatively easily identified. The chief properties aiding recognition are *colour, streak, lustre, diaphaneity, form, hardness, cleavage, fracture* and *specific gravity*.

Colour

The colour of a mineral is one of its most obvious characters. Unfortunately in many examples the colour is a non-diagnostic property. It may result from the chemical composition of the pure mineral, in which case the property is described as inherent and can be utilized in the mineral identification. Thus galena is lead-grey and pyrite brassy yellow. More commonly the colour of a mineral is exotic, that is due to impurities or minute alteration products of the original mineral. Pure quartz is colourless or transparent but most varieties have exotic coloration. For instance, the colour of amethystine quartz is attributed to the presence of minute amounts of manganese dioxide. Another common variety is milky quartz, which owes its whitish coloration to the light reflection from large numbers of small cracks or inclusions within the crystal. Even the same crystal may exhibit a variety of colours, as in Blue John, the local Derbyshire variety of fluorite; the coloration of which is now considered to be due to mineral hydrocarbon impurities.

Streak

When a mineral is crushed the resulting powder is often of a lighter or different colour than that of the solid specimen. The powder can also be obtained by scratching an edge of the mineral across a metal file or a piece of unglazed porcelain, termed a streak plate. The streak is a very useful property in mineral identification, particularly with respect to the dark-coloured minerals. For instance, galena and the darker varieties of sphalerite are sometimes confused by the student, though they may be easily distinguished by their respective grey and yellow streaks. The light-coloured minerals frequently have a whitish streak despite their sometimes exotic colours; thus the blue varieties of fluorite have a white streak.

Lustre

The lustre of a mineral is determined by its power of light reflection. Minerals of a similar colour may have different lustres. Descriptive terms are given, the more important of which are the following.

Metallic. Having a high degree of reflection on untarnished surfaces. Example, galena.

Vitreous. Having the lustre of glass. Example, quartz.

Resinous. Having the lustre of resin. Example, some varieties of sphalerite.

Pearly. Possessing a tendency to iridesce. Example, labradorite, a variety of plagioclase felspar.

Silky. Having a silky lustre, a property peculiar to fibrous minerals. Example, satin spar, a variety of gypsum.

Sometimes the lustre may be imperfect, which may be indicated by a prefix, e.g. sub-metallic, sub-vitreous.

Diaphaneity

Diaphaneity concerns the power of light transmission of a mineral. Regarding this property there are three mineral groups.

Transparent. Objects can be clearly discerned when viewed through the mineral.

Translucent. Light passes through the mineral. A property common to many minerals.

Opaque. No light is transmitted through the mineral.

Naturally the property is partly related to the thickness of the specimen, so where possible a small cleavage fragment should be used for identification. Certain minerals are opaque in the mass but translucent along the edges.

Form

Under certain conditions minerals may be crystallized, that is, they occur as crystals having a definite geometric arrangement of flat crystal faces. The simplest crystal is the cube, a form in which pyrite is often found. Depending on the size of the crystals a mineral may be either macrocrystalline or microcrystalline. Generally the crystals of a particular mineral have constant shapes, and therefore crystallography is an important adjunct to advanced mineralogy.

A mineral is *massive* if individual crystals cannot be recognized in the specimen. A large number of shapes or forms may be assumed by minerals which do not necessarily depend on the shape of the crystal. The following descriptive terms are used in this connexion.

Columnar. Appearing as a series of thin columns. Example, hornblende.

Fibrous. Formed of parallel elongated strands. Example, satin spar.

Foliaceous. Consisting of thin cleavable sheets. Example, muscovite.

Pyramidal. Having a tendency to develop pyramidal crystals. Example, quartz.

Radiating. Displaying a radial arrangement of needle-like crystals. Example, marcasite.

Reniform. Occurring as rounded, kidney-shaped masses. Example, hematite.

Tabular. Composed of a number of flat plates. Example, barite.

Hardness

Minerals vary individually in hardness; consequently this property is an important aid in their identification. The relative hardness of a mineral may be compared with a standard scale of minerals arranged in order of their hardness (Table 3). The hardness of a mineral is expressed numerically with reference to this scale: thus pyrite, hardness 6–6·5, signifies that this mineral will scratch apatite but will itself be scratched by quartz. In testing for hardness, certain precautions should be taken. A mineral softer than another may leave a powder on the harder one which may on a cursory examination appear to be scratched. The scratch should be made on an unweathered surface, as some minerals may be thinly coated with a soft alteration product. As most mineral collections can be replaced only with difficulty, care should be taken so that the specimen is not grossly disfigured.

Cleavage

If a mineral breaks readily along a smooth surface, it possesses cleavage. The cleavage surfaces have a definite orientation determined by the crystal structure. If the surfaces are closely spaced and shining, the mineral has *perfect cleavage*. Alternatively the cleavage may be *good*, *poor* or *absent*. Minerals may cleave in one or more directions. Thus muscovite, an outstanding example of perfect cleavage, will readily split in one direction. Galena, with perfect cleavage,

TABLE 3

Scale of Hardness

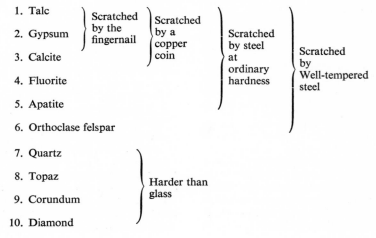

has three cleavage directions parallel to the original cubic faces.

Fracture

The surface obtained by breaking a mineral in a direction other than that of the cleavage displays fracture. The chief descriptive terms used are as follows.

Conchoidal. When the broken surface is curved as a fragment of glass. Example, quartz.

Splintery. If the surface is wood-like. Example, satin-spar.

Irregular. When the fracture surfaces are rough and uneven. Example, muscovite.

Specific gravity

The specific gravity of a mineral may be defined as its weight divided by the weight of an equal volume of water. An accurate determination may be made by the use of various instruments or solutions of known specific gravity. For most purposes it is sufficient to estimate the weight by handling the specimen. Naturally some practice is required but, after a little time, the approximate specific gravity of a mineral may be estimated in this way. In the practical examination of minerals their specific gravities may be classified as *average* (e.g. quartz, calcite), *high* (e.g. barite, pyrite) and *very high* (e.g. galena).

OCCURRENCE OF MINERALS

The more common minerals, particularly from a coal mining viewpoint, are described on the following pages. Since many of the minerals described are important constituents of igneous, sedimentary and metamorphic rocks, some of the terms used in this chapter with regard to their occurrence are only defined in Chapters 4, 5 and 6. The student should, whenever possible, examine actual specimens and make his own notes, based on his own observations. These may frequently differ, because of the presence of impurities, for instance, from the properties described below or recorded in a mineralogical textbook (Hurlbut, 1959; Hurlbut, 1963; Read, 1948).

Quartz

Composition: Silicon dioxide, SiO_2. *Crystal system:* Hexagonal. *Form:* commonly massive. *Colour:* colourless, when pure. *Lustre:* vitreous. *Diaphaneity:* transparent to opaque. *Hardness:* 7. *Fracture:* conchoidal. *Cleavage:* nil. *Specific gravity:* 2·65.

Occurrence: An important constituent of oversaturated igneous rocks. Common in many metamorphic rocks. Major component of sandstones. A common gangue mineral.

Uses: Glass manufacture, abrasives, ceramics, radio industry.

Varieties: Flint (massive, vitreous, conchoidal fracture. Occurs as beds or nodules in Mesozoic strata). Chert (massive, dull, sub-conchoidal or variable fracture. Occurs as beds or nodules in Palaeozoic strata). Amethyst (crystalline, purple). Cairngorm (crystalline, smoky-yellow). Milky quartz (milk-white colour, crystalline or massive).

Felspars

Of variable composition, the common felspars may be divided into two groups: orthoclase and plagioclase. The main varieties may be shown as a triangular diagram (Fig. 2.1). The plagioclase series

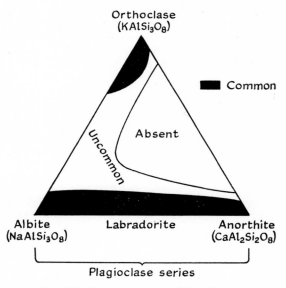

Fig. 2.1 The composition of the felspars.

shows a continuous gradation in chemical and physical properties. The individual members may be distinguished by microscopic tests.

Orthoclase

Composition: Potassium aluminium silicate, $KAlSi_3O_8$. *Crystal system:* monoclinic. *Form:* crystalline. *Colour:* often flesh-pink. *Lustre:* vitreous to pearly. *Diaphaneity:* translucent to opaque. *Hardness:* 6. *Fracture:* conchoidal to irregular. *Cleavage:* two sets at right angles. *Specific gravity:* 2·57.

Occurrence: A common constituent of oversaturated and saturated igneous rocks.

Uses: Ceramics, glass manufacture, abrasives.

Plagioclase

Composition: variable (see Fig. 2.1). *Crystal system:* triclinic. *Form:* crystalline, often tabular. *Colour:* often white, may be obscured by iridescent lustre. *Diaphaneity:* translucent to opaque. *Hardness:* 6–6·5. *Specific gravity:* 2·60 (albite)–2·76 (anorthite).

Occurrence: An important constituent in saturated igneous rocks.

Biotite ('Black' mica)

Composition: A complex silicate containing potassium, magnesium, iron and aluminium, $K(MgFe)_3(AlSi_3)O_{10}(OH,F)_2$. *Crystal system:* monoclinic. *Form:* crystalline, characteristically foliaceous. *Colour:* black, dark brown. *Lustre:* vitreous. *Diaphaneity:* transparent to opaque. *Hardness:* 2·5–3. *Fracture:* irregular. *Cleavage:* perfect in one direction, a diagnostic feature. *Specific gravity:* 2·7–3·1.

Occurrence: An important constituent of igneous and some metamorphic rocks.

Muscovite ('White' mica)

Composition: A complex silicate containing potassium and aluminium, $KAl_2(AlSi_3)O_{10}(OH,F)_2$. *Crystal system:* monoclinic. *Form:* crystalline, characteristically foliaceous. *Colour:* white. *Lustre:* pearly. *Diaphaneity:* transparent to translucent. *Hardness:* 2–2·5. *Fracture:* irregular. *Cleavage:* perfect in one direction, a diagnostic feature. *Specific gravity:* 2·76–3.

Occurrence: A common constituent of oversaturated igneous rocks and arenaceous sedimentary rocks.

Uses: Electrical insulators, heat-resisting windows.

Augite

Composition: A silicate containing variable amounts of calcium, iron, magnesium and aluminium. *Crystal system:* monoclinic. *Form:* commonly crystalline, prismatic. *Colour:* dark green to black. *Streak:* grey-green. *Lustre:* vitreous. *Diaphaneity:* opaque. *Hardness:* 5–6. *Fracture:* irregular. *Cleavage:* good, in two directions nearly at right angles, an important distinction from hornblende. *Specific gravity:* 3·2–3·5.

Occurrence: An important constituent of saturated and undersaturated igneous rocks. The commonest member of the *pyroxene* family of minerals.

Hornblende

Composition: A silicate containing variable amounts of calcium, magnesium, iron, aluminium, sodium and hydroxyl. *Crystal system:* monoclinic. *Form:* commonly crystalline, prismatic, columnar. *Colour:* dark green to black. *Streak:* grey-green.

Lustre: vitreous. *Diaphaneity:* commonly opaque. *Hardness:* 5–6. *Fracture:* irregular. *Cleavage:* good, in two directions meeting at angles of 125 degrees and 55 degrees. *Specific gravity:* 3–3·5.

Occurrence: A primary *amphibole* mineral in oversaturated and saturated igneous rocks.

Leucite

Composition: Potassium aluminium silicate, $KAlSi_2O_6$. *Crystal system:* orthorhombic, occasionally cubic. *Form:* crystalline. *Colour:* white or grey. *Lustre:* vitreous. *Diaphaneity:* translucent to opaque. *Hardness:* 5·5–6. *Fracture:* conchoidal. *Cleavage:* poor. *Specific gravity:* 2·5.

Occurrence: A constituent of some undersaturated lavas.

Olivine

Composition: Silicate of magnesium and iron, $(MgFe)_2SiO_4$. *Crystal system:* orthorhombic. *Form:* rarely crystalline, massive or granular. *Colour:* often green. *Lustre:* vitreous. *Diaphaneity:* transparent to opaque. *Hardness:* 6·5–7. *Fracture:* conchoidal. *Cleavage:* nil. *Specific gravity:* 3·5.

Occurrence: Common in undersaturated igneous rocks.

Uses: Refractory materials, moulding sands.

Carbonate minerals

The carbonate minerals form an important assemblage of rock-forming and gangue minerals. The most common are calcite, dolomite and siderite. Their composition may be shown diagrammatically as in Fig. 2.2. Excepting calcite, the carbonate minerals are difficult to differentiate by normal

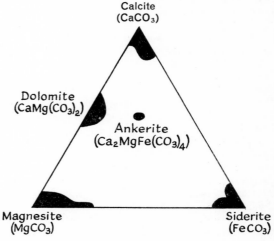

Fig. 2.2 The composition of the major carbonate minerals.

physical characteristics and it is usual to resort to chemical methods of determination. For laboratory use a number of staining techniques have been developed, a most comprehensive scheme having been devised by Warne (1962).

Calcite

Composition: Calcium carbonate, $CaCO_3$. *Crystal system:* hexagonal. *Form:* considerable variation of crystalline forms, also massive, stalactitic and fibrous. *Colour:* generally white or colourless. *Streak:* white. *Lustre:* vitreous to dull. *Diaphaneity:* transparent to opaque. *Hardness:* 3. *Fracture:* conchoidal. *Cleavage:* perfect in three planes at oblique angles to each other. *Specific gravity:* 2·71.

Effervesces freely in *cold* dilute hydrochloric acid.

Occurrence: The major constituent of limestone and marble. A common gangue mineral.

Uses: Lime and cement manufacture, chemical industry.

Dolomite

Composition: Carbonate of calcium and magnesium, $CaMg(CO_3)_2$. *Crystal system:* hexagonal. *Form:* rhombohedral crystals having curved surfaces —an important distinction from calcite, also massive and granular. *Colour:* white when pure, often brownish. *Lustre:* pearly. *Diaphaneity:* translucent to opaque. *Hardness:* 3·5–4. *Fracture:* conchoidal. *Cleavage:* perfect in three directions parallel to the faces of the rhombohedral crystal. *Specific gravity:* 2·87.

Effervesces freely in *warm* dilute hydrochloric acid.

Occurrence: The major constituent of dolostone. A common gangue mineral.

Uses: Cement manufacture, refractory material.

Siderite

Composition: Iron carbonate, $FeCO_3$. *Crystal system:* hexagonal. *Form:* rhombohedral crystals having curved faces, also massive. *Colour:* yellow to brown. *Streak:* white. *Lustre:* vitreous or pearly. *Diaphaneity:* translucent to opaque. *Hardness:* 3·5–4·5. *Fracture:* irregular. *Cleavage:* perfect in three directions parallel to the faces of the rhombohedral crystal. *Specific gravity:* about 3·8.

Occurrence: A common gangue mineral, also as a bedded sedimentary deposit, e.g. the *clay ironstones* of the Coal Measures.

Uses: An ore of iron.

Ankerite

Composition: Carbonate of calcium, magnesium and iron, $Ca_2MgFe(CO_3)_4$. Other properties essentially similar to siderite and dolomite. Can be satis-factorily distinguished only by staining (Warne, 1962) or analysis.

Occurrence: Commonly as white 'spar' developed along the cleat in coal seams.

Galena

Composition: Lead sulphide, PbS. *Crystal system:* cubic. *Form:* crystalline or massive. *Colour:* lead-grey. *Streak:* greyish-black. *Lustre:* metallic on freshly cleaved surfaces. *Diaphaneity:* opaque. *Hardness:* 2·5. *Fracture:* generally obscured by perfect cleavage. *Cleavage:* perfect, in three planes at right angles to each other forming cubes. *Specific gravity:* about 7·5.

Occurrence: In veins and associated deposits.

Uses: The chief ore of lead. Some argentiferous varieties are important sources of silver.

Sphalerite (Zinc blende)

Composition: Zinc sulphide, ZnS. *Crystal system:* cubic. *Form:* crystalline or massive. *Colour:* commonly black or reddish brown, occasionally yellow or white. *Streak:* yellowish. *Lustre:* vitreous to resinous. *Diaphaneity:* translucent to opaque. *Hardness:* 3·5–4. *Fracture:* irregular. *Cleavage:* perfect in six directions. *Specific gravity:* about 4.

Occurrence: Commonly distributed in veins and associated deposits. Often occurs with galena.

Uses: The major ore of zinc.

Pyrite (Iron pyrites)

Composition: Iron sulphide, FeS_2. *Crystal system:* cubic. *Form:* cube, massive or radiating. *Colour:* brassy-yellow. *Streak:* greenish-black. *Lustre:* metallic, duller when tarnished. *Diaphaneity:* opaque. *Hardness:* 6–6·5. *Fracture:* conchoidal or uneven. *Cleavage:* nil. *Specific gravity:* about 5.

Occurrence: Occurs mainly in rocks and mineral veins, as nodules in sedimentary strata and as an incombustible constituent of coal seams.

Uses: Worthless as iron ore, but of importance in the production of sulphuric acid.

Hematite (Kidney iron ore)

Composition: Iron oxide, Fe_2O_3. *Crystal system:* hexagonal. *Form:* commonly reniform. *Colour:* steel-grey to reddish-black. *Streak:* reddish-brown. *Lustre:* metallic. *Diaphaneity:* opaque. *Hardness:* 5·5–6·5. *Fracture:* sub-conchoidal or irregular. *Cleavage:* poor. *Specific gravity:* about 5.

Occurrence: In veins, irregular pockets and beds.

Uses: An important ore of iron.

Gypsum

Composition: Hydrated calcium sulphate, $CaSO_4.2H_2O$. *Crystal system:* monoclinic. *Form:*

crystalline, radiating, fibrous, massive. *Colour:* colourless, white, yellow or red. *Streak:* white. *Lustre:* sub-vitreous, pearly, silky. *Diaphaneity:* transparent to opaque. *Hardness:* 1·5–2. *Fracture:* conchoidal or irregular. *Cleavage:* one direction of perfect cleavage. *Specific gravity:* 2·3.

Varieties: Alabaster—fine-grained or massive. *Satin Spar*—fibrous variety with a silky lustre.

Occurrence: Often in thick beds resulting from the evaporation of semi-enclosed bodies of sea water. Occasionally as small stellate aggregates in weathered marine shales.

Uses: Plaster of Paris, plasterboards, quick-setting cement.

Barite (Barytes)

Composition: Barium sulphate, $BaSO_4$. *Crystal system:* orthorhombic. *Form:* crystalline, tabular, massive. *Colour:* commonly white or pinkish. *Streak:* white. *Lustre:* vitreous or pearly. *Diaphaneity:* transparent to opaque. *Hardness:* 3–3·5. *Fracture:* irregular. *Cleavage:* perfect in three directions. *Specific gravity:* 4·5.

Occurrence: A common gangue mineral in lead and zinc veins.

Uses: A filler in various products, e.g. wallpaper. Mud flush boring for oil wells.

Fluorite (Fluorspar)

Composition: Calcium fluoride, CaF_2. *Crystal system:* cubic. *Form:* frequently cubes. *Colour:* colourless, yellow, blue. *Streak:* white. *Lustre:* vitreous. *Diaphaneity:* transparent to translucent. *Hardness:* 4. *Fracture:* irregular to conchoidal. *Cleavage:* perfect in eight directions. *Specific gravity:* 3–3·2.

Variety: Blue-John—a blue and white banded variety found in Derbyshire.

Occurrence: A vein mineral associated with lead and zinc ores.

Uses: A flux in steel manufacture. Source of hydrogen fluoride.

REFERENCES

HURLBUT, C. S. (1959) *Dana's Manual of Mineralogy,* 17th revised ed., New York, Wiley.

HURLBUT, C. S. (1963) *Dana's Minerals and How to Study Them,* 3rd ed., Science Editions, New York, Wiley.

READ, H. H. (1948) *Rutley's Elements of Mineralogy,* 24th ed., London, Allen and Unwin (Murby).

WARNE, S. S. J. (1962) A quick field or laboratory staining scheme for the differentiation of the major carbonate minerals, *J. sedim. Petrol.* **32,** 29–38.

3

THE OPTICAL PROPERTIES OF MINERALS

THE PETROLOGICAL MICROSCOPE

The ordinary microscope is a relatively simple instrument for the examination usually of transparent material under high magnifications in normal light. Using such an instrument the geologist may identify a few of the common rock types but, for the precise determination of the constituents of transparent rock sections, a more specialized microscope fitted with polarizing equipment is essential. For the full utilization of the petrological microsocpe a comprehensive knowledge of crystal optics is required, but fortunately the common rock-forming minerals may be identified in the course of relatively simple microscope work.

The petrological microscope (Plate 1) is essentially an instrument for studying minerals in polarized light. Below the microscope stage a sheet of Polaroid or, in older models, a specially cut calcite crystal, a Nicol prism, causes the light reflected from the mirror to become *plane-polarized*. That is, the light vibrations, instead of occurring in all possible planes, are reorientated to a constant direction by the *polarizer*. Above the stage a second Polaroid screen, the *analyser*, may be slotted into position. If no thin section interferes with the polarized light, the analyser will *extinguish* all light so that the field of view will be dark (Fig. 3.1). However, if a thin section is placed on the stage, the different mineral particles produce a variety of diagnostic effects on the polarized light as it passes through them, so that some light will reach the eyepiece forming a characteristic *interference colour*. The functions of the polarizer and analyser may be likened to the effects caused by slotted screens, being respectively orientated E–W and N–S, that is, parallel to the cross wires contained in the microscope eyepiece. If the light path is unobstructed the E–W plane-polarized light will be blocked by the 'slots' of the analyser orientated N–S. Thus there is total darkness or *extinction*. The effect of most minerals is to alter the polarized light so that some can pass through the analyser, rendering them visible to the observer.

Immediately below the stage are mounted the condenser and the iris. The aperture of the latter can be varied to give the particular illumination required. In most cases the aperture should be only partly open to give adequate illumination and cause relief effects in the minerals. If the iris is fully open a normal rock section will have a flat appearance, and if strong artificial illumination is used the observer's eyesight may be impaired. The stage itself may be rotated and

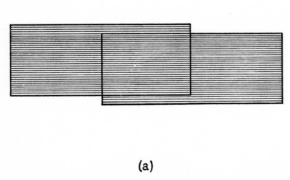

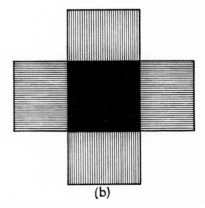

(a)
(b)

Fig. 3.1   Effect of polarizing filters on light, (a) partly superimposed and parallel, (b) one filter rotated 90 degrees and causing extinction in the superimposed area.

TABLE 4

The Diagnostic Optical Properties of the Major Rock-forming Minerals

Mineral	Plane-Polarized Light						Crossed Polars		
	Colour	Pleochroism	Form	Cleavage	Refractive Index and Relief	Alteration	Extinction	Twinning	Interference colours
Quartz SiO_2	Colourless	None	Commonly anhedral, sometimes hexagonal crystals	None	1·55 low	None[1]	Sometimes undulose	None[1] visible	Greys or yellows
Orthoclase $KAlSi_3O_8$	Colourless when fresh	None	Commonly anhedral, sometimes rectangular crystals	Occasionally rectangular	1·52 low	Commonly[1] turbid and brownish due to formation of kaolinite	Commonly oblique	Common,[1] Carlsbad or Baveno[2]	Greys
Plagioclase (see Fig. 2.1)	Colourless when fresh	None	Anhedral or lath shaped crystals	Rarely seen	1·53–1·58 low	Kaolinization often not as greatly[1] developed as in orthoclase	Oblique	Common[1] lamellar[2]	Greys
Leucite $KAl(SiO_3)_2$	Colourless when fresh	None	Euhedral octagonal sections with inclusions[3]	None	1·51 low	Occasionally turbid and brownish	Commonly wavy	Complicated lamellar[3] giving a cross-hatched appearance	Very dark grey or isotropic
Nepheline $(NaK)(AlSi)_2O_4$	Colourless	None	Small[3] euhedral crystals with rectangular or hexagonal sections	Rarely seen	1·54 low	Turbid	Straight	None[3]	Greys

Mineral	Colour	Pleochroism	Form	Cleavage	Refractive index	Alteration	Extinction	Twinning	Interference colours
Nosean $3(NaAlSiO_4)$ Na_2SO_4	Colourless with dark brown border due to inclusions	None	Commonly anhedral, sometimes hexagonal crystals	Rarely seen	1·46 very low	Occasionally turbid	ISOTROPIC		
Muscovite $KAl_2(AlSi_3)O_{10}(OH,F)_2$	Colourless to very pale green	Very feeble in some varieties	Commonly anhedral, shapeless plates or shreds	Generally one direction	1·58 moderate	None	Straight	Rarely apparent	Often bright pinks or greens
Biotite $K(MgFe)_3(AlSi)_3O_{10}(OH,F)_2$	Brown	Strong, pale brown to dark brown	Commonly anhedral, shapeless plates or shreds	Generally one[4] direction	1·6 moderate	Decomposes to green chlorite	Straight[4]	Rarely apparent	Masked by body colour
Augite $Ca(MgFe)(SiO_3)_2[(AlFe)_2O_3]x$	Slight brownish hue	Occasionally exhibits feeble pleochroism[5]	Commonly euhedral with octagonal sections	Two[5] directions at 87° & 93°	1·72 high	Sometimes altered to green chlorite, occasionally to hornblende	Commonly oblique	Occasionally simple lamellar	Bright blues, greens and pinks
Hornblende $Ca_2(MgFeAl)_5(OH)_2[(SiAl)_4O_{11}]_2$	Often brown occasionally green	Strong,[5] commonly light to dark brown	Often euhedral crystals with hexagonal sections	Two[4] directions at 56° and 124°[5]	1·65 rather high	Sometimes altered to green chlorite	Commonly[4] slightly oblique	Occasionally simple lamellar	Often masked by body colour
Olivine $(MgFe)_2SiO_4$	Colourless when fresh	None	Commonly anhedral, sometimes polygonal sections	Rarely seen, irregular cracks common	1·68 high	Decomposes to serpentinite (pale green) & magnetite	Rarely apparent	Rare and ill defined	Bright greens, blues and yellows
Calcite $CaCo_3$	Colourless	None, but a 'twinkling' effect seen when stage is rapidly rotated	Commonly anhedral[6]	Often two sets intersecting at oblique angles	c. 1·5 Variable, depending on orientation of section	None	Symmetrical	Common, lamellar	White, pale pinks or greens

[1] Distinction between quartz and felspars
[2] Distinction between orthoclase and plagioclase
[3] Distinction between leucite and nepheline
[4] Distinction between biotite and hornblende
[5] Distinction between augite and hornblende
[6] Distinction between calcite and dolomite

TABLE 4 (*continued*)

The Diagnostic Optical Properties of the Major Rock-forming Minerals

Mineral	Plane-Polarized Light						Crossed Polars		
	Colour	Pleochroism	Form	Cleavage	Refractive index and relief	Alteration	Extinction	Twinning	Interference colours
Dolomite $CaMg(CO_3)_2$	Brownish	None, but a slight 'twinkling' effect seen on rapid rotation of stage	Often euhedral, crystal faces[6] slightly curved	Often two sets intersecting at oblique angles	c. 1·5 Variable, depending on orientation of section	None	Symmetrical	Occasionally lamellar	White or pearl grey

[6] Distinction between calcite and dolomite

is provided with a graduated scale and index. Thus the angles of cleavage intersections of crystal faces can be measured by comparison with the eyepiece cross wires. Also rotation between crossed polars will result in the formation of differing interference effects of various minerals.

The total magnification depends upon the microscope tube length and the focal lengths of the eyepiece or *ocular* and the objective. It may be determined by the multiplication of the figures engraved on the objective and ocular. Thus, if the magnification numbers of the objective and ocular are respectively $\times 9$ and $\times 10$, then the total magnification is $\times 90$. On most student microscopes the objectives are placed in a turret-head mount so that different magnifications can be readily acquired. The oculars may also be changed. It is often unnecessary to use a high magnification and, for the preliminary investigation of a rock slice, a low magnification of about $\times 30$ should be used. For the identification of a particular mineral, especially in fine-grained rocks, it may be necessary to change to a higher magnification.

THE MICROSCOPICAL EXAMINATION OF A THIN SECTION

The examination of a mineral in thin section should follow a standard procedure and the specific characteristics noted as described below. Identification should not be based on one isolated property but on the sum total of the optical tests carried out on several sections of the same mineral contained in the slice. The optical properties of a mineral may vary with its orientation, which is seldom constant in thin sections. In most cases reference to Table 4 will prove sufficient to identify the major rock-forming minerals, although, for the rarer and accessory minerals, reference should be made to one of the standard works (Rogers & Kerr, 1942; Smith, 1949; Winchell, 1951).

Plane-polarized light

It is first necessary to examine the mineral in plane-polarized light using the polarizer alone. This must be correctly orientated by rotation and for this purpose is usually provided with click stops at 90-degree intervals. The orientation of the polarizer may be checked by inserting the analyser. With this in place and the stage empty, the polarizer is correctly positioned when there is complete extinction.

Colour. The majority of rock-forming minerals are transparent in thin section. In some cases all the constituents of white light are allowed to pass through so that the minerals are colourless. Other minerals may absorb some parts of the spectrum, in which case they are coloured. The colour may sometimes vary in different sections of the same mineral depending on the orientation of the section.

Certain minerals are opaque in thin section, the commonest in igneous rocks being magnetite and pyrite, and should be examined in reflected light. The sub-stage area is shielded to exclude any transmitted light and the microscope lamp arranged to shine obliquely on the section. Under these conditions magnetite will have a steely-blue colour and pyrite a brassy yellow.

Pleochroism. In plane-polarized light on rotation of the stage certain minerals change colour. This phenomenon is well developed in biotite and hornblende which change from pale to dark brown in a 90-degree rotation. The change is most noticeable, and these minerals are described as exhibiting *strong pleochroism*. In certain varieties of augite and muscovite a very *feeble pleochroism* can be observed.

Form. In certain rocks, particularly those of igneous and metamorphic origin, individual well-formed *euhedral* or *idiomorphic* crystals of a particular mineral may occur. In many cases, however, the minerals are *anhedral* or *allotriomorphic*, their shapes being determined, in the case of an igneous rock, by its cooling history; the last-formed minerals, commonly quartz and felspar, forming an interlocking mass of indeterminate shapes. A euhedral crystal in thin section will exhibit a number of straight sides, the intersections of the crystal faces with the thin section. The actual form (Fig. 3.2) or shape of the crystal section depends on the particular system to which the crystal belongs and also on the orientation of the rock section. Thus, a transverse section of a cube will appear as a square, whereas an oblique section will appear as a triangle. However, in most thin sections one or more characteristic forms can be seen.

Cleavage. The cleavage of a mineral may be evident as a series of fine parallel lines formed by the intersection of the cleavage planes with the surface of the thin section. There may be several directions of cleavage, in which case the angle formed by their intersection is a specific characteristic (Fig. 3.3.). Thus the cleavage traces of augite intersect at approximately 90 degrees, whereas those of hornblende form angles of 56 and 124 degrees. In measuring the cleavage angles the student should make sure that the slice is perpendicular to the cleavage planes because, if they are not, the apparent angle of intersection may differ from the true angle. In a perpendicular section the cleavage trace will remain in the same position when the focus of the microscope is altered, whereas there will be a slight lateral shift if the cleavage surface is oblique. A mineral possessing only one cleavage direction may not always exhibit the property in thin section if the slice was cut parallel to the cleavage. This commonly occurs in the examina-

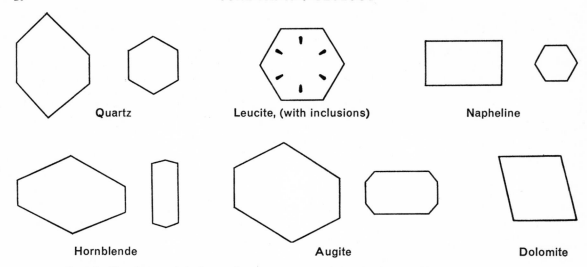

Fig. 3.2   The characteristic forms of some common rock-forming minerals as seen in thin section.

tion of micaceous sections, when some of the mica fragments may appear uncleaved.

Distinct from cleavage, but sometimes of diagnostic importance, are the irregular cracks developed either from alteration or by strain features during grinding. Olivine in thin section commonly shows an irregular series of cracks which are rendered conspicuous by the development of greenish alteration products.

Refractive Index. The refractive index determines the appearance of a transparent mineral examined in thin section. When mounted in a medium of identical colour and refractive index, a mineral will be invisible in ordinary light. Thus the refractive indices of quartz and Canada balsam, a common mountant, are 1·55 and 1·54 respectively, so that the boundary of a quartz grain along the margin of a rock section will be extremely difficult to see. If, however, quartz and augite, the latter having a refractive index of 1·72, are in contact, then the boundary will be clearly visible since the respective indices differ greatly. Also,

the augite will have a brilliant appearance and will appear to stand out in relief; thus augite, and likewise other minerals with a high refractive index, have a *high relief.* Conversely, minerals with low indices appear to be sunk below the surface of the section and therefore have *low relief.*

A comparison of the relative refractive indices of two adjacent minerals may easily be made by the Becke method. A junction is first chosen which is perpendicular, or nearly so, to the rock slice. Such a contact will be sharply in focus as compared with others oblique to the slice which may appear blurred. The illumination is limited by closing down the sub-stage iris diaphragm and top light reflections are excluded by shading the microscope stage with the hand. Particularly under high-powered magnification the junction will be evident as a narrow band of bright light, the *Becke line.* As the microscope tube is slightly raised the Becke line moves inside the mineral with the higher refractive index. If the microscope tube is lowered the Becke line moves inside the

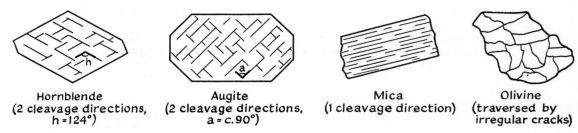

Hornblende
(2 cleavage directions,
h =124°)

Augite
(2 cleavage directions,
a = c.90°)

Mica
(1 cleavage direction)

Olivine
(traversed by
irregular cracks)

Fig. 3.3   Cleavage types as aids to mineral identification in thin section.

mineral with the lower refractive index (Fig. 3.4). Extremely small differences of refractive index as low as 0·001 can be detected by this method. The estimation of relative refractive indices is of great importance in the optical identification of minerals and the student should familiarize himself with the indices of the common rock-forming minerals.

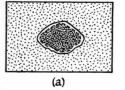 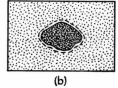

Fig. 3.4 The Becke Line effect. In a mineral of higher refractive index than the matrix, the position of the Becke Line varies as the microscope tube is respectively raised (a) and lowered (b).

Alteration. Certain minerals are prone to decomposition either as a result of surface weathering or the circulation of deep-seated solutions and vapours. Thus orthoclase is commonly seen in thin section to be altered either totally or partially to a mass of kaolinite which causes the mineral to appear brownish and turbid. All felspars are liable to alteration but generally orthoclase is more affected than plagioclase. On the other hand, quartz, which in plane-polarized light is otherwise virtually indistinguishable from the felspars, is always unaltered. Other rock-forming minerals particularly prone to alteration are olivine and biotite. In the former, greenish serpentine minerals, sometimes associated with magnetite, commonly infill irregular cracks in the crystal. The familiar brown colour of biotite may be

completely masked by the green decomposition product chlorite which commonly fringes an unaltered biotite core.

Inclusions. The presence of inclusions, either gaseous, liquid or solid, are sometimes useful in mineral identification. Thus leucite often contains included fragments which may be arranged radially or concentrically, giving a characteristic 'death's head' appearance to the mineral. Again, quartz may be packed with minute liquid and gas inclusions visible under high magnifications.

Between crossed polars

The student must ensure that the polarizer is correctly positioned. With the analyser in place there should be total darkness when the stage is empty. In such conditions the thin section is viewed between *crossed polars*.

Extinction. In thin section most rock-forming minerals alter the polarized light so that part of the spectrum is allowed through the analyser. On a complete rotation of the stage such *anisotropic* minerals extinguish at four positions at right angles to each other. Extinction may occur when a cleavage trace or crystal edge is parallel to one of the cross wires. Thus biotite and muscovite are said to possess *straight extinction*. In other cases, as for instance the plagioclase felspars, the extinction position is *oblique* to the linear features of the mineral. Other minerals, notably the carbonates, having rhombic cross-sections or cleavage intersections, extinguish parallel to the diagonals of the rhombic patterns and are said to exhibit *symmetrical extinction*. Quartz is often characterized by *undulose extinction*, that is, a single

Straight extinction of micas
N.B. Cleavage traces

Oblique extinction of plagioclase
N.B. Lamellar twinning

Symmetrical extinction of calcite

Undulose extinction of a single quartz grain

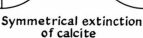

Fig. 3.5 The major classes of extinction.

grain or crystal may not darken uniformly since different parts extinguish separately as the stage is rotated (Fig. 3.5). Such an effect is due to strain developed during the formation of the rock and is commonly seen in thin sections of metamorphic rocks.

An important group of minerals are *isotropic*. As such they have no effect upon polarized light and are quite dark throughout a complete rotation of the microscope stage. All cubic minerals have this property; it may be observed occasionally in basal sections of minerals crystallizing in certain other systems.

Twinning. Twinned crystals consist of a number of portions which are so joined that one part is in reverse position to another. Such twinning is easily detected under crossed polars since the individual twin parts extinguish at different positions. Twinning is commonly exhibited by the felspars, which can therefore often readily be distinguished from the typically untwinned mineral, quartz. Moreover, the type of felspar may usually be determined by the nature of the twinning. Thus plagioclase exhibits lamellar twinning revealed between crossed polars as an alternating series of light and dark stripes, whilst the twin form of orthoclase is most commonly a simple two-fold division (Fig. 3.6). Of more specialized use, the plagioclase series may be subdivided by means of the varying extinction angles in the two alternating sets of lamellae (Harker, 1954, pp. 9–13; Hatch and Wells, 1949, pp. 93–5).

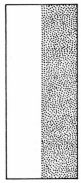 

Orthoclase showing Carlsbad twinning

Plagioclase showing Lamellar twinning

Fig. 3.6   The common twin forms of the felspars.

Interference colours. Any section of an anisotropic mineral, except when in one of the extinction positions, allows the passage of a certain amount of light to the objective. Some of the constituents of white light may be withheld so that many minerals appear coloured. The *interference* or *polarization colour* depends on the thickness, orientation and nature of the mineral. Since geological thin sections are all cut to a standard thickness of 0·03 mm, the comparative interference colours are important aids to mineral identification.

The rock slice

So far the minerals occurring in thin section have been subjected to separate study, but the student must always consider the correct identification of the component minerals to be only a part of the examination. The mutual relationships, size and degree of crystallinity and relative proportions of the various minerals should also be noted. Only then can a name and possible mode of origin be suggested for the rock. For that is the main object of the microscopic examination.

PREPARATION OF A ROCK SECTION

The preparation of rock sections is a specialized procedure (Holmes, 1921, pp. 231–49), the methods employed varying according to the type of rock and the individual preferences of the technician. The basic procedure described is suitable for most rocks and it is suggested that the advanced student be familiar with the basic techniques, at least in theory, though preferably in practice also.

The specimen to be sectioned should be fresh and unweathered since the development of secondary minerals may obscure the primary characters of the rock. A small flake should be taken, approximately $1 \text{ in} \times 1 \text{ in} \times \frac{1}{2} \text{ in}$. This may be obtained by careful hammering or by using one of the several rock-cutting machines on the market. If the former method is used a flat surface should be prepared by hand grinding over a thick sheet of plate glass not less than 12 in² and using a coarse carborundum powder (about 90 grade). The rough surface is now finely ground using successively finer carborundum powders (220, then 600 grades). The utmost care must be taken in changing from one abrasive to a finer grade; the rock fragment, operator's hands and grinding plate should be carefully washed and scrubbed because a residual grain of coarse powder, left by chance, will prevent the formation of a finely polished surface. If possible a different grinding plate should be used for each operation. After the final grinding the specimen should have a smooth, finely polished surface. This is then cemented face down to a glass microscope slide using Canada balsam as the mountant. In normal temperatures the balsam is commonly viscous when placed on the slide. This should therefore be heated at approximately 105 °C on a hotplate until a small drop of balsam, collected on a pin point, hardens when chilled. Care should be taken not to overheat the cement which, in this state, becomes brittle and discoloured. The warmed

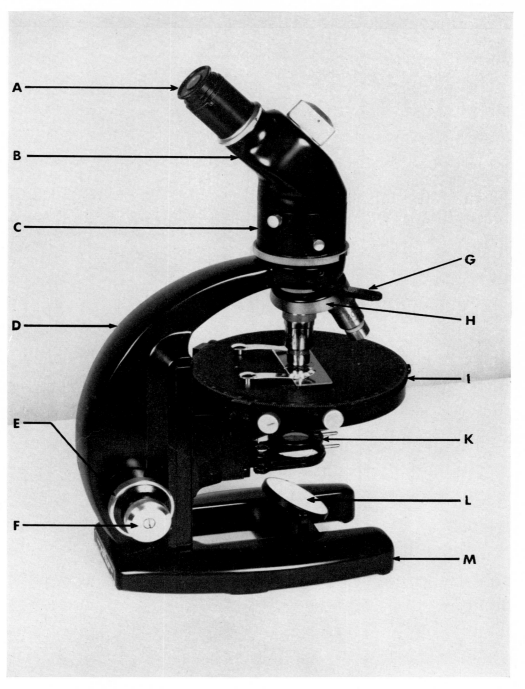

Plate 1 The essential features of a modern petrological microscope. (A) Eyepiece. (B) Inclined monocular head. (C) Analyser. (D) Limb. (E) Coarse focus control. (F) Fine focus control. (G) Quartz wedge. (H) Triple objective carrier. (I) Revolving stage. (K) Swing-out polarizing unit. (L) Mirror unit. (M) Base.

Plate 2(b) Dolerite sills with columnar jointing intruded into horizontal sandstones with some coal seams, Theron Mountains, Antarctica.

Plate 2(a) Tertiary dolerite dyke intruded into sandstone, Port Leacach, Arran, Scotland.

slice, at a slightly higher temperature than the cement, is then carefully lowered into position and any trapped air bubbles gently pressed out. A small weight is placed on the slice which is cooled in contact with a flat surface.

The mounted slice is thinned in a similar manner to that described previously. When the section approaches transparency the finer grades of carborundum powder must be used. Constant checks should be made, examining the slice under crossed polars so that its thickness may be estimated by the interference colours. Most igneous rocks contain either quartz or felspars and, when the interference colours of these minerals are pale greys, then the slice is of a standard thickness of 0·03 mm. Before this stage, when the interference colours are bright yellows, the worker must change over to the finest abrasive and use a very light hand pressure. In this final stage of polishing it is not uncommon for the student to destroy the slice completely by overgrinding—one must concentrate and have patience! If at some part of the treatment the slice becomes uneven, a slight extra pressure of the fingers should be exerted on the thicker area until a constant thickness is reached. The cover glass is then mounted on a carefully washed, dried and polished surface. A drop of Canada balsam in xylol is placed on the section and the cover glass allowed to settle into place, the slide being heated gently at about 65 °C on the hot plate. After cooling, the excess balsam around the cover glass may be removed by cleaning with methanol or xylol.

Preparation of coal sections

In comparison with the preparation of thin sections of rocks, such as granite or sandstone, the making of a thin section of coal is extremely difficult and, in the case of anthracites, often impossible. Owing to the greater opacity of coals the section must be at least 10 times as thin (0·003 mm) as those of other rocks so that specialized techniques, only acquired with considerable practice, need to be used (Francis, 1961, pp. 760–8; Raistrick and Marshall, 1939, pp. 260–70). Owing to the difficulties still experienced and despite much research into techniques, it is truly remarkable that some of the first sections of coal, made over 130 years ago, compare favourably with our modern products (Hickling, 1936, pp. 243–53).

The coal must first be impregnated by heating it for over 24 hours in a bath of paraffin wax at 105 °C.

This preliminary treatment both acts as a binder to an often otherwise fragmentary material and also drives off any moisture and gases contained in cracks in the coal. Following this the specimen is ground with succeedingly finer grades of carborundum powder. The surface must then be honed and finally polished on a damp Selvyt cloth impregnated with a polishing cream. The surface is then cemented to a microscope slide with a mixture of Canada balsam and refined marine glue.

The procedure is repeated on the opposite face, the final polishing stage being done over an illuminated table, thereby enabling one to observe and control the final stages. A cover glass is finally placed in position using a water soluble cement (gum arabic: 4 parts; glycerine: 4 parts; water: 2 parts). Canada balsam should not be used because the contained solvents will weaken the section and cause disintegration.

Fortunately the basic constituents of coal, the macerals, can be distinguished in reflected light when a microscope fitted with a special illuminator is used. This method does not necessitate the preparation of thin sections; all that is required is a finely polished coal surface. This may be prepared by initial grinding with carborundum powder followed by polishing on finer grades of alumina powder. In the case of friable coals, the specimens must be first impregnated.

REFERENCES

Francis, W. (1961) *Coal*, 2nd ed., London, Arnold.

Harker, A. (1954) *Petrology for Students*, 8th ed., Cambridge Univ. Press.

Hatch, F. H., M. K. & A. K. Wells (1949) *The Petrology of the Igneous Rocks*, 10th ed., London, Allen and Unwin (Murby).

Hickling, H. G. A. (1936) William Hutton's 'Observations on coals', 1833, *Trans. Instn Min. Engrs* **90**, 243–53.

Holmes, A. (1921) *Petrographic Methods and Calculations*, 1st ed., London, Allen and Unwin (Murby).

Raistrick, A. & C. E. Marshall (1939) *The Nature and Origin of Coal and Coal Seams*, 1st ed., London, Eng. Univ. Press.

Rogers, A. F. & P. F. Kerr (1942) *Optical Mineralogy*, 2nd ed., London, McGraw-Hill.

Smith, H. G. (1949) *Minerals and the Microscope*, 4th ed., London, Allen and Unwin (Murby).

Winchell, A. N. (1951) *Elements of Optical Mineralogy*, Pt. 2. *Descriptions of Minerals*, 4th ed., New York, Wiley.

4

PETROLOGY: IGNEOUS ROCKS

INTRODUCTION

Igneous rocks are formed by the cooling and solidification of an originally molten silicate melt or *magma*. The final stages in the formation of volcanic lavas can be observed during modern eruptions. Intrusive rocks, because of their subterranean mode of emplacement, cannot be so studied and consequently, particularly with regard to the larger, deep-seated or plutonic bodies, their exact mode of origin may be problematical. Many such rocks owe their final composition to the effects and interaction of several factors during their intrusive development. Thus a deep-seated magma intruded into a sedimentary series may partly or wholly assimilate masses of the country rock, thereby altering its own original composition and converting some of the intruded sediments into ultra-metamorphic rocks indistinguishable from igneous (Fig. 1.1). In this respect the precise nature of the granitic rocks has stimulated geological thought for over 100 years and still results in much discussion (Read, 1957; Shand, 1949, pp. 252–65). There is less conflict of opinion as to the origin of the basic rocks such as gabbro and basalt. Even so during a prolonged cooling phase a variety of rock types may originate from a basic magma by the gravitational settling of the first-formed or denser minerals. This will enrich the residual magma in more acidic material. Evidence for such *magmatic differentiation* may be observed in many intrusions as, for instance, in the Inner Hebrides of Scotland, where gradual passages are recorded from quartz-gabbro at the base through various intermediate rock types into granite in the upper levels of the same intrusion (Richey, 1948, p. 61).

All igneous rocks are popularly imagined as originating under extremely high temperatures in a fiery state. Indeed such an origin is suggested by the rock name (L. *igneus*, fiery). From the occurrence of certain mineral varieties in the rocks the temperatures of formation can now be proved to be far lower than originally believed. Thus quartz when heated over 870 °C transforms into tridymite, which again changes to cristobalite at 1 470 °C. Since the latter two high temperature varieties of quartz are absent in deep-seated intrusive rocks we may conclude from such evidence and that supplied by similar mineral inversions that the larger intrusive masses were never at temperatures higher than 870 °C (Shand, 1949, pp. 52–63).

CLASSIFICATION OF IGNEOUS ROCKS

There are several classifications in present-day use, each being based on a few properties considered to be important. No single scheme is perfect, and indeed never can be, for there are few rigid boundaries in nature. Many rock types grade into one another so that the ever present problem is where to place an artificial boundary between one rock type and another. The problem is sometimes evaded by the coining of new names for every minor variety discovered. It is therefore perhaps not surprising that petrological nomenclature appears stifled with hosts of strange-sounding and often unpronounceable titles, including such horrors as jacupirangite and kalitordrillite. A comprehensive list of definitions of such rocks is that of Johannsen (1939, pp. 238–88). In order to incorporate the numerous varieties of the major rock groups a classification should have a flexible rather than a rigid framework. Unfortunately the very term suggests a series of clear cut and accurately defined divisions. This is further emphasized by the pigeon-hole effect of many classifications with the rock names neatly and sharply framed.

A SIMPLE CLASSIFICATION

A simple classification should be applicable to both laboratory and field studies, and therefore only require the use of uncomplicated equipment. Much can still be learnt by using a hammer and a hand lens! Such a classification should express both the crystallinity, from which may be derived the probable mode of occurrence, and the mineralogical composition which expresses the mutual relationships of the rock members. Accordingly that to be followed is based on the degree of crystallization, the silica saturation and the nature of the felspars (Table 5).

TABLE 5

A Simple Classification of Igneous Rocks

Component minerals	Major rock group						
	Acid		Intermediate		Basic	Ultrabasic	
Quartz	X	X	R¹	R¹	R³	A	
Orthoclase	X	O	X	O	R	A	
Plagioclase	O	X	O	X	X	X	
Muscovite	X	R	A	A	A	A	
Biotite		X	O	O	R	A	
Augite	R	O	O	O	X	X	
Hornblende	O	X	O	X	R	O	
Olivine	A	A	A	A	O⁴	X⁶	
Felspathoids (mainly leucite and/or nepheline)	A	A	R²	A	O⁵	R	CRYSTALLINITY
	Granite	Granodiorite	Syenite	Diorite	Gabbro, Dolerite	Picrite	EUCRYSTALLINE
	Rhyolite	Dacite	Trachyte	Andesite	Basalt	Undersaturated rare lavas	DYSCRYSTALLINE

X—Essential mineral   O—Subsidiary mineral (may not always be present)   A—Absent   R—Rare

¹ Generally less than 10 per cent of the rock. Some varieties of diorite have more than 10 per cent, e.g. tonalite. Where quartz is present, prefix rock name, e.g. quartz syenite
² Where felspathoid is present, prefix rock name e.g. nepheline trachyte (phonolite)
³ Where quartz is present, prefix rock name e.g. quartz dolerite
⁴ Where olivine is present, prefix rock name e.g. olivine basalt
⁵ Where felspathoid is present, prefix rock name e.g. leucite basalt
⁶ In peridotites, olivine is the essential mineral. Plagioclase is absent

Degree of crystallization

Most early classifications were partly based on the actual mode of occurrence of the igneous rocks so that three major groups, plutonic, hypabyssal and extrusive, were established. These were respectively more or less equivalent to coarse-, medium- and fine-grained rocks. The terminology is however difficult to apply as the worker is often unaware of the actual field occurrence of the specimen. Even when in the field it may be difficult to distinguish between plutonic or deep-seated, and hypabyssal or shallow intrusions. Moreover, fine-grained rocks may be de-

rived from an extrusive lava or a small hypabyssal intrusion and it is certainly unnecessary and confusing to apply two names to what is virtually the same rock type.

Accordingly a two-fold division, based on the degree of crystallinity, is used as defined by Shand (1949, pp. 225–6). *Eucrystalline* rocks are coarse-grained so that all the essential minerals can be distinguished either by the unaided eye or with the use of the hand lens. The *dyscrystalline* rocks are so fine-grained that the components cannot be identified without using a microscope. In the case of porphyritic varieties containing one or more minerals attaining a relatively large size, termed *phenocrysts* or *porphyritic crystals*, the rock is classified according to the crystallinity of the groundmass.

Certain general inferences may be made with regard to the two groups. Eucrystalline rocks cooled slowly, thereby enabling large crystals to develop. Favourable conditions are a thick cover of overlying rocks which prevent a rapid heat loss. It may be inferred that eucrystalline rocks are therefore intrusive. Crystal growth in the dyscrystalline rocks is inhibited by rapid chilling as they form as either extrusive surface flows or as small intrusions. In both cases the heat loss will be rapid. Thus at the margins of eucrystalline intrusions it is not uncommon to find a thin dyscrystalline and sometimes glassy selvage representing the rapidly chilled margin.

Owing to their crystallinity the dyscrystalline rocks cannot be accurately determined in the field. An approximate identification can however, in most cases, be made. Many are porphyritic rocks and the nature of the phenocrysts will indicate the mineralogical affinities of the specimen. Also there is a general increase in specific gravity and a darkening towards the ultrabasic group. To utilize the latter criterion fresh unweathered material should be examined.

Silica saturation

Since silica is a constituent of all the major minerals in igneous rocks their silica content is of use in classification. The actual quantities of silica may be expressed as percentages. Thus the groups—acid, intermediate, basic and ultrabasic—were originally defined in order of decreasing silica percentages. Modern usage (Hatch & Wells, 1949, pp. 184–5) whilst retaining the group names, employs more qualitative characters determined by the presence or absence of certain key minerals. Thus minerals such as olivine, leucite and nepheline have relatively low silica contents; that is they are *unsaturated*. They do not normally occur in rocks containing quartz, since during the cooling of a magma they would combine with any excess silica to form either augite or one of the felspars.

$$KAlSi_2O_6 + SiO_2 = KAlSi_3O_8$$
$$\text{(Leucite)} \quad \text{(Quartz)} \quad \text{(Orthoclase)}$$

or $\quad NaAlSiO_4 + 2SiO_2 = NaAlSi_3O_8$
$\qquad\qquad$ (Nepheline) $\quad$ (Quartz) $\qquad$ (Albite)

Since leucite and nepheline have such chemical similarities to the felspars they are termed felspathoids. The presence of quartz or one or more unsaturated minerals clearly expresses the silica saturation of a rock and is of major use in classification.

Acid group. The group is defined by the presence of over 10 per cent free quartz. That is, quartz is an essential mineral to the classification. Other such minerals are one or more of the felspars and biotite and/or muscovite. By definition no unsaturated minerals may be present.

Basic group. Ideally quartz is absent and frequently one or more of the unsaturated minerals occur. The presence of such minerals is usually indicated by a prefix (Table 5, ff. 3, 4 & 5). Minerals essential to the group classification are plagioclase and augite.

Intermediate group. Containing less than 10 per cent quartz, the group is of intermediate composition between the acid and basic groups. The dioritic varieties are exceptional in that they may contain more than this amount. The essential minerals are either orthoclase or plagioclase with one or more of the coloured silicates: biotite, hornblende or augite.

Ultrabasic group. The group has a characteristically low silica content so that the common minerals are all unsaturated. One of these may be so predominant that the rock is almost monomineralic. Thus *dunite* is a rock composed almost entirely of olivine. Quartz is always absent.

Type of felspar

The felspars are present in the majority of igneous rocks and consequently can be used in classification. The acid and intermediate groups can each be reduced into orthoclase- or plagioclase-rich divisions. More detailed classifications employ a third division containing approximately equal amounts of plagioclase and orthoclase. In the basic and ultrabasic groups orthoclase is absent. Some difficulty may be experienced in distinguishing between the two minerals in rock specimens. Sometimes plagioclase may appear faintly striated and lacks the pinkish coloration often developed by orthoclase.

COMMON IGNEOUS ROCKS

The nature, occurrence and uses of the more abundant igneous rocks are described below. Excepting dolerite the eucrystalline rocks are rarely, if ever, encountered in coal mining. Their intrusive size and consequent large metamorphic aureoles preclude any coal-getting in their proximity. Most mining courses however, and quite rightly, require a practical study of the commoner eucrystalline types, for it is by their examination that a knowledge of the mineralogy and properties of the igneous rocks can most readily be acquired. The dyscrystalline rocks on the other hand may be fairly common in some mining areas.

Granite (Fig. 4.1a)

Crystallinity. Eucrystalline, frequently very coarse grained.

Essential minerals. Quartz, orthoclase, muscovite

and/or biotite. (The rock name may be prefixed by the name of the predominant mica).

Subsidiary minerals. Often a small amount of plagioclase. Occasionally hornblende and more rarely augite. Frequently minor accessories such as pyrite, zircon and tourmaline occur.

Colour. The colour of eucrystalline rocks is seldom uniform owing to the large crystals of individual minerals. Generally granites have a predominant white, grey or reddened colour.

Occurrence. Large intrusions, batholiths, stocks, laccoliths (for descriptions of the various types of intrusions see pages 28–32).

Varieties. Porphyritic granite – with large euhedral crystals of orthoclase.

Varieties. Obsidian—with an entirely glassy groundmass, and black colour. Pitchstone—with a partly microcrystalline ground-mass and generally dark green colour.

The above glassy varieties have irregular or conchoidal fractures and vitreous lustres. They may develop by devitrification into rhyolite. In this respect it is pertinent that obsidian occurs only in recent lavas.

Uses. Roadstones, ballast, etc.

Granodiorite

Crystallinity. Eucrystalline, often porphyritic.

Essential minerals. Quartz, plagioclase, biotite and hornblende.

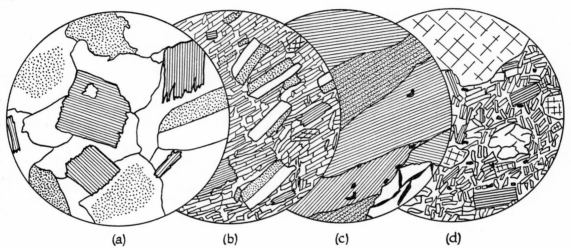

| (a) | (b) | (c) | (d) |

Fig. 4.1 (a) Biotite-granite. The biotite exhibits characteristic ragged edges. Orthoclase felspar with some Carlsbad twinning and containing turbid patches of kaolin may be distinguished from clear quartz. (Crossed polars.) (b) Trachyte. Phenocrysts of orthoclase felspar, biotite and hornblende occur in a matrix composed principally of sub-parallel orthoclase laths. (Crossed polars.) (c) Olivine gabbro. Composed essentially of augite, olivine and plagioclase felspar. (Crossed polars.) (d) Olivine dolerite. Phenocrysts of olivine and augite occur in a ground mass composed of the latter mineral and plagioclase felspar. (Crossed polars.)

Granophyre – with complex intergrowths of quartz and felspar.

Uses. Building and ornamental stones, concrete products, ballast etc.

Rhyolite

Crystallinity. Groundmass dyscrystalline, may be porphyritic with orthoclase and/or quartz phenocrysts.

Minerals. Mineralogical composition similar to granite. The groundmass minerals may only be distinguished by high power microscopic examination.

Colour. Pinkish or greenish, sometimes streaky.

Occurrence. Lava flows and sometimes small intrusions.

Subsidiary minerals. Orthoclase (up to one third of the total felspar content), and/or augite. The minor accessories, magnetite, pyrite, apatite and sphene, may be present.

Colour. Slightly darker than granite.

Occurrence. Similar to granite.

Uses. Similar to granite.

Trachyte (Fig. 4.1b)

Crystallinity. Dyscrystalline, usually porphyritic, the phenocrysts being of orthoclase.

Essential minerals. Orthoclase and one or more of the coloured silicates, biotite, hornblende and/or augite. The felspars are commonly in parallel alignment due to flowage.

Subsidiary minerals. Up to 10 per cent quartz may occur as in quartz-trachytes. Plagioclase (up to one third of the total felspar content). Occasionally one or more of the felspathoids.

Colour. Usually light or dark grey.

Occurrence. Lava flows and small intrusions.

Varieties. Phonolite—a felspathoidal trachyte containing nepheline.

Uses. Roadstones.

Andesite

Crystallinity. Dyscrystalline, usually porphyritic, the phenocrysts being of plagioclase.

Essential minerals. Plagioclase with one or more of the coloured silicates, biotite, hornblende and/or augite. It is usual to prefix the rock name with that of the dominant coloured silicate, e.g. hornblende-andesite.

Subsidiary minerals. Some quartz may be present. Magnetite is common as a minor accessory.

Alteration. Andesites are particularly prone to alteration, so that many of the original constituents may be replaced by kaolinite, chlorite and carbonate minerals.

Colour. Commonly dark green.

Occurrence. Lava flows.

Uses. Roadstones.

Gabbro (Fig. 4.1c)

Crystallinity. Eucrystalline, frequently very coarse grained.

Essential minerals. Plagioclase and augite. In hand specimens the latter may appear micaceous.

Subsidiary minerals. Olivine or quartz may occur in some varieties. Commonly magnetite or ilmenite is an abundant minor accessory.

Colour. Usually dark grey or dark green.

Occurrence. Large intrusions such as stocks and laccoliths.

Varieties. Troctolite—composed essentially of plagioclase and olivine. Anorthosite—a plagioclase-rich variety which is almost monomineralic.

Uses. Building and ornamental stones.

Dolerite (Fig. 4.1d)

Crystallinity. Just eucrystalline, so that the components can only be distinguished with a hand lens.

Minerals. Mineralogical composition similar to gabbro. Groups of lath-shaped plagioclase crystals are frequently enclosed by plates of augite. The resulting *ophitic* texture is characteristic of the rock.

Colour. Dark grey, dark green or black. A slight speckled effect, caused by the pin-point reflections of small quartz crystals, is sometimes noticeable.

Occurrence. Common as sills and dykes. The dolerite forming such intrusions in the British coalfields is locally termed *whin* or *whinstone*.

Uses. Roadstones, ballast, etc.

Basalt

Crystallinity. Dyscrystalline, sometimes porphyritic.

Minerals. Mineralogical composition similar to gabbro.

Colour. Usually black.

Occurrence. The commonest extrusive rock, though occasionally found as small dykes and sills.

Varieties. Tachylyte—with a glassy texture, brown or green colour and developed as a thin selvage to a dyke or sill. Tholeiite—with some interstitial patches of glass.

Uses. Roadstones, ballast, etc.

IGNEOUS INTRUSIONS

A mass of magma is either extruded as lava on the Earth's surface or it may be emplaced within the crustal rocks to form an igneous intrusion. Both extrusive and intrusive igneous rocks frequently occur together in the same geological succession, though they may be usually distinguished (Fig. 4.2) by several criteria.

(1) Owing to the longer cooling history of an intrusive magma the resulting rocks are generally eucrystalline, whereas lavas are typically dyscrystalline.

(2) The invaded or *country rock* surrounding an intrusion commonly shows marginal contact metamorphism. The relative width of the zone of alteration, or *metamorphic aureole* (page 46, Fig. 6.1), varies with the size and type of intrusion and the nature of the country rock. In the case of tabular intrusions, which are parallel to the stratification of the intruded rocks, some difficulty may be experienced in proving an intrusive as opposed to an extrusive origin. Generally this may be determined by the nature of the upper contact between the igneous and sedimentary rocks, since only when the former are intrusive will the overlying sediments be metamorphosed.

(3) Many intrusions are transgressive, that is the intrusive contacts cut across the sedimentary or other country rock structures. Even concordant intrusions normally having contacts parallel to the stratification may be locally transgressive. Such a discordant contact is in most cases sufficient evidence of an intrusive nature. Only rarely does a lava plough into the underlying sediment, thus simulating an intrusion, and even so the scale of such a feature precludes its confusion with a true intrusive transgression.

(4) Inclusions or *xenoliths* composed of fragments of partly or completely indurated country rock are found in many intrusions and may be abundant in the marginal parts. If it is possible to match the more unaltered xenoliths with the overlying country rock an intrusive origin is proved. This may also be indi-

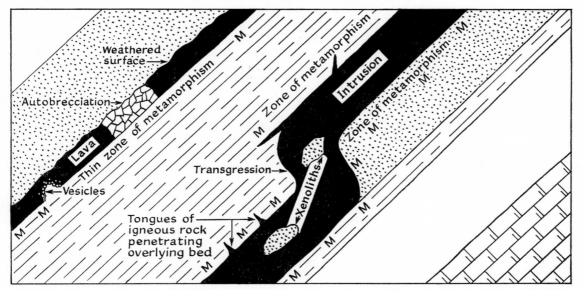

Fig. 4.2 Diagram illustrating the differences between a tabular and essentially concordant intrusion and a sill.

cated by the presence of thin tongues or strings from the main intrusion penetrating the overlying rocks.

(5) Usually some time elapses between the eruption of a lava and its subsequent burial, so that the upper parts of the flow may become weathered. Basic lavas are particularly prone to rapid weathering, so that they may possess an upper weathered layer or *bole*. Weathered surfaces are absent over intrusions in a normal sedimentary sequence. Again certain lavas, notably andesites, may suffer *autobrecciation*. That is, during effusion the volatile constituent gases were released so quickly that the lava rapidly solidified and therefore accumulated as a blocky autobrecciated mass. Other typical extrusive structures are *vesicles* or former gas cavities of an ovoid or spherical shape and commonly a few millimetres in maximum dimension. These may be subsequently infilled with secondary minerals, chiefly hydrous silicates or carbonates, to form an *amygdaloidal* lava.

The age of an intrusion is generally assessed as relative to that of the surrounding strata (Fig. 4.3). Thus the Shap granite of Westmorland is intruded into and metamorphoses Ordovician and Silurian rocks, whilst the nearby basal Carboniferous conglomerate contains fragments of felspar phenocrysts derived from the granite. Therefore the age of the intrusion is post-Silurian and pre-Carboniferous, that is, Devonian (Harker & Marr, 1891, p. 267). A modern development, based on radiological dating, is being increasingly used for the estimation of the absolute ages of igneous rocks. By this method the

Shap granite has been established as of Lower Devonian age or more particularly as 397 ± 8 million years old (Sabine & Watson, 1965, p. 494).

Intrusions are classified according to their shapes.

Dykes

Generally composed of dolerite, dykes are the commonest intrusions and the most likely to be encountered in mining. They are of a discordant

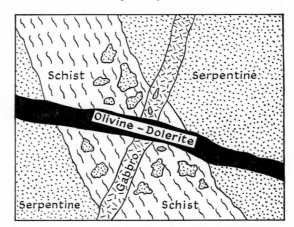

Fig. 4.3 Section at Coverack Cove, Cornwall, illustrating the relative order of several igneous intrusions. Gabbro was intruded into serpentine and subsequently metamorphosed into a schist. At a later stage successive dykes of gabbro and olivine dolerite were intruded. (After H. Dewey.)

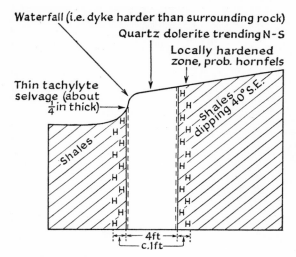

Waterfall (i.e. dyke harder than surrounding rock)

Quartz dolerite trending N-S

Locally hardened zone, prob. hornfels

Thin tachylyte selvage (about ¼ in thick)

Shales

Shales dipping 40° S.E.

4ft
c.1ft

Fig. 4.4   Field sketch showing the outcrop of a dyke in a stream bed.

nature and in an otherwise sedimentary sequence normally transgress the stratification at considerable angles (Fig. 4.4). They are essentially of vertical tabular form (Plate 2a). Consequently their outcrops are unaffected by topographic variations so that on the geological map they possess a noticeably straight trace. Many dykes average between 3 and 20 ft in width, and greater thicknesses are unusual. In contrast to their relatively narrow widths, individual dykes can frequently be traced for considerable distances and some, as for instance the Armathwaite—Cleveland dyke of Northern England, are over 100 miles long. It is probable that such extensive dykes were filled by the lateral migration of magma along pre-existing tensional fissures rather than by a continuous upwelling throughout the length of the feature.

In some areas dykes occur in linear groups composed of parallel and closely adjacent intrusions (Fig. 4.5). *Dyke swarms* of this type are common on the Isle of Arran, Scotland, where in one measured section 525 dykes, with an aggregate thickness of 6050 ft were counted in 14·8 miles. Clearly a crustal extension of this magnitude is indicative of dyke

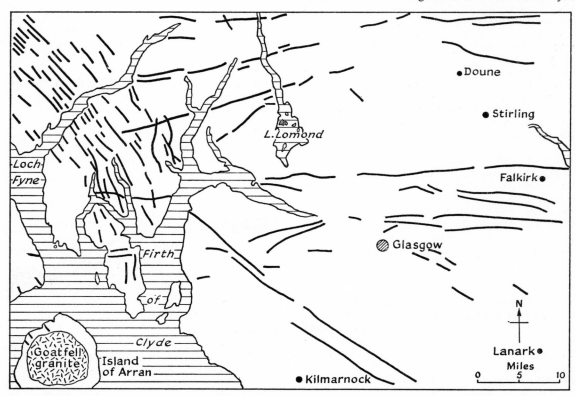

Fig. 4.5   Dyke swarms of Tertiary (NW–SE) and Permo-Carboniferous (E–W) age in central Scotland.

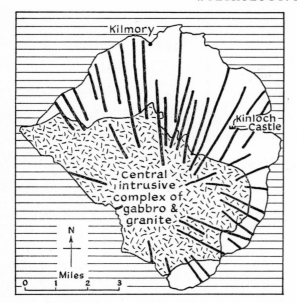

Fig. 4.6 Radial dykes on the Island of Rhum, Scotland.

formation during phases of lateral tension. Dykes developed radially around a large igneous intrusion are the result of the igneous infillings of former tension cracks situated above a rising igneous mass (Fig. 4.6).

Sills

Sills are tabular intrusions, commonly of dolerite, which largely conform to the bedding of the intruded stratified rocks (Plate 2b). It should be noted that the intrusions are not necessarily horizontal, for as with stratified rocks they can be greatly inclined. Locally they are transgressive, that is, the strati-

graphical horizon of the intrusion may change along a dyke-like step, termed a *transgression*. The vertical range may be large and transgressions of over 1000 ft along pre-intrusion fault surfaces have been recorded in the Stirling Sill, Scotland (Reid, 1959, pp. 53–9), (Fig. 4.7).

Sills may vary from a few to hundreds of feet in thickness, and this may also differ in an individual intrusion. Thus the Great Whin Sill of Northern England varies from about 70 ft to over 240 ft. Often the intrusions cover large areas and the dolerites of the Karroo in South Africa, averaging up to 500 ft in thickness, occupy as much as 5000 mile². Undoubtedly the relatively low viscosity of basic, as compared with acid magma, renders such a widespread intrusion possible. Acid sills are neither so numerous nor as widespread.

Laccoliths

Usually with plane lower and gently arched upper surfaces, laccoliths are concordant intrusions. They may develop as a local thickening of a sill, an origin now considered to be more probable than the originally suggested central feeder pipe. In contrast to sills and dykes the rocks most commonly forming laccoliths are intermediate or acidic in composition. The viscosities of such magmas would determine the dome-like shapes of the intrusions, which therefore crop out over comparatively small surface areas. Frequently the intrusions are composite, having a layered structure due to a successive sequence of magma injections (Fig. 4.8).

Stocks

Stocks or *bosses* are discordant, usually granitic, intrusions, of irregular shape and with surface areas up to about 40 mile². Their sides are steeply plunging

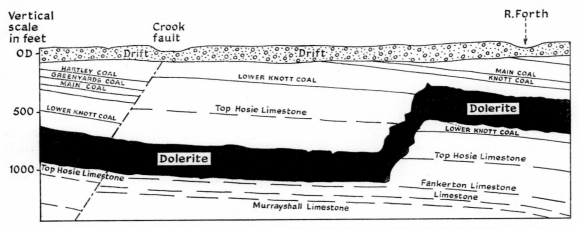

Fig. 4.7 Section illustrating a transgression in the Stirling Sill, Scotland. (After M. & A. G. Macgregor.)

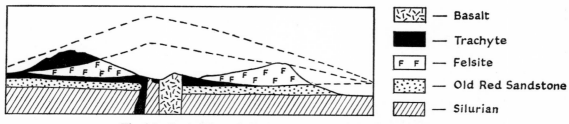

	— Basalt
	— Trachyte
F F	— Felsite
	— Old Red Sandstone
	— Silurian

Fig. 4.8   Section through the laccolith of the Eildon Hills, Scotland.

and many such masses may be merely projections of the irregular upper surfaces of batholiths. A consequence of the upwelling of magma is that the country rocks may become domed and therefore strike approximately parallel to the margin of the intrusion despite its discordant nature. This apparent suggestion of conformity is not generally supported by detailed mapping (Fig. 4.9).

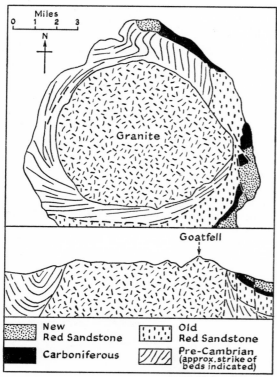

	New Red Sandstone		Old Red Sandstone
	Carboniferous		Pre-Cambrian (approx. strike of beds indicated)

Fig. 4.9   Sketch map and section of the Northern Granite, Island of Arran, Scotland.

Batholiths

Batholiths are intrusive masses of irregular shape and are composed of eucrystalline acid rocks, of which granodiorite is the most common type. Their scale is immense and the largest, the Coast Range Batholith of North America, has a surface area of at least 100000 mile². With steep sides plunging rapidly into sub-crustal depths, the nature of their floors is problematical (Fig. 4.10). Many appear to have formed in the cores of fold mountain systems so that they are only visible in deeply eroded areas.

There is much discussion and speculation as to the origin and mode of emplacement of an intrusion of batholithic dimensions. Certainly they cannot be intruded by simply wedging the country rocks aside. For such an origin would require unprecedented expansions of the Earth's crust. It may be that masses of country rock were incorporated in the igneous magma. In some cases the granitization of the surrounding rocks *in situ* is indicated by the gradational sequence of rock types between undoubted country and igneous rocks. In such examples no sharp boundary can be drawn around the intrusion, and within the batholith itself there may be relic traces of bedding and other structures characteristic of the country rock. Clearly the acceptance of an ultra-metamorphic origin of the 'intrusive' rock solves the space problem, even if we must then return to the perennial arguments concerning the origin of granites (page 24).

VULCANISM

Vulcanism is the surface manifestation of igneous activity. Extrusive igneous rocks or lavas pour out from fissures or pipes through the Earth's crust. This may be accompanied by the deposition of pyroclastic material derived from the explosive fragmentation of pre-existing rocks.

VOLCANOES

By the accumulation of lavas and pyroclastic material a characteristic land form, the volcano, is built up (Table 6).

Central Volcanoes

Central volcanoes are fed by a vertical pipe, around the orifice of which material will accumulate to form a conical deposit. On erosion, only the volcanic pipes may remain as agglomerate and/or

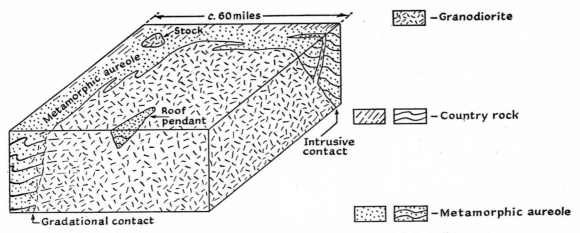

Fig. 4.10   Block diagram to illustrate the major features of a batholith.

lava-filled *necks* and *vents*. Such residual features are not uncommon in the Scottish coalfields.

Pyroclastic cones. Entirely composed of volcanic debris, pyroclastic cones are steep sided fragmental accumulations. The coarser fragments are situated immediately around a central crater, away from which there is an outward gradation to finer material (Fig. 4.11a). Naturally such accumulations when unconsolidated may be rapidly eroded, so that the initially high-angled slopes are modified before burial by later rocks. In a recent off-shore bore in the Firth of Forth, Scotland, a pyroclastic cone at least 536 ft thick was proved in a Carboniferous sequence. Several workable coals in adjacent areas thin out and are locally absent in the vicinity of the deposit (Francis and Ewing, 1961, Figs 2 & 3).

Lava volcanoes. The appearance of a lava volcano depends primarily on the fluidity of the magma. Thus lava domes may be distinguished from shield volcanoes. The latter were formed by successive flows of extremely viscous lava which piled up as

sluggish masses around the central crater. Since therefore the areal extent of such a lava is limited, the resulting volcano will be dome-like. This shape may be further emphasized by later magma failing to reach the surface and so forming a series of intrusive blisters within the volcano. Other lavas, of more basic composition, flow more readily so that they spread out as thin, nearly horizontal sheets covering large areas. Many such shield volcanoes are extremely low in proportion to their great surface area. The term originates from their similarity in shape to a warrior's shield.

Composite volcanoes. Composite volcanoes are composed of lenticular sheets of both pyroclastic and igneous rocks which form a complex interdigitating series (Fig. 4.11b). In some cases the central pipe may become totally blocked with solidified material. New volcanic activity is then confined to the development of minor *parasitic cones* on the flanks of the main volcano. In rarer cases, blockage of the central pipe results in the opening of lateral cracks on the flanks

TABLE 6

Classification of Volcanic Types

Feeder	Volcanic material		Type
Central Pipe	Pyroclastic		Pyroclastic cones
	Lava	Acidic and Intermediate Igneous Rocks	Lava domes
		Basic Igneous Rocks	Shield volcanoes
	Pyroclastic and lava		Composite volcanoes
Fissure	Basic lava		Fissure eruptions

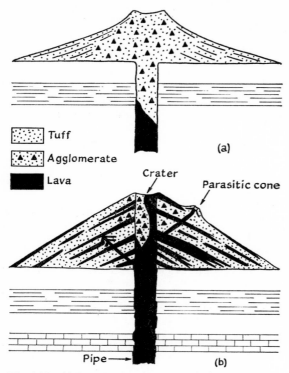

Tuff

Agglomerate

Lava

(a)

Crater

Parasitic cone

Pipe

(b)

Fig. 4.11 (a) Pyroclastic cone (b) Composite volcano.

from which pour gaseous masses of lava and ash. In 1902 such a *nuée ardente* erupted from the West Indian volcano, Mt Pelée, and totally annihilated the 30000 inhabitants of St Pierre which lay in its path (Holmes, 1965, pp. 333–6).

Fissure eruptions

All the present-day volcanic eruptions are of the central type, but some of the most widespread lava flows have originated from long continuous fissures tapping a sub-crustal basaltic layer. Such an origin is probable for the basaltic lavas of the Indian Deccan, which total over 7000 ft in thickness and have a surface of over 200000 mile². As compared with the products of normal volcanoes, those of fissure eruptions have a more regional distribution.

PYROCLASTIC ROCKS

Fragmental materials formed by settling from the atmosphere and resulting from explosive vulcanicity are collectively termed *pyroclasts*. Depending on the size of fragments two major rock types are recognized.

Agglomerate

Agglomerates or *volcanic breccias*, chiefly occurring in and around the volcanic necks, are composed

of extremely coarse fragments set in a finer matrix. The fragments are frequently angular and may consist of blocks of lava, tuff or country rock torn from the volcanic pipe and crater area during the eruption. Occasionally large clots of still molten lava may be ejected during an eruption. Such *volcanic bombs* often have ovoid or spherical shapes developed by their rotation as they fell through the atmosphere. The agglomerate type is termed *bomb-rock*.

Tuff

The finer-grained pyroclastic material may be deposited in a sub-aerial or sub-aqueous environment to form tuff, which may therefore possess a normal sedimentary structure. Depending on the nature of the material several types are recognized. Thus *vitric tuffs* are made up principally of glassy shreds formed by the rapid cooling of minute lava fragments. *Lithic tuffs* are composed of finely crystalline stony material, whilst *welded tuffs* of a streaky appearance may have been deposited by *nuées ardentes*.

Owing to their extremely fine-grained nature, tuffs are generally distributed over a wider area than other volcanic material. They may occur at great distances from their source. In such cases the presence of rare layers of tuff in a sedimentary sequence may be of use in correlation.

REFERENCES

DEWEY, H. (1948) South-West England, *Regional Handbook geol. Surv. G.B.*

FRANCIS, E. H. & C. J. C. EWING (1961) Coal Measures and volcanism off the Fife coast, *Geol. Mag.* **98**, 501–10.

HARKER, A. & J. E. MARR (1891) The Shap granite and associated igneous and metamorphic rocks, *Q. Jl. geol. Soc. Lond.* **47**, 266–327.

HATCH, F. H., M. K. & A. K. WELLS (1949) *The Petrology of the Igneous Rocks*, 10th ed., London, Allen and Unwin (Murby).

HOLMES, A. (1965) *Principles of Physical Geology*, 2nd ed., London, Nelson.

JOHANNSON, A. (1939) *A Descriptive Petrography of the Igneous Rocks, Vol. I, Introduction, Textures, Classifications and Glossary*, 1st ed., Chicago, University of Chicago Press.

MACGREGOR, M. & A. G. (1948) The Midland Valley of Scotland, *Regional Handbook geol. Surv. G.B.*

READ, H. H. (1957) *The Granite Controversy*, 1st ed., London, Allen and Unwin (Murby).

READ, W. A. (1959) The economic geology of the Stirling and Clackmannan coalfield, Scotland, *Coalfld Pap. geol. Surv. G.B.* **2**.

RICHEY, J. E. (1948) Tertiary Volcanic Districts, Scotland, *Regional Handbook geol. Surv. G.B.*

SABINE, P. A. & J. V. WATSON (1965) Isotopic age-determinations of rocks from the British Isles, 1954–64, *Q. Jl. geol. Soc. Lond.* **121**, 477–523.

SHAND, S. J. (1949) *Eruptive Rocks*, 3rd ed., London, Allen and Unwin (Murby).

5

PETROLOGY, SEDIMENTARY ROCKS

INTRODUCTION

Sedimentary rocks (Hatch, *et al.*, 1965; Pettijohn, 1957), which cover over two-thirds of the world's total land surface, are composed of fragments of pre-existing rocks and minerals, organic materials and chemical precipitates. They are deposited as lenticular sheets or strata under marine or continental conditions. Marine sediments accumulate in three major environments which can be related to their relative depths below sea level—coastal, shelf or deep-water. Under normal conditions the progressive decrease in component size, from pebble beach through sand to fine mud, deposited in progressively deeper water conditions may be seen in most coastal areas. The non-marine sediments are principally the result of deposition in fluvial, lacustrine, desert, and more rarely, glacial environments. Since the position of sea level relative to the land surface is rarely constant for any length of time, the products of the marine and non-marine environments may be interdigitated, as in many Carboniferous sequences.

CLASSIFICATION OF SEDIMENTARY ROCKS

The general remarks concerning igneous rock classifications are also applicable to the sedimentary rocks. For, despite the wealth of data which has accumulated from detailed observations of sedimentary processes throughout the world, considerable difficulty is still experienced in forming a suitable and comprehensive classification. One sediment grades imperceptibly into another, and artificial boundaries are clearly unsatisfactory in a sequence such as limestone, sandy limestone, calcareous sandstone and sandstone. The end members may be easily defined, but what of the intermediate grades? It would appear logical to classify sedimentary rocks according to their origins so that three main groups can be recognized: detrital or fragmental accumulations, organic accumulations and chemical precipitates. However such a grouping is unsatisfactory with regard to many rocks. For example, limestones, which

are composed almost entirely of calcite, can be formed in all of the three ways.

Accordingly the classification employed (Table 7) is a simple descriptive type based primarily on their chemical and mineralogical compositions and secondly on the actual modes of origin of the rocks. Another criterion, that of grain size, is used for the important clastic siliceous group.

SILICEOUS SEDIMENTS

The siliceous group forming the majority of all sedimentary rocks is largely composed of quartz and other silicate minerals. Two main classes, clastic and non-clastic, are recognized.

Clastic siliceous sediments

The commonest sediments are of the clastic siliceous class. They consist of fragments and grains derived from pre-existing rocks and minerals set in a finer-grained matrix. The latter may have been deposited at the same time as, or formed subsequently to the deposition of the sediment. Subdivisions are made according to the size, shape and nature of the component particles.

Rudaceous rocks. The sub-class includes the coarsest sediments with a minimum particle size of 2 mm. Generally the fragments or *phenoclasts* attain much larger dimensions. Two principal rock types, conglomerates and breccias, are distinguished.

Conglomerates are composed of rounded phenoclasts which accumulate chiefly as pebble beds. The interstices between the pebbles are usually occupied by finer-grained material of similar composition and a natural cement, often of quartz or calcite. The most typical conglomerates are ancient beach deposits. They are therefore often associated with unconformities, as for instance in the basal-Carboniferous beds at Ingleton, Yorkshire (page 89, Fig. 9.3). Other conglomerates represent former stream channel deposits, so they are therefore encountered in many Coal Measure washouts. In the Southern Hemisphere certain conglomerates of Permo-Carboniferous age are attributed to a glacial origin. Such ancient glacial deposits or *tillites* have many characters similar to the as yet unconsolidated Pleistocene tills

TABLE 7

A Classification of the Common Sedimentary Rocks

Group		Class			Rock types
SILICEOUS		Clastic	Rudaceous sub-class	*Grain size* > 2 mm	Breccia, conglomerate
			Arenaceous sub-class	0·062 mm to 2 mm	Sandstone, flagstone, greywacke
			Argillaceous sub-class	< 0·062 mm	Siltstone, mudstone, shale
		Non-clastic			Flint, chert
CARBONATE	Calcareous sub-group	Clastic			Clastic limestone
		Organic			Shelly limestone
		Chemical			Oolitic limestone
	Dolomitic sub-group	Primary			Primary dolostone
		Secondary			Secondary dolostone
EVAPORITES					Anhydrite, gypsum, halite
FERRUGINOUS					Ironstones
CARBONACEOUS					Coals (see Chapters 18 and 19)

of Europe and North America. Most conglomerate beds vary considerably in thickness and lateral distribution.

In the above examples the contained pebbles are considerably older than the actual bed. Thus the basal-Carboniferous conglomerate at Ingleton is largely composed of pebbles and boulders derived from the erosion of the immediately underlying Pre-Cambrian rocks. However in certain cases the difference in age between the phenoclasts and the bed as a whole is negligible. Thus the *mud-flake conglomerates* of the English Coal Measures were formed by the local erosion of a clay bed and the almost contemporaneous deposition of the eroded fragments nearby.

Breccias are distinguished by the shapes of the phenoclasts, for unlike the water-worn and rounded pebbles of conglomerates those of breccias are noticeably angular. Fault and sedimentary breccias are the major types. The former are situated along fault surfaces and are formed by earth movements (page 76). Fault breccias are composed entirely of fragments derived from strata adjacent to the faults,

and are often cemented by quartz, calcite and other minerals deposited by solutions percolating along the dislocation. Sedimentary breccias, which are notably lenticular and have a restricted local distribution, commonly form as ancient scree deposits composed of rock chips and fragments which collect at the foot of cliffs. Such breccias must occur *in situ*, as the phenoclasts would have become rounded had they been transported any distance.

Arenaceous rocks. Arenaceous rocks have an average grain size of between 2 and 0·0625 mm (Table 8). The wide variety of constituent grains, matrices and cements permits the distinction of several important rock types.

The dominant constituents of *sandstones* are quartz fragments, which frequently comprise over 90 per cent of the mineral grains. The remainder are principally rock fragments, micas and felspars, together with a small percentage of 'heavy minerals' of little importance in the rock classification but sometimes useful in correlation (pages 208–9). Aeolian (wind-deposited) and aqueous (water-deposited) sandstones are characterized by the nature of the

TABLE 8

Grades of Arenaceous Sediments

Limiting dimensions in mm	Sandstone type
1–2	Very coarse sandstone
0·5–1	Coarse sandstone
0·25–0·5	Medium sandstone
0·125–0·25	Fine sandstone
0·0625–0·125	Very fine sandstone

individual sand grains. Those of aqueous sands have angular shapes since during transportation the individual grains were knocked against each other and so developed sharp and well-chipped edges. Conversely, aeolian sand grains were rolled over a desert surface thereby acquiring rounded outlines. The Permian 'millet-seed' sandstones of N.W. England are of this type (Fig. 5.1). An aeolian origin is also suggested by their red coloration, which is due to the presence of finely divided iron oxide. It should however be emphasized that such a coloration may only be used as supporting evidence for the deposition of a sediment under arid conditions (Dunbar & Rodgers, 1957, pp. 209–18).

Fig. 5.1 Microscopic structure of aeolian sandstone. The sediment is a well-sorted aggregate composed of rounded quartz grains.

The cementing media of sandstones are most commonly siliceous, calcareous, dolomitic or ferruginous. Sandstones having a quartz cement are generally light-coloured hard rocks which form durable building stones. Carbonate cements, commonly either calcite or dolomite, because of their soluble natures form less durable and softer sandstones. The presence of a ferruginous cement is often indicated by a brownish or red coloration of the weathered sandstones. Less common cements, usually having a patchy and local distribution, include barite, gypsum, fluorite and the copper carbonates, malachite and azurite.

Arkoses are arenaceous rocks with felspars forming over 20 per cent of the fragmentary material. The presence of a smaller felspar content may be indicated by a prefix—e.g. felspathic sandstone. Under normal conditions of temperature and humidity felspar rapidly decomposes to the soft clay mineral, kaolinite. Its occurrence in a rock indicates either rapid sedimentation outstripping the decay rate, or else deposition in an arid climate. Thus the locally arkosic sandstones of the Namurian, which formed in a warm humid climate, owe their felspar content to very rapid deposition and burial under deltaic conditions. Again the Upper Pre-Cambrian Torridonian Series of N.W. Scotland contain felspathic sandstones and arkoses. In this case there is contributary evidence for the derivation of the sediments from a desert land mass.

By the increasing abundance of mica a sandstone passes, through a micaceous variety, into a *flagstone* which may easily be split into thin layers. The parting surfaces are thinly covered with small silvery plates of muscovite. The particular structure of flagstone results from the differential settling of quartz and mica, the latter mineral subsiding more slowly than quartz from an aqueous suspension and being selectively concentrated as a distinct layer.

Normally sediments are naturally sorted into beds of more or less uniform grain size. This is because coarse debris is deposited nearer to the source than finer material, which accumulates farther away. Thus a shale may pass laterally into a sandstone; hence the many problems of correlation. *Greywackes* are therefore unusual rocks in that their components range from coarse sands and even pebbles to extremely fine-grained argillaceous material. It is considered that many have been deposited by dense sediment-laden masses of water, termed turbidity-currents, flowing down and eroding into an off-shore slope. Ultimately the current velocity is decreased as the slope lessens so that the unsorted sediment is deposited *en masse* to form a greywacke. Alternatively it has recently been suggested that in some cases the clay matrix may be secondary in origin, being formed by the decomposition of unstable grains in the original sediment (Cummins, 1962).

Argillaceous rocks. Having a maximum dimension of 0·062 mm, the constituent particles of the argillaceous rocks cannot be so readily determined as those of the other clastic sediments. Indeed, with the exception of the coarser siltstones, normal microscopic methods of mineral identification are usually impossible. Argillaceous rocks are composed of a number of hydrous aluminium silicates, the clay minerals, together with minor amounts of quartz and other silicate particles. Since a study of the mineralogy of the sediments is a highly specialized subject (Grim, 1953) involving chemical, radiographic and electron microscopic techniques, the following descriptions are based on their simple macroscopic properties.

Having grain sizes between 0·062 and 0·005 mm *siltstones* are intermediate rocks between sandstones and mudstones. They may be distinguished from other argillaceous rocks by their rough feel when rubbed with the finger. This property is due to their considerable quartz content. Their finely laminated nature (page 41) is in most cases due to alternating quartzose and clay layers.

Shales and *mudstones* possess extremely fine-grained textures since the constituent clay minerals are less than 0·005 mm in maximum dimension. Both are smooth to the touch and usually are bluish-black or dark grey in colour. Shales are highly fissile rocks which, particularly when weathered, may be separated into paper-thin layers. *Oil shales* are a variety which on distillation yield quantities of oil derived from organic material present in the rock. They are often brown to black in colour and have a brown streak when scratched. When freshly cut with a knife thin peels of oil shale will sometimes curl up at the edges.

Mudstones are relatively massive rocks which cannot be easily split into layers. They often break with a conchoidal or semi-conchoidal fracture. Those with a calcite content of over 25 per cent are termed *marl*, though some ambiguity has arisen from the use of the name in a stratigraphical sense, as for instance the Keuper Marl which is essentially non-calcareous.

Non-clastic siliceous sediments

This class contains what are virtually monomineralic rocks composed of quartz or its varieties. They form by either chemical precipitation or by organic action. *Chert* and *flint* (page 11) are the most abundant types. Both are locally common in calcareous rocks but may also occur in arenaceous or argillaceous sediments. They occur as either thin and discontinuous beds up to about 1 ft thick or as isolated nodules.

CARBONATE SEDIMENTS

The greater proportion of the carbonate sediments is composed of calcite or dolomite. Two major rock types, limestone and dolostone, are defined according to the nature of their mineralogical composition.

Limestones

Limestones are almost entirely composed of calcite and are usually light-coloured rocks distinguishable from most others by their marked solubility in cold dilute hydrochloric acid. On complete solution of the calcite, a small percentage, commonly less than 5 per cent, of insoluble argillaceous, siliceous or ferruginous material remains. Some limestones, as for example those of Lower Carboniferous age in England and Wales (pages 178–80), may form thickly bedded units of considerable thicknesses in which other rock types are absent. Alternatively they may be thinly bedded, in which case they are often members of an alternating shale-limestone sequence.

Since most limestones have been subjected to subsequent recrystallization, the primary structures, by which their origins may be determined, are often extremely difficult to recognize. Accordingly although they may form as organic accumulations of fossil material, clastic accumulations of pre-existing limestone fragments and grains, and as chemical or biochemical precipitates, a simple genetic classification is in most cases unsatisfactory. It is moreover apparent that many limestones result from a complex interaction of processes.

Shelly limestone is a term which may be applied to any highly fossiliferous bed. Such limestones, whose outcrops form the Mecca of the fossil collector, are composed of both macroscopic and microscopic fossils included in a carbonate matrix. This may be either chemical or clastic in origin. It is usual to prefix the name of an essentially organic limestone with that of the predominant fossil member (e.g. crinoidal limestone, coral limestone, foraminiferal limestone (Fig. 5.2a), *Syringothyris* limestone). Some of the most fossiliferous limestones have a

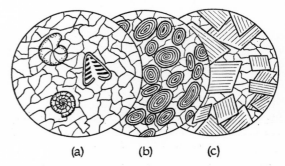

Fig. 5.2 Microscopic structure of (a) foraminiferal limestone, (b) oolitic limestone and (c) dolostone.

markedly lenticular character. They accumulated as isolated reefs or shell-banks surrounded by deeper waters in which argillaceous sediments were deposited.

Chemical precipitation has undoubtably played a major role in the formation of *oolitic limestones* (Carozzi, 1960, pp. 238–60), (Fig. 5.2b). These are composed of small spherical or ovoid bodies (ooliths)

Plate 3(a) Well-bedded bituminous limestones and shales, Clitheroe, Lancashire.

Plate 3(b) Cross-stratification in the Falsebedded Sandstones, Enugu, Nigeria.

Plate 4(a) Oblique aerial photograph of a large plunging anticline, Kuh-I-Pabda, Iran.

Plate 4(b) Asymmetrical syncline, Bude, Cornwall.

up to 2 mm in diameter. *Pisolitic limestone* is a related type in which the ooliths are over 2 mm in diameter. The ooliths have a nucleus of either clastic or organic material surrounded by a series of concentric bands of calcite. They form in turbulent shallow-water conditions by the precipitation of calcite around sand and other chance grains.

Chalks, of Mesozoic or recent age, are porous, fine-grained and light-coloured rocks frequently composed of over 98 per cent calcium carbonate. They may be distinguished from other limestones by their more friable and softer natures. Many can easily be scratched with the finger nail, and in collecting some of the more recent examples a trowel may be of more use than a hammer! They are mainly composed of microscopic organic remains and were probably formed in a shallow-water or moderately deep-water environment (Hatch *et al.*, 1965, pp. 197–9).

Dolostones

Dolostones (dolomites) (Fig. 5.2c) are composed of the mineral dolomite (page 13). Many authorities use the same name for both the mineral and the rock type, and it is suggested that the ambiguity be removed by restricting the usage of the term dolomite to the mineral alone (Dunbar and Rodgers, 1957, p. 219 ff.). Dolostones are creamy-yellow, weathering to brown, rocks with a sandy texture. Compared with limestones they are less soluble, only effervescing in *warm* dilute hydrochloric acid. From their stratigraphic relations (Fig. 5.3) dolostones may be classified into primary and secondary types.

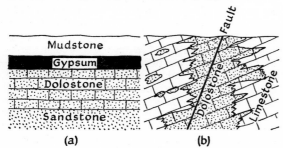

(a) (b)

Fig. 5.3 Diagrammatic sections showing the non-transgressive and transgressive relationships of (a) primary dolostones and (b) secondary dolostones.

Primary dolostones are bedded deposits with constant stratigraphic horizons. Since they are rarely observed forming at the present day their precise origins are uncertain (*op. cit.*, pp. 237–44). Their common association with evaporites is however indicative that dolostone formation is favoured by an arid climate and considerable salinity of the sedimentary environment. They may have formed by

C.M.G.—4

the direct chemical precipitation of dolomite or else by the penecontemporaneous replacement of a calcite deposit by magnesia-rich fluids. The Magnesian Limestone of N.E. England appears to be largely of the latter type, as in places considerable masses of unaltered limestone remain. Also, the contained fossils represent a fauna which could certainly not have existed in a sea with a salinity such that dolomite was contemporaneously being precipitated. The fissured nature of the series, which is locally associated with hydrogeological problems in the underlying Coal Measures, would result from the penecontemporaneous dolomitization of a limestone, since there is a 12 per cent volume decrease during the conversion of limestone to dolostone.

Secondary dolostones have no constant stratigraphic horizon and form markedly transgressive units. Isolated patches, often rendered conspicuous by their brownish coloration, may occur in limestones, or a zone of dolomitized rock may be situated adjacent to a fault or mineral vein. Clearly secondary dolostones form by the subsequent dolomitization of a limestone by magnesia-rich fluids percolating along fault fissures and mineral veins.

EVAPORITES

The evaporites are bedded deposits formed by the precipitation of soluble salts contained in sea water. Of importance as the source of raw materials for the chemical industry, they are chiefly composed of sulphates and chlorides of calcium, sodium and potassium. The commonest mineral salts are gypsum ($CaSO_4.2H_2O$) (page 13), anhydrite ($CaSO_4$) and halite (NaCl). Apart from gypsum they rarely crop out because of their soluble nature, and are either extracted by brine pumping or mining.

Since they form under arid climatic conditions they are often associated with red mudstones, aeolian sandstones and dolostones. The important British evaporite sequences are therefore confined to the Permian and Triassic systems (Sherlock, 1921; Sherlock & Hollingworth, 1938). The deposits, many hundreds of feet thick, are not simply the result of the total evaporation of a static water mass. It has been calculated that the complete evaporation of a deep body of water such as the Mediterranean would only form about 80 ft of salts, and there are many indications that evaporites form as shallow-water deposits. An essential condition for the development of a thick evaporite series is a steady replenishment of the evaporating sea by an inflowing saline current (Fig. 5.4). In this way an extremely thick deposit may form. Usually the salts are precipitated in the inverse order of their solubilities so that in many sequences a vertical zonation may be identified. Thus the Permian deposits of East York-

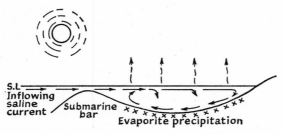

Fig. 5.4   Conditions for evaporite formation.

shire possess a number of cycles, each having an upward succession from dolostone, anhydrite and halite to potassium salts (Fig. 5.5). In the same field a lateral zonation is also apparent. The most soluble

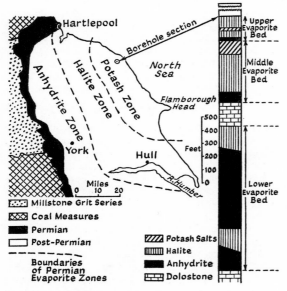

Fig. 5.5   Sketch map and section illustrating the Permian evaporite deposits of N.E. Yorkshire.

potassium salts are confined to the extreme east of the county, westwards from which only the less soluble evaporites occur (Dunham, 1960, pp. 264–84).

FERRUGINOUS SEDIMENTS

Various iron compounds are common as minor impurities and isolated nodules in many sediments, but their concentration in iron-rich beds of economic importance is relatively rare. Ironstones are ferruginous sediments in which the iron content is over 15 per cent. Usually they may be recognized in hand specimens by their high specific gravities. The more important types are clay and chamosite ironstones.

Clay ironstones are the typical ferruginous sedi-

ments of the Coal Measures (pages 61–3). They are chiefly composed of siderite (page 13) and clayey material.

The *chamosite ironstones* contain the green iron-silicate mineral, chamosite. This is often associated with siderite, as in the important British Jurassic ironstones of Cleveland, Frodingham and Northampton. Oolitic textures are commonly developed but their origin cannot be simply explained by the replacement of an oolitic limestone. It is considered that chamosite develops independently of siderite in a marine environment by a series of extremely complex precipitation processes (Dunham, 1960, pp. 250–64).

SEDIMENTARY STRUCTURES

The truth of the maxim that 'the study of the present is a key to the past' can rarely be more evident than in sedimentary petrology. From the observation of modern sedimentary structures we can logically deduce that identical features preserved in ancient sediments originated in similar conditions. Many sedimentary structures, recently most comprehensively described and illustrated (Potter & Pettijohn, 1963; Pettijohn & Potter, 1964), are of directional significance and as such are of importance to the mining geologist engaged in the assessment of face conditions and the prediction of discontinuities such as washouts.

NORMAL STRATIFICATION

The most obvious feature of a sedimentary series is its stratification (Plate 3a); that is, the possession by rocks of a layered structure which results from their original mode of deposition (Twenhofel, 1950, pp. 546–50). In most cases the layers were originally horizontal or nearly so, but due to subsequent earth-movements, they are now generally inclined. Apart from highly folded areas there is an orderly sequence of stratified units with the first-formed layers overlaid by later deposits. The stratification of a sedimentary sequence is most often rendered apparent by selective weathering emphasizing the original differences in hardness, composition and texture of the rock units. Bedded rocks may be distinguished from laminated rocks by the closer spacing of the latter's stratification surfaces (Table 9).

Bedding

Most sedimentary rocks may be easily split along their bedding surfaces. If the latter are dominant features in a rock, it is described as *well-bedded*. Alternatively the feature is only weakly developed in *massive* rocks. When the bedding surfaces are even, in which case the often erroneously used term *bedding-plane* is applicable, the bed itself may be

TABLE 9

Classification of Stratification (according to Ingram, 1954)

Unit	Class	Thickness in cm
Bed	Very thick-bedded	
		100
	Thick-bedded	
		30
	Medium-bedded	
		10
	Thin-bedded	
		3
	Very thin-bedded	
		1
Lamina	Laminated	
		0·3
	Thinly laminated	

constant over a wide area. Alternatively the surfaces are irregular and undulating, as below many coarse and medium sandstones, so that the beds may rapidly thin out. A study of the exact nature of the bedding may therefore enable some prediction to be made as to the possible extension of a bed into an unproved area. Moreover a markedly irregular base of a sandstone is often indicative of its erosional nature and if developed above a coal seam may suggest the proximity of a washout (pages 193–5). Until recently the detailed study by the mining engineer of such bedding features has been ignored, with a consequent failure to use an important aid to predicting future conditions.

Lamination

As distinct from bedding, the possession of lamination does not always enable the rock to be split into thin individual units or *laminae*. For example, shales are well laminated rocks which, particularly when weathered, break along the lamination surfaces into often paper-thin sheets, whereas many fine sandstones though distinctly laminated often only separate into beds. Again, some massive mudstones may be *colour-laminated*. The laminae may be even or uneven; those of shales are frequently planar and have a remarkably uniform development over considerable areas. Some siltstones however possess laminae which form small-scale cross-stratification units. When the lamination surfaces are micaceous, parting frequently occurs, so that adverse roof conditions may be experienced below a flagstone series.

GRADED BEDDING

Graded bedding, a structure most commonly developed in arenaceous sediments, is characterized by a vertical gradation of grain size within the bed. Normally there is a gradual change from coarse material at the base of the bed to fine at the top. Beds with such *positive grading* possess a sharply defined lower contact which may be of an erosional nature. The structure is sometimes present in sandstones forming washouts, in which case it clearly results from the silting of river channels. In some cases *inverted* or *negative grading* has been recorded (Clarke, 1963, p. 674), where the bed exhibits an upward coarsening in grain size. Much of the graded bedding in non-coal-bearing sequences is associated with greywackes and is attributed to sediment deposition from turbidity-currents (Pettijohn, 1957, pp. 170–8).

CROSS-STRATIFICATION

Cross-stratification (current-bedding, false-bedding, foreset-bedding) as developed in clastic rocks consists of a series of variously shaped layers or *sets* varying in size from small-scale features less than 1 in thick to massive large-scale units several feet in thickness. Each set lies between, and is inclined up at about 30 degrees to the normal stratification surfaces (Plate 3b). The latter may be the least apparent feature, so that in an isolated exposure, the cross-stratification may be mistaken for the bedding and so result in a complete misconception of the geological structure (Fig. 5.6).

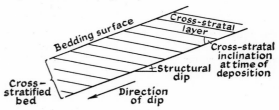

Fig. 5.6 Cross-stratal and structural dip.

From the cross-sectional appearance two common types may be recognized in the interseam sediments (Clarke, 1963, pp. 696–7). In the *rectilineal* type the cross-strata appear as series of tabular sheets terminating abruptly against the bedding (Fig. 5.7a). Where several such sets (cosets) are developed their inclination is commonly in a similar direction, although occasionally a chevron-effect is given by cosets inclined in opposite directions. *Festoon* sets of cross-strata have rounded bases which are concave upwards and appear to have been deposited in a series of troughs (Fig. 5.7b).

Cross-stratification is formed by the uneven deposition of sediments in either aqueous or aeolian environments. Its mode of formation appears to be related to that of asymmetrical ripple marks (Allen,

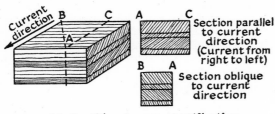

(a) Rectilineal cross-stratification

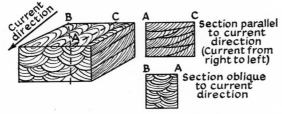

(b) Festoon cross-stratification

Fig. 5.7 Diagrams illustrating the three-dimensional nature of cross-stratification.

1963) and in some cases is analogous to a workman tipping successive barrowloads of sand and so building a ramp-like feature, with each load inclined away from the source and separated by a depositional slope—equivalent to a cross-stratal surface. The recording of cross-stratification is clearly of importance in stratigraphical studies, for it is indicative of the source direction of the sediments. Thus studies of the rectilineal variety, occurring in Namurian sandstones in the English Pennines, show that the beds were deposited by rivers having a north-easterly source (Gilligan, 1920, pp. 283–4; Shackleton, 1962, pp. 113–16). Furthermore, since cross-stratification is frequently encountered in channel deposits, as for example in washouts, the estimation of current direction is of considerable economic importance in the prediction of the trends of such discontinuities. Unfortunately the current direction cannot be simply estimated by the random measurement of the cross-stratal dip of a bed (Fig. 5.7). With the rectilineal type the current direction is indicated by the 'true dips' of the cross-strata measured at right angles to their strike. In the case of the festoon type the current direction can be estimated by noting the trend of the confining troughs. Furthermore, corrections must be applied when there has been subsequent tilting of the beds, for in areas of folded strata directional sedimentary structures no longer retain their original orientation (Bouma, 1962, pp. 25–7; Potter & Pettijohn, 1963, pp. 259–62).

RIPPLE MARKS

Ripple marks are groups of small wave-like troughs and ridges commonly occurring on the bedding surfaces of sandstones and more rarely on limestones and argillaceous beds. They vary in size from almost microscopic forms to large undulations with amplitudes of hundreds of yards. Of the many varieties described (Shrock, 1948, pp. 92–127) there are three major types.

Oscillation ripples (Fig. 5.8a) are symmetrical in cross-section and consist of a series of broadly rounded troughs with sharp or truncated intervening crests. They are produced by wave action, and since normal waves have little effect below about 30 ft are indicative of shallow-water deposition. *Current ripples* are composed of asymmetric ridges and hollows spaced fairly regularly up to about 12 in apart in the case of *small-scale* ripples and many feet apart in that of *large-scale* ripples (dunes, megaripples, sandwaves). They are transverse to the current direction with the steeper slopes on the downstream side. In plan, *straight forms* of fairly constant direction can be distinguished from the concentric *linguoid* and *lunate forms* which possess curved crest lines (Allen, 1963, pp. 189–203). Ripples formed by aqueous currents (Fig. 5.8b) are more prominent features than the rarer aeolian-current forms. *Interference ripples* may form by the interaction of wave and current forces so that two or more sets of

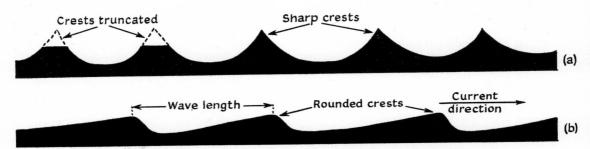

Fig. 5.8 Types of ripple marks, (a) oscillation ripples, (b) current ripples.

ripples develop at angles to each other. Consequently the bedding surfaces have an indented appearance.

CONTEMPORANEOUS DEFORMATION STRUCTURES

Sometimes one or more intensely crumpled beds occur in an otherwise normally bedded sequence. Most of the deformation structures were formed during, or soon after, the deposition of the bed and can be attributed to sedimentary rather than tectonic forces.

Slumped structures

The slumping of a bed occurs when it is deposited as an unstable saturated mass on an inclined surface. A slight earthquake shock, or local erosion at the foot of the slope, may start the whole mass moving down the slope. Common internal structures, revealed by lamination or bedding traces, are discontinuous asymmetrical folds of irregular trend and often broken by reverse faults. If more than one sediment has been affected, rafts or pillow-shaped masses of differing rock types may be grouped in juxtaposition. Prior to the deposition of the overlying beds the upper surface of the slumped sheet may be eroded, in which case the internal structure are frequently sharply truncated (Fig. 5.9). A slumped bed can be distinguished from other contemporaneous structures by its limited lateral extent, a markedly lenticular nature and an often 'intrusive' lower contact.

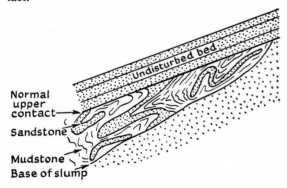

Fig. 5.9 Section illustrating the haphazard internal structures of a slumped bed.

Upper Carboniferous slumped sediments have been recorded from Derbyshire and S. Wales (Broadhurst, 1953, pp. 240–5; Keunen, 1948, pp. 365–80).

Load casting

Load casts are irregularly shaped, steep-sided projections on the undersurface of a sandstone bed. They are often of coarser grain size than the rest of the bed. Laminations in the underlying argillaceous rocks bend around the casts. Load casting most often originates by the differential loading of a soft sediment overlaid by sand. The irregular contact between the beds is also sometimes interpreted as having an erosional origin.

Earthquake disturbances

Occasionally beds of uniform thickness are deformed over a wide area. The internal structures may vary from minor contortions to highly complex overfolded and thrust masses involving several rock types. These, although originally deposited as distinct beds, may form a considerably intermixed mass with no regular lamination or bedding. The laminations of a mudstone may be so broken up as to make an incoherent *clod* which, when overlying a coal seam, results in extremely poor roof conditions. In a coal measure sequence the structures may be associated with stone intrusions developed within a coal (page 196). One such disturbed horizon, about 25 ft thick, occurs above the Fox Earth Coal of the East Midlands Coalfields and is recorded over a distance of 50 miles (Shirley, 1955).

The uniform thickness of such structures and the absence of any erosional features may suggest that they formed *in situ* rather than by any lateral movement. Their regional distribution may be most satisfactorily explained as resulting from earth tremors shaking up a partly consolidated or unconsolidated group of sediments.

Differential compaction

During the vertical compression of a sedimentary series various rock types will compact at different rates and by different amounts. Differential warping will occur over a wide area together with local minor distortions. Compaction effects may be negligible in sands as the grains are deposited in contact with one another. Argillaceous sediments on the other hand are deposited together with large quantities of water, so that large reductions in their original thicknesses are made by compaction effects. Consequently the interval between two coal seams may vary considerably depending on lateral variations in the interseam strata. It is often impossible to separate the effects of differential compaction and subsidence. In Fig. 5.10, by accepting the Upper and Lower Florida Seams to have been formed on an originally level surface, the thickness variations of the interseam strata may be interpreted in two ways.

(1) They may be a result of the greater compaction of the shale sequence in borehole No. 3. On deposition the sediments represented in the three boreholes had similar thicknesses.

(2) The compaction effects may have been accen-

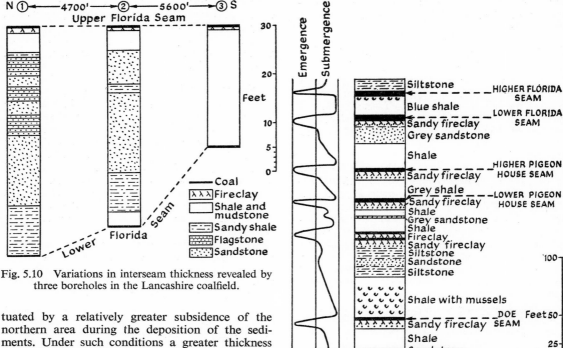

Fig. 5.10 Variations in interseam thickness revealed by three boreholes in the Lancashire coalfield.

Fig. 5.11 Typical Coal Measure cyclothems in the Lancashire coalfield. (Note the general decrease in grain size towards the base of each cyclothem.)

tuated by a relatively greater subsidence of the northern area during the deposition of the sediments. Under such conditions a greater thickness would accumulate in that area.

CYCLOTHEMS

The constant repetition of the interseam strata is a most noticeable feature of a Coal Measure succession as recorded in a shaft or borehole section (Fig. 5.11). Each rhythmic unit or *cyclothem* is composed of a sequence of rock types, usually characterized by an upward increase in the grain size of the clastic components, and is repeated many times in a stratigraphical succession. Cyclothems containing coal seams were first noted in the Lower Carboniferous of N. England, where the fully developed units, usually over 100 ft thick, are as follows:

COAL;
Seat earth with plant rootlets;
Fine- and medium-grained cross-stratified sandstones;
Flaggy sandstones;
Alternating thin sandstones and siltstones;
Siltstones;
Shales and mudstones, the lower beds containing marine fossils;
Limestone, containing marine fossils.

In the British Coal Measures the basal limestone is absent, so that the generalized sequence, on an average between about 20 ft and 60 ft thick, is:

COAL $\left\{\begin{array}{l}\text{Cannel;}\\ \text{Dull coal;}\\ \text{Bright Coal;}\end{array}\right.$

Seat earth with plant rootlets and ironstones;
Fine- and medium-grained cross-stratified sandstones;
Flaggy sandstone;
Siltstones and thin sandstones;
Unfossiliferous mudstones and shales;
Shale with non-marine fossils (mussel bands);
Pyritic shale with marine fossils (marine bands);
Shale with plant fossils and ironstones.

It is only in exceptional cases that the cyclothem is complete and usually several beds are absent. Thus in a statistical analysis of 1200 cyclothem records in the East Pennine coalfield, over 400 lacked a sandstone member, and in 154 cases only mudstones or shales occurred between adjacent coal horizons (Duff & Walton, 1962, p. 248). Similarly out of thirty-four cyclothems examined in two boreholes in the Durham coalfield (Clarke, 1963, Fig. 10) only three possessed the mudstone or shale, siltstone and sandstone interseam succession often quoted as the 'normal' sequence. From such studies it is apparent that variability is the keynote. Of all the cyclothem members the seat earths are the most consistent in their occurrence and the marine phase is only seldom developed.

The Carboniferous cyclothems reflect the relative oscillations of land and sea level. Thus coal formation wanes and finally ceases on submergence of the Coal Measure swamps. By the deposition of successive argillaceous and arenaceous beds in a deltaic environment (Moore, 1958, pp. 127–34) the surface is again built up above water level. In some cyclothems initially slow subsidence or compaction rates are indicated by the composition of the coal seam. The upper layers may be of dull and cannel coals which form in shallow-water conditions. Coal formation would cease at once on a rapid submergence of the coal swamps so that bright coal of essentially non-aqueous formation would be immediately followed by marine shale. Such sharp changes in sedimentation and rapid oscillations of sea level are primarily due to unstable crustal conditions. The progressive decrease in thickness and consequent greater frequency of the Upper as compared with the Lower Carboniferous cyclothems may therefore be a measure of the progressive build-up of forces which culminated in the Armorican orogeny (pages 128–9).

REFERENCES

ALLEN, J. R. L. (1963) Asymmetrical ripple marks and the origin of water-laid cosets of cross-strata, *Lpool Manchr geol. J.* **3**, 187–236.

BOUMA, A. H. (1962) *Sedimentology of some Flysch Deposits*, 1st ed., Amsterdam, Elsevier.

BROADHURST, F. M. (1953) A note on contorted gritstones in the Rowarth area of North Derbyshire, *Lpool Manchr geol. J.* **1**, 240–5.

CAROZZI, A. V. (1960) *Microscopic Sedimentary Petrography*, 1st ed., New York, Wiley.

CLARKE, A. M. (1963) A contribution to the understanding of washouts, swalleys, splits and other seam variations and the amelioration of their effects on mining in South Durham, *Trans. Instn Min. Engrs* **122**, 667–99.

CUMMINS, W. A. (1962) The greywacke problem, *Lpool Manchr geol. J.* **3**, 51–72.

DUFF, P. McL. D. & E. K. WALTON (1962) Statistical basis for cyclothems: A quantitative study of the sedimentary succession in the east Pennine coalfield, *Sedimentology* **1**, 235–55.

DUNBAR, C. O. & J. RODGERS (1957) *Principles of Stratigraphy*, 1st ed., New York, Wiley.

DUNHAM, K. C. (1960) Syngenetic and diagenetic mineralisation in Yorkshire, *Proc. Yorks. geol. Soc.* **32**, 229–84.

GILLIGAN, A. (1920) The petrography of the millstone grit of Yorkshire, *Q. Jl geol. Soc. Lond.* **75**, 251–92.

GRIM, R. E. (1953) *Clay Mineralogy*, 1st ed., London, McGraw-Hill.

HATCH, F. H., RASTALL, R. H. & J. T. GREENSMITH (1965) *The Petrology of the Sedimentary Rocks*, 4th ed., London, Allen and Unwin (Murby).

INGRAM, R. L. (1954) Terminology for the thickness of stratification and parting units in sedimentary rocks, *Bull. geol. Soc. Am.* **65**, 937–8.

KEUNEN, P. H. (1948) Slumping in the Carboniferous rocks of Pembrokeshire, *Q. Jl. geol. Soc. Lond.* **104**, 365–85.

MOORE, D. (1958) The Yoredale Series of upper Wensleydale and adjacent parts of north-west Yorkshire, *Proc. Yorks. geol. Soc.* **31**, 91–148.

PETTIJOHN, F. J. (1957) *Sedimentary Rocks*, 2nd ed., New York, Harper.

PETTIJOHN, F. J. & P. E. POTTER (1964) *Atlas and Glossary of Primary Sedimentary Structures*, 1st ed., Berlin, Springer-Verlag.

POTTER, P. E. & F. J. PETTIJOHN (1963) *Palaeocurrents and Basin Analysis*, 1st ed., Berlin, Springer-Verlag.

SHROCK, R. R. (1948) *Sequence in Layered Rocks*, 1st ed., London, McGraw-Hill.

SHACKLETON, J. S. (1962) Cross-strata in the Rough Rock (Millstone Grit Series) in the Pennines, *Lpool Manchr geol. J.* **3**, 109–18.

SHERLOCK, R. L. (1921) Rock salt and brine, *Spec. Rep. Miner. Resour. Gt Br. geol. Surv.* **18**, vi + 123 pp. London.

SHERLOCK, R. L. & S. E. HOLLINGWORTH (1938) Gypsum and anhydrite & celestine and strontianite, *Spec. Rep. Miner. Resour. Gt. Br. geol. Surv.* **3**, v + 98 pp. London (3rd ed.).

SHIRLEY, J. (1955). The disturbed strata on the Fox Earth Coal and its equivalents in the East Pennine coalfield, *Q. Jl. geol. Soc. Lond.* **111**, 265–79.

TWENHOFEL, W. H. (1950) *Principles of Sedimentation*, 2nd ed., London, McGraw-Hill.

6

PETROLOGY: METAMORPHIC ROCKS

INTRODUCTION

Metamorphic rocks are formed from the alteration of pre-existing igneous or sedimentary rocks by the effects of high temperatures and/or intense pressure or stress differences. In most cases metamorphic processes are aided by aqueous catalytic fluids either present in the original rock or derived from an external source. The straightforward catalytic action of such fluids must be distinguished from the introduction of secondary igneous material. In such *metasomatic metamorphism* the original chemical composition of the rock is changed. Where no such new material is introduced, then the total chemical composition of the rock remains unchanged. Mineralogical and textural changes will however cause the resulting metamorphic rock to be very different from its parent. Traces of the primary structures of the original rocks sometimes remain despite severe metamorphism and hence indicate their former nature. Metamorphosed sedimentary rocks may therefore possess relic traces of bedding, cross-stratification, ripple marks and other such structures of great importance in establishing the geological succession of a highly folded metamorphic area (Read, 1958). In exceptional cases the discovery of highly contorted fossils will prove the sedimentary origin of a metamorphic rock.

METAMORPHISM OF NON-CARBONACEOUS ROCKS

Excepting the alteration of coal seams and adjacent strata by minor intrusions, the products of metamorphism are of little direct concern to the mining engineer. Consequently a detailed treatment of this part of the subject is unwarranted and the principal metamorphic processes and rocks are only briefly discussed. In the following account three major classes of metamorphism, contact, dislocation and regional, are recognized. Under these headings examples are given of a few characteristic rock types. Should the reader's appetite be stimulated, two excellent introductions to the study of this rapidly expanding subject are those of Read & Watson (1962, pp. 500–87) and Williams, *et al.* (1955, pp. 161–247).

CONTACT METAMORPHISM

Contact metamorphism results from the thermal and sometimes metasomatic effects of cooling igneous intrusions. The zone of affected rock, or *metamorphic aureole*, is of variable width depending on the nature of the intrusive and country rocks, and on the shape and size of the intrusion. Argillaceous sediments are some of the most sensitive indicators of metamorphic changes as they contain minerals which are stable only at low temperatures. Consequently the thermal effect of an intrusion creates many new metamorphic minerals. The aureoles around most dykes and sills may usually be measured in inches and feet, whereas aureoles over a mile in width are sometimes developed around a large intrusive mass. In such cases a zonary distribution of progressive grades of metamorphism may be traced towards the intrusion (Fig. 6.1).

Hornfels

Hornfelses are commonly developed in the argillaceous country rocks immediately adjacent to intrusions. They are crystalline rocks with equidimensional grains which are arranged haphazardly. Flaky

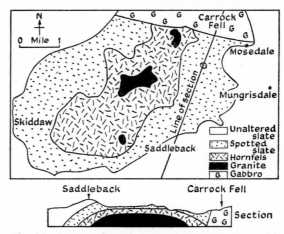

Fig. 6.1 Map and section showing the metamorphic aureole developed around the Skiddaw granite intrusion, Cumberland.

minerals, such as biotite, have an irregular arrangement so that they lie in all directions (Fig. 6.2). The consequent interlocking texture gives the rock a notable toughness and hackly fracture. During the

Fig. 6.2   The microscopic structure of hornfels. Biotite flakes occur in a quartz matrix.

metamorphism, new minerals, such as garnet, may be developed by reactions between the original minerals in the rock.

'Spotted rocks'

In the outer parts of the aureole the metamorphism may be insufficient to destroy the sedimentary laminations of the original rocks. If these were originally argillaceous a series of *spotted slates* may be formed. These are foliated rocks breaking along well marked cleavage and lamination surfaces. Various alumino-silicate minerals may form, as in *chiastolite slate*. In this example the metamorphic mineral chiastolite is easily identified by its markedly needle-like form. At the margin of the aureole, where the formation of new minerals is inhibited by low temperatures, metamorphic effects are confined to the concentration of organic matter into carbon-rich clots forming the typical *spotted slate*.

Quartzite

Normally the contact metamorphism of a pure quartz sandstone will merely cause recrystallization since, without metasomatic action, no new minerals may form. The resulting quartzite is a hard equigranular and light-coloured rock in which the recrystallized quartz forms an interlocking mosaic. The original distinction between mineral grains and groundmass is completely destroyed, so that the rock will break across the grains rather than around them, as in most ordinary sandstones (Fig. 6.3). Since some authorities designate as quartzite *any* pure quartz rocks, the terms *metaquartzite* and *orthoquartzite* are nowadays used to distinguish between true metamorphic quartzites and quartz sandstones respectively.

Occasionally an extreme stage of contact metamorphism is present in sandstone xenoliths within an intrusion and more rarely at the immediate margins.

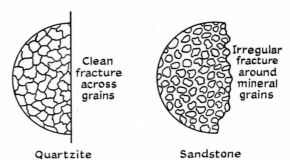

Fig. 6.3   The microstructures of metaquartzite and sandstone.

Under such conditions of very high temperatures the rocks may be completely fused to form the glassy rock *buchite*.

Marble

The term marble is here applied to carbonate metamorphic rocks, although the term is often loosely used in the building industry to include many non-metamorphic rocks which will take a high polish. Marbles are metamorphosed limestones and dolostones, and from their composition may be classed as calcite-marbles and dolomite-marbles. They are equigranular, light-coloured massive rocks which may be distinguished from quartzites, which in hand specimens they often resemble, by their solubility in dilute hydrochloric acid. Thin marbles may form by the contact metamorphism of limestones (Fig. 6.4),

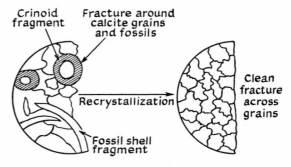

Fig. 6.4   Micro-sections of limestone and marble illustrating their major textural differences.

but the world's major deposits, much used in statuary and the building industries, were formed by regional metamorphism.

DISLOCATION METAMORPHISM

Dislocation or cataclastic metamorphism is confined to relatively narrow zones along major reverse and wrench faults. Normally, in superficial parts of the Earth's crust, faulting only results in the formation of breccias and gouges. Where movement occurs at depth in conditions of high pressures and temperatures, the latter partly generated by frictional heat, more complete breakdown of the country rocks occurs.

Mylonite

Mylonites are extremely fine-grained flinty rocks commonly composed of quartz and felspar. Rounded masses or 'eyes' of uncrushed country rock give the rock a patchy appearance. Some internal welding of the components may be apparent in thin section. In the extreme case of dislocation metamorphism, *pseudotachylite* is developed. This is a dark glassy structureless rock closely resembling its igneous namesake. Occasionally thin veins of pseudotachylite, injected into neighbouring rocks, indicate that complete melting of the parent rock occurred.

REGIONAL METAMORPHISM

During the development of the great fold mountain systems of the world, the rocks of these areas were subjected to widespread regional metamorphic effects. They accumulated in deep buckles of the Earth's crust, the lower parts of which were affected by exceptionally high temperatures and stresses. Indeed the former were so great that local melting and complete regeneration of rocks occurred. From the base of these deep crustal flexures there was a progressive upward decrease of temperatures and pressures, with consequent lessening of metamorphic effects (Fig. 6.5). On the subsequent erosion of a fold mountain system a series of metamorphic grades

may therefore be apparent, each being characterized by a particular metamorphic mineral assemblage.

Innumerable rock varieties, including those previously described, may form during regional metamorphism. The most characteristic rocks, in order of increasing metamorphic grade, are slates, schists, gneisses and migmatites.

Slate

Slates form by the regional metamorphism of argillaceous or fine-grained pyroclastic sediments under conditions of relatively low temperatures but great stresses. They are very fine-grained rocks frequently of a bluish-black or grey colour. Characterized by a well developed cleavage, they may easily be split into extremely thin sheets. In most cases slates cannot be broken along their original sedimentary partings, although their bedding and lamination may be apparent on cleavage surfaces as bands of different colour or hardness (Fig. 6.6). Slaty cleavage results from the recrystallization of the mineral components of the parent rock. Under the effect of strong directional pressures the tabular micaceous minerals develop a parallel alignment at right angles to the major stress direction. Since this was not a local effect the orientation of the minerals and therefore the strike of slaty cleavage is constant over a wide area and is, moreover, usually parallel or sub-parallel to that of the fold structures themselves.

Schist

The products of medium-grade regional metamorphism, schists are course-grained shiny rocks. Some cleavage may be apparent but the property is less well developed than in slates. Moreover, the parting surfaces are often irregular and may be developed

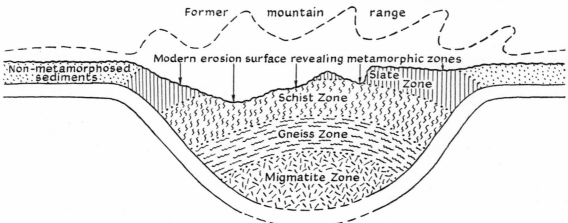

Fig. 6.5 Diagrammatic section illustrating the relationship between regional metamorphic zones and mountain building.

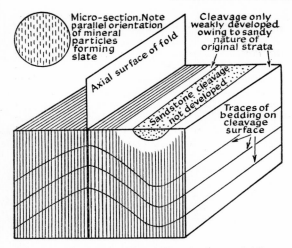

Fig. 6.6   The relationship of slaty cleavage to folding.

parallel to the original bedding structures. When de-rived from argillaceous sediments the mineral as-semblages are characterized by muscovite or biotite micas, the latter forming at slightly higher tempera-tures. *Garnetiferous mica-schists* of higher metamor-phic grade still, are truly beautiful rocks often containing perfect crystals, up to about the size of a thumb-nail, of pinkish garnet embedded in biotite mica.

Gneiss

Gneisses are formed by high-grade regional meta-morphism. They are coarse-grained rocks often containing mica but more characterized by felspar, quartz and sometimes hornblende. Cleavage is not usually developed although they often possess a roughly layered structure due to the metamorphic segregation of the various minerals. Some varieties, *augen-gneisses*, have an eyed or clotted structure developed by the flowage of micaceous material around less easily deformed crystals of felspar and quartz.

Migmatite

The most extreme products of regional meta-morphism, migmatites, are a half-way stage between metamorphic and igneous rocks. They may form from any pre-existing rocks by injection or permea-tion with granitic emanations. Migmatites have a typically banded or streaky appearance consisting of layers or patches of quartz and felspar in a darker matrix of the original rock. They grade on one side into gneisses, many of which were originally sedi-mentary rocks, and on the other into granites which are classed as igneous. Thus, once more, we arrive

back at the concept of the petrological cycle (Fig. 1.1) in which we see 'neither the beginning nor the end'.

CONTACT METAMORPHISM OF COALS

Local masses of altered coal are common where igneous intrusions occur within a coal-bearing se-quence. The alteration of an ordinary coal to a mass of hard natural cinder adjacent to an intrusion is clearly the result of contact metamorphism. Again the *coal apples* of roughly spherical shape, sometimes over 12 inches in diameter and occurring in some Scottish, Indian, American and Australian coals can also be attributed 'in some mysterious way' (Briggs, 1935, p. 189, Fig. 1; Moore, 1940, pp. 247–50) to the igneous alteration of coal. Less obvious, perhaps, but sometimes of similar origin, are the chemical changes involved in the conversion of bituminous coals to anthracites. Relatively minor and local oc-currences of the latter may be attributed to contact metamorphism, though the regional developments of anthracite, as in the South Wales or Pennsylvanian coalfields, undoubtedly result from other causes (Chapter 19).

The temperatures attained during the contact metamorphism of coals have been variously sug-gested as being from about 300 °C to 1 000 °C. From recent studies on the optical and radiological proper-ties of coke samples carbonized in the laboratory, it now appears likely that many coals, such as those recently described from Antarctica (Brown & Taylor, 1960) were altered at temperatures between 600 °C and 900 °C.

Numerous terms, many of local usage, have been given in the various coalfields to heat-altered coals. The commonest (taken from Tomkeieff, 1954) are listed below.

Blind coal	Coke coal	Dundy
Burnt coal	Columnar coal	Grey maggie
Cinder coal	Dandered rock	Natural coke
Clinker	Deaf coal	Smudge

The contact metamorphism of workable coals can usually be attributed to the intrusive effects of either dykes or sills. In most cases, the intrusion is of basic composition, being either dolerite or basalt. The initial temperatures of minor acidic intrusions ap-pear to be insufficient to affect coals seriously. Some-times the igneous rock is itself altered into a bleached and softened *white trap* of a greyish colour. Ap-parently more rare are the occurrences of heat-altered coals arranged around axes along which only minor, if any, intrusions are present. In NE. Durham such a progressive alteration of coals towards north-easterly trending fractures are interpreted as resulting from the effects of high temperature gases of igneous origin (Edwards & Tomlinson, 1958). In every respect the alteration phenomena are similar, though more widespread, to those observed along dykes.

EFFECT OF DYKES

The physical effects of dykes vary in the numerous recorded examples. The stage reached in the contact metamorphism of a coal is dependent on many factors, the most important of which are the initial temperatures, compositions and sizes of the intrusions, the presence or absence of water, the original nature of the coal and the thermal conductivity of the interseam sediments.

As a dyke is approached by mining the general alteration stages (Fig. 6.7) of the coal seams are:

Ultimately the cinder coal develops a columnar structure with the column axes generally at right angles to the dyke surface and therefore parallel to the direction of heat flow. In the Grey Seam at Westerhope colliery, Northumberland, a less usual orientation occurs (*op. cit.*, p. 240). Here, the columns dip away from the dyke, thus making acute angles with the floor and roof of the seam. Clearly the associated sedimentary rocks possess a greater thermal conductivity than the coal.

(4) At the actual margin the coal in contact with the intrusion may be rendered extremely tough and highly mineralized, forming a thin skin to the dyke itself.

(5) Xenoliths of coal are occasionally incorporated within the intrusion and may be altered to graphite. A notable example is that at Craigman, Ayrshire

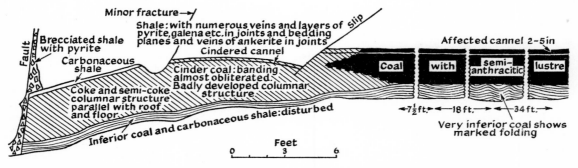

Fig. 6.7   Section illustrating contact metamorphism in the Hutton Seam, Co. Durham. (After Edwards and Tomlinson.)

(1) The coal first becomes brighter and anthracitic in lustre. At this stage the seam may be more friable than the unaltered coal.

(2) Traces of incipient cindering may then appear, so causing a decrease in the lustre of the coal.

(3) The total change to cinder coal is usually abrupt and takes place within a variable distance from the dyke. In some cases the cindering extends only a few feet, although in others over 100 ft of cinder coal may be encountered. Cindering of coal is often accompanied by mineralization, so that secondary carbonate minerals usually occur within the cindered mass.

At first the cinder coal may retain traces of its original layered nature, although the laminae are distorted and often acutely folded. Towards the intrusion the laminae are less apparent and the coal becomes vesicular, the vesicles being commonly in-filled by secondary minerals. That the coal is rendered plastic during this stage is indicated by the small-scale intrusive behaviour of the coal within the intrusion itself (Marshall, 1936, pp. 239–40, Plate 1).

(Simpson & MacGregor, 1932, p. 155) where 101 ton of impure graphite were mined in 1908.

In some cases thickness reductions of over 40 per cent accompany the alteration to cinder coal. Such decreases result from the distillation of the volatiles present in the normal coal (Table 10), (Edwards and Tomlinson, 1958, p. 63). Nearer the dyke there may be a slight increase in the original thickness of the seam owing to the extensive deposition of secondary minerals. Changes in the seam thickness are frequently accompanied by a rapid deterioration in roof conditions.

No relationship has been positively established between the intrusion thickness and the width of the zone of contact alteration. For instance, three dykes in the Durham and Northumberland coalfield, 50, 17, and 19 ft thick, produced respectively 30, 2 and 11 ft of cinder coal (Marshall, 1936, p. 250). On the other hand, certain dykes examined in the Natal coalfield appear to affect coals within a distance approximately equal to the thickness of the intrusion.

In a comparison of analyses showing different

TABLE 10

Variations in Thickness, Ash Content and Specific Gravity with Volatile Matter
(Maudlin Seam, Washington Glebe Pit, Co. Durham; Edwards and Tomlinson, 1958, p. 64, Table 4)

Sample	Total height of seam (in)	Section analysed (in)	Volatile matter (dry, ash-free coal, corrected for CO_2; per cent)	Ash (per cent)	Specific gravity
1	65½	58½	27·5	4·9	1·32
2	65½	59	25·2	5·2	1·32
3	66½	63	19·6	4·8	1·34
4	59	57½	17·1	5·1	1·34
5	58½	55½	13·4	5·9	1·37
6	48	44½	12·7	7·6	1·43
7	33	23½	5·8	9·2	1·65
8	31	29	5·8	14·3	1·75
9	43	31	5·7	12·0	1·64
10	33	21½	5·4	11·3	1·71

stages in the contact alteration of a coal seam (Table 11), the most obvious guide to the progressive alteration is the decrease in volatile content (Fig. 6.8). This must be estimated for the dry ash-free coal and suitably corrected for CO_2 (Edwards & Tomlinson, 1958, pp. 53–4). Otherwise the effects of secondary mineralization may obscure the change. The degree of chemical alteration of a coal may not necessarily be equivalent to the stage reached in its physical alteration. Thus in Table 11 there is a rapid decrease in volatile content between 2 ft and 3 ft from the dyke, whereas the cindering appeared between 4 ft and 5 ft.

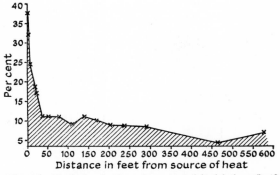

Fig. 6.9 Variation in the ash content (air-dried coal) of contact-altered coal in the Hutton Seam, Co. Durham. (After Edwards and Tomlinson.)

carbonates, the CO_2 content of the coal is also increased. Furthermore, the specific gravity of the altered coals is also related to the degree of secondary mineralization.

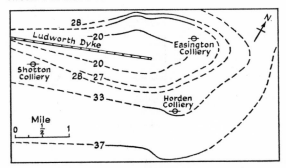

Fig. 6.8 Isovol map for the Hutton Seam, Co. Durham, showing variations in the volatile content around the Ludworth Dyke. (After Edwards and Tomlinson.)

Large quantities of secondary minerals, deposited from residual igneous gases and liquids, are introduced within the coal as infillings of vesicles and cleat partings. Therefore the ash content is considerably increased in the vicinity of the intrusion (Fig. 6.9). The ash is chiefly derived from the decomposition of calcite, dolomite, ankerite, gypsum and pyrite. Since the bulk of such secondary minerals are

EFFECT OF SILLS

Following Raistrick & Marshall (1939, p. 250) two general cases may be distinguished.
(1) The sill is intruded within the seam.
(2) The sill is intruded within the interseam sediments.
In the first case the intrusion either completely replaces the coal or else renders the seam entirely worthless. Such intrusions are frequently transgressive so that laterally a sill may vary in position from one being entirely within a seam to one situated along the seam's upper or lower contacts. The effects are similar, though more widespread, to those in the immediate contact zones of dykes. Thus the seam is highly cindered with low volatile and high

TABLE 11

Proximate Analyses of Cinder-coal Samples from the Brockwell Seam, Denton Burn, Northumberland
(Marshall, 1936, p. 237, Table 1)

Sample No.	1	2	3	4	5	6	7	8	9	10	11
Position*	Contact	1	2	3	4	5	6	10	15	24	30
Moisture	2·4	2·1	1·1	0·6	0·6	1·1	0·9	1·0	1·3	1·2	1·4
Volatile, less moisture	18·6	19·7	19·6	26·3	27·8	31·8	30·5	33·7	34·7	33·8	35·1
Ash	23·9	22·6	23·1	13·5	19·3	11·0	9·9	11·1	8·9	5·9	6·7
Volatile, ash-free dry	25·2	26·2	25·9	30·6	34·7	36·2	34·2	38·3	38·6	36·4	38·2
Carbon dioxide	12·2	13·2	10·9	4·4	6·5	7·2	3·4	3·7	3·8	3·8	3·1
Volatile, less carbon dioxide	6·4	6·5	8·7	21·9	21·3	24·6	27·1	30·0	30·9	29·9	33·0
True volatile†	10·4	10·5	13·4	26·9	28·9	30·5	31·6	35·6	35·9	33·6	37·2

* The position of the samples is measured from the contact of the coal with the dyke and is stated in feet

† *True volatile*, unless otherwise stated, is used in all cases to indicate the volatile matter corrected for the carbon dioxide of the ash

ash contents. Immediately above a dolerite sill in Linlithgowshire, the Smithy Coal had a 67 per cent ash content as compared with a normal one of about 3 per cent (Cadell, 1920, p. 278).

An interesting example showing the effect of a dirt band on coal alteration is described by Raistrick & Marshall (1939, p. 252), (Fig. 6.10). A thin basalt

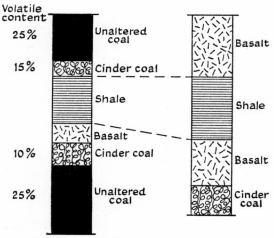

Fig. 6.10 Sections within the same colliery showing the replacement and alteration of coal by a basalt sill. (After Raistrick and Marshall.)

sill or 'float' was intruded immediately below a dirt band. Below the sill 9 in of cinder coal having a 10 per cent volatile content was produced. This was sharply demarcated from more or less unaltered coal with a volatile content of 25 per cent. Above the dirt band a slightly thinner development of cinder coal with 15 per cent volatiles was less sharply separated from the overlying unaltered coal. Clearly the dirt band acted as a partial insulator, lessening the effect

of the intrusion. In the same colliery, as the intrusion thickened, the upper coal became totally replaced.

When a sill is intruded into the interseam strata the effect is less severe than in the first case and may, in certain cases, improve the quality of the coal (Fig. 6.11). This is so in the Yampa Coalfield,

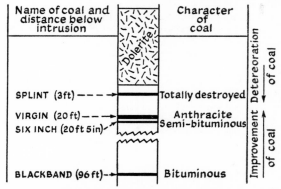

Fig. 6.11 The effects of a dolerite sill on underlying coals at Queenslie Colliery, Lanarkshire. (Section based on Briggs, 1935, p. 204.)

Colorado, where normally black lignites and low-rank bituminous coals are altered by olivine basalt sills into high-rank bituminous coals and anthracites. In one example, a dolerite sill over 75 ft thick affected coals up to an average of 80 ft above it. Anthracites were formed up to 45 ft above the intrusion (Eby, 1925, pp. 249–50). It has been suggested that in this field the influence of a sill is greater on coals above than below it. One intruded immediately above the Wolf Creek Coal, hereabouts a 'super-anthracite', caused the alteration of coals 160 ft above it and only 90 ft below. Evidently the anthracitized Wolf Creek Coal was a poorer heat conductor than the interseam sediments (McFarlane, 1929, p. 3).

REFERENCES

BRIGGS, H. (1935) Alteration of coal-seams in the vicinity of igneous intrusions, and associated problems, *Trans. Instn Min. Engrs* **89**, 187–211.

BROWN, H. R. & G. H. TAYLOR (1960) *Metamorphosed coal from the Theron Mountains*, Trans-antarctic Expedition 1955-58, Scientific Report **12**.

CADELL, H. M. (1920) A whinstone laccolite in the Bo'ness coalfield, *Trans. Instn Min. Engrs* **59**, 271–80.

EBY, J. B. (1925) Contact metamorphism, of some Colorado coals by intrusives, *Trans. Am. Inst. Min. mettal. Engrs* **71**, 246–50.

EDWARDS, A. H. & T. S. TOMLINSON (1958) A survey of low volatile coals in north-east and south-east Durham, *Trans. Instn Min. Engrs* **117**, 49–73.

MCFARLANE, G. C. (1929) Igneous metamorphism of coal beds, *Econ. Geol.* **24**, 1–14.

MARSHALL, C. E. (1936) The alteration of coal-seams by the intrusion of some of the igneous dykes in the Northumberland and Durham coalfield, *Trans. Instn Min. Engrs* **91**, 235–52.

MOORE, E. S. (1940) *Coal*, 2nd ed., New York, Wiley.

RAISTRICK, A. & C. E. MARSHALL (1939) *The Nature and Origin of Coal and Coal Seams*, 1st ed., London, E.U.P.

READ, H. H. (1958) A centenary lecture: stratigraphy in metamorphism, *Proc. geol. Ass., Lond.* **69**, 83–102.

READ, H. H. & J. WATSON (1962) *Introduction to Geology*, Vol. 1., 1st ed., London, Macmillan.

SIMPSON, J. B. & A. G. MACGREGOR (1932) The Economic Geology of the Ayrshire Coalfields, Area IV, *Mem. geol. Surv. Scotld.*

TOMKEIEFF, S. I. (1954) *Coals and Bitumens*, 1st ed., London, Pergamon.

WILLIAMS, H., TURNER, F. J. & C. M. GILBERT (1955) *Petrography*, 1st ed., San Francisco, Freeman.

INTERSEAM ROCKS

Various estimates have been made as to the percentage of coal in the total thickness of the coal-bearing formations. Of course, such figures can be accurate only for a stated locality since most coal-bearing sequences are extremely variable in both thickness and rock types. It is however apparent that coal makes up an extremely small proportion, usually less than 4 per cent, of the total rock thickness, and even this figure includes many seams too thin to work. For example, in a borehole at Whittington, South Staffordshire, 1624 ft of productive Coal Measures contained 3·3 per cent of coal of which only half formed seams of workable thickness. Besides having a direct influence on methods of working (most obviously in determining roof and floor conditions) some of the interseam sediments are of economic importance in their own right and are mined and quarried together with the associated coals. Clearly such rocks are not simply to be classified as 'dirt'. Moreover, a knowledge of the nature of the interseam strata is often important in correlation (page 205). Detailed observations of the exact natures and thicknesses of strata penetrated in drivages, boreholes and shafts are of primary importance in the development of a coalfield area. It is unfortunate that in some cases a wealth of potential knowledge has been lost to the mining industry through insufficient records being made at the time. The use of some loose term such as 'measures' to describe the varied and often complex interseam sections is of little use to the geologist concerned with correlation problems.

In the examination of old borehole logs and shaft sections much local descriptive terminology, often peculiar to particular coalfields, is revealed. Though modern mining opinion, most certainly supported by coalfield geologists, is that such terminology should be discarded, old habits die hard. It is to be hoped that the many vernacular terms still in common usage will be appropriately consigned to the dialect dictionaries in favour of the more accurately defined geological names. The commoner descriptive terms are listed in Table 12, which is largely based on Arkell & Tomkeieff (1953), to which further reference can be made.

CONGLOMERATES AND BRECCIAS

Rudaceous rocks are of fairly frequent occurrence as patchy or markedly lenticular bodies in the interseam strata. Both conglomerates and breccias occur, although many might be more correctly termed *breccia-conglomerates* since they contain considerable admixtures of both rounded and angular fragments, as for instance in the 'espleys' of the W. Midlands coalfields. They often form the basal parts of an otherwise arenaceous bed and are sometimes associated with washouts. In the former case there may be an erosional contact with the underlying bed, and a 'rolling-roof', causing particular trouble in mechanized mining, is found typically where a conglomeratic sandstone overlies a coal. In parts the latter may be completely washed out or rendered unworkable.

The phenoclasts, which may be orientated so that their longer axes exhibit a common alignment parallel to the direction of the former transporting current, are most commonly quartz or quartzite and more rarely include ironstones, various igneous rocks and coal. The occurrence of the latter is particularly interesting since it indicates both the penecontemporaneous erosion of the coal deposits and their relatively rapid hardening. Otherwise, on transportation the original peaty material would have been completely disintegrated rather than eroded to distinct pebbles. Other varieties include the *mud-flake* or *clay-gall conglomerates* characterized by small pellets and flakes of shale or mudstone in a sandy matrix.

SANDSTONES

Sandstones are most inconsistent members of the Coal Measure cyclothems. Owing to rapid variations in thickness it is preferable to regard sandstones as forming lenticular bodies rather than tabular sheets. This is well seen by a study of a thickness or iso-pachyte map (Fig. 9.11), (Mitchell, *et al.*, 1947, Figs 12, 18, 19, 20, 21 & 22). For example, within one mile between Thrybergh Hall and Roundwood Collieries, Yorkshire, the Abdy Rock completely thins out from 148 ft at the former colliery. In the same collieries, the underlying Barnsley Rock varies from

TABLE 12

Local Descriptive Terms used for Sedimentary Rocks in the British Coalfields

Approximate rock type	Local term
Conglomerate	Espley, pudding-stone
Sandstone	Burr, cank[1], cuttery, cwar, freestone, kingle, peldon, pennant, post, rag, rock[2], warden
Sandy shale	Bind, fakes, feaks, rock-bind, wool
Siltstone	Fakey-blaes, linsey, linstey, linn and wool
Shale or Mudstone	Bannock, bind, blaes, calmstone, clift, lemon, metal
Shale	Boards, clives, flue, flue-legs, leys, shiver, slate clay, slate metal
Carbonaceous shale	Bass, bast, batt[3], blacks, callis, callus, chitters, criggling, hubb, jabez, marden, pouncil, rashings[3], scale, sclit, slatter
Oil-shale	Honks, shale[4]
Fireclay	Cat, clod, clunch, daugh, dauk, dawk, duns, gubbin, pounson, seat-clay, seat-earth, seggar, sod, spavin, thill, underclay, warrant, warren-earth
Ganister	Calliard, crowstone, galliard
Ironstone	Balls, black-band, blond-metal, cank[1], cannock, catsheads, checks, curdly, dogger, flat-stone, mush, pins, raddle, ruft

[1] Depending on the local area the term may refer to fine-grained sandstones, clay ironstones or impure limestones
[2] A sandstone unless otherwise stated
[3] Batt and rashings are approximately synonymous for shale containing thin coal streaks
[4] In the Scottish mining areas the term is restricted to oil-shale

105 ft at Roundwood to 43 ft at Thrybergh. Such variations are chiefly of depositional origin. A thick sandstone lens may have formed as a local sandbank surrounded by muds, in which case there may be a progressive lateral decrease in grain size through siltstones into shales or mudstones, so that margins of the lens are indistinct (Fig. 7.1a). Alternatively a

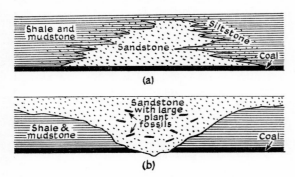

Fig. 7.1 The development of lenticular sandstones as (a) sandbank accumulations and (b) as channel infillings. (Note the marked gradation of rock types in (a).)

local swelling of a sandstone may arise from the infilling of an erosional channel. In this case the base of the bed may show erosional phenomena so that partial or complete washouts may be developed in an underlying coal (Fig. 7.1b). In some cases the sandstone may have been deposited close to the

land margin and by a gradual diminution in grain size it may pass into more argillaceous strata.

Mostly the interseam sandstones are fine- to medium-grained although occasional coarse beds, passing locally into conglomerates, may form highly distinctive horizons, as with some members of the Pennant Measures of S. Wales. Others may form well laminated flagstones or cross-stratified beds. Many of the sandstones have silica percentages between 80 and 90 per cent and, particularly in the Lower Coal Measures, the percentage may rise to over 90, in which case the rock is more properly termed an orthoquartzite or in some cases a ganister (see below). The major clastic components are generally subangular quartz fragments. Small amounts of felspar may also occur although generally in insufficient quantities for an arkosic designation to be given. The cements are varied, commonly being siliceous, calcareous, ferruginous or argillaceous. Normally a siliceous cement forms an extremely hard rock. This is often advantageous for its use as a building stone but results in slow drivage rates when encountered underground. In some beds, decomposed, highly ferruginous and often ovoid masses occur sporadically distributed throughout the rock. Such *red-horses* are troublesome in quarrying as they form worthless patches in otherwise good quality stone. Many of the coarser sandstones contain coaly debris, and *coal scars* occurring as streaks on the outer surfaces of fossil trees are fairly common. Usually the latter, chiefly Stigmarian rootlets, although occasionally branches of *Lepidodendron* and *Sigillaria*, are crushed flat and lie parallel to the stratification. More rarely the plants remain in the position of growth, that is vertical to the bed. Above some seams, vertical tree-casts or *potholes* are dangerous, for they may slide out along thin coal films into the workings and therefore may require individual supports.

Economically the interseam sandstones were more important in the past. Formerly beds were extensively worked as sources of building, paving and roofing stones. Apart from a limited demand for facing materials the sandstones have been largely superseded by the cheaper (though not necessarily inferior) artificial building products. Some of the more important building stones are the Elland Flags of W. Yorkshire, once mined as well as quarried near Bradford, the Upholland Flags of Lancashire, the Cefn Rock of N. Wales and the Pennant Sandstones of S. Wales. Most of the quarries at present being worked produce concrete products and aggregate from the crushed stone. Small quantities of moulding sands have sometimes been produced, as for instance east of Glasgow, although the main source of this material is from more recent rocks. Other uses include the manufacture of grindstones for the steel industry, as for example from the Grenoside Sandstone at Sheffield, and for glass polishing as from the Dyneley Knoll Flags near St Helens, Lancashire.

Many of the more porous beds, such as the Elland Flags in W. Yorkshire, form important sources of underground water and both private and public wells in the industrial towns of the coalfields draw water from such sources. The benefits derived from these relatively easily accessible water supplies are somewhat offset by the difficulties experienced in penetrating heavily watered sandstones underground (pages 102–3). Furthermore, since the melting-point of quartz is above the ignition temperature of methane-air mixtures it is apparent that the penetration or impact of sandstones during coal-getting, ripping, or as a result rock falls may cause the ignition of such mixtures (Rae, 1964). Such a firedamp ignition by the impact of a quartzitic rock onto a steel girder was considered to have caused the coal dust explosion at Six Bells Colliery in South Wales on June 28th, 1960, when forty-five men were killed (*Explosion at Six Bells Colliery, Monmouthshire*, Ministry of Power, 1961. H.M. Stat. Off., p. 36). The bulk of petroleum production in the small North Nottinghamshire and Lincolnshire oilfields is obtained from Lower Coal Measure sandstones (Brunstrom, 1963, pp. 11–18; Falcon & Kent, 1960), and most of the oil seepages recorded from collieries are derived from similar beds. Thus at Manvers Main Colliery, Yorkshire, in 1902 a seepage from a coarse sandstone above the Parkgate Seam yielded 7800 gallons in 3 days. Further seepages have occurred since then and the thick dark green oil was sold regularly by the colliery until 1916 (Strahan, 1920, pp. 2–3).

SILTSTONES

Siltstones are common members of the interseam sequence despite their apparent absence upon the examination of many colliery records. Some of the so-called shales or mudstones as recorded during routine colliery surveys are actually siltstones. That such incorrect interpretations should be made is surprising for siltstones have many distinctive characters.

(1) Siltstones are slightly rough to the touch whereas shales and mudstones are smooth.

(2) Owing to their quartz content, siltstones will scratch steel.

(3) On being scratched with a knife or hammer point they emit a gritty sound.

(4) Siltstones are more massive than shales and split into much thicker laminae.

(5) If the above distinctions are insufficient the oral test can always be applied! When chewed, a siltstone feels distinctly gritty, whereas there is no marked dental abrasion on the application of the test to other argillaceous rocks.

Siltstones may occur either as thick groups of sediments passing upwards into sandstones or sandy fireclays, as relatively thin beds interleaved with fine sandstone ribs, or more rarely as dirt partings within a coal seam. They may possess fine cross-stratification, in which case there is a definite layering into greyish quartzose and darker carbonaceous layers. Fine quartz fragments of pin-point size form between 50 and 20 per cent of the rock, the rest being composed of extremely fine carbonaceous and argillaceous materials. Some finely comminuted fossil plant material may be scattered on the lamination surfaces, although other fossils are rare. *Tuffaceous siltstones*, of some use in correlation, contain small amounts of pyroclastic material. Individual beds, up to 20 ft thick, have been traced for about 10 miles in the Fife Coalfield (Francis, 1961, pp. 201–8).

MUDSTONES AND SHALES

The argillaceous sediments form the bulk of most interseam successions. In the Lower Coal Measures, siltstones are particularly well developed, although these are replaced in the higher sequences by shales and mudstones. These are of widespread and uniform occurrence, forming beds sometimes over 100 ft thick and traceable throughout a coalfield. Certain horizons, notably the Etruria or Ruabon Marl of the Upper Coal Measures are over 1000 ft thick. It should be noted that these so-called marls, having low calcareous contents (Table 13), should be more correctly termed mudstones.

Mudstones and shales are extremely fine-grained, being chiefly composed of various clay minerals. Small quantities of detrital material including micas, quartz grains and carbonaceous debris are also present. Of increasing interest are the microscopic pyritic bodies which sometimes form visible aggre-

commonly, oil, on the surface of stream waters. The iron hydroxide is derived from the weathering of the pyritic material present within many marine beds, which, in some cases, also contain small quantities of oil. Non-marine shales may contain 'mussels', either as distinct bands or occurring more sporadically, and those immediately above coal seams often contain plant debris. In such beds the plant content is sufficiently high to form a black carbonaceous shale

TABLE 13

Chemical Analyses of some Carboniferous Brick Clays

Chemical composition	Shale (Lancashire)	Etruria Marl (Staffordshire)	Colliery shale (Staffordshire)
Silica SiO_2	61·66	58·38	46·42
Titania TiO_2	0·91	1·09	1·00
Alumina Al_2O_3	17·50	20·60	22·15
Ferric oxide Fe_2O_3	3·33	6·25	2·23
Ferrous oxide FeO	3·12	0·19	5·89
Ferrous sulphide FeS_2	nil	nil	0·31
Calcium oxide CaO	1·17	0·65	1·03
Magnesia MgO	1·18	0·71	1·28
Potash K_2O	2·52	1·02	1·90
Soda Na_2O	1·17	0·56	0·39
Sulphur trioxide SO_3	0·57	0·72	1·65
Loss	6·60	9·79	14·26
Total	99·73	99·96	100·00

gates up to about pin-head size. In some cases the pyrite grains enclose ultra-microscopic forms of organic material (Love, 1965, pp. 189–95). Pyritic shales are particularly common above marine horizons and should always be recorded in the measured section. Indeed it is the author's experience that the proximity of a marine band may be indicated by a noticeable increase in the pyrite content of an otherwise unfossiliferous dark shale. In the argillaceous beds above coal seams a series of ironstone bands and concretions are usually developed.

Although highly specialized techniques are necessary to examine the detailed mineralogical contents of the argillaceous rocks, simple distinctions can be made on the basis of their more obvious characters. Thus shales may be distinguished from mudstones by the marked fissility of the former. Similarly, should they be fossiliferous, marine and non-marine beds may be readily distinguished. In this respect the colours are often significant. Usually marine shales or mudstones are black and certainly in the British Lower Coal Measures it is generally useless searching for marine fossils in the lighter coloured beds. Furthermore the proximity of a surface exposure of a marine bed is sometimes indicated by the occurrence of iridescent films of iron hydroxide or, less

which may, by its colour, be at first confused with a marine deposit. The highest Carboniferous rocks, such as the Etruria Marl of the W. Midlands coalfields, have distinctive chocolate-red, purple or pinkish colorations attributed in some cases to their deposition and in others to their weathering in semi-arid conditions (pages 64–5).

The Carboniferous shales and mudstones are a major source of brickclay, over 31 per cent of the British output of bricks being derived from these beds (Table 14). Most of the final products are of a better quality than those obtained from the more recent systems, and hence the bulk of British engineering bricks of high crushing strengths and low porosities are from Carboniferous sources. For example, the engineering bricks manufactured from the Accrington Mudstones in the Lancashire coalfield have crushing strengths from 12 000 lbf/in² to 20 000 lbf/in². Even common bricks have strengths from 2 000 lbf/in² to 10 000 lbf/in². These figures may be compared with those of common London bricks, derived from more recent systems and having strengths of between 500 lbf/in² and 1 500 lbf/in². The numerous argillaceous horizons are mostly worked by quarrying although some brickclays are also extracted from colliery tips, in which case they

TABLE 14

Output of Building Bricks from Carboniferous Shales and Mudstones
(based on Bonnel & Butterworth, 1950, Table 108)

Area	Major horizons	Total output of bricks (millions per year)	Percentage of national total
Scotland and N.E. England	Barren Red Measures, Productive Coal Measures Scremerston Coal Group	791·0	9·4
Lancashire and Yorkshire	Lower and Middle Coal Measures	899·0	10·7
Midlands and N. Wales	Etruria Marl, Ruabon Marl, Blackband Group, Lower and Middle Coal Measures	782·5	9·3
S.W. England and S. Wales	Lower and Middle Coal Measures	189·0	2·2

are termed *colliery shales*. Considerable variations are possible in the chemical compositions of brick-clays (Table 13). Many contain approximately 50–60 per cent silica, 15–22 per cent alumina and 5–8 per cent total iron. A clay's suitability for brick making is largely determined by its physical characters. The major property required is a good degree of plasticity, which enables a brick to be moulded and allows a retention of shape during drying and burning. When freshly quarried, the Carboniferous shales and mudstones are hard coherent rocks; their plasticity is acquired either on crushing and mixing with water and sometimes other clays, or by natural weathering.

FIRECLAYS

Fireclays are typically associated with coal seams, usually occurring below them as seat earths or under-clays, often occurring within them as dirt bands and occasionally developed on their own. In the latter case an independent fireclay horizon in one area may well be an important marker band representing a known coal horizon in other parts of the coalfield. They often grade vertically downwards and some-times laterally into shales or mudstones and by an increase in quartz content into sandstones. When overlaid by a seam the contact between the two beds is usually sharp, although sometimes it is gradational so that the lowest coal may be a markedly impure variety with a high ash content. Considerable varia-tions in thicknesses frequently take place sometimes within the same colliery and there is no relationship between the thickness of a coal and that of the under-lying fireclay (Fig. 7.2).

Fossil roots, principally *Stigmaria*, are common, so that most fireclays have a streaky appearance due to

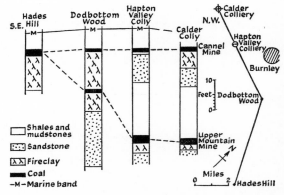

Fig. 7.2 Variations in fireclay thickness in the Cannel–Upper Mountain Seam sequence of the north-east Lancashire coalfield.

the thin carbonaceous films on the outer surfaces of the fossils. In rare cases fossil tree stumps within the coal are continuous with their roots within the fire-clay. It is because of their fossil content that many fireclays are called 'rootlet beds' although it should be clearly noted that the term also embraces some siliceous seat earths.

Chiefly composed of clay minerals, fireclays are fine-grained rocks with particle sizes of usually less than 0·003 mm diameter. Small quantities of detrital minerals are invariably present and commonly in-clude quartz, felspar and muscovite. The more sandy varieties containing noticeable amounts of quartz, and hence usually gritty to the touch, grade into siltstones or sandstones. Irregular or ellipsoidal ironstone nodules are frequently present, particularly in their lower layers. Some fireclays have a smooth waxy feel due to their clay-mineral content. This also results in their marked plasticity when wet, therefore creating problems of strata control in mining. The normal face supports may have to be adapted to prevent penetration into a soft floor. Fireclays with low quartz contents are characteristically highly slickensided and non-laminated rocks which break easily along randomly arranged listric surfaces. The latter were probably formed by compaction during the dehydration of the strata but in some cases may result from induced stresses during mining.

A vertical variation of the lithological characters within fireclay beds often occurs. Since these variations may have considerable effect on roof control, they should most certainly be recorded during development work. Such variations were demonstrated in a study of the seat earths of the South Wales coalfield, where the following units (Wilson, 1965a, pp. 392–3; 1965b, pp. 93–4) can often be recognized:

COAL

Unit	Usual thickness	
1	0–6 in	Shale, dark and carbonaceous. Occasionally coarse and micaceous, contains rootlets and sometimes plants—*Sigillaria*. This unit is sometimes represented by an impersistent sandstone, in which case it may be as thick as 2 ft. Contact usually sharp.
2	0–2 in	Clay, plastic and unconsolidated. Frequently contains coaly material and may show faint bedding. Contact generally sharp.
3	3–4 ft	Pale grey, unbedded, fine-grained and traversed by slickensides and rootlets. May contain small and sporadic ironstone nodules. Gradational contact.
4	1–2 ft	Base of underclay. Rather coarse and sandy. Contains fewer rootlets and slickensides but usually more ironstone nodules. Grades down into shale or sandstone

The occurrence of unit 2, by reason of its marked plasticity—a property which if not immediately apparent is revealed by soaking the specimen in water for a few hours—may result in difficult support con-

ditions, which in some cases could be alleviated by a limited amount of floor cutting.

Wide ranges in the chemical composition of fireclays are apparent in the many published analyses (Table 15). Their major components are silica (chiefly as the combined form in the clay minerals) between approximately 50 and 75 per cent, and alumina between approximately 15 and 35 per cent. Their total iron content is usually below 5 per cent. A rough guide to the purity of a particular bed is its colour at outcrop. Fireclays with high iron contents are yellowish, and similarly those containing much organic matter are dark grey to black as in most partings within seams. The chief chemical differences between the fireclays and other argillaceous rocks are the extremely low concentrations of lime, soda, potash and magnesia in the former. The titanium content is usually higher in the fireclays.

From their close association with coal seams and the common occurrence in them of fossil roots, fireclays appear to have functioned as ancient soils on which at least the initial coal-forming vegetation accumulated. Indeed their lack of internal stratification is usually attributed to the 'churning effect' of generations of plant roots. Their exact mode of origin has been variously explained. Until recently the principal theory was that they represent *in situ* or autochthonous deposits which formed in a waterlogged environment from the modification of previously unaltered sediment as a result of leaching by acid swamp waters and plant roots (Huddle & Patterson, 1961, pp. 1651–2). However, fireclays differ in many respects from modern soils, most noticeably in the absence of any normal soil profile. Furthermore, evidence such as the occurrence of faulting not affecting the overlying coal suggests that the fireclays may have formed prior to the main phase of coal formation. Consequently, in a study of certain North American fireclays it was suggested that they are composed of materials which were altered outside the depositional basin and that their mineral composition was chiefly determined by the source rocks from which they were derived (Schultz, 1958). They were in effect deposited as fireclays. In support of this, the allochthonous theory, Wilson (1965b), in a study of the fireclays of the South Wales coalfield, considers the occurrence of chlorite to be especially significant. Chlorite, although present only in small amounts, is highly sensitive to weathering and would not occur in fireclays had the latter been formed *in situ* as a result of extensive weathering and leaching. Similarly the lack of any correlation between the thickness of a coal and that of its underclay can hardly be explained by the autochthonous theory. Had fireclays originated and functioned as soils during peat formation then some fairly constant relationship between

FIRECLAYS (Ennos and Scott, 1924)

LOCALITY:	Glenboig, Lanarkshire	Hoddlesden, Lancashire	Amblecote, Worcestershire	Trevor, Denbighshire
HORIZON:	*Passage Group*	*Lower Mountain Mine*	*New Mine*	*Chwarelau Coal*
Chemical composition				
Silica SiO$_2$	53·19	53·87	62·67	70·40
Titania TiO$_2$	1·55	1·34	1·15	1·19
Alumina Al$_2$O$_3$	28·14	29·51	22·30	16·43
Ferric oxide Fe$_2$O$_3$	2·84	1·76	2·90	2·35
Manganous oxide MnO	0·20	0·02	0·03	0·05
Calcium oxide CaO	0·47	0·07	0·23	0·20
Magnesia MgO	0·36	0·53	0·66	0·66
Potash K$_2$O	0·14	0·88	0·48	1·74
Soda Na$_2$O	0·06	0·36	0·38	0·15
Lithia Li$_2$O	trace	trace	trace	trace
Water H$_2$O	12·08	11·27	9·47	5·93
Phosphoric acid P$_2$O$_5$	0·12	0·06	0·07	0·07
Ferrous sulphide FeS$_2$	0·25	0·09	0·02	—
Organic matter	0·02	0·39	0·12	0·58
Carbon dioxide CO$_2$	0·64	0·06	0·04	0·36

the thicknesses of the two deposits might be expected. On the other hand, if sediments were primarily deposited as fireclays before the formation of most, if not all, of the overlying peat, then the thickness of the former would be controlled by sedimentation and would be independent of coal thicknesses (Wilson, 1965b, p. 98).

Of considerable economic importance, many fireclay horizons are both mined and quarried (Special Reports on the Mineral Resources of Great Britain, **14**, Refractory Materials: Fireclays, *Mem. Geol. Surv.*, 1920). In some mines both the coal and underlying fireclay are extracted and utilized. About 1 300 000 ton are worked yearly in Great Britain for the production of refractories, over half of which are used in the iron and steel industry. A further 250 000 ton are supplied annually to the pottery industry for the manufacture of sanitary ware, glazed tiles and acid-proof products. Economically, fireclays can be classed according to their alumina content, of which increasing amounts add to their refractoriness and plasticity. Impurities that reduce refractoriness are chiefly alkalis, lime, magnesia and iron. In the glazed products ferruginous or carbonaceous matter may cause unsightly brown or bluish disfigurations of the glaze. Several clays may be blended to produce the required properties.

SILICEOUS SEAT EARTHS

Siliceous seat earths, with a silica content over 90 per cent, occur below some Lower Coal Measure and older coals. Seldom exceeding 5 ft in thickness, their quality deteriorates vertically so that their basal layers may be valueless. Their upper parts are often rootlet beds containing usually abundant and well preserved remains of *Stigmaria*. Some beds called *pencil-ganisters*, are crowded with small pencil-like markings of minor plant debris.

The term *ganister* is applied to the more siliceous varieties and was first used in the Sheffield area for several hard beds at the base of the Coal Measures. Indeed, in the Yorkshire and Lancashire coalfields this part of the sequence is occasionally still called the Ganister Group. Many siliceous seat earths bearing little resemblance to the original rock type are often loosely called ganister since there is little agreement as to the specific properties which determine the designation (Table 16). It is suggested that the term be restricted to those rocks approaching, in composition and texture, those from the Sheffield localities. Mineralogically these are composed of angular quartz grains, in a silica cement, having a marked uniformity of grain size ranging from 0·05 mm to 0·15 mm (Thomas, *et al.*, 1920, p. 4). Small quan-

15

Carboniferous Seat Earths

Beaufort, Monmouthshire	SILICEOUS SEAT EARTHS (Thomas, *et al.* 1920)				
	Bonnybridge, Stirlingshire	Rookhope, Co. Durham	Sheffield, Yorkshire	Pott Shrigley, Cheshire	Guisley, Yorkshire
Old Coal	Passage Group	Lower Millstone Grit	Ganister Coal	Lower Mountain Mine	Stanningley Rock
64·77	93·49	97·77	97·02	93·42	99·26
1·32	0·24	0·06	0·22	0·52	0·13
22·01	2·31	0·26	0·34	2·69	0·28
1·29	0·74	0·34	0·31	0·56	0·10
0·06	0·04	0·06	0·10	0·08	not found
0·16	1·17	0·13	0·05	0·48	0·02
0·69	0·17	0·11	0·13	0·08	0·01
1·88	0·68	0·20	0·09	0·24	0·08
0·04	0·35	0·18	0·17	0·21	0·34
trace	not found	trace	not found	trace	not found
7·55	0·63	0·51	0·44	1·20	0·13
0·06	not found	not found	0·02	0·11	not found
0·05	0·01	not found	0·49	not found	not found
0·34	0·03	0·69	0·44	0·27	not found
0·10	0·25	0·04	0·04	0·12	not found

tities of carbonaceous material may be present giving the rock a light to dark grey colour. Other minerals which are commonly present in clastic rocks are however rare. Owing to their angularity, the quartz grains are closely packed so that porosity is reduced to a minimum. Laminae or beds are seldom present and the rock possesses an irregular to sub-conchoidal fracture. In the less siliceous seat earths, mica fragments and altered felspars may occur together with a variety of cements, the commonest being ferruginous, calcareous or dolomitic. By increasing amounts of clay minerals they pass into sandy fireclays or siltstones.

The chemical analyses of the siliceous seat earths (Table 15) show less variation than those of the fireclays. All have a silica content of over 90 per cent. Their alumina content falls to below 1 per cent. A most noticeable difference between the fireclays and siliceous seat earths is in the higher silica and lower alumina contents of the latter.

From their constant association with coal seams and the occurrence of Stigmarian rootlets it is apparent that, like fireclays, the siliceous seat earths functioned, for a time at any rate, as soils upon which the coal-forming plants grew. The marked predominance of quartz may be interpreted as either indicating their formation from the original quartzose sandstones or as resulting from the prolonged weathering, leaching and probable redeposition of an originally more argillaceous deposit. In the British Carboniferous sequence siliceous seat earths are confined to several comparitively rare horizons. It may be that they reflect phases of comparative crustal stability when the prolonged emergent conditions necessary for their formation occurred.

Siliceous seat earths are mined and quarried in most British coalfields, (Special Reports on the Mineral Resources of Great Britain, **6**, Refractory Materials: Ganister and Silica-rock, *Mem. Geol. Surv.*, 1920). Their major use is for the production of silica-bricks and high temperature moulding sands. For high grade refractories the silica content of the raw material should exceed 97 per cent, since the presence of impurities increases the fusibility of the finished product which should be refractory up to about 1700 °C. Similarly the porosity should be less than 3 per cent as otherwise the products will be mechanically weak.

IRONSTONES

Carboniferous ironstones most commonly occur in argillaceous beds and more rarely in arenaceous strata. All are associated with carbonaceous matter and many though not all contain fossils. Some may

TABLE 16

Major Chemical Composition and Grain-sizes of Gainister according to Three Definitions

	Silica percentage	Alumina percentage	Grain size in mm
Raistrick and Marshall, 1939, pp. 138–9	87–99	0–5·0	0·05–0·25
Thomas, *et al.* 1920[1]	97–99	0·17–1·0	0·1–0·3
Trueman, 1954, p. 27	95–98	0–1·0	0·05–0·025

[1] Chemical properties based on nine quoted analyses

be composed entirely of non-marine lamellibranchs, as for instance the Bassey Mine Ironstone of the North Staffordshire coalfield. Usually their fossiliferous nature is apparent only in weathered or broken material. Ironstones may be distinguished from other interseam rocks by their higher specific gravities and hardness. The iron content of the yellow ochreous waters drained or pumped from many collieries may be attributed to the solution of the ironstones which usually occur in close proximity to coal.

The dominant iron mineral is siderite (page 13), although from analyses and optical determinations (Dunham, 1960, p. 238) it is apparent that small quantities of calcium, magnesium and manganese are present as impurities (Table 17). Due to their carbonate content ironstones, when crushed, are partly soluble in dilute hydrochloric acid. The insoluble residue is chiefly composed of clay minerals, since ironstones contain over 30 per cent clay minerals. The total metallic iron content is usually between 20 and 30 per cent although occasionally this may rise to about 40 per cent. Many ironstones, especially the nodular varieties, possess a *septarian structure*. This is formed by a series of internal cracks, tapering towards the outer margin, which are developed within the body of the rock. The cracks are chiefly infilled with calcite or other carbonate minerals, although small amounts of pyrite, limonite, sphalerite and galena have sometimes been recorded.

Bedded ironstones can be distinguished from nodular varieties (Trotter, 1953a, pp. 2–5). The former may be further subdivided into *clayband* and

TABLE 17

Chemical Analyses of some Carboniferous Ironstones

	CLAYBAND IRONSTONES			BLACKBAND IRONSTONE
LOCALITY:	Low Moor, Yorkshire	Sheffield, Yorkshire	Butterley, Derbyshire	Shelton, Staffordshire
HORIZON:	Black Bed	Dogtooth rake	Brown rake	Red shagg
Chemical composition				
Ferrous oxide FeO	36·14	28·27	37·99	46·53
Ferric oxide Fe_2O_3	1·45	1·42	1·49	0·05
Manganese oxide MnO	1·38	1·02	1·51	2·54
Alumina Al_2O_3	6·74	2·31	5·57	1·22
Calcium oxide CaO	2·70	13·94	4·59	2·44
Magnesia MgO	2·17	9·27	3·37	1·39
Silica SiO_2	17·37	3·55	10·04	1·93
Potash K_2O	0·65	0·16	0·55	0·20
Carbon dioxide CO_2	26·57	37·61	29·92	26·57
Phosphoric acid P_2O_5	0·34	0·74	0·80	0·69
Ferrous sulphide FeS_2	0·10	0·04	0·06	
Water H_2O	1·77	0·91	2·21	1·47
Organic matter	2·40	0·92	1·42	10·46

blackband ironstones. They differ in carbonaceous content (Table 17), as much as 20 per cent occurring in some of the latter. Clayband ironstones when unweathered are greyish or grey-blue, whereas the blackband ores are commonly dark brown to black. Both are usually a few inches thick but since they occur in thinly bedded shale-ironstone sequences several distinct beds have been worked as one. Thus the Low Moor Ironstone, a once important source of ore in the Yorkshire coalfield, is really a series of nodules and thin beds never exceeding 22 inches in total thickness and situated in some 10 ft of shale (Wray, *et al.*, 1930, pp. 58–9). Since the upper layers are of inferior quality only about 10 in of ore was ever worked. A section of the lower beds is as follows.

	Inches
Shale	
Ironstone nodules (Top Balls)	2
Shale	7½
Bedded ironstone (Top Flats)	1½
Shale	4½
Ironstone nodules (Middle Balls)	1½
Shale	10
Bedded ironstone (Bottom Rufts)	1
Shale	7
Bedded ironstone (Low Measures)	¾
Shale	7
BLACK BED COAL	

Nodular ironstones may be symmetrical or irregular in shape. The former consist of pear-shaped or flattened discs seldom more than 1 ft in maximum diameter and distributed parallel to the bedding. Irregular nodules occurring in the underlying fireclays have no constant orientation and may be *sphaerosiderites*. These are composed of ferruginous spherulitic bodies of about pin-head size surrounded by an argillaceous matrix.

Economically the interseam ironstones are of no importance at the present time. They were much mined in the early nineteenth century, since which time production has declined. The blackband ironstones of the W. Midlands and Scottish coalfields were the most prized ores since their carbonaceous content is such that they require little if any coal for smelting. In 1947 only 2 000 ton of Carboniferous ironstones were produced, as compared with the total United Kingdom production, largely from Jurassic sources, of over 11 million ton. None are at present being worked. Their decline may be attributed to their relatively low iron content and the development of the more profitable Jurassic ironstones of E. England.

LIMESTONES

In contrast to the N. American coalfields where they may occur at several horizons in an individual cyclothem, limestones are rarely found in the British Upper Carboniferous interseam strata. If developed they are usually impure argillaceous limestones occurring as rich fossil accumulations. Apart from the light-coloured fossil shells, the limestones are often dark-bluish rocks. They may be of marine origin, as for example the dark and often discontinuous limestone associated with the Mansfield or Dukinfield Marine Band, important marker horizons in the E. Midlands and Lancashire coalfields respectively.

In the non-productive Carboniferous red beds limestones are of more frequent occurrence. Seldom over 6 ft in thickness, the light grey limestones are of fresh-water origin. They sometimes persist as definite horizons and may therefore be of use as marker bands. Thus the Index Limestone, about 2 ft thick, is a consistent bed in the Halesowen Group of the Warwickshire coalfield. Although often referred to as 'Spirorbis' limestones' from the occurrence of small spirally coiled worm tubes, other fossils, including ostracods and lamellibranchs, are often present in them. In texture they vary from coarse-grained limestones to fine-grained calcite mudstones with conchoidal fractures (Trotter, 1953b, p. 265). Some are dolomitic in composition. Many have brecciated structures which originated soon after their precipitation as lime-muds, when desiccation cracks developed during a dry phase prior to subsequent flooding and the deposition of succeeding layers. Local erosion is evidenced by the occurrence of penecontemporaneous limestone-conglomerates (Barrow, *et al.*, 1919, pp. 47–8). Of no present-day importance, occasional outcrops may have formerly been worked as local sources of agricultural lime, and in Lancashire some of the thin limestones in the Upper Coal Measures were once mined for the manufacture of a slow-setting cement.

COAL-BALLS AND BULLIONS

Although both are associated, either directly or indirectly, with marine strata, coal-balls and bullions are distinct concretionary types. The latter occur in the roof of certain seams, whilst coal-balls are confined to positions strictly within coal.

Coal-balls occur only within seams directly overlaid by marine strata and even so are not found in every such seam. They contain masses of plant material completely petrified by secondary carbonate minerals so that even the most delicate tissues are preserved and may be examined in thin section. Consequently much of our detailed knowledge of

Carboniferous plant structures is obtained from various studies of coal-ball material, notably from the Upper Foot Mine of the Lancashire coalfield. Besides several British occurrences they have also been noted from seams in other European coalfields and also those of Japan and North America. Of variable size, coal-balls are roughly circular or elliptical concretions usually between a few inches and 2 ft in diameter. Exceptionally large masses of irregular shape and weighing several tons sometimes occur (Stopes & Watson, 1908, pp. 174–6). The coal laminae bend around the nodules and, as a result of compaction effects, their outer coaly surfaces are often slickensided. Coal-balls have a patchy distribution and locally occur in sufficient proportions to render seams unworkable. Furthermore their particularly hard nature renders machine mining either difficult or impossible.

Many coal-balls are composed of dark bituminous limestones, the carbonate minerals of which sometimes approach the composition of dolomite. Small percentages of ferruginous matter, chiefly as pyrite, and carbonaceous debris also occur. Detrital minerals are virtually absent.

There is no doubt that coal-balls were formed within the seams and not transported into the coal-forming areas. Their *in situ* formation is indicated by the continuity of plant stems through several adjacent nodules and also by a similar continuity of plant tissues through the concretions into the surrounding coal. These delicate fossil structures would not in such cases have been otherwise preserved. The perfect petrifaction of the fossils is attributed in the British examples (Stopes & Watson, 1908, pp. 210–12) to the deposition of secondary carbonates during the marine inundation of the coal-forming swamps. Such minerals would be precipitated by CO_2, generated by decaying plant debris, reacting with soluble magnesium and calcium salts in the sea water. A slightly different origin is proposed for the coal-balls within the Herrin Coal, Illinois, where they occur as accumulations confined to funnel-shaped hollows within the coal. The underlying sediments show disturbance features below the funnel apices and it is suggested that the mineralizing solutions were derived from springs tapping a saliferous aquifer below the peat swamp (Evans & Amos, 1961).

Bullions (baum pots, bobbers) are usually highly fossiliferous marine roof concretions which vary in size from a few inches to a yard or more in diameter. They are smooth ovoid nodules breaking cleanly from the enclosing rocks. Occurring above the coal, the larger specimens may be dangerous, occasionally falling from the roof without warning. Their presence is sometimes indicated by slight 'blisters'

in the roof measures, which may also be ironstained immediately below. Within the bullions a laminated structure is sometimes apparent, the laminae and greatest diameter being parallel to the bedding. Bullions are composed of fine-grained dark argillaceous limestones having conchoidal fractures and spintering into knife-sharp fragments. Freshly broken specimens sometimes yield small quantities of a thick green oil. The included fossils, usually arranged along the laminae and conspicuous on the surface of weathered specimens, are chiefly marine forms, although plant tissues also occur. Many of the fossils, beautifully preserved in their original form, have a thin external 'shell' of secondary pyrite. The conditions of formation of bullions are essentially similar to those of coal-balls. Gases evolved by decaying organic material on the sea floor caused the precipitation of the calcium and magnesium salts contained in the sea water.

ERRATIC BOULDERS

Well rounded pebbles and boulders of non-carbonaceous rocks are sometimes encountered within the seam. They may occur singly or in groups embedded either completely in the coal or else partly within it and the adjacent strata. On casual inspection they may be mistaken for coal-balls since they are often covered by thin tenacious films of coal which obscure their diagnostic characters. Presumably the boulders and pebbles were trapped in the root systems of Carboniferous trees and so rafted along rivers into the coal-forming swamps (Dix, 1942, pp. 49–52). Whenever possible, specimens should be collected and submitted to competent geological opinion. For if their sources can be proved, a more accurate understanding of the palaeogeographical features at the time of their deposition can be arrived at.

RED AND REDDENED BEDS

In some coalfields there exists a reddened or partly reddened zone in the strata close to the Permo-Trias. That this zone is frequently a secondary feature and not of contemporaneous origin is indicated by its transgressive character in the Carboniferous beds. In some areas the reddened beds may extend into the Lower Carboniferous and are certainly not characteristic of any one horizon (Fig. 7.3). The coloration is due to the presence of small amounts of finely divided ferric oxides, chiefly haematite (Fe_2O_3)—red, turgite ($2Fe_2O_3.H_2O$)—red, geothite ($Fe_2O_3.H_2O$)—yellowish-brown, and limonite ($2Fe_2O_3.3H_2O$)—yellow. The *reddened beds* of no constant horizon should be distinguished from the Upper Coal Measure *red beds*, such as the Etruria Marls, of constant horizon and with a colora-

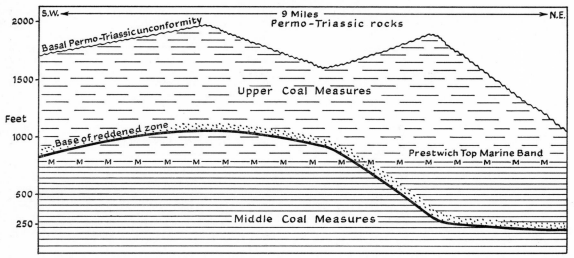

Fig. 7.3 Diagrammatic section illustrating the transgressive nature of the Reddened Beds in the Coal Measures of the South Lancashire coalfield.

tion considered to be of primary origin (Hoare, 1959, pp. 190–1). In a humid environment, such as that in which coal measure strata formed, iron is precipitated as colourless or brownish ferrous minerals owing to the strong reducing conditions caused by decaying organic material. Since the Carboniferous reddened beds contain considerable amounts of organic matter, their coloration must be a secondary feature. It is significant that the Etruria Marls are lacking in much organic matter.

A distinction may also be made between reddening due to staining and that due to oxidation of primary ferrous minerals (Trotter, 1953a, pp. 10–13). The percolation of iron-bearing solutions may result in the deposition of ferric oxide with consequent staining of the rocks. Porous beds, such as sandstones, are more susceptible to staining than impervious shales and mudstones. Oxidation on the other hand most strongly affects those beds rich in iron; consequently shales and mudstones are markedly reddened but non-ferruginous sandstones may be almost unaffected. Coal seams themselves may become totally oxidized, passing through limey coals into complete carbonate sediments (Mykura, 1960).

It is considered that the reddening of the Carboniferous strata was chiefly produced during a pause in sedimentation on the pre-Permian land surface. During this interval oxidizing conditions penetrated into the underlying beds. In the N. Staffordshire and Lancashire coalfields the reddened zone exceeds 1 600 ft in depth and in Ayrshire may extend to 2 000 ft below the base of the Permian. The particular depth to which reddening is developed is considered by Trotter (1953a, pp. 18–19) to have

been determined by the position of the pre-Permian water-table, since oxidizing conditions rarely occur in saturated sediments.

REFERENCES

ARKELL, W. J. & S. I. TOMKEIEFF (1953) *English Rock Terms*, 1st ed., London, O.U.P.

BARROW, G., GIBSON, W., CANTRILL, T. C., DIXON, E. E. L. & C. H. CUNNINGTON (1919) The Geology of the Country around Lichfield, *Mem. geol. Surv. Engld & Wales*.

BONNELL, D. G. R. & B. BUTTERWORTH (1950) *Clay Building Bricks of the United Kingdom*, London, H.M.S.O.

BRUNSTROM, R. G. W. (1963) Recently discovered oil-fields in Britain, *Proc. Sixth World Petrol. Cong.*, Section 1, Paper **49**.

BUTTERWORTH, B. (1948) *Bricks and Modern Research*, 1st ed., London, Crosby Lockwood.

DIX, E. (1942) Interesting Boulders found in and associated with coal seams in the South Wales coalfield, *Proc. S. Wales Inst. Engrs* **58**, 21–56.

DUNHAM, K. C. (1960) Syngenetic and diagenetic mineralisation in Yorkshire, *Proc. Yorks. geol. Soc.* **32**, 229–84.

ENNOS, F. R. & A. SCOTT (1924) Special Reports on the Mineral Resources of Great Britain, **28**, Refractory Materials: Fireclays. *Mem. geol. Surv.*

EVANS, W. D. & D. H. AMOS (1961) An example of the origin of coal-balls, *Proc. geol. Ass., Lond.* **72**, 445–54.

FALCON, N. L. & P. E. KENT (1960) Geological results of petroleum exploration in Great Britain 1945–1957, *Mem. geol. Soc. Lond.* **2**.

FRANCIS, E. H. (1961) Thin beds of graded kaolinised tuff and tuffaceous siltstone in the Carboniferous of Fife, *Bull. geol. Surv. Gt Br.* **17**, 191–215.

HOARE, R. H. (1959) Red beds in the Coal Measures of the W. Midlands, *Trans. Instn Min. Engrs* **119**, 185–95.

HUDDLE, J. W. & S. H. PATTERSON (1961) Origin of Pennsylvanian underclay and related seat rocks, *Bull. geol. Soc. Am.* **72**, 1643–60.

LOVE, L. G. (1965) Micro-organic material with diagenetic pyrite from a Carboniferous shale, *Proc. Yorks. geol. Soc.* **35**, 187–202.

MITCHELL, G. H., J. V. STEPHENS, C. E. N. BROMEHEAD & D. A. WRAY (1947) Geology of the Country around Barnsley, *Mem. geol. Surv. Engld & Wales.*

MYKURA, W. (1960) The replacement of coal by limestone and the reddening of Coal Measures in the Ayrshire coalfield, *Bull. geol. Surv. Gt Br.* **16**, 69–106.

RAE, D. (1964) The role of quartz in the ignition of methane by the friction of rocks, *Res. Rep. Saf. Mines Res. Bd* **223**.

RAISTRICK, A. & C. E. MARSHALL (1939) *The Nature and Origin of Coal and Coal Seams*, 1st ed., London, E.U.P.

SCHULTZ, L. G. (1958) Petrology of underclays, *Bull. geol. Soc. Am.* **69**, 363–402.

STOPES, M. C. & D. M. S. WATSON (1908) On the present distribution and origin of the calcareous concretions in coal seams known as 'coal balls', *Phil. Trans. R. Soc. (Ser. B)* **200**, 167–218.

STRAHAN, A. (1920) Special Reports on the Mineral Resources of Great Britain, **7**, Mineral Oil, Kimmeridge Oil-shale, Lignites, Jets, Cannel Coals, Natural Gas. England and Wales, *Mem. geol. Surv.*

THOMAS, H. H., A. F. HALLIMOND & E. G. RADLEY (1920) Special Reports on the Mineral Resources of Great Britain, **16**, Refractory Materials: Ganister and Silica-rock, *Mem. geol. Surv.*

TRUEMAN, A. (1954) *The Coalfields of Great Britain*, 1st ed., London, Arnold.

TROTTER, F. M. (1953a) Reddened beds of Carboniferous age in north-west England and their origin, *Proc. Yorks. geol. Soc.* **29**, 1–20.

TROTTER, F. M. (1953b) Exploratory borings in south-west Lancashire, *Trans. Instn Min. Engrs* **112**, 261–81.

WILSON, M. J. (1965a) The underclays of the South Wales coalfield east of the Vale of Neath, *Trans. Instn Min. Engrs* **124**, 389–403.

WILSON, M. J. (1965b) The origin and geological significance of the South Wales underclays, *J. Sedim. Petrol.* **35**, 91–9.

WRAY, D. A., J. F. STEPHENS, W. N. EDWARDS & C. E. N. BROMEHEAD (1930) Geology of the Country around Huddersfield and Halifax, *Mem. geol. Surv. Engld & Wales.*

8

STRUCTURAL GEOLOGY, FAULTS AND FOLDS

Some of the most striking examples of the intensity of natural forces are seen in the often fantastic distortions of strata in a heavily folded area. Immense thicknesses of seemingly hard and unyielding rocks have buckled and fractured like so many sheets of Plasticene. Many coalfields are affected by such folds and faults so that their exploitation is controlled to a large extent by structural considerations.

DIP AND STRIKE

Commonly the stratified rocks, originally deposited as flat or gently dipping beds, have been folded and tilted so that they are now considerably inclined. The measurement of the direction and amount of such inclinations is the primary stage in the analysis of the structural complexities of a district.

The angle made by the intersection of an inclined bed with the horizontal is termed the *dip*. It may be expressed in degrees or as a ratio. The *strike* is the bearing of a line formed by the intersection of a bed with an imaginary horizontal surface. Thus, a strike line joins all points of equal height on a bedding surface. If the direction and amount of dip is uniform over an area, then the strike lines at unit intervals, for any geological horizon, are straight, parallel and equidistant. Most simple map exercises are based on this assumption, but it should be noted that such uniformity is rarely the case in practice. Whenever possible the direction and amount of *true* or *full dip* of a bed is measured; this is the maximum angle of inclination and is at right angles to the strike. It will be seen that if the direction of true dip is given, the strike may be found. In the opposite case, given the strike, the true dip may be in one of two possible directions at right angles to the strike. Often it is impossible to measure the true dip and the surveyor may estimate an *apparent dip* which is a lesser angle and not in the same direction. The relationship of dip and strike can perhaps be better understood if the terms are applied to a gabled house roof (Fig. 8.1). The ridge trends in the direction of strike and the gables are the directions of full dip. Points X and Y are of similar height; therefore XY may be shown

as a strike line. A line YB at right angles to XY is the direction of true dip. Any other slope from Y is an apparent dip direction with a lesser gradient. It is easiest to ascend a house roof from one corner to the opposite ridge end.

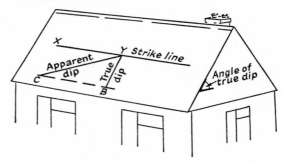

Fig. 8.1   Diagram to illustrate the meaning of true dip, apparent dip and strike.

Given two directions and amounts of apparent dip of a bed, it is possible to calculate the true dip.

Problem. To find the direction and amount of true dip from two apparent dip observations (Fig. 8.2).

Given. The apparent dips of a bed are 1 in 8 south and 1 in 5 east.

Solution. From a point A construct two lines AC and AB trending east and south. Measure 5 units along AC and 8 units along AB. Join the eighth unit D along AB with the fifth unit E along AC. Construct AF at right angles to DE. The length of AF is 4·2 units.

The direction and amount of true dip is 1 in 4·2 south-east by east.

It is frequently necessary to construct a horizontal section across a geological map in a direction other than that of true dip. The apparent dip in any direction may be found graphically.

Problem. To find the apparent dip along the line AC (Fig. 8.2).

Given. The true dip is 1 in 4·2 south east by east.

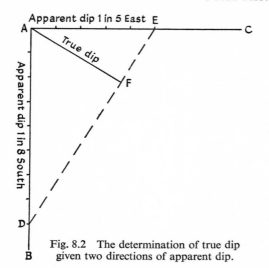

Fig. 8.2   The determination of true dip given two directions of apparent dip.

where A is the angle of apparent dip, T is the angle of true dip and H is the horizontal angle between the direction of true dip and that of the required apparent dip. It will be seen that as the strike direction is approached the apparent dip progressively decreases.

If strike lines are superimposed for two geological horizons in a given area, the vertical distance between the horizons may be found (Fig. 8.3). For instance, if the 100-ft strike line of one seam is plotted on a plan as halfway between the positions of the 200-ft and 300-ft strike lines of another seam, then the first seam lies 150 ft below the second.

Assuming the dip to be uniform over an area and given the position and height of three points on a bed, the strike lines and bearing and rate of true dip may be found. Such a 'three-point problem' is a standard exercise in geological mapwork.

Problem. The plan (Fig. 8.4) shows certain roadways in two seams. The roadway in the lower seam is indicated by dashed lines and the roadways in the upper seam by solid lines. The levels on the floors of the seams are given in feet above Ordnance Datum. The thickness of the strata between the seams, direction and rate of dip is uniform.

State: (1) The bearing and rate of true dip.

       (2) The vertical distance between the seams.

Solution. From the levels given construct the 160-ft and 140-ft strike lines for the upper seam. The

Solution. At point A the true dip is known. Construct AF 4·2 units in length. A line from F at right angles to AF intersects AC at E.

AE is 5 units; thus the apparent dip along AC is 1 in 5 east.

Often the true dip is given in degrees. In this case the required apparent dip may be calculated from the formula:

$$\tan A = \tan T \times \cos H,$$

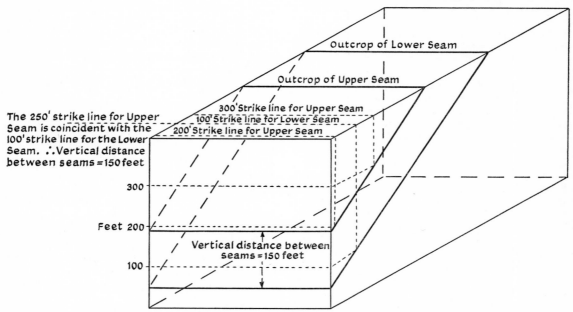

Fig. 8.3   Block diagram illustrating strike lines for two geological horizons.

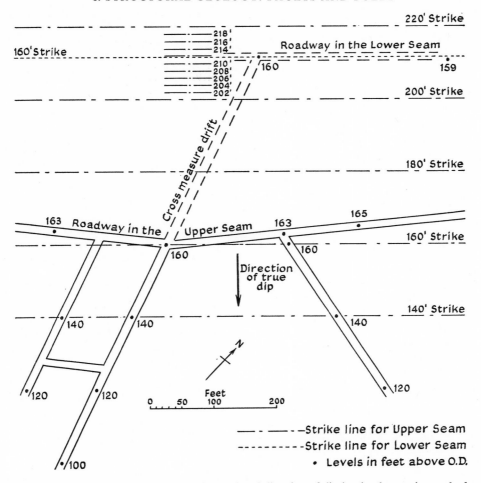

Fig. 8.4 The determination of seam interval and direction of dip by the three-point method.

true dip is at right angles to the strike and the seam is inclined from the 160-ft to the 140-ft strike line. Therefore since the seam is 20 ft lower in a horizontal distance of 120 ft (i.e. the distance between, and measured at right angles to the two strike lines), the bearing and rate of true dip is 1 in 6 south-east.

Construct a series of strike lines for the upper seam. Since the direction and rate of dip is uniform the strike lines will be parallel and equidistant. The 212-ft strike line for the upper seam is coincident with the 160-ft strike line for the lower seam. The vertical distance between the seams is therefore 52 ft.

On a plan with topographic contours the 'three-point' procedure is frequently used to plot the outcrop of a bed or beds.

Problem. The Roger Coal is worked from outcrop by two drift mines at *A* and *B* (Fig. 8.5). The seam was proved in a borehole at *C* at a depth of 100 ft.

Assuming a uniform rate and direction of dip, plot:

(1) the outcrop of the Roger Coal;

(2) the outcrop of the Sussi Coal, which is 100 ft above the Roger Coal;

(3) give the direction and rate of true dip and also state the depth of the seams in a borehole at *Z* (starting level of bore at 650 ft O.D.).

Solution. Seeing that points of equal height are situated on strike lines, the 200-, 300- and 400-ft strike lines for the Roger Coal will pass through *B*, *A* and *C* respectively.

Join *CB*.

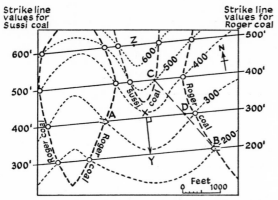

Fig. 8.5   The plotting of seam outcrops as a three-point problem.

Since the 400-ft and 200-ft strike lines pass through *C* and *B* respectively, then the 300-ft strike line will pass through a point *D* situated halfway along *CB*. The same strike line also passes through A. Therefore *AD* is the 300-ft strike line.

Since the direction and rate of dip is uniform all the strike lines are parallel and equidistant. Accordingly, construct the 200-ft, 400-ft and 500-ft strike-lines for the Roger Coal. The seam will outcrop where the corresponding strikes lines and topographic contours intersect.

Because the Sussi Coal is 100 ft above the Roger Coal, increase the value of the plotted strike lines by this amount and repeat the procedure.

The true dip is obtained by considering any two adjacent strike lines. The horizontal distance between *X* and *Y* is 1000 ft. The vertical distance between the two strike lines is 100 ft. Therefore the true dip is 1 in 10 south.

The 500-ft and 600-ft strike lines for the Roger and Sussi Coals respectively pass through the point *Z* at 650 ft O.D. The Sussi Coal will be at a depth of 650 ft − 600 ft = 50 ft in the borehole. Similarly, the Roger Coal will occur at a depth of 150 ft.

FOLDS

The forms of fold structures are exceedingly numerous and vary from broad open folds with gentle stratal dips to narrow closed structures characterized by steeply dipping beds which may sometimes be overturned. The scale of folding is also variable, in that some folds may have amplitudes of many miles in contrast to others developed only upon a microscopic scale.

THE ELEMENTS OF A FOLD

There is unfortunately considerable variance amongst authorities with regard to the definition of

the various structural terms required for the description of individual folds (Fleuty, 1964). Accordingly students are advised to make sure of the particular usage employed when consulting structural accounts. The fold components noted below (Fig. 8.6) are defined in accordance with common British practice.

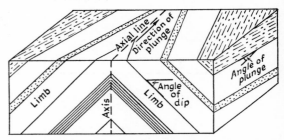

Fig. 8.6   Block diagram of a plunging anticline to illustrate the descriptive terms employed.

Axial Surface or *Axial Plane*. A surface equidistant from either limb of the fold. The axial surfaces and axes (see below) are vertical in symmetrical folds and inclined in asymmetrical folds (Fig. 8.7).

Axial Line or *Axial Trace*. The intersection of the axial surface with a horizontal-datum or topographic surface. Of importance in map interpretation. The bearing of the axial line is the same as the *trend* of a fold.

Axis. It is suggested that this term be restricted to the trace of the axial surface on a cross-section of a fold (Hills, 1953, p. 79). Also wrongly used for the direction in which the fold trends.

Crest. A line joining the highest points of a bed in an anticline.

Trough. A line joining the lowest points of a bed in a syncline. In non-plunging folds the crests and troughs are horizontal.

Plunge or '*Pitch*'. The inclination of the trough or crest of a fold from the horizontal is the *angle of plunge*. *Plunging* folds (Plate 4a) may be recognized on the geological map from the non-parallelism of their limbs and resulting broad, V-shaped, outcrop patterns (Fig. 8.11). On the geological map of an area of gentle topography the apex of the V is towards the direction of plunge in the case of an anticline. Conversely, in synclines the outcrops of opposite limbs open out towards the plunge direction.

Limb. The side or flank of a fold. Strictly defined as an area in folded strata between adjacent axial surfaces.

SIMPLE CLASSIFICATION OF FOLDS

The yielding of rocks by folding in the upper levels of the Earth's crust is a primary result of the effects

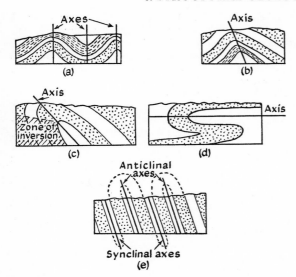

Fig. 8.7 Types of folds: (a) Symmetrical anticlines and synclines. (b) Asymmetrical anticline. (c) Overturned anticline. (d) Recumbent folds. (e) Isoclinal folds.

of differential pressure, and many fold types originate from the effect of essentially horizontal forces. Folds may be classified either genetically or descriptively. The former method requires a specialized study of structural geology (De Sitter, 1964) outside the field of the mining student. Accordingly, we may classify folds into a number of standard types based primarily upon their shapes.

Anticline

An anticline is an upwardly convex flexure in which a given geological horizon intersects a horizontal plane in both limbs. A fold may be *symmetri-*

cal, when opposite limbs dip at the same angle and therefore the axis is vertical (Fig. 8.7a). More commonly folds are *asymmetrical*, in which case the dips of opposite limbs are of different values so that the axes are inclined (Fig. 8.7b). If the axial inclination is considerable, the fold may be *overturned*, when the strata forming part of one limb are inverted (Fig. 8.7c). In extreme cases when the folds are *recumbent* (Fig. 8.7d), the axial planes may be horizontal or nearly so. As a rule, overturned beds have been greatly compressed so that opposite limbs may be parallel. Such structures are *isoclinal folds* (Fig. 8.7e) and when partly eroded and composed of an unfossiliferous sequence of similar rock types may be extremely difficult to recognize. Thus at Ingleton, Yorkshire, the exposed Pre-Cambrian slates were formerly estimated as about 10000 ft thick. The demonstration of isoclinal folding in this area has reduced this apparent thickness to about 2500 ft (Leedal & Walker, 1950).

The Pennine anticline—The low-lying Lancashire and Yorkshire coalfields are separated by a moorland area, the Central Pennines, developed along a broad anticlinal uplift of Armorican age. Originally the Coal Measures were continuous between the two areas, certain seams being correlated across the Pennines. The principal factor in the separation of the coalfields is the Pennine Anticline, erosion having removed the once overlying Coal Measures in the crestal parts of the fold (Fig. 8.8).

The anticline, trending principally north-northwest over a length of some 30 miles, is a markedly asymmetrical structure. A comparison of the outcrop widths measured along the dip of identical horizons on opposite flanks of the fold clearly indicates this. For instance, although of similar thickness on both flanks of the anticline the Rough Rock outcrop along the Lancashire flank is less than ¼

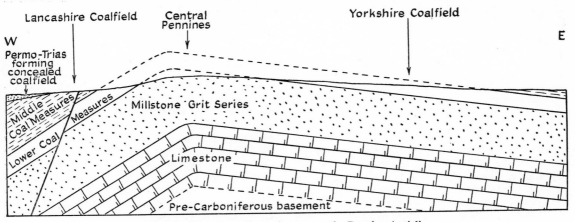

Fig. 8.8 Diagrammatic section across the Pennine Anticline.

mile in width, in contrast to a width of over 2½ miles on the Yorkshire flank (Geological Survey 1-Inch Sheets, 76 (Solid) and 77). From its crest the strata dip between 20 and 40 degrees west, whereas the dips along the eastern limb are between 5 and 10 degrees. A consequence of the asymmetry is the differing mining conditions in the Lancashire and Yorkshire coalfields. In the former, deep mining (up to 4200 ft at Parsonage Colliery, west of Manchester) has been extensively practised for many years so that reserves of economically workable coals are approaching exhaustion in some areas. In Yorkshire, mining is generally shallower, the dips beings much smaller, so that the coalfield reserves are considerably greater.

Syncline

Complementary to an anticline, a syncline (Plate 4b) is a downwardly convex flexure in which a given bed intersects a horizontal surface in both limbs. Many coalfields have a general synclinal nature, the structure being responsible for the preservation of the coals and associated strata which have been removed by erosion from the flanking anticlines.

The South Wales coalfield syncline. An excellent example of the preservation of the Coal Measures by folding, the S. Wales coalfield lies in a major syncline (Fig. 8.9) trending east–west and about 85 miles

of the coalfield. The anticlines bring up the rich Lower Coal Series within working limits; hence the important mining area of Rhondda situated along the Pontypridd Anticline. In the western half of the coalfield owing to the absence of such folds the Lower Coal Series in the centre of the main syncline are below the depth of economic working. The Caerphilly Syncline preserves a workable area of Upper Coal Series and is itself a small-scale repetition of the main coalfield structure (Jones & Walker, 1948, Plate 18). The steep inclination of the southern limb renders conditions ideal for horizon mining as at Nantgarw Colliery (*op. cit.*).

In the highly folded areas the essentially soft or incompetent shale sequences of the Lower Coal Series, sandwiched between the strong sandstones of the Namurian and overlying Pennant Series, have been intensely sheared and broken as a result of differential movement which may take place along the seams. Because of this, considerable difficulties in working are encountered in the central zones of the folds. Locally, *disharmonic folding* which cannot be traced into the overlying beds, occurs in the Lower Coal Series (Fig. 8.10). Such minor structures, particularly in the anthracite area of the north-western part of the coalfield, may be associated with large outbursts of coal and firedamp (Pescod, 1948).

Along the southern edge or 'South Crop' of the

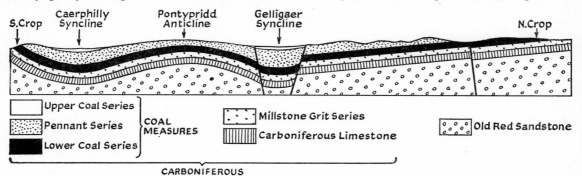

Fig. 8.9 Diagrammatic section across the South Wales coalfield.

in length. The fold is asymmetrical, with a northern limb dipping gently about 10 degrees south, whereas along the southern limb the dips are consistently over 40 degrees north and the beds are sometimes locally overturned. The disparity in outcrop widths of the Lower Coal Series on the northern and southern flanks of the coalfield is a result chiefly of the asymmetry. East of the Neath Disturbance, several important 'ripples' are situated upon the southern limb of the main syncline. These are the Maesteg and Pontypridd Anticlines, with the Caerphilly Syncline situated between the latter and the southern margin

coalfield, the gently inclined Triassic beds are unconformable upon the steeply dipping Carboniferous, the base of the unconformity overstepping locally across the Lower Carboniferous onto the Coal Measures. Hence the coalfield syncline was clearly formed in pre-Triassic time during the Armorican orogeny. Furthermore, evidence based upon thickness variations supplemented by sedimentological studies suggest that the present structural form of the coalfield was developing during the deposition of the Upper Carboniferous.

The North Staffordshire coalfield. The triangular

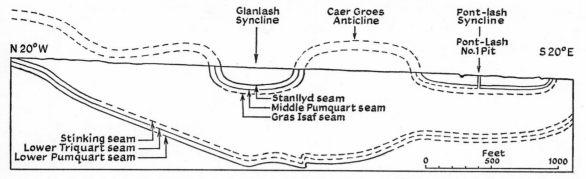

Fig. 8.10 Disharmonic folding in the Ammanford area of the South Wales coalfield. (After F. M. Trotter.)

shape of the coalfield with a northern apex near Biddulph (Fig. 8.11) results from the south–south-westerly plunge of the asymmetrical Potteries Syncline which forms the major part of the field. The flanking Western and Werrington Anticlines both converging to the north emphasize the principal structure. Resulting from the plunge of the syncline the outcrop of the productive Lower and Middle Coal Measures widens southwards, and it is in this

direction that the major seams are carried to depths below 5000 ft B.O.D., being overlaid by barren Upper Coal Measures. Considerable reserves of high-grade coking coals exist, there being a close relation-ship between coal rank and geological structure (Millot, 1941, Figs 2, 3 and 4; Crofts, 1953), the higher rank coals lying in the deeper southern parts of the syncline.

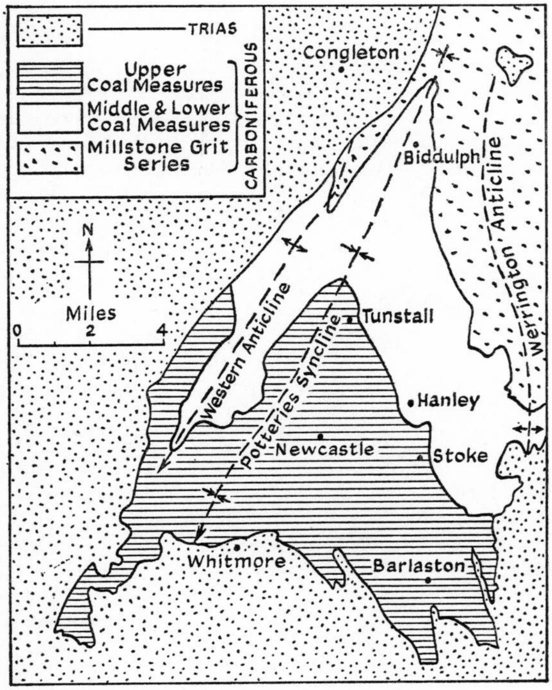

The Armorican age of the folding is clearly apparent from the unconformable relationship of the Triassic System along the southern margin of the coalfield. Thickness variations within the coalfield indicate some early-Armorican movement contem-poraneous with the deposition of the Coal Measures.

Basin

Ideally a basin is a structure in which the dip is radially inclined towards a central point; most basins are in fact elongated in one direction. Thus the intersection of a bed with a horizontal surface forms an oval outcrop pattern. Such basins may be formed by a 180-degree rotation of plunge direction in a plunging syncline. A horizontal section across a basin in any direction will indicate a synclinal ar-rangement of the beds.

The Skelmersdale basin. Situated on the western edge of the Lancashire coalfield 4 miles south-east of Ormskirk, the Lower and Middle Coal Measures of the Skelmersdale Basin are characterized by rela-tively gentle dips of less than 15 degrees. The basinal nature of the fold is most apparent in the west, where the Park Mine has an almost semicircular outcrop (Fig. 8.12). The eastern side of the basin is affected by a series of large north–north-westerly trending faults, the easterly downthrows of which increase in amount southwards. A consequence of this is to displace the centre of the basin southwards across the faults and so give a false impression of horizontal displace-ments along what are undoubtedly normal faults (Jones, *et al.*, 1938, pp. 68–70).

Fig. 8.11 Geological map of the North Staffordshire coalfield. An example of the effect upon outcrops of plunging folds.

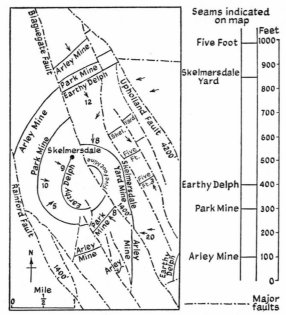

Fig. 8.12 Sketch map of the Skelmersdale Basin, Lancashire.

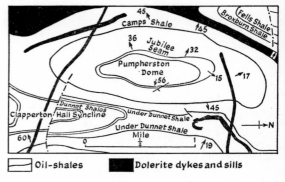

Fig. 8.13 Sketch map of the Pumpherston Dome, Scotland.

Dome

An opposite type of structure to a basin, a dome or *pericline* is characterized by a radial arrangement of dip directions away from a central area or point. As with basins, the outcrop pattern around a dome may be circular or ovoid. A dome may form above an igneous intrusion (Fig. 4.9) or from a reversal of plunge direction in a plunging anticline. The Pumpherston 'Anticline' (Fig. 8.13), 11 miles west–south-west of Edinburgh, is considered to be of the latter type (Anderson, 1942, p. 5).

Monocline

Defined as a local increase of dip in an otherwise horizontal or gently inclined series of strata, a monocline may often be associated with faulting (Fig. 8.14). Thus in the Stirling and Clackmannan coalfield, the Campsie and Carnock Faults of similar trend and in direct line are separated by a monoclinal flexure in which the amplitude of the monocline is equal to the vertical displacement of the faults (Read, 1959, p. 52).

FAULTS

Almost all coalfields are affected by the stratal dislocations termed faults. Usually they have an adverse effect upon mining, which in a heavily faulted field may be rendered exceedingly difficult and expensive by such structures. On the other hand the repetition by faulting of a group of seams may create conditions especially favourable to horizon mining. It is therefore important that the mining engineer and surveyor be fully acquainted with the nature and effects of faults.

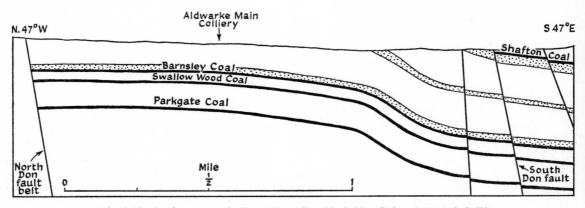

Fig. 8.14 Section across the Don Monocline, Yorkshire. (After G. H. Mitchell.)

THE ELEMENTS OF A FAULT

A detailed and clear description of any fault met with underground is of great importance, for based on such an account, inferences may be made as to the possible extension and character of the fault outside the district in which it has so far been proved. Such evidence is therefore vital to the planning of any new development. The principal descriptive terms employed (Fig. 8.15) are as follows.

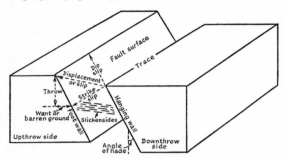

Fig. 8.15 Block diagram showing the descriptive terminology applied to faults.

Throw. The throw is the amount of vertical displacement between two formerly adjacent points and may vary from a few inches to thousands of feet. It is usual to describe the opposite faces of a fault as the *downthrow* and *upthrow* sides, depending on the relative direction of movement. In horizontal strata the throw is the vertical interval between two opposite horizons across the fault. Sometimes the estimation of the throw along a fault may not give a true picture of the total effect, since particularly along large faults, beds may be 'dragged' (see below) so that the overall effect is greater than appears from the throw.

In the concealed coalfields, the throw of a fault in the Coal Measures may differ from that in the overlying post-Carboniferous beds. Thus in the Yorkshire coalfield at Cadeby the Coal Measures are thrown 378 ft by the South Don Fault, whilst the throw of the same fault in the overlying Permian is only 60 ft (Mitchell, 1947, p. 130). Similarly, the Minney Moor Fault at Conisbrough throws the Coal Measures 75 ft south-east and the Permian 60 ft north-west! In such cases the faults are clearly affected by two or more phases of movement, and this possibility should always be considered in mining developments based on borehole evidence in the Permo-Trias. Indeed, it is believed that most large faults have been affected by many small movements rather than by a sudden 'overnight' displacement of hundreds or thousands of feet.

Hade. The inclination of a fault surface from the vertical is termed the hade. The angle of hade depends on the origin of the fault and type of rocks affected. It is often greater in the relatively soft or incompetent argillaceous rocks than in harder and more competent strata. Rarely constant along a single fault, the hade may often increase at depth.

Complementary to the hade, the *dip* is the inclination of the fault surface from the horizontal. On the Continent and in America many workers use this term in preference to hade.

Displacement. Measured across the fault surface, the displacement or *slip* of a fault is the distance between two formerly adjacent points. It may be resolved into the *strike slip*, that is, the horizontal displacement, and the *dip slip* or the vertical displacement.

Want. The want, *barren ground* or *gape* is the area along a fault in which a particular bed is absent. Thus a vertical borehole or drivage will miss a seam completely if it passes through the barren ground of that seam. The width of the barren ground (Fig. 8.16) is a function of the hade, stratal dip and throw, and its position differs from one seam to another.

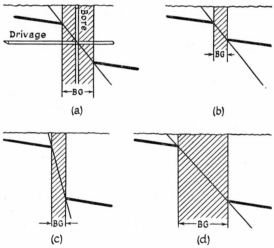

Fig. 8.16 Diagrams to illustrate the relationship of the barren ground (BG) to the throw (a, b) and hade (c, d) of a normal fault.

In a heavily faulted coalfield the coal reserves may be seriously depleted owing to the width of barren ground. Thus the total expansion of the Arley Mine across the $3\frac{1}{2}$ mile wide Wigan Fault Belt of the Lancashire coalfield due to barren ground is some 21 per cent (Jones, *et al.*, 1938, Fig. 19). Such a figure may render the economic winning of coal impossible.

Fault surface. Often loosely termed the 'fault plane', the actual face of a fault is rarely planar but is more commonly an undulating surface. A study of the minor structures which are frequently developed on a fault surface may give some indication as to the relative direction of movement of opposite sides (B. & R. Willis, 1934, pp. 483–92). *Slickensides* are polished surfaces due to friction, with the striations parallel to the direction of the last phase of fault movement. Unfortunately, along many faults of proved vertical displacement the fault surface is horizontally slickensided. In such cases the last movement was clearly a slight horizontal settling and therefore such slickensides cannot be used to identify the true character of the displacement. Small step-like interruptions of the slickensides may be sometimes found, and are usually interpreted as being formed by movement down the steps of the opposite face, as otherwise they would have been abraded. Again, grooves may be formed which deepen in the direction of movement of the opposite fault face.

Between the fault surfaces there may be masses of angular broken-up fragments of the country rock, which are sometimes associated with pyrite, calcite and other minerals deposited along the fault. Such *fault breccia* is common along faults affecting thick sequences of hard rocks. In an argillaceous sequence there may be a thin layer of *gouge*, *listing*, or a *leather bed*, composed of finely pulverized and slickensided clay materials.

Fault Trace. The intersection of the fault surface with a topographic surface or bed is the fault trace. Its form on the geological map may sometimes provide a clue as to the hade and type of fault. For example, faults with zero hade are unaffected by topographic variations and therefore may plot out as straight lines, whereas those with a considerable hade will have a sinuous trace in areas of considerable relief (Fig. 8.17). The general bearing of the trace is the *trend* of the fault.

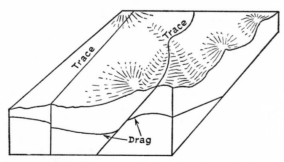

Fig. 8.17   Block diagram showing the effect of hade on the fault trace.

Fault Zone. Frequently large faults are characterized by a disturbed area, the fault zone, in which the normal dip of the strata may be increased or locally reversed by 'drag' of the strata produced by move-

ment (Fig. 8.17). Where the drag is considerable the throw may lead to erroneous conclusions as to the total effect of the fault. The drag effect along the Southern Uplands Fault was a fundamental cause of the conditions which led to the Knockshinnoch Castle Colliery disaster of 1950 (page 106, Fig. 10.14). Here a coal heading was holed through into waterlogged superficial strata though it had been estimated that there would be at least 100 ft of cover when the Southern Uplands Fault was reached. Owing to drag, the normal gradient of the coal increased from 1 in 4 to 1 in 2 so that the seam cropped out.

In studies of large-scale faulting it is often impossible to identify a single dislocation as the main surface of movement. Many 'faults' are really wide *smash zones* composed of large numbers of minor dislocations. Such zones are rarely in evidence on the surface, and the single trace of a large fault on the geological map is often a misleading feature. The Bradford Fault (Magraw, 1960, p. 488), a major fault in the Lancashire coalfield with a throw of 2600 ft, was recently proved in two horizon tunnels 590 ft vertically apart. In the lower and upper drivages the smash zone was 200 ft and 300 ft wide respectively (Fig. 8.18).

Hanging and Foot Walls. Except in faults with zero hade, one fault surface, the hanging wall, projects over the other, the foot wall.

ORIGIN AND CLASSIFICATION OF FAULTS

Dislocations may be simply classified as *normal*, *reverse* and *wrench* faults. In the first two the nature of the displacement is essentially vertical whereas that along a wrench fault is horizontal. Normal and reverse faults may be distinguished from one another by the relationship of the hanging and foot walls (Table 18).

According to Anderson (1951, pp. 13–16), the three major fault types differ only in the relationship of the three principal stresses to the Earth's surface. All faults are shear surfaces forming an acute angle

TABLE 18

A Simple Classification of Faults

Nature of displacement	Direction of movement of hanging wall relative to foot wall	Type of fault
VERTICAL	Downthrown	Normal
	Upthrown	Reverse
HORIZONTAL		Wrench

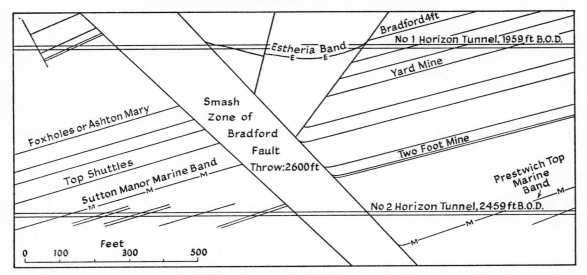

Fig. 8.18   The Bradford Fault at Bradford Colliery, Lancashire. (After D. Magraw.)

with the maximum principal stress, and are parallel to the intermediate stress. Theoretically two shear directions are possible, ideally at 45 degrees to the maximum stress, but generally only one shear surface forms, which lies closer to the maximum stress axis, forming an angle with it of about 30 degrees. This approximates to the hade of normal faults and the dip of reverse faults. In the former, the maximum stress is vertical and elongation of strata occurs in the direction of least stress, which lies in the horizontal plane (Fig. 8.19a). The stress conditions are very different during the formation of a reverse fault,

when there is a vertical extension of strata and a horizontal decrease. In this case the direction of least stress is vertical, the intermediate and maximum stress axes lying in the horizontal plane (Fig. 8.19b). Wrench faults are similarly formed by horizontal compression, when the least and maximum stresses lie in the horizontal plane (Fig. 8.19c). Since both reverse and wrench faults are formed by lateral pressures it will be apparent that although such faults may be contemporaneous with folding, normal faults are developed independently and at a different time.

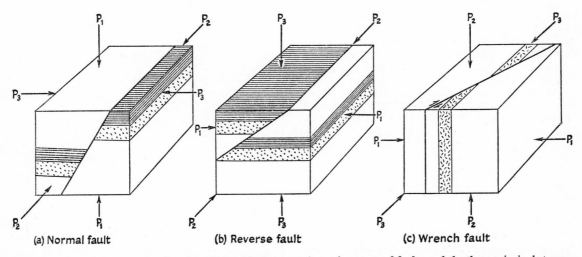

Fig. 8.19   Block diagrams showing the relationship between the major types of faults and the three principal stresses.

NORMAL FAULTS

Normal faults (Plate 5a) are formed by the effects of gravity and tension in the Earth's crust causing a horizontal extension of strata. They are the most common type of fault, and are defined as dislocations in which the hanging wall is displaced downwards relative to the foot wall. The hade is frequently between 50 and 30 degrees and in the majority of cases it is nearer the latter figure. Some normal faults may, however, have an almost zero hade, whilst others, *lag faults*, may hade over 50 degrees. Breccia or gouge is commonly developed and clean-cut fractures are rare, particularly in the case of larger faults where a wide smash zone is sometimes developed. In most examples the occurrence of barren ground is a characteristic feature, though repetition of strata can occur when the beds are steeply inclined towards the fault (Fig. 8.20). Examples have been described from the French coalfields (Hurst, 1962).

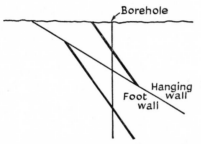

Fig. 8.20   An unusual case of a normal fault associated with repetition of strata.

Some faults of relatively small throw cannot be traced throughout a vertical sequence. Thus in the Durham coalfield (Clarke, 1962, p. 211) numbers of small faults with displacements often of less than 2 ft occur in belts of which the overall throw is negligible. Each fault cannot be proved in more than one seam, though the area of disturbed ground which fails at deeper levels may be traced to the surface. Conversely in the Lancashire coalfield certain faults, rarely exceeding 60 ft in throw and proved in the lower seams, die out verticallly upwards. The largest such structure, a 90-ft fault at Bradford Colliery, Manchester, is absent in a seam 1 100 ft above. There is no evidence for contemporaneous faulting and it is suggested that the faults result from an excess of vertical over lateral pressure, the determining factor being the thickness of superincumbent strata (Jones, 1938, pp. 72–3). On the other hand, in some seams relatively small faults with a throw of a few feet may 'run out' along the stratification surfaces of the roof strata and within the underlying seat earths. Such

structures may account for the intensely slickensided zones of gouge which are noticeable in some inter-seam sequences.

The effect of particularly large faults may be altered by the development of secondary faults which downthrow and hade towards the major dislocation. Such *antithetic faults* terminate abruptly against the principal fault and enclose a minor downthrown trough (Fig. 8.21). They may result from secondary

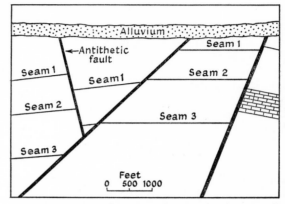

Fig. 8.21   Geological section illustrating an antithetic fault proved in a colliery.

strain effects developed during the formation of the principal fault. A series of parallel *step faults*, of similar displacement and sometimes individually of relatively small throw, but collectively of significant effect, are common in many collieries (Fig. 8.22). Faults of this type may occur as a group along a coal face, each only throwing the coal a few inches, but they are of deleterious effect in mining since they reduce the efficiency of machine mining and furthermore often create difficult roof conditions.

The Butterknowle Fault. Affecting the South Durham coalfield, the Butterknowle Fault of approximate east–north-east trend has most recently been described by Clarke (1962, pp. 213–14). Over the area examined the throw decreases from about 950 ft south to 300 ft south in about 5½ miles. The hade is about 45 degrees and the fault is a clean-cut dislocation along which is developed between 2 ft to 8 ft of gouge. Within the actual fault zone drag effects occur, the stratal dip being irregular; and in one section overturning is recorded. There is considerable flexuring up to 2 miles away from the fault on the downthrow side. Up to about 150 yd from the fault its direct effects are conspicuous. Groups of minor faults, striking roughly parallel to the Butterknowle Fault but not always having the same direction of throw, are common. Bedding surfaces in shales are highly polished, and close proximity to

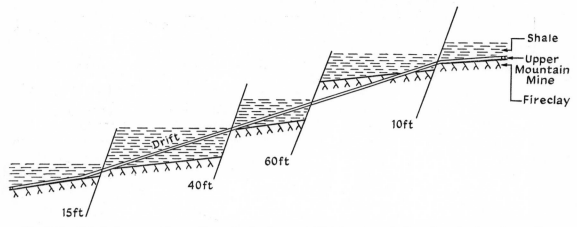

Fig. 8.22   Step faults proved in a colliery rise development. The throws are indicated on the downthrow sides.

the fault is indicated by a marked increase in joint and cleat frequencies resulting in difficult working conditions.

From its effect on Carboniferous sedimentation it is suggested (Bott, 1961) that the Butterknowle Fault originated on a monoclinal flexure in early Carboniferous or possibly Devonian time. The major movement of the fault was during the Armorican orogeny, though a small post-Permian movement phase is also indicated.

Faults and problem-maps

Some of the map work attempted by the student will concern the solution of problems involving normal faults. Usually such problem-maps require the estimation of the throw of the fault and the plotting of the area of barren ground for a particular seam:

Problem. The plan (Fig. 8.23) shows the observed outcrops of the Earnshaw Coal, the true dip of which is 1 in 7·5 north. A fault also crops out at *A* and *B*, and a boring at *C* has proved it at a depth of 300 ft from the surface.

(1) Plot the fault trace and complete the outcrop of the seam.

(2) Determine the direction and amount of throw of the fault.

(3) Shade the barren ground of the seam.

Solution. (1) Strike lines for the fault are constructed using the three-point technique, since the fault at *A*, *B* and *C* is at 400 ft, 600 ft and 200 ft respectively. From the intersection of the strike lines with equivalent surface contours the trace can be plotted. Since the outcrop positions of the Earnshaw Coal at 500 ft and 600 ft on the west and east sides

of the fault are given with the direction and amount of true dip, the appropriate strike lines and hence the full seam outcrops can be drawn. It should be noted that strike lines for opposite sides of the fault have different values.

(2) The 600-ft strike line of the coal east of the fault is equivalent to the 500-ft strike line on the west. The seam is therefore downthrown 100 ft west.

(3) Two sets of strike lines for the fault and seam have previously been constructed. The points of intersection (e.g. points *X*, *Y*, *Z*) made by the fault and seam strike lines of similar value mark the boundaries of the area of barren ground.

For the solution of this type of problem it is necessary to consider the fault surface as being planar.

REVERSE FAULTS

A reverse fault in which the hanging wall is displaced upwards relative to the foot wall, is almost the opposite of a normal fault. Formed by compression, reverse faults may be extreme results of folding originating through the failure of the steeper limb of an asymmetrical fold. They therefore commonly occur in heavily folded areas such as Pembrokeshire where the trends of reverse faults and folds are similar.

The hade is generally greater than that of most normal faults, being often between 40 and 60 degrees. Where it is greater than 45 degrees the fracture is termed a *thrust*, and it is possible that many reverse faults flatten out at depth into such faults. The latter include very large structures, for instance along the Moine Thrust of North-West Scotland (Fig. 12.5) the Pre-Cambrian rocks have been thrust approximately 10 miles over the Cambrian. Structures of this size,

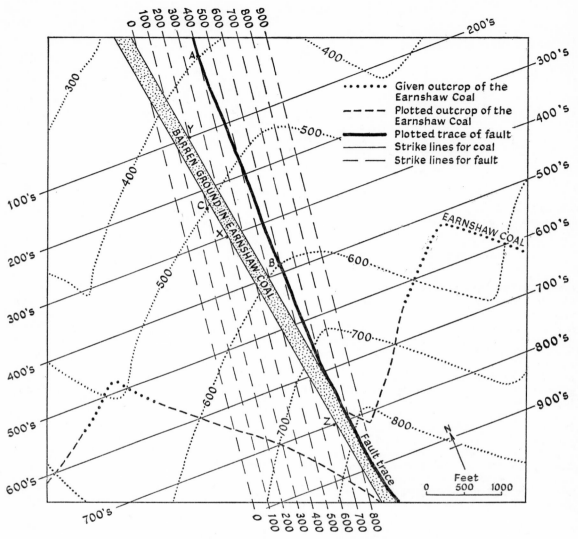

Fig. 8.23 Geological problem map based on faulting.

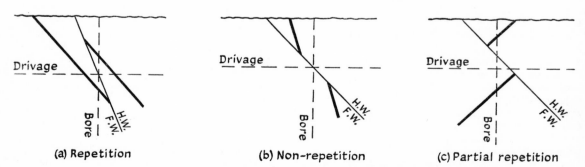

Fig. 8.24 Sections illustrating the effects of reverse faulting.

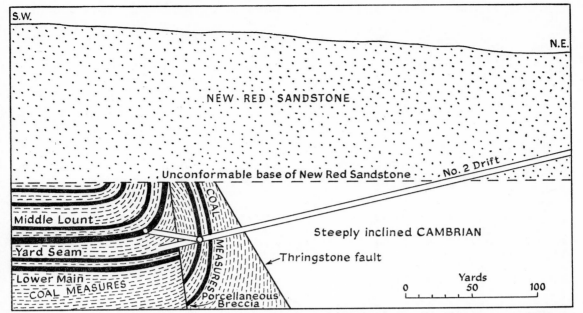

Fig. 8.25   Section across the Thringstone Fault, at the Merry Lees Colliery, Leicestershire. (After Butterley and Mitchell.)

typically developed in the highly folded orogenic areas, may cause great inversions of strata. Along some of the larger reverse faults and thrusts, *mylonite*, a fine-grained streaky metamorphic rock, may have developed from the intense crushing of the country rocks.

Reverse faults in most cases cause repetition of strata (Fig. 8.24a), though in a steeply dipping series, non-repetition of beds may occur (Hurst, 1962, pp. 497–8). Thus in *conforming faults*, that is where the strata are inclined in the same direction as the fault, if the beds are steeper than the fault surface, an area of barren ground is formed. In this case a seam may be missed entirely by a horizontal drivage or vertical borehole (Fig. 8.24b). In *contrary faults*, where the strata dip against the hade, repetition is only partial, since, although the seam may be penetrated twice in the borehole, it may be missed completely in a drivage (Fig. 8.24c).

The Thringstone Fault. Of general north–north-west trend, the Thringstone Fault forms the eastern boundary of the Leicestershire coalfield. Clearly the structure is pre-New Red Sandstone, since the fault has no apparent effect on that system. At the Merry Lees Colliery the fault was intersected by two drifts from the surface (Butterley & Mitchell, 1945, pp. 703–9). After commencement in superficial deposits the headings were driven through almost horizontal New Red Sandstone beds which were resting un-

conformably on highly inclined Cambrian shales. At the Thringstone Fault (Fig. 8.25), hading at 40 degrees, the Cambrian was thrust over Coal Measures which were overturned in a zone up to 80 yd wide. A related fault in this zone is associated with the development of an unusual rock type, the Porcellaneous Breccia, from 10 ft to 3 ft wide, in which the fragments are surrounded by a basaltic matrix. It is considered that an original fault breccia was later injected with basaltic magma intruded along the fault.

In view of the great geological interest of the Merry Lees Drifts it is fortunate that through the insight of the late A. D. Butterley, the major exposures may still be examined in special insets.

The Nanticoke Thrust. Many examples proving the close relationship between folding and reverse faulting occur in the highly flexured part of the North Anthracite Coal Basin of Pennsylvania, U.S.A. (Darton, 1940). A typical structure is at Nanticoke, where in parts an overturned anticline is broken by the Nanticoke Thrust, hading at 65 degrees and clearly developed by failure of the northern limb of the fold (Fig. 8.26).

FAULT TROUGHS AND RIFT VALLEYS

Consisting of central downthrown areas bounded by normal or reverse faults, fault troughs and rift valleys are respectively minor and major features.

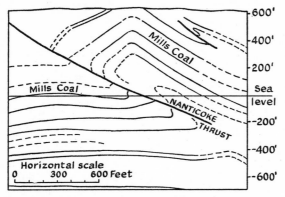

Fig. 8.26 Section across the Nanticoke Thrust, Pennsylvania. (After N. H. Darton.)

A rift valley is of large dimensions, up to about 50 miles wide and, as the name implies, is bordered by much higher ground. Undoubtably the largest such structures are those of the African Rift Valley sys-

tem, which extend for at least 1 800 miles and form the major topographic features of the continent. Several interpretations based on the nature of the boundary faults have been made as to the origin of these large structures. Although a compressional origin was formerly considered, it is now accepted that the major rift valleys are bounded by normal faults (Fig. 8.27) and so have tensional origins.

Of more local effect, a fault trough is flanked by normal faults hading towards one another and enclosing a wedge-shaped block (Fig. 8.28). Such features have often no topographic expression and are of frequent occurrence in mining areas. They commonly vary from between a mile to a few hundred yards in width, and a consequence of the faulting is the general downward attenuation of coal reserves within the trough.

The Midland Valley of Scotland. About 50 miles wide, the Midland Valley is bounded on the north and south respectively by the north-easterly trending Highland Boundary and Southern Uplands Faults. Much of the valley is below 500 ft O.D., the relief

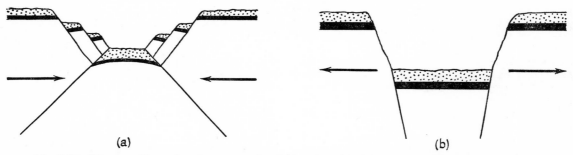

Fig. 8.27 Diagrams illustrating the compressional (a) and tensional (b) theories of rift valley formation.

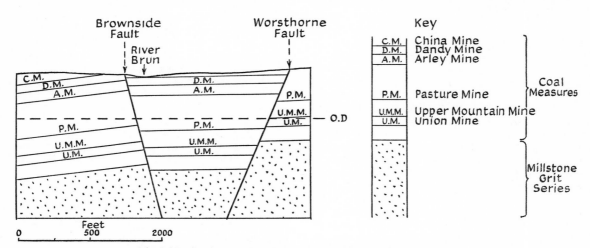

Fig. 8.28 Section across a fault trough near Burnley, Lancashire.

being of marked contrast to the bordering areas of the Grampian Highlands and Southern Uplands. Essentially the valley is a wide compound syncline of Carboniferous rocks underlaid by Old Red Sandstone beds which crop out on the margins, and are faulted against Pre-Cambrian and Lower Palaeozoic strata on the north and south. Thus the area is a rift valley which has subsided relative to the bordering districts. From stratigraphic evidence the subsidence was initiated in Silurian times, the boundary faults having functioned intermittently since this time. Their exact nature is uncertain, although surface exposures suggest the Highland Boundary Fault to be a reverse fault of low hade, whereas the Southern Uplands Fault appears in parts to be a normal fault.

WRENCH FAULTS

The major displacement along wrench or *transcurrent* faults is horizontal. When viewed in plan the direction of movement appears to be either clockwise, as along *dextral* wrench faults, or anticlockwise, as along *sinistral* wrench faults (Fig. 8.29). When other than vertical strata are affected, there will be an apparent vertical displacement, though this is exceedingly variable. Owing to their apparent throw, wrench faults are often difficult to recognize and this is probably why they appear to be rare. Since they are essentially compressional features the possibility of their occurrence should always be considered in highly folded or reverse faulted areas. During the formation of wrench faults the principal and least stresses lie in the horizontal plane so that any vertical extension is restricted by the position of the mean stress. Resulting from movement along a wrench fault, secondary strain effects may form a number of associated features. Thus many wrench faults are accompanied by parallel compression ridges or drag folds forming a small angle with the

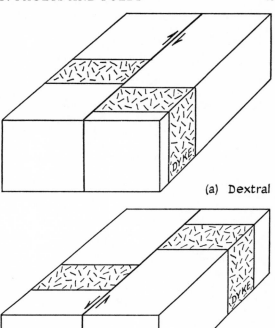

(a) Dextral

(b) Sinistral

Fig. 8.29   Dextral and sinistral wrench faults.

fault. Again the major fracture may be horizontally displaced by second order wrench faults. Such systems have been comprehensively described by Moody and Hill (1956), (Fig. 8.30).

Ideally of zero hade, wrench faults are therefore characterized by a trace unaffected by topographic

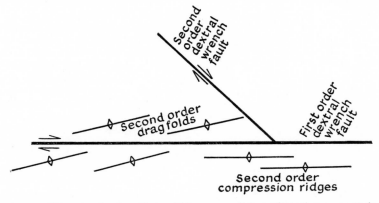

Fig. 8.30   Plan showing possible second order effects which may result from dextral movement along a primary wrench fault.

variations and which is in many cases remarkably straight. Horizontal slickensides are developed, though as discussed previously these may also form along normal or reverse faults! The fault zone is generally wider than along other faults and may have extensive developments of mylonite. Along the Great Glen Fault of Scotland (Fig. 12.4), with a sinistral displacement of 65 miles (Kennedy, 1946), the fault zone is over a mile wide and has been deeply eroded to form an impressive topographic feature. Undoubtedly the safest criterion for the recognition of wrench faults is the displacement of vertical strata, though such absolute evidence is unfortunately all too rare! The geologist has frequently to rely on less specific evidence, and later vertical movements along an original wrench may confuse the issue even further. Evidence which has been used include the presence of second order effects, the offsetting of structures and, along recent faults, stream displacements.

Commonly the terms 'tear' and 'wrench faults' are used as synonyms, though the former was originally defined as a distinct fault type (Marr, 1900, pp. 465–7). A *tear fault* is an essentially superficial structure along which horizontal displacement has taken place which does not continue to any great depth. Tear faults are situated above thrust surfaces and originate through unequal movement of different parts of a thrust. Thus one area moving at a different rate than another will become separated from it by a tear fault (Fig. 8.31).

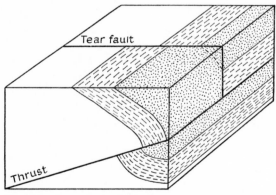

Fig. 8.31 The relationship between tear faulting and thrusting.

The Neath Disturbance. Trending east–north-east across South Wales, the Neath Disturbance is apparent for at least 40 miles from Neath to beyond Crickhowell. The structure is a compression belt along which a series of west–south-westerly plunging folds are arranged *en echelon* and parallel to the Dinas Fault (Fig. 8.32). It is significant that the fault has a noticeably straight trace over undulating topography. This indication of a low hade is born out by that observed at Penderyn of 18 degrees. Along that part of the fault mapped in detail by Owen (1954) there is a great variation, between 30 ft and 700 ft, in amount and direction of throw, far more than might be expected along normal or reverse faults. Numbers of north–north-westerly trending faults, for instance the Clyngwyn and Penderyn Faults, are displaced laterally, some ¾ mile, by the Dinas Fault, which is therefore a sinistral wrench. It is probable that the flanking folds, occurring in a belt up to 2 miles wide, are secondary compression features formed during the sinistral movement. Similarly, faults such as the Tredegar Fault, along which the Dinas Fault is dextrally displaced some 350 yd, may also be interpreted as rejuvenated second order effects.

JOINTS

Joints are rock fractures along which there has been little or no displacement. Frequently they occur as *systems*, formed by two or more *sets* of joints, each set having a constant strike and dip. One particular joint, the *master joint* of the quarryman, may be the dominant line of parting in the rock. A well jointed rock will split readily into regular blocks and the frequency or spacing of the jointing is of importance with regard to the working characters of a rock. The joint faces in fresh unweathered beds, as met with underground, are often of smooth appearance and may be discerned only with difficulty. They may sometimes be coated with secondary minerals precipitated from percolating solutions. Thus weathered Upper Carboniferous shales often have thin crusts of brownish iron compounds developed along the joints.

The major joint types may be classified according to their origins into:

(1) *Dehydration joints.* Developed chiefly in argillaceous rocks, such joints originate from the shrinkage of clays on drying. The resulting *mudcracks*, of polygonal plan, clearly predate the overlying bed, the undersurface of which may show casts of the cracked layer.

(2) *Expansion joints.* A volume increase and the formation of expansion joints often result from the growth of new minerals during the weathering of a rock. Alternatively the joints may form by thermal metamorphism. Thus cinder coals close to igneous intrusions often have well developed columnar jointing caused by the swelling of the coal on heating.

(3) *Igneous joints.* Many joints in igneous rocks are primary structures developed as either contraction cracks during the cooling of the rock or formed

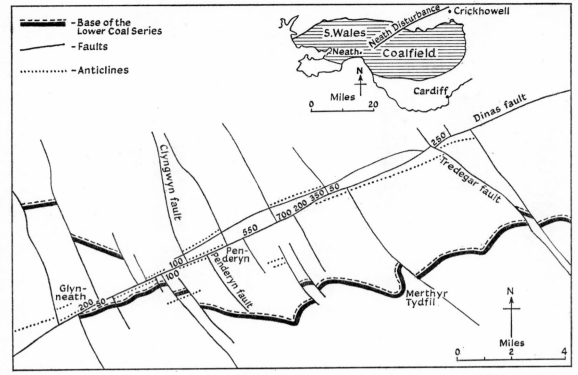

Fig. 8.32 The major structural elements along part of the Neath disturbance. (After T. R. Owen.) The apparent throws in feet along the Dinas fault are shown upon the downthrow side.

by stresses during the intrusive phases. Common contractive effects are the columnar joints typically developed in basalt lavas and magnificently exposed in the Giants' Causeway, N. Ireland.

(4) *Tectonic joints*. The major joints in sedimentary strata are chiefly formed by the effects of compression and tension during earth movements, particularly folding. Such joints form systems of constant orientation and may be classified as *shear* or *tension* joints depending on their origin.

Cleat

Important joints, of great effect in mining operations, are the cleat fractures or *slynes* predominant in bituminous coals and occurring to a lesser degree in lignites and anthracites. The fractures consist of well marked parallel breaks along which the coal most easily parts. They may be lined with thin films of 'spar' (mainly calcite or ankerite), and in the more sulphurous coals, with pyrite. Such secondary mineral infillings contribute greatly to the ash content of the coal. The cleat fractures are generally normal to the bedding, although rare cases have been

described (Dron, 1925, p. 116) where the cleat is inclined at a small angle to the seam.

Cleat is developed in the thinnest coals and has even been demonstrated in a streak less than 1/500 in thick. Generally there are two sets intersecting at a little less than 90 degrees, although occasionally up to four directions have been recorded. Along one set, the *main, face or master cleat*, the coal parts most easily. The conjugate set is termed the *cross or bord cleat*. The cleat frequency depends on the type of coal, being greatest in the bright coals. In a study made of several seams in the Yorkshire coalfield (Fig. 8.33), the durain bands thicker than 6 in had less than five fractures per foot, whereas in the clean, bright coals there is a frequency per foot of up to 70 (Macrea & Lawson, 1954). Similarly it was shown (*op. cit.*, p. 241), that the cleat frequency may determine the size of run of mine coal. Given the former, it seems possible to predict the percentage of various coal sizes separated by screening. In many areas the direction of main cleat shows a remarkable uniformity, but the often quoted north-westerly trend in the British coalfields, although fairly common, is

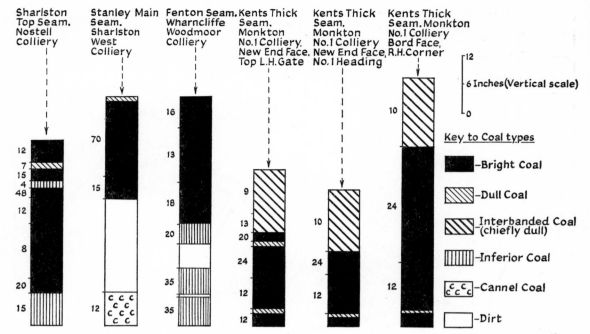

Fig. 8.33   Cleat frequency in various seams of the Yorkshire coalfield. The small figures besides the columns represent the number of cleat fractures per horizontal foot of end face. (Macrea and Lawson, 1954, Fig. 2.)

liable to considerable variation in some localities. This is particularly so in the Scottish coalfields where the cleat direction may even vary between upper and lower seams in the same colliery (Dron, 1925, p. 116).

Although it is generally believed that cleat is caused by shearing, there is great uncertainty as to the nature of the primary stress. Cleat directions, unlike more normal joints, show little relationship to other structures and therefore it is likely that the cleat formed independently of these. It has been suggested that the common north-westerly orientation of the main cleat is a fatigue feature originating from the persistent, though minute, tidal torque of the Earth (Kendall & Briggs, 1933). A more probable idea is that the feature developed by horizontal compressive stress when the coals were subject to great hydrostatic pressures due to the weight of superincumbent strata. Most certainly the precise origin is as yet undiscovered.

Slips

Slips (Dix, 1941, pp. 234–7) are surfaces of parting diagonal to the seam and with a hade of between 25 and 60 degrees. In Britain they are most common in the S. Wales coalfield where they create conditions highly favourable to the use of ploughs in coal extraction. They are clean-cut fractures, sometimes slickensided, and may be covered with thin layers of carbonate minerals. Their spacing varies from 6 in to 6 ft with a common interval less than 2 ft. Usually the slips have a uniform strike over an area, and occasionally two sets occur. Depending on the direction of working, the partings are termed *face slips* when the coal overhangs the cut, or *back slips* if the coal is worked opposite to their dip. In rare cases the slips of the lower part of a seam hade in the opposite direction to those in the upper part. Some slips behave as small normal faults with a throw of about 2 in, and as such affect the roof and floor of a seam as minor step faults. More commonly the slip fractures are confined entirely to the coal.

Frequently striking parallel to the north or north–north-westerly trending faults of the S. Wales coalfield, the slips may have formed under similar stress conditions. Alternatively, they may have originated by bedding plane slip developed during a compressive phase in the coalfield. Movements in opposite directions of the beds above and below a seam would form a shear couple which would create slip surfaces in the coal.

Riders

Described from S. Wales (Dix, 1941, p. 237; Robertson, 1933, p. 220) and particularly common in the anthracite area, *riders* or *backs*, are crush fractures frequently inclined at about 45 degrees to

Plate 5(a) Normal fault in shales, Todmorden, Yorkshire.

Plate 5(b) Angular unconformity: Lower Carboniferous limestones resting on steeply inclined Silurian flagstones, Horton in Ribblesdale, Yorkshire.

Plate 6(a) Torrent tract of a river, near Todmorden, Yorkshire.

Plate 6(b) Glaciated valley, Great Langdale, Westmorland.

the bedding of the seams. They are more irregular than slips, occurring in two sets at right angles and forming an acute angle with the slips. Most marked in the thicker seams where they may mask the slips almost completely, backs are often accompanied by a layer of powdery crushed coal sometimes containing shale inclusions.

REFERENCES

ANDERSON, E. M. (1951) *The Dynamics of Faulting*, 2nd ed., Edinburgh, Oliver and Boyd.

ANDERSON, J. G. C. (1942) *The Oil Shales of the Lothians*, Geol. Surv. Scotld, Wartime Pamphlet **27**.

BOTT, M. H. P. (1961) A gravity survey of the coast of North-East England, *Proc. Yorks. geol. Soc.* **33**, 1–14.

BUTTERLEY, A. D. & G. H. MITCHELL (1945) Driving of two drifts by the Desford Coal Co., Ltd., at Merry Lees, Leicestershire, *Trans. Instn Min. Engrs* **104**, 703–12.

CLARKE, A. M. (1962) Some structural, hydrological and safety aspects of recent developments in South-East Durham, *Trans. Instn Min. Engrs* **122**, 209–221.

CROFTS, H. J. (1953) Coking coals of North Staffordshire, *Trans. Instn Min. Engrs* **112**, 719–27.

DARTON, N. H. (1940) Some structural features of the northern anthracite coal basin, Pennsylvania, *Prof. Pap. U.S. geol. Surv.* **193D**, 69–80.

DE SITTER, L. U. (1964) *Structural Geology*, 2nd ed., London, McGraw-Hill.

DIX, E. (1941) Some minor structures in the anthracite coal seams of South Wales, *Proc. geol. Ass., Lond.* **52**, 227–44.

DRON, R. W. (1925) Notes on cleat in the Scottish coalfield, *Trans. Instn Min. Engrs* **70**, 115–17.

FLEUTY, M. J. (1964) The description of folds, *Proc. geol. Ass., Lond.* **75**, 461–92.

HILLS, E. S. (1953) *Outlines of Structural Geology*, 3rd ed., London, Methuen.

HURST, G. (1962) The La Mure coal basin, *Colliery Engr* **39**, 494–500.

JONES, I. I. & L. WALKER (1948) The reorganisation of Nantgarw Colliery, *Trans. Instn Min. Engrs* **107**, 652–66.

JONES, R. C. B., L. H. TONKS & W. B. WRIGHT (1938) Wigan District, *Mem. geol. Surv. Engld & Wales*.

KENDALL, P. F. & H. BRIGGS (1933) The formation of rock joints and the cleat of coal, *Proc. R. Soc. Edinb.* **53**, 164–87.

KENNEDY, W. Q. (1946) The Great Glen fault, *Q. Jl geol. Soc. Lond.* **102**, 41–72.

LEEDAL, G. P. & G. P. L. WALKER (1950) A restudy of the Ingletonian Series of Yorkshire, *Geol. Mag.* **87**, 57–66.

MACRAE, J. C. & W. LAWSON (1954) The incidence of cleat fractures in some Yorkshire coal seams, *Trans. Leeds geol. Ass.* **6**, 227–42.

MAGRAW, D. (1960) Coal Measures proved underground in cross-measure tunnels at Bradford Colliery, Manchester, *Trans. Instn Min. Engrs* **119**, 475–489.

MARR, J. E. (1900) Notes on the geology of the English Lake District, *Proc. geol. Ass., Lond.* **16**, 449–83.

MILLOTT, J. O'N. (1961) Regional variations in properties of the Eight Foot Banbury or Cockshead Seam in the North Staffordshire Coalfield, *Trans. Instn Min. Engrs* **101**, 2–13.

MITCHELL, G. H., J. V. STEPHENS, C. E. N. BROMEHEAD & D. A. WRAY (1947) Geology of the Country around Barnsley, *Mem geol. Surv. Engld & Wales*.

MOODY, J. D. & M. J. HILL (1956) Wrench-fault tectonics, *Bull. geol. Soc. Am.* **67**, 1207–46.

OWEN, T. R. (1954) The structure of the Neath disturbance between Bryniau Gleision and Glynneath, South Wales, *Q. Jl geol. Soc. Lond.* **109**, 333–58.

PESCOD, R. F. (1948) Rock bursts in the western portion of the South Wales coalfield, *Trans. Instn Min. Engrs* **107**, 512–36.

READ, W. A. (1959) The Economic Geology of the Stirling and Clackmannan Coalfield, Scotland, *Coalfld. Pap. geol. Surv. G.B.* **2**.

ROBERTSON, T. (1932) The Geology of the South Wales Coalfield. Part V, The Geology of the Country around Merthyr Tydfil, *Mem. geol. Surv. Engld & Wales*.

WILLIS, B. & R. (1934) *Geologic Structures*, 3rd ed., London, McGraw-Hill.

9

STRUCTURAL GEOLOGY: STRATIGRAPHIC RELATIONS

The mutual relationship between stratigraphy and structural geology is typical of the interdependence of the geological sub-sciences. The student must avoid regarding the various aspects of geology as separate studies which are complete in themselves. Thus the relative ages and therefore stratigraphic relations of a series of unfossiliferous and highly folded beds can only be derived from a correct knowledge of their geological structure. Again without the utilization of stratigraphic principles it is often impossible to arrive at a reasoned interpretation of a structural problem. For example, the throw of a fault is usually the sum effect of a number of movements each of a relatively minor amount. These are often difficult to distinguish, but as with the South Don and Minney Moor Faults (page 75), where pre-Permian and post-Permian displacements occurred, two movement phases can be proved by stratigraphic means. Moreover in many coalfields two sets of faults at right angles to each other are commonly developed. One set usually offsets the other, which is therefore apparently the older. In Fig. 9.1a two such sets are shown trending north–south and east–west. The former appears to be the oldest in the Carboniferous

beds. However the east–west faults have no effect on and therefore preceded the deposition of the Permian. Faulting along north–south lines certainly continued after cessation along the other set. The apparent off-setting of the north–south faults may have resulted from their deflexion along pre-existing and east–west faults. In Fig. 9.1b the north–south faults are undoubtedly the older since they affect only the Carboniferous beds.

UNCONFORMITY

An unconformity is a break or time gap in the geological succession. As such it may be of minor effect and only marked by the local non-deposition of a few feet of strata, or it may be developed on a regional scale in which case whole systems and even erathems may be missing. Its actual position is either a surface of erosion or of non-deposition so that the beds in contact along such a surface are *unconformable*. Although the unconformable relations of strata had been figured in the early eighteenth century, as for instance in the Somerset coalfield, the significance of the features as records of previous mountain-building phases and also of former movements of

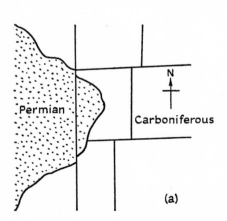

(a)

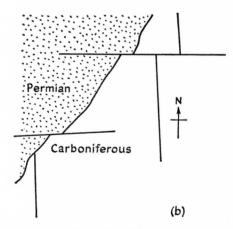

(b)

Fig. 9.1 Sketch maps illustrating the offsetting and age relationships of faults.

land and sea was not realized until Hutton, in 1787, (Tomkeieff, 1962, pp. 393–401) described and illustrated several Scottish examples.

Of the many criteria utilized for proving the unconformable relations of beds, some of the more important (Fig. 9.2) are as follows.

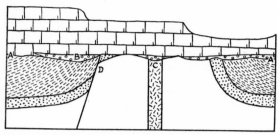

Fig. 9.2 Diagrammatic section illustrating some of the criteria enabling recognition of an unconformity. Note the irregular surface of the unconformity (A–A), the basal conglomerate (B), probably containing phenoclasts derived from underlying beds, and the truncation of the igneous dyke (C) and fault (D).

(1) An angular discordance between the beds in contact along an unconformity may be most marked. In such a case the discordance may vary from a maximum of 90 degrees (vertical strata overlaid by horizontal). When folded strata are overlaid by horizontal beds considerable variation in discordance often occurs as the unconformity is traced laterally.

(2) Faulting may take place prior to the deposition of the overlying strata, in which case the dislocations are confined to the beds below the unconformity and have no effect above it. Alternatively, if a subsequent phase of movement occurred, differing displacements may be proved in the strata above and below the unconformity (page 75).

(3) Again transgressive igneous intrusions may be also restricted to the lower group.

(4) The surface of an unconformity is often irregular, and locally the overlying beds may form deep *swilleys* or *washouts* into the older strata. Alternatively ridges and hillocks of the latter may project upwards. Thus in the South Staffordshire coalfield, where Coal Measures rest unconformably on the Silurian, 'banks' of the latter are sometimes encountered in the colliery workings (Eastwood, *et al.*, 1925, pp. 15–18).

(5) Conglomerates occur above many unconformities and are particularly associated with those developed by a marine transgression over a former land surface. The conglomerates frequently have a patchy distribution and the phenoclasts are usually composed of the underlying rocks.

(6) Major unconformities representing consider-

able time gaps are usually characterized by marked lithological contrasts. This is well seen in the British coalfields where the Upper Carboniferous rocks of essentially aqueous deposition are unconformably overlaid by the Permo-Triassic rocks often of aeolian origin.

(7) If the beds associated with an unconformity are fossiliferous then the feature can be proved by palaeontological methods. It is only by such palaeontological work that the relative age of the feature may be proved.

Several distinct types of unconformity may be distinguished. Since there is as yet no agreement on the precise terminology employed (Tomkeieff, 1962, Table 1) the use of the descriptive adjective, angular or parallel, is advocated.

ANGULAR UNCONFORMITY

An angular unconformity, characterized by an angular discordance of strata, is a significant record of former fold movements. Let us examine the sequence of events which led to the formation of the basal Carboniferous unconformity at Thornton Force, Ingleton, W. Yorkshire (Fig. 9.3). Here almost

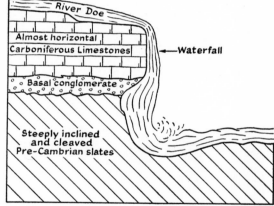

Fig. 9.3 Diagrammatic section across the basal Carboniferous unconformity at Thornton Force, Yorkshire.

horizontal limestones of the Lower Carboniferous age rest unconformably on steeply inclined Pre-Cambrian sandstones and slates. In adjacent areas the basal Carboniferous rests with similar discordance on Ordovician and Silurian strata (Plate 5b). Clearly the Lower Palaeozoic and Pre-Cambrian strata were considerably folded and eroded prior to submergence below the Lower Carboniferous sea. The basal conglomerate represents an ancient shingle beach deposit, which as the area became progressively more submerged was succeeded by the deposition of limestone. The actual unconformity represents a time gap of at least 260 million years since the *lowest* Carboniferous beds are also absent.

Because of the folding and erosion of the underlying beds during the development of an angular

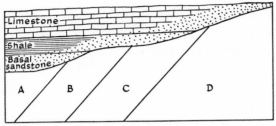

Fig. 9.4 Section showing unconformity with overstep and overlap.

unconformity, various geological horizons may be transgressed by the overlying strata. The latter therefore *overstep* (Fig. 9.4) beds of varying age. Moreover, due to the initial slope of the unconformity progressively younger strata may *overlap* across each other as a former land surface is gradually submerged. Consequently although the beds immediately above the unconformity may everywhere be a conglomerate or similar shallow-water beach deposit its age may not be constant. Thus the basal sandstone of Fig. 9.4 is *diachronous*, that is, it transgresses time planes. On the southern fringe of the S. Wales coalfield, Triassic and Jurassic beds are developed as a northerly overlapping series across the Carbonifer-

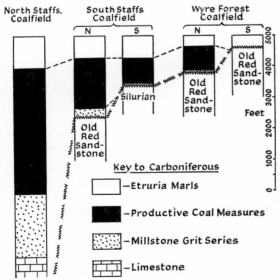

Fig. 9.5 Vertical sections illustrating the progressive southerly overlap of the Carboniferous beds in the West Midlands coalfields of England.

ous. A basal conglomerate is everywhere developed although its age decreases from Triassic in the south to Jurassic in the north (Pringle & George, 1948, pp. 82–6). Conversely the Carboniferous rocks of the West Midlands coalfields show progressive overlap to the south (Fig. 9.5). In this region a land mass composed of pre-Carboniferous rocks and sometimes termed 'St George's Land' had a great influence on sedimentary deposition. The land mass was slowly buried beneath Carboniferous sediments. In North Staffordshire a more or less complete Carboniferous sequence is developed but, as the succession is traced to the south, progressively higher horizons overlap across each other and so rest unconformably on older rocks. Thus in the Warwickshire coalfield Coal Measures rest unconformably on Cambrian orthoquartzites and shales and no representatives of the Lower Carboniferous rocks occur.

PARALLEL UNCONFORMITY

Parallel unconformities are more common although less obvious than the angular type, since no discordance is developed between the adjacent strata. They therefore appear as bedding surfaces and may be extremely difficult to recognize. Usually however some erosional phenomena in the underlying stratum, associated with a marked lithological change, may suggest the occurrence of a parallel unconformity. Palaeontological work is however necessary to prove their existence. They should not be confused with the local *washout* (Chapter 16) encountered in many Coal Measure successions. Washouts are chiefly contemporaneous or penecontemporaneous features of usually limited lateral extent which do not mark any significant change in environmental conditions. Unconformities on the other hand are of more regional effect.

CONCEALED COALFIELDS

In some coalfields the productive beds have no outcrop either at the surface or immediately below the superficial deposits and are therefore concealed beneath later rocks. Usually a coalfield is considered only to be concealed when the coal-bearing sequences are covered by later systems, which in Britain are usually of Permian, Triassic and Jurassic age. However, where an especially thick nonproductive sequence of Upper Coal Measures occurs the latter are regarded by some authorities as a concealing cover, although where such rocks are perfectly conformable it is preferable to consider the coalfield as exposed.

Many coalfields, including those of the East Midlands (Fig. 9.6) and South Lancashire, have both exposed and concealed portions. Owing to their accessibility most of the seams have been worked out

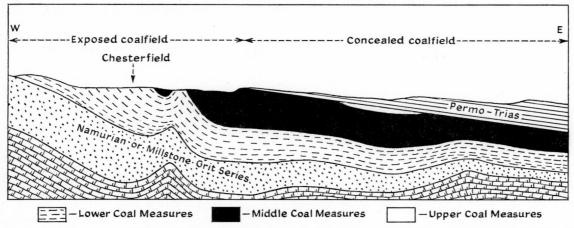

Fig. 9.6 Section across the East Midlands coalfield, England, showing the concealed and exposed parts. (Length of section about 24 miles.)

in the former areas so that modern development is now concentrated in the concealed parts. In the British concealed coalfields the cover rocks rest unconformably on the Carboniferous which were folded, faulted and eroded prior to burial beneath the younger beds. Consequently the structures developed in the cover may give little indication as to the structural complexities of the coalfield. Furthermore the cover is often composed of highly permeable strata so that shaft-sinking through it is often beset by water problems. Considerable inrushes may occur as mine workings approach the unconformity, so that its position and that of the seam *incrop* against it should be accurately proved. As it is approached the *Statutory Precautions against Inrushes* come into effect.

The small but important E. Kent coalfield, producing over $1\frac{1}{2}$ million ton of coking and steam coals per annum, is the only British example of a totally concealed coalfield at present being worked. Coal Measures were initially proved at 1 151 ft beneath the Jurassic and Cretaceous cover at Dover in 1890 in connexion with an early Channel Tunnel project. The probable existence of the field had been previously predicted from its location on a line joining the S. Wales and Somerset coalfields with those of north-western France. The Coal Measures (Dines, 1933, pp. 19–22) form a basin elongated and plunging towards the south-east (Fig. 9.7). Some major faulting affects the field and at least one fault has a post-Carboniferous component. Angular unconformities are developed at the bases of the Jurassic (dipping south-west) and overlying Cretaceous (dipping north-east) systems, so that the latter oversteps the Jurassic directly on to the Coal Measures in the extreme north-east (Fig. 9.8). Owing to the saturated

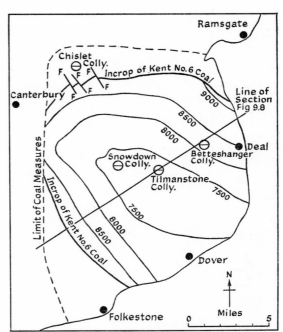

Fig. 9.7 Structure contours of the No. 6 coal of the Kent coalfield. (After H. G. Dines.)

nature of several horizons in the cover rocks water seepage into the Coal Measures is continuous and even at depths of 2000 ft may be encountered in the workings (Plumtre, 1959).

It may be noted that recent geophysical exploration in southern England suggests a strong possibility of other totally concealed coalfields, particularly between Worcester and Swindon and also

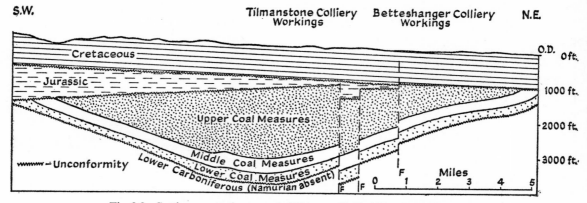

Fig. 9.8   Section across the concealed Kent coalfield. (After J. H. Plumtre.)

Oxford and Reading (Falcon & Tarrant, 1951, Plate XXIII, pp. 153–6).

INLIERS AND OUTLIERS

An *inlier* is an area of rocks completely surrounded by geologically younger strata. Inliers may be either composed of rocks of the same system as the surrounding strata or may belong to an older system. In both cases the overlying beds may be, although not necessarily, unconformable upon the older. Essentially the structures are of erosional origin, recent denudation having removed the formerly continuous cover. They are therefore often located in valleys, as for instance the Pre-Cambrian inlier at Ingleton (Fig. 9.9). Others may occur within the

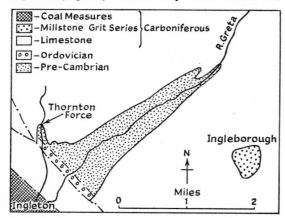

Fig. 9.9   Geological sketch map showing a Pre-Cambrian inlier and a Millstone Grit outlier near Ingleton, Yorkshire.

crestal areas of denuded anticlines, as for example the large Cambrian inlier of the Harlech area of N. Wales. Some of the more interesting types are formed

Fig. 9.10   Digrammatic section across part of Charnwood Forest, Leicestershire.

by local projections of the rocks below an unconformity, as for instance the hundreds of Pre-Cambrian masses rising above the Triassic plain of Leicestershire (Fig. 9.10). Here the Triassic sediments buried an area of considerable relief, the inliers representing the tips of an ancient mountain system.

Conversely *outliers* are composed of areas of younger strata completely surrounded by geologically older rocks. That is, they are erosional remnants of a formerly continuous sedimentary cover. Thus in the Yorkshire coalfield a number of small outliers of Lower Magnesian Limestone occur a few miles west of the present Permian escarpment. As such they indicate a former western extension of the Permian over at least part of the exposed coalfield. Similarly, the sandstone cap-rock of Ingleborough (Fig. 9.9) is but one of a series of such small outliers forming the summits of adjacent hills. Other outliers occur in synclines, and indeed the S. Wales coalfield is of this type. Again others may be preserved by faulting and so form the central parts of rift valleys and trough faults.

SUB-SURFACE MAPS

The normal geological map is essentially a record of outcrop data and so illustrates the surface position of various geological horizons. Thus a coal seam is shown as a narrow line in the position at which it crops out. In coal mining it is frequently necessary to portray other information, including variations in thickness and structure for a selected horizon over a wide area and not merely confined to its outcrop. Much of this information may be shown in the form of sub-surface maps (Bishop, 1960) relevant to one particular seam.

STRATAL CONTOUR MAPS

Stratal contour maps are composed of a series of strike lines, in this context termed contours, for a particular horizon (Fig. 9.7), and so permit a visual appreciation of the structure of an area. The selected horizon should be stratigraphically constant and therefore non-diachronous. It is now usual mining procedure to contour seams as working progresses. The standard British (National Coal Board) practice is to relate all underground levels to a datum of 10 000 ft below Ordnance Datum, so that the seam contours are shown with positive values. Thus elevations in a seam below O.D. are subtracted from 10 000 ft, whilst those above O.D. are added to 10 000 ft. Formerly when O.D. itself was used some confusion was possible, for in the same colliery there could be two contours of the same figure although with positive and negative values. For example, a 300-ft seam contour above O.D. now becomes the 10 300-ft contour, whilst if below O.D. it becomes the 9 700-ft contour.

Within the colliery, seam contours are based on underground levels and bench marks within the seams being worked, and a high standard of accuracy is possible. Outside the worked area less accurate contours may be projected from various information sources. Thus if the interval is known to be constant between two seams, one extensively worked and the other to be developed in the same area, then contours may be constructed for the latter seam by simple addition or subtraction of the seam interval. However the common variation in interseam strata renders this method and one based on borehole data liable to considerable inaccuracy. Naturally such contours are speculative and the final accuracy is in all cases less than that to be expected from normal topographic contouring.

ISOPACHYTE MAPS

An *isopachyte* or *isopach* is a line connecting the points where a particular bed or group of beds are of equal thickness. Consequently a series of such lines presented as an isopachyte map may be used to illustrate variations in thickness and areal extent of a particular sedimentary unit (Fig. 9.11). Coal seam isopachyte or thickness maps are being prepared for most workable British seams and some have now been published (Adams, 1956; Fenton, *et al.*, 1962, pp. 457–8) in the form of Coalfield Survey Folios (page 260).

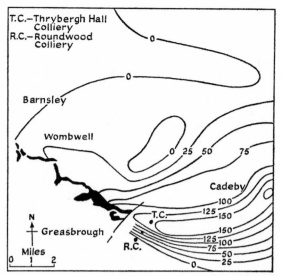

Fig. 9.11 Isopachytes (in feet) of the Abdy Rock in the East Midlands coalfield. (After G. H. Mitchell.)

The accuracy of the map depends primarily on the amount of information available during its construction. Isopachytes of actual worked seams are the most accurate since large numbers of seam sections are measured during routine colliery surveying. Even so, some difficulty may be experienced in the measurement of a seam section underground, owing chiefly to coal being left as roof or floor supports, crushing at the face and the commonly ill-defined vertical limits of a workable seam (Elliott, 1953). Away from the worked area the reliability of isopachyte maps diminishes as borehole information becomes scanty. Nevertheless, isopachytes should be prepared well in advance of the coal workings for such information enables future mining conditions to be predicted.

In the construction of an isopachyte map the control points, at which thicknesses are known, should whenever possible be evenly spaced. They should not be grouped in isolated clusters separated by comparatively large areas in which no information is recorded. Indeed an even distribution of a few points will enable the construction of a more accurate map than another based on a much larger number of unevenly spaced control points. In the projection of isopachytes from an area with great control to one with little, as, for instance, from a colliery into unworked ground, the minor local variations recorded in the colliery workings should be ignored and the regional trend of the isopachytes established by the moving average method (Clarke, 1963, p. 686, Fig. 14a). Such local variations in

94   COAL MINING GEOLOGY

seam thickness cannot be accurately predicted in an area where the control is scanty.

Isopachytes may also be prepared by the superposition of levels or strike lines for the top and bottom of a bed or group of beds. At the strike-line intersections the thickness can be calculated by the subtraction of the lower from the higher values if both figures are above or below the datum used. Where one set has negative and the other positive values then the two figures are added. Usually the isopachyte problem encountered by the student is of this type:

Problem. On the plan provided (Fig. 9.12) three boreholes at *A*, *B* and *C* were drilled to establish the thickness of the Coal Measures below the Permo-

Trias. From the information given construct the Coal Measure isopachytes at 100-ft intervals.

Solution. Construct by the three-point method two sets of strike lines for the bases of the Permo-Trias and Coal Measures respectively. Since all levels are below Ordnance Datum the Coal Measure thicknesses at the strike intersections are obtained by subtracting the Permo-Trias values from those of the Coal Measures.

The isopachytes are constructed by joining points (e.g. *X* and *Y*) at which the Coal Measures are of equal thickness. It will be seen that the Coal Measures thin south-eastwards.

REFERENCES

ADAMS, H. F. (1956) Seam structure and thickness in the South Wales coalfield, *Trans. Instn Min. Engrs* **115**, 839–57.
BISHOP, M. S. (1960) *Subsurface Mapping*, 1st ed., New York, Wiley.
CLARKE, A. M. (1963) A contribution to the understanding of washouts, swalleys, splits and other seam variations and the amelioration of their effects on mining in south Durham, *Trans. Instn Min. Engrs* **122**, 567–99.
DINES, H. G. (1933) Contributions to the geology of the Kent coalfield, (1) The sequence and structure of the Kent coalfield, *Mem. geol. Surv. Summ. Prog.* for 1932, 15–43.
EASTWOOD, T., T. H. WHITEHEAD & T. ROBERTSON (1925) Geology of the Country around Birmingham, *Mem. geol. Surv. Engld & Wales.*
ELLIOTT, R. E. (1953) The preparation of coal seam isopachytes and a résumé of seam thickness variations, *Trans. Inst. Min. Surv.* **33**, 40–53.
FALCON, N. L. & L. H. TARRANT (1951) The gravitational and magnetic exploration of parts of the Mesozoic-covered areas of south-central England, *Q. Jl geol. Soc. Lond.* **106**, 141–67.
FENTON, G. W., H. F. ADAMS & P. L. RUMSBY (1962) The mapping and appraisal of the characteristics of British coal seams, *Trans. Instn Min. Engrs* **121**, 454–64.
PLUMTRE, J. H. (1959) Underground waters of the Kent coalfield, *Trans. Instn Min. Engrs* **119**, 155–64.
PRINGLE, J. & T. N. GEORGE (1948) South Wales, *Regional Handbook geol. Surv. G.B.*
TOMKEIEFF, S. I. (1962) Unconformity—an historical study, *Proc. geol. Ass., Lond.* **73**, 383–416.

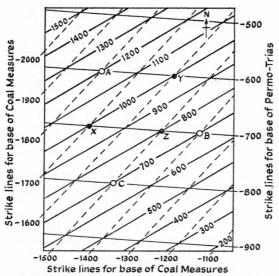

Fig. 9.12   Isopachyte problem map.

Borehole	Ht. above O.D.	Depth to base of Permo-Trias	Depth to base of Coal Measures
A	150 ft.	750 ft.	1950 ft.
B	250 ft.	950 ft.	1650 ft.
C	150 ft.	950 ft.	1650 ft.

10

SOME GEOMORPHOLOGICAL CONSIDERATIONS

Geomorphology is concerned with the study of landscape development as resulting from a number of differing erosional and depositional processes. It is the depositional aspects of the science that are most important to the mining engineer. As the land surface is naturally sculptured and eroded, so the resulting fragmentary materials are laid down as discontinuous and unconsolidated *superficial deposits* over the bedrock, and thereby present considerable hazards to shallow mining. In order to identify and distinguish between the various types of such deposits, and consequently somewhat lessen the dangers in mining, we must first consider the origin of the materials.

MASS MOVEMENTS

Most superficial deposits show evidence of widespread transportation from a relatively distant source. A few, however, are found adjacent to and often immediately below the source from which they were transported by simple gravitational movements.

CREEP

Slow and imperceptible movement of the soil and underlying broken rock mantle takes place everywhere on hillside slopes. The more striking results of the process of *creep* are most apparent on the steeper slopes. Movements of this kind primarily result from gravitational force supplemented by the presence of pore water and burrowing organisms.

Creep is evidenced by a number of effects, the more common of which are illustrated in Fig. 10.1. Boundary walls situated parallel to the contours often appear at first sight to have been built as retaining structures, since, after their construction, downslope movements cause the accumulation of soil on their upper sides. On well wooded slopes trees often have characteristic 'kinks' in their lower trunks. These were caused by soil creep which pushed the young saplings from the vertical, until later movements, when the root-system had firmly anchored the tree into the undisturbed bedrock, ceased to affect the growing trees. A similar effect is sometimes noticed on a series of fencing posts, which may be moved out

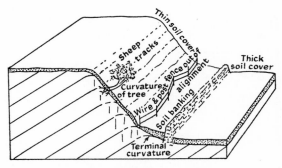

Fig. 10.1   The effects of soil creep.

of lateral and vertical alignment. 'Though misnamed 'sheep tracks' some may be used by animals, but they are certainly not created by them. All occur on steep grass-covered slopes and give a small-scale stepped appearance to the hillsides with individual 'treads' up to a few feet apart. They are undoubtedly formed by minor superficial movements. Occasionally in a quarry or similar natural section beds at outcrop may be locally overturned, showing *terminal curvature*. This is usually a result of gravitational movement although it may sometimes be formed by frictional effects at the base of a glacier or ice sheet.

PERMAFROST

Permafrost or 'perennially frozen ground' (Black in Trask, 1950, pp. 248–75) has a widespread development at the present in high latitudes and, formerly, a much greater distribution during the Ice Age. It extends to considerable depths in both superficial deposits and bedrock, as for instance in the Sveagruvan Colliery, Spitzbergen, where permafrost conditions are encountered at 1 050 ft. Its occurrence raises considerable problems in civil engineering projects because the construction of buildings and roads may cause local melting, which leads to the damage of structures by subsidence effects. Usually a thin superficial layer thaws out during the summer season and forms a highly saturated deposit because percolation of the water is inhibited by the permanently frozen underlying layer. Consequently such sheets, of the consistency of mud, will readily flow down slopes and accumulate at their bases as *solifluction deposits.*

During the Pleistocene glaciation of Britain permafrost conditions were developed at the edge of the ice sheets. The local folds, parallel to the present-day topographic features originally described from the ironstone field of the East Midlands and more recently from the Yorkshire coalfield (Cook, 1959; Shotton & Wilcockson, 1951), are most likely to have developed in the former permafrost zone. In the latter district both the Adwalton Stone and Barnsley Coals display in opencast sites a series of minor thrusts and folds (Fig. 10.2) in otherwise gently

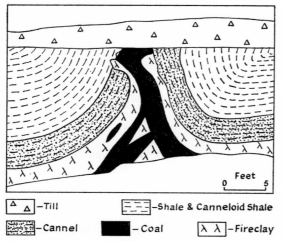

Fig. 10.2　Section illustrating a permafrost structure in the Adwalton Stone Coal, Yorkshire. (Cook, 1959, Fig. 2B.)

dipping strata. The structures are entirely surface features which die out at depth and are considered to have been formed by the sliding of a thin upper layer of thawed-out rocks over the permanently frozen substrata.

LANDSLIPPING

The most rapid mass movements are those associated with landslipping. Often they may be catastrophic, as in October, 1963, when a large section of Mount Toc in northern Italy became unstable and slipped into the Vaiont reservoir. The volume of debris was such that the reservoir overflowed and caused the death of over 2 000 local inhabitants.

Basically three types of land slipping—rock falls, landslides and rotational slips—can be distinguished. *Rock falls* accumulate below cliffs as *screes* or *block-*

fields. They may be caused by the undercutting of an outcrop by river or marine erosion, but many result from frost-wedging. During the formation of ice, expansion takes place (this may easily be proved by placing a tightly stoppered bottle of water in the empty freezing compartment of the household refrigerator), and water contained within the pores or joints of a rock acts as a powerful wedge on freezing.

Landslides are caused by the detachment of larger rock masses along bedding surfaces (Fig. 10.3). If a

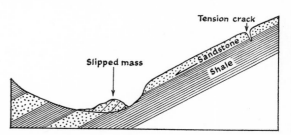

Fig. 10.3　Landsliding developed in an inclined series of sedimentary rocks.

sedimentary sequence is inclined valleywards and becomes undercut, either by natural erosion or an artificial cutting, sliding of one or more beds may take place. A steeply dipping sandstone-shale sequence, of the type common in the Carboniferous, is particularly prone to this type of movement, since the sandstone bases, along which the sliding occurs, are often lubricated by groundwater. The movements may be sudden or more prolonged, in which case some warning is given by the occurrence of *tension cracks*, delimiting the slipped mass; bulges also develop in any retaining walls. *Rotational slips* (Fig. 10.4) break across the bedding along curved slip-

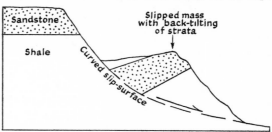

Fig. 10.4　Rotational slipping developed in a horizontal series of sedimentary rocks.

faces and are accompanied by back-tilting of the strata. They may form along slopes composed of consolidated rocks, which are usually almost horizontal as compared with the steeper dips of the slipped masses, or may form in unconsolidated material. A natural amphitheatre or semicircular hollow is in most cases developed at the rear of the feature. Landslipped masses themselves often form a series of hummocky mounds which are sometimes confused with morainic deposits. Some of the larger slipped masses may be hundreds of feet high and cover several square miles. Indeed, in the lower Taff valley of the S. Wales coalfield seams have been worked within actual landslips.

RIVERS

River action plays a major part in the erosion of the land surface and even small streams may, in suitable conditions, excavate deep gorges or broader valleys. The eroded materials, carried by the rivers as their *load*, are redeposited in the lower reaches or carried directly into the sea. Erosion and valley development can only take place if a river is capable of transporting the eroded material.

EROSION AND VALLEY DEVELOPMENT

Most large river valleys when examined along their length can be divided into three major reaches. Near their source they are narrow and steep-sided with swiftly flowing streams. Along their middle reaches the slopes are more gentle, the valleys correspondingly wider and the water-flow less rapid. In the lower reaches the relief is insignificant and broad sluggish rivers flow across it before entering the sea. Let us follow a hypothetical river from its source.

Torrent tract

Developed in the source area of the river the torrent tract (Fig. 10.5) is essentially an area of steep-sided valleys with narrow V-shaped cross-profiles (Plate 6a) and containing swiftly flowing mountain streams. A consequence of the steep slopes and under-cutting action of the streams is the common occur-

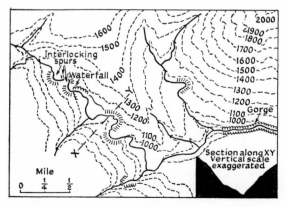

Fig. 10.5   Sketch map of the torrent tract of a river.

rence of mass-movements. Corrasion is rapid, and exposures of solid rock often occur in the beds and steep banks of streams. The stream courses tend to be winding so that a series of *interlocking spurs* are developed which restrict the view of the observer on the valley floor. The occasional straight sections often owe their nature to outcrops of softer beds which are easily eroded along their strike. Again, abrupt deviations in the stream courses may be determined by the effects of faulting or jointing. During periods of spate the streams may transport very large rock fragments, so that under normal conditions their channels are occupied by accumulations of boulders to be moved and worn down a little more at the next flood.

Waterfalls are commonly developed, usually occurring at the outcrop of a hard bed overlying a softer one. Thus the Carboniferous Limestone, overlying the relatively softer Pre-Cambrian slates, is the *fallmaker* for Thornton Force (Fig. 9.3). Another type may be formed by igneous intrusions (Fig. 4.4). Ultimately the fallmaker is eroded back so that its initial cliff-like edge disappears and is replaced by a zone of rapids.

Valley tract

Along the middle reaches or valley tract (Fig. 10.6) the slopes are more subdued, the valley wider and the volume of the river considerably greater than that in the torrent tract. Since the longitudinal profile is relatively gentle the river velocity is correspondingly less. Interlocking spurs have been replaced by relatively straight bluffs which edge the broad flat floor of the valley, across which the river swings along a series of loops or *meanders* within the river deposits, so that bedrock is seldom exposed. Often a meander may become breached at its narrowest part so that a temporary crescentic lake or *oxbow* (or, should the reader sing 'Waltzing Matilda', a *billabong*) remains. Sometimes, owing to relative uplift of the land at this stage, the river may recommence the erosion of its bed so that the meanders, originally shallow features, become *incised* as deep gorges into the bedrock. A further consequence of such uplift is the isolation of small remnants of the former valley deposits forming *river terraces* well above the present floor. After a period of heavy rain the river may locally overflow on to the adjacent *floodplain*, over which is deposited a layer of alluvium.

Lowland tract

In the lowland tract erosion is almost completely inhibited, whereas deposition is a major function since, because of the insignificant longitudinal gradient, the river cannot carry the same sediment load as in its higher reaches. The sluggish sediment-laden river is a marked contrast to the swift-flowing

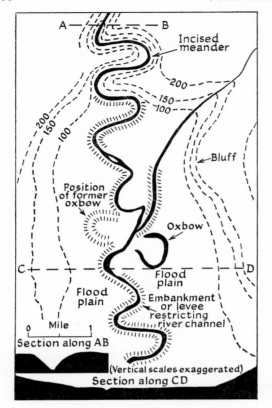

Fig. 10.6   Sketch map of a typical valley tract.

Pre-Cambrian, Permo-Carboniferous and Pleistocene periods has extensive glaciation of the land surface occurred. During the latter period, in the lifetime of prehistoric man, over half the northern hemisphere was glaciated, so that the present distribution of ice is insignificant in comparison (Figs 10.7, 12.13). Because this great Ice Age, during which time there were several interglacial phases having milder climates, is so recent, its erosional and depositional effects have as yet been little modified by more normal erosional processes.

GLACIERS

Glaciers are relatively narrow tongues of ice extending below the snowline of mountain ranges. Most glaciers (Fig. 10.8) originate in *corries*, also called *cirques*, *cwms* or *combes*, which are deep hollows on the mountainsides and formed by frost wedging and sub-glacial erosion. Often a series of corries, separated by sharp *arêtes*, contribute ice to a common glacier. Many are eroded into natural rock basins often with precipitous head-walls. Thus on the melting of the ice they are occupied by small lakes or tarns which are so numerous in formerly glaciated areas. Usually the corries are situated well above the main glaciers so that a highly fissured or crevassed ice fall links the two. One of the major problems in the ascent of Everest is the successful traverse of the 'Great Ice Fall' between the South Cwm and the Khumbu Glacier. On the melting of the ice a series of waterfalls or rapids are commonly formed between the corrie and valley floor.

Below the ice falls the glaciers are continuous although some crevassing occurs wherever the sub-glacial floor is locally steeper. Considerable glacial erosion takes place and a deep trough with a U-shaped cross profile (Plate 6b) is formed. Frost-wedged debris accumulates on the glacier surface as *surface moraine*, which may be either marginal or medial, the latter forming at the confluence of two glaciers. Some of the surface moraine ultimately becomes incorporated with the rock fragments eroded from the sub-glacial surface to form *ground moraine*. The latter, the 'teeth of the glacier', add to its power and may deeply score and polish the underlying bedrock. Such *glacial striae*, parallel to the direction of former ice flow, are occasionally seen in quarries during the removal of the superficial deposits prior to extension of the working faces. Below the confluence of several glaciers the erosive power of the ice is increased, so that a rock step in the valley floor may be formed. This, in post-glacial time, is the site of another waterfall. Again, softer rocks may be more readily eroded so that sometimes deep basins are formed which are later occupied by numerous elongated lakes.

clear mountain streams near its source. Visible relief is confined to a number of bluffs forming erosional remnants, and a monotonous floodplain is developed. Shoaling is a frequent cause of obstruction in the main channel, which if not artificially controlled is constantly changing its course over the wide floodplain.

At the mouth of the river the load may be rapidly deposited as a *delta* forming an arcuate or tongue-like extension of the land. Prolonged deltaic deposition builds up an extremely thick and widespread gently sloping fan of sediment. Similar deltas, although generally smaller in size, may form wherever a stream or river enters a lake. The deposits of such lacustrine deltas usually form ill-drained 'flats' at the heads or lateral margins of most lakes.

GLACIERS AND ICE SHEETS

The occurrence of large masses of ice on the Earth's surface, as at present in the Polar ice caps, is abnormal in that, throughout much of its geological history, the planet has been ice free. Only in the late

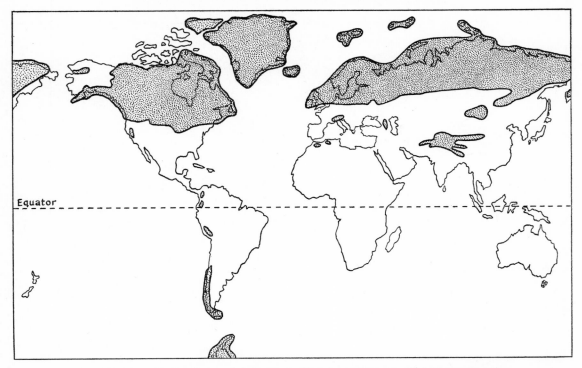

Fig. 10.7 Map showing the maximum extent of ice-sheets during the Pleistocene glaciation.

In its lower reaches, as the *snout* is approached, melting of the glacier is accentuated so that the ice becomes heavily loaded with moraine which may entirely cover its surface. At the snout itself vast mounds of *terminal moraine* accumulate. Former extensions of the glacier may be indicated by similar masses, often impounding lakes, well below the present ice margin.

ICE SHEETS

Ice sheets are masses, sometimes of continental extent, which are little affected by pre-glacial topography. Only the tips of the highest mountains may rise above the ice surface as isolated *nunataks*. Below the ice the land surface tends to be smoothed and planed down. Any pre-existing valleys and hollows are filled with the eroded debris so that an often monotonous landscape is revealed on the melting of the ice. Much of the Pleistocene glaciation was of this type; hence the widespread occurrence of ground moraine or *till* as a superficial deposit.

GROUNDWATER

Groundwater is that which occurs below the land surface in the zone of saturation. Most of it is of *meteoric* origin, that is, derived from rain and snow-fall by percolation from the surface into the Earth's crust. Small quantities of *connate water*, trapped in the sediments at the time of deposition and usually of high salinity, together with *juvenile water* of igneous origin, make up the sum total.

CIRCULATION

The circulation of groundwater is an important stage in the hydrological cycle (Fig. 10.9). By evaporation, water is abstracted from the world's seas, oceans and larger lakes, to be precipitated on the land surface as rain or snow. Some of this flows back directly in the form of rivers. Another part percolates through the rocks as groundwater ultimately to emerge as springs and seepages forming the sources of most rivers. Thus the cycle is repetitive.

Permeable and pervious rocks

Permeable rocks allow the passage of water under pressure through their bulk. Their permeability is primarily dependent on the shape, size and degree of cementation of their components. Most clastic sediments are only partially cemented so that a percentage of their total volume is made up of small interconnected open spaces or *pores* which may allow the free passage of water. Unconsolidated sediments,

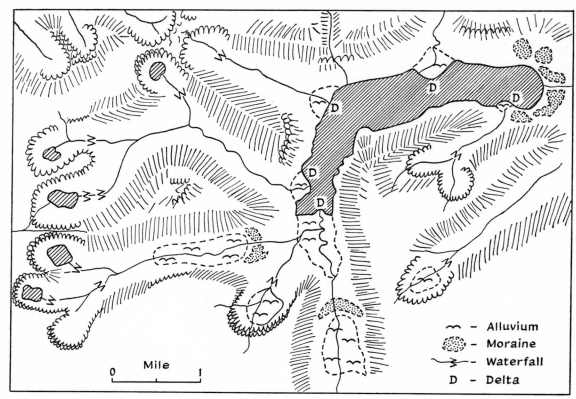

Fig. 10.8 Sketch map of a formerly glaciated area illustrating typical erosional and depositional features.

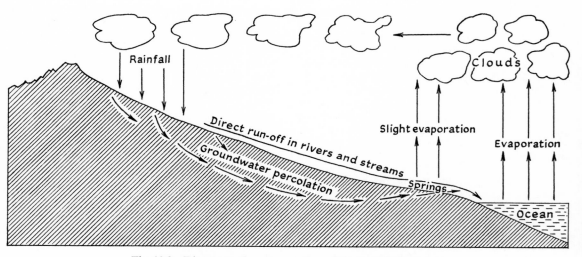

Fig. 10.9 Diagrammatic representation of the hydrological cycle.

in which cementation is hardly developed, are the most porous. Therefore the superficial deposits of sand and gravel of high porosity, sometimes encountered in glacial washouts (pages 197–8), may rapidly yield large quantities of water as dangerous inrushes. The grain size of the clastic components is an important factor in assessing the permeability of a bed. Usually the coarser sediments have a higher permeability, though not necessarily porosity, than their finer-grained equivalents. Some of the least permeable sediments are the unconsolidated clays which may nevertheless have porosities of more than 50 per cent. Although such sediments may be saturated, their contained water is effectively trapped because of surface tension effects due to the extremely small volumes of the individual pores. The shape of the clastic grains has a marked effect on the porosity of a sediment. Angular grains often form a tightly interlocking mass with consequent low porosity, whilst more rounded grains have a more porous 'billiard ball' type of packing. It is therefore not surprising that, before the development of cementation and refrigeration techniques of shaft-sinking through the British Permian aeolian sandstones, great quantities of water were frequently encountered.

A bed may however be composed of impermeable rock and yet contain and permit the passage through it of great volumes of water. Such rocks are termed *pervious*. Thus granite is a compact crystalline non-porous rock which may nevertheless be highly jointed and so contain water. Similarly, limestones, although often non-porous, are usually highly jointed and form important sources of ground-water. Furthermore, since carbonate rocks are relatively soluble, vast subterranean channels and caves may allow the rapid passage of continuous flows as underground rivers. In working the concealed parts of the East Pennine coalfields, the overlying Magnesian Limestone is an ever-present source of ground-water necessitating the strict observance of the *Statutory Precautions against Inrushes* when working close to the Permian base.

Water zones

In most areas, and at varying distances from the surface, permeable or pervious beds are saturated with water. Such beds which yield appreciable quantities of water are termed *aquifers*. The surface below which saturation occurs, that is, the *water-table* (Fig. 10.10), approximately follows the topographic surface. In ground-water studies three major zones (Fig. 10.10) are recognized.

(1) In the *vadose zone* the water content is variable and the superficial deposits and bedrock are never saturated. Meteoric water percolates through this zone from the surface. It should be noted that in humid regions the zone is often absent in the vicinity of river valleys.

(2) Below the water-table there exists the *ground-water zone* in which may be distinguished the sub-zones of permanent and intermittent saturation. The latter has a variable vertical distribution and fluctuates with the seasonal rainfall, the water-table being highest during the wet season. The permanently saturated sub-zone is of variable thickness.

(3) In the *dry zone* the rocks are free from ground-water. No absolute depth to the zone can be estimated since the local geological structure is an important determinitive factor. Thus a colliery in non-faulted ground may be dry at 1000 ft whilst a neighbouring colliery at 3000 ft may have exceptionally wet areas in the vicinity of large faults or steeply inclined aquifers along which water may percolate freely.

SPRINGS AND WELLS

If the water-table intersects the surface a series of free-flowing *springs* or the less dramatic *seepages* which are marked by patches of swampy ground may be developed along the intersection. Alternatively should the water-table lie below the surface then the ground-water may be tapped by the sinking of wells. Springs are not haphazard occurrences for in most cases their positions are determined by geological factors, so that their distribution is a major help to

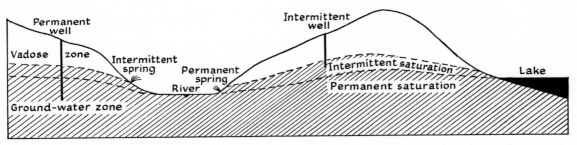

Fig. 10.10 Diagram showing the ground-water distribution in homogeneous and pervious rocks.

the geological surveyor (page 113). The most common are those developed along sedimentary junctions formed by permeable and impermeable beds. In Fig. 10.11a the lateral migration of water occurs through a sandstone overlying an impervious shale. Consequently a *spring-line* is developed along the junction between the two beds. Other springs

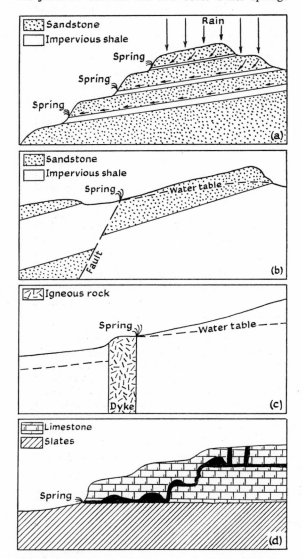

Fig. 10.11   Major types of springs. (a) Bedding springs developed in an alternating pervious and impervious series. (b) Fault spring. (c) Spring formed by an igneous dyke. (d) A limestone cave system with drainage concentrated on the surface of an unconformity below which occur impervious slates.

may be situated along fault traces (Fig. 10.11b), along the contacts of igneous intrusions (Fig. 10.11c) or at the mouths of limestone cave systems (Fig. 10.11d). Both springs and wells may be of a seasonal nature if they are supplied from the sub-zone of intermittent saturation. Since the dry season is generally the one in which ground-water supplies are most needed, wells are usually sunk to depths below the permanent water-table.

In *artesian* systems the aquifers, confined within impervious beds or *aquicludes*, are inclined so that the catchment area and the water-table may be situated above the well sites. If so, the ground-water is under hydrostatic pressure and may rise to the surface forming a free-flowing well. A classic example of an artesian system is the London Basin (Fig. 10.12) where the Chalk aquifer, with catchment at outcrop on the Chilterns and North Downs, lies between aquicludes formed by the Gault and London Clays. During the early utilization of the artesian water the wells were free-flowing although, as a result of over-extraction, the water-table has now been lowered to such an extent that water extraction is dependent on pumping.

GROUND-WATER IN MINING

Owing to the occurrence in the normal coal-bearing sequence of porous and often well jointed and bedded sandstones, hydrological troubles are common in mining. Indeed the make of water, expressed in tonnages, may be greater than the total coal production. Thus in 1948 it was calculated that about 1½ ton of water were drawn for every ton of coal in the S. Yorkshire coalfield (Saul, 1948, p. 295), whilst ten collieries in the Wigan area of the Lancashire coalfield were, in 1947, pumping 4 ton of water for each ton of coal mined. Furthermore, relatively insignificant seepages, although having little influence on the pumping load, may have significant effects on the humidity and accordingly the ventilation of a colliery. Since the hydrological features are rarely constant, even in adjacent collieries, it is not considered possible to present a detailed treatment of the subject. Some of the more important factors which determine the distribution of mine water are briefly described.

Climatic effects

If the coalfield is situated within either an arid or arctic climatic region few if any hydrological problems will be encountered. For example, in the Spitzbergen coal mines, developed within the permafrost zone, the mines are dry as a consequence of the sub-zero temperatures. In other areas the effect of heavy rainfall may be experienced within a few days in shallow workings. In some of the major Indian coal-

Plate 7 Subsidence crater in basin peat at Knockshinnoch Castle Colliery, Ayrshire.

Plate 8 Cross-stratified fluvio-glacial sands and gravels, Appleby, Westmorland.

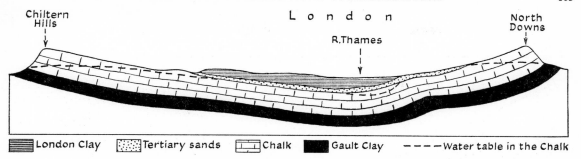

Fig. 10.12.   Diagrammatic section across the London artesian basin.

fields the rapid increase in ground-water during the heavy seasonal rains of the monsoons may cause temporary abandonment of workings. Within a month of the cessation of the monsoons the mines may, however, be dewatered and mining be resumed. Such effects are usually limited to relatively shallow mines within a few hundred feet of the surface.

Structural effects

In an inclined series lateral migration of water may take place from the surface along aquifers to their intersections with mine workings. Particularly large feeders occasioned in this way are sometimes encountered during the construction of cross-measures drivages. Similarly, the nature of the roof and floor strata is of importance in assessing the possible water problems likely to be encountered in the development of new districts. Obviously a sandstone aquifer lying above a seam may cause very wet working conditions. These are not necessarily restricted to seams in immediate contact with aquifers. Roof breaks associated with long wall methods of extraction may extend through normally impervious argillaceous beds to the base of an overlying water-laden sandstone and hence form considerable feeders. The occurrence of larger roof falls over wide gate-end roads and crossings and extending upwards of 90 ft to the base of the water-saturated Permian is considered to be possible in the Durham coalfield (Clarke, 1962, p. 218).

Ground-water is encountered at greater depths in the concealed than in the non-concealed coalfields. The cover of the former contain many highly pervious horizons including the Bunter Sandstone of South Lancashire, the Magnesian Limestone of North Eastern England and the Hastings Beds of East Kent. Pervious Carboniferous horizons incropping against such beds may carry water to considerable depths. In the E. Kent coalfield at Betteshanger Colliery a major inrush occurred at over 2 000 ft from the surface and 750 ft below the Mesozoic cover from which the water is considered

to be derived (Plumtre, 1959, pp. 159–63). In deeper parts of the same coalfield highly saline water, making 190 000 gallons per day at 3 000 ft in the Snowdown Colliery, and very different in composition from that at higher levels (*op. cit.*, Table 1) is probably connate in origin, issuing from highly fissured Coal Measure sandstones.

Seepages and inrushes are particularly liable in faulted ground since the often fissured smash zones may form ideal conduits for the percolation of groundwater. Even at 2 000 ft feeders associated with faults may be encountered in normally 'dry' collieries. Similarly faulting may cause the juxtaposition of pervious and impervious beds, thereby causing inrushes on the penetration of the former across the fault. One such inrush occurred at Mossbeath Colliery, Cowdenbeath, where a 72-fathom fault was penetrated by workings in the Glassee Coal (Reid & Brown, 1937, pp. 310–12). On the downthrow side (Fig. 10.13) a sandstone aquifer yielded water which after 8 hours was flowing at the rate of 300 gallons per minute. The effect of an impervious gouge is described from the Yorkshire coalfield (Saul, 1948, pp. 300–1) where the gouge developed along a 2-ft fault effectively prevented water migration across it. On penetration from the dip side, at 3 000 ft below the surface, a feeder of 200 gallons per minute was encountered. In this and similar cases there may be a time lag between the proving of the dislocation and the onset of water flow since the gouge may adhere to the fault for a short period before disintegrating under seepage.

SUPERFICIAL DEPOSITS

The unconsolidated or only partly consolidated superficial deposits derived from comparatively recent erosion are common over most coalfields. In some areas, particularly those of little relief, they may entirely or partially obscure the underlying rock types and geological structure, so that two geological maps are often published. The *Drift Edition* illustrates the nature and distribution of the superficial

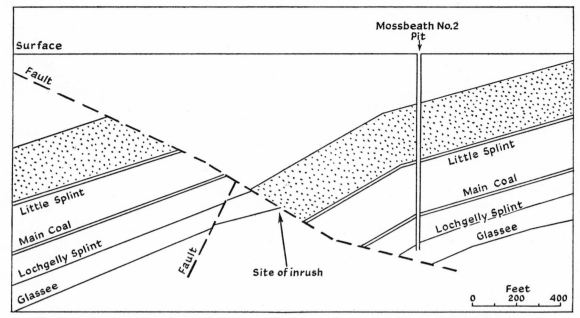

Fig. 10.13   Section at the Mossbeath Colliery, Fife, showing the site of an inrush. (After Reid and Brown.)

deposits which are omitted from the *Solid Edition*. Since the deposits are frequently waterlogged and may therefore either flow themselves or yield sudden and large quantities of water on being penetrated by mine workings, a number of statutory regulations concern mining development in their vicinity. Many varieties of superficial deposits occur but of these, alluvium, peat, till and fluvio-glacial materials are predominant in the coalfields and consequently are described in some detail.

ALLUVIUM

Alluvium is composed of the disintegrated and weathered material carried by rivers and deposited by them. It is a well sorted deposit in which the material at any one level is more or less of uniform grain size. However, it may vary vertically in grade from components of gravel size to fine clay particles. *Fluviatile alluvium* is the most abundant type being formed on the floodplains marginal to river channels in the valley and lowland tracts. Many deposits show a vertical gradation from coarse- to fine-grained deposits. The basal pebbly layers overlying rock head or older superficial deposits, and similar lenticular masses sometimes more sporadically distributed, accumulated in the actual river channel. On the occasions during which the rivers overflow the fine silt-size sediments are deposited across the floodplains. *Alluvial cones* forming fan-shaped deposits of coarser sands and gravels may occur at the points

where tributary streams enter the floodplain. The velocities and therefore load-bearing capacities of such streams are abruptly lowered by the usually sharp change in gradient so that the bulk of their load is rapidly deposited.

During glacial and early post-glacial time the sea level was considerably lower than it is at present. Thus many valleys were eroded to below the present sea level and, as this finally rose, were infilled with alluvium. Consequently, although the alluvial surface may be almost at sea level one cannot reason that the deposit is necessarily thin. The base of the alluvium is not therefore limited by the present sea level. For example, the early post-glacial gorge of the River Tees at Middlesbrough contains about 100 ft of alluvium, the surface of which is just above sea level (Agar, 1954, pp. 245–52).

Lacustrine alluvium is that deposited in lakes from the load of tributary streams. It is a basinal deposit with, usually, a convex base. Frequently the alluvium may grade laterally from fine to coarse materials, the latter often deltaic in origin, along the margins. Some of the finer-grained lacustrine deposits are characteristically laminated. Such *varved clays* are composed of alternations of clays and silts forming, respectively, thin and thick laminae, which formed during cold climatic conditions. In these conditions during the spring and summer months the coarser materials carried by tributary rivers and streams are rapidly deposited on the lake floors as the thick silt layers. The finer material is held in suspension in the lake waters until the freezing of the tributaries during the winter season, when it settles to form the clay layer. Consequently each couplet or *varve* represents an annual deposit.

Since alluvial deposits occur within valleys, close to or even below the water-table, they are often saturated in their lower parts. Consequently they may flow *en masse* or otherwise yield inrushes of water on their penetration by mine workings. Fortunately, when they occur as the uppermost superficial deposit they form extremely flat topographic features with well defined margins and may therefore be easily identified. Usually an abrupt break in slope, often emphasized by a vegetation change, demarcates the edges of the flood-plains or lake flats.

PEAT

Peat is a light-brown to black spongy mass of more or less decomposed plant debris in a waterlogged environment. The upper layers are fibrous and often contain still recognizable woody material sometimes consisting of the stumps and roots of what were once large trees. In thick accumulations the lower layers are more compact so that the fibrous structure is lost. All peat deposits have extremely high water contents exceeding 90 per cent of their total weight prior to drainage, and are therefore a potential danger in shallow mining. Their true nature may be sometimes confused by local nomenclature. This was apparent during the Knockshinnoch Inquiry (see below) where it appeared that the peat and its Scottish equivalent, moss, had been erroneously considered to be distinct sedimentary types. The more common names (Tomkeieff, 1954, p. 110) locally applied to peat deposits are:

bog muck, divet, moor, moss and turf

Two major types of peat accumulations may be distinguished. *Climatic peat* forms in areas of abundant rainfall and therefore may have a regional development, as for example in northern Britain where the deposits are seldom over 12 ft thick and commonly less. Deposits of *basin peat* are of more local occurrence and form in a waterlogged environment, either where underlying impervious material restricts free drainage or, more usually, in the infillings of former lakes. The deposits are commonly thicker than the climatic types.

Because of their high moisture content, peat deposits are extremely soft and particularly mobile sediments. The consistency of their somewhat dehydrated surface layers is no guide to the essentially sloppy nature of their bulk. Usually they are uncultivated and the margins of peat deposits may be indicated by a slight break in slope and a vegetation change.

Influx at Knockshinnoch Castle Colliery

Owing to the frequency of basin peat in the Scottish coalfields, influxes involving a number of fatalities have occurred in Scottish mines from time to time. The most serious was that on September 7, 1950, when thirteen men were killed and 116 trapped at Knockshinnoch Castle Colliery, Ayrshire (*Accident at Knockshinnoch Castle Colliery, Ayrshire*, Ministry of Fuel & Power, 1951, H.M. Stat. Off., p. 48).

The disaster occurred in a heading in the Main Coal which was holed through on August 30 into about 38 ft of superficial deposits (Fig. 10.14). These consisted of glacial material overlaid by lacustrine alluvium below 12 ft of waterlogged basin peat. On the initial holing through, water flowed into the heading until, on the morning of the accident, the yield increased prior to a large fall of glacial material, quickly followed by the influx of waterlogged peat. Widespread subsidence occurred above the heading (Plate 7) and a sludgy mass of peat rapidly filled the roadways and blocked all means of exit from the colliery.

Although the occurrence of peat was indicated on the relevant geological map, the subsequent inquiry (*op. cit.*) revealed a startling ignorance of this fact among many of the colliery officials. Furthermore the drag effects of the adjacent Southern Uplands Fault which resulted in the Main Coal cropping out (page 76) had clearly not been taken into consideration. Following this accident it became statutory to include the extent and type of superficial deposits within 150 ft of any working on the plans of all collieries.

TILL

Although often loosely termed *boulder clay*, till is composed of an unstratified and unsorted mass of pebbles and boulders set in a fine-grained matrix and deposited as the ground moraine of the Pleistocene ice sheets.

The matrix, which may be predominantly sandy or clayey, varies in colour according to that of the predominant local bedrock. Those with clayey matrices are light-coloured or bluish and because of their impervious nature form waterlogged and ill-drained soils. The more sandy and therefore pervious tills form better-drained soils. Occasionally a till contains highly waterlogged lenses or beds of fluvio-glacial sands. The rudaceous components are of variable size and range from small pebbles to rare detached rafts of local rock of immense proportions. One such sandstone raft, separated from bedrock by a thin layer of clay, and about 350 ft in length, was encountered in opencast workings south-west of Leeds (Cook, 1959, p. 90). Boulders of all shapes

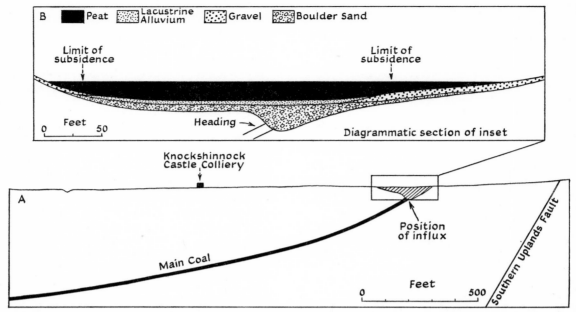

Fig. 10.14   Section at Knockshinnoch Castle Colliery, Ayrshire, showing (A) the position of the influx and (B) an enlarged section across the superficial deposits. (*Accident at Knockshinnoch Castle Colliery, Ayrshire*, Ministry of Fuel and Power, 1951.)

occur and some may have polished and striated surfaces resulting from their abrasion at the actual base of the ice. In many sections a rough orientation of the larger components is apparent in that their longer axes are approximately parallel to the direction of glacial flow. Besides the more abundant local material, far-travelled rocks, of types foreign to the area, also occur. These *glacial erratics* are mostly hard igneous boulders and pebbles which resist the erosional effects of transportation. The sources of certain rocks having characteristic features may often be identified and therefore enable the direction of ice flow to be determined. Some of the more distinctive *indicator erratics* are those derived from the small granitic boss of Shap in Westmorland, which are traceable in northern England on both sides of the Pennines, and those of riebeckite (a bluish mineral) granite derived from Ailsa Craig, a small island off the south-west coast of Scotland, and traceable as far as South Wales. In parts of the Yorkshire coalfield, pebbles of undoubted Scandinavian rocks indicate deposition from a large ice sheet originating in the latter area.

Head deposits (Dines *et al.*, 1940) of rubbly masses of unbedded stoney clay are sometimes mistaken for true till, from which they may be distinguished by the entirely local origin of their components. Usually a few feet thick, although sometimes swelling out as thicker hump-like mounds, accumulations of head are confined to valley bottoms or along hillside slopes. They formed as solifluction material developed under permafrost conditions in the *periglacial areas* along the edges of Pleistocene ice sheets.

Most commonly till deposits form a gently undulating topography and effectively mask that of the underlying pre-glacial land surface. Pre-glacial valleys are commonly infilled by thick accumulations of till which, in the coalfields, form the potentially dangerous glacial washouts (pages 197–8). Sometimes the till was moulded by the ice into a series of whale-backed mounds or *drumlins* of which some form significant landscape features over 200 ft high. Less common accumulations are the morainic ridges or mounds developed across valleys and formed at the ice margins. All till deposits are of extremely variable thickness so that an accurate estimation of the position of rock head below them can be made only by a high-density boring programme or a geophysical survey. Particularly in lowland areas sudden increases in thickness and the consequent depression of rock head, as in the case of buried valleys, should always be considered possible until proved otherwise.

Influx at Brancepeth Colliery

On July 11, 1949, an influx of till, at one stage flowing at 'about walking pace' and preceded by a small roof fall, occurred at Brancepeth Colliery, Co. Durham (Salmon & Simpson, 1951, pp. 22–36). The area affected was the main haulage road in the Three-quarter Seam, hereabouts some 127 ft from the surface. By July 17 about 67 yd of roadway were completely blocked. The influx had little effect on the surface but subsequent boring revealed a 35 ft × 24 ft cavity in till some 7 ft below a small surface depression.

The primary reason for the influx was the unforeseen depression of rock head along the course of a drift-filled pre-glacial valley (Fig. 10.15). Only a thin

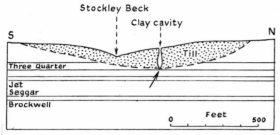

Fig. 10.15 Geological section at Brancepeth Colliery, Co. Durham, showing the position of the influx. (After Salmon and Simpson.)

crust of strata separated the base of the valley and the roadway. Ultimately this collapsed and the influx of sandy till occurred. As at Knockshinnoch there was a slight time lag between the initial roof fall and the influx. Consequently, however innocuous and immobile a superficial deposit may appear, measures should immediately be taken on its discovery to prevent or localize any subsequent movement.

FLUVIO-GLACIAL DEPOSITS

Fluvio-glacial deposits of sands and gravels accumulate as outwash material deposited by rivers emerging from a glacier or ice sheet. Consequently they frequently occur above the till of the last glacial phase. Some may, however, occur within it as isolated lenses or more regionally developed beds, such as the Middle Sands of north-western England. These were deposited during an inter-glacial period and were buried during a subsequent ice advance. Since fluvio-glacial materials are most commonly stratified and cross-bedded (Plate 8) they may easily be distinguished from the unbedded and ill-sorted tills. Accumulations of fluvio-glacial material, forming important sources of building sands and similar constructional materials, have a variety of topographic forms. They sometimes occur as gently sloping outwash plains developed fairly continuously

along the former ice margins. Other forms include the more local conical mounds (*kames*), sinuous ridges (*eskers*) and deltas.

Because of their porosity, fluvio-glacial deposits form highly waterlogged layers when situated below the water-table. Inrushes of water or influxes of 'running sand' should be anticipated on their penetration by mine workings. Above the water-table they form particularly well-drained soils. In fact any vegetation developed on them may rapidly become parched during a relatively short dry spell and so give some indication as to their nature.

REFERENCES

AGAR, R. (1954) Glacial and post-glacial geology of Middlesbrough and the Tees estuary, *Proc. Yorks. geol. Soc.* **29**, 237–253.

CLARKE, A. M. (1962) Some structural, hydrological and safety aspects of recent developments in south-east Durham, *Trans. Instn Min. Engrs* **122**, 209–21.

COOK, A. (1959) Superficial structures in the Adwalton Stone Coal at Rods Wood, West Yorkshire, *Trans. Leeds geol. Ass.* **7**, 88–99.

DINES, H. G., HOLLINGWORTH, S. E., EDWARDS, W., BUCHAN, S., & WELCH, P. B. A. (1940) The mapping of head deposits, *Geol. Mag.*, **77**, 198–226.

PLUMTRE, J. H. (1959) Underground waters of the Kent coalfield, *Trans. Instn Min. Engrs* **119**, 155–64.

REID, W. & P. W. BROWN (1937) Notes on an unusual occurrence of inrush of water at Mossbeath Colliery, Fife, *Trans. Instn Min. Engrs* **93**, 310–12.

SALMON, F. R. & J. A. SIMPSON (1951) Influx of clay into an underground roadway at Brancepeth Colliery, *Trans. Instn Min. Engrs* **110**, 22–36.

SAUL, H. (1948) Mine water. *Trans. Instn Min. Engrs* **107**, 294–307.

SHOTTON, F. W. & W. H. WILCOCKSON (1951) Superficial valley folds in an opencast working of the Barnsley Coal, *Proc. Yorks. geol. Soc.* **28**, 102–11.

TOMKEIEFF, S. I. (1954) *Coals and Bitumens*, 1st ed., London, Pergamon.

TRASK, P. D. (editor) (1950) *Applied Sedimentation*, 1st ed., New York, Wiley.

Suggestions for general reading

The student may be interested to learn more about the development of the scenery of his area. Of the many geomorphological textbooks the following are some of the more accessible to British readers.

DURY, G. (1959) *The Face of the Earth*, Harmondsworth, Penguin.

HOLMES, A. (1965) *Principles of Physical Geology*, 2nd ed., London, Nelson.

STAMP, L. D. (1955) *Britain's Structure and Scenery*, 4th ed., London, Collins.

TRUEMAN, A. E. (1949) *Geology and Scenery in England and Wales*, 1st ed., Harmondsworth, Penguin.

11

GEOLOGICAL SURVEYING

The geological map or plan, depending on the scale used, is the essential prerequisite to the geological study of an area. Thus the preparation of such maps is one of the most important tasks of the geologist. A geological map may be defined as an illustration of the three-dimensional distribution of lithologies, and the age relationships of strata in a particular area. The value of such maps to the mining industry is obvious and in all but the most recently discovered coalfields they are readily available to the mining engineer. This does not mean however that the student should ignore the various techniques used in their production, for the maximum amount of information can only be derived from the geological map if the reader has at least an elementary knowledge of geological surveying. It is with this requirement in mind that a brief introduction is given to the techniques involved in the preparation of geological maps. For a more comprehensive treatment the student is referred to one of the several textbooks on the subject (e.g. Forrester, 1946; Lahee, 1961; Himus & Sweeting, 1955). If at all possible the reader should prepare a simple map of an area where rock exposures are common. Alternatively the basic methods of geological surveying can be derived from the field examination of a published map by noting the evidence for the structures and geological boundaries shown. It is best to attempt this type of field work in other than mining areas where much information shown on the maps may have been derived from underground surveys and consequently with little surface evidence. Moreover, since many coalfields are in predominantly lowland districts, their 'solid' geology is often obscured by a thick cover of superficial deposits.

EQUIPMENT

The most important item of equipment is the *base map* on which the geological information is recorded. Apart from reconnaissance mapping in which a small scale is used, the usual base maps in Britain are the Six Inch to One Mile Ordnance Survey sheets. In other countries different scales may be used. The field map should always be protected in a case of convenient size. As notes are made directly on the map the case should be of the open folder type with a rigid cover. In Britain a complete Six-Inch sheet measures 18·84 in by 18·64 in and it is customary to divide the sheet into two halves in order to reduce its bulk when in the field. Accordingly when open the map case should measure about 19 in by 9·5 in. The actual size may be suitably modified for other countries where different-sized maps are published. In the field, observations are recorded on the map with a well sharpened pencil which should preferably be about 2H hardness. A harder pencil line can seldom be completely erased whereas those produced by softer pencils in the HB or B range may easily smudge and furthermore produce rather thick and consequently inaccurate lines. After the day's work has been concluded all field notes and boundaries should be rendered permanent in waterproof inks. Usually blue or black inks are sufficient for this purpose although, where a wealth of detail is recorded, it is advisable to use other colours to denote specific features such as faults or igneous contacts. Neatness is essential if much detail is to be recorded and therefore a good standard of draughtsmanship should be attained. There are now some excellent reservoir-type drawing pens available which obviate the risk of ruining a map by spilling a bottle of ink and, moreover, are easier to use than the standard fine mapping pen.

The next requirement is a suitable *hammer*. It is often amazing to see the varied assortment of hammers carried by an inexperienced student party. A carpenter's claw hammer or the family coal pick are of as much use in field work as a cold chisel is to a brain surgeon! The choice of the hammer varies with the individual, but whatever is chosen it should be well balanced, weighing about 2 lb and have a chisel edge perpendicular to the shaft. A pointed pick or one with a chisel edge parallel to the shaft is unsuitable for most field investigations. In Carboniferous studies, particularly when 'levering out' masses of fossiliferous shale, the writer has found a bricklayer's hammer particularly useful. Alternatively an orthodox geological hammer may be purchased from a firm of geological suppliers.

The amount of stratal dip is measured by a *clinom-*

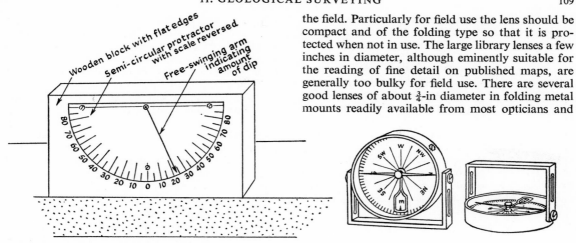

Fig. 11.1 A simple clinometer constructured from a semi-circular protractor.

Fig. 11.2 A compass-clinometer.

the field. Particularly for field use the lens should be compact and of the folding type so that it is protected when not in use. The large library lenses a few inches in diameter, although eminently suitable for the reading of fine detail on published maps, are generally too bulky for field use. There are several good lenses of about ¾-in diameter in folding metal mounts readily available from most opticians and

eter. This in its simplest form consists of a pendulum swinging within a protractor graduated into two 90-degree quadrants (Fig. 11.1). If the straight edge of the protractor, or a parallel edge of the mount, is held against a bedding surface, the amount of dip will be indicated by the position of the pendulum. Care should be taken to ensure that the maximum angle is recorded. On a bedding surface this will be the full dip and the bearing of the latter should be determined with a compass. Alternatively a more sophisticated combined *compass-clinometer* of the type commonly sold as the 'Royal School of Mines Clinometer' may be used (Fig. 11.2). In this the pendulum hangs from the centre point which also carries the compass needle. The straight base attached to one side of the compass, and parallel to its N–S or E–W line, is placed on either the under or upper surface of a bed, so that the amount of dip is indicated by the position of the pendulum. A compass bearing is then taken in the direction of full dip. Sometimes a bedding surface is so uneven that it is necessary to measure the dip of a map case or straight edge placed over the irregularities (Fig. 11.3).

A *lens* is a necessary adjunct to almost all geological practical work whether it be in the laboratory or

large pharmacies. For general purposes the magnification should be about ×8. Those with higher magnifications are less useful since the areas and depths of field are very restricted. Furthermore such lenses have to be held so close to the object that their use is often prevented by insufficient illumination.

The *auger* is a hand boring outfit capable of obtaining samples of argillaceous rocks or relatively fine-grained unconsolidated sediments such as sands, alluvium and peat. Where weathering extends to considerable depths, as for example in many tropical countries, the raising of auger samples may be one of the most important aids to geological mapping. By the use of lightweight tubular scaffolding it is sometimes possible to drive auger holes to depths of over 50 ft (Milner, 1962, pp. 58–60). A simple instrument is readily constructed from a carpenter's auger of about 1-in diameter. Its length may be extended by using sections of slightly lesser diameter gas pipe culminating in a T-piece into which a tommy-bar is inserted for hand turning. As the auger is successively lowered or raised in the hole further sections of pipe are added or removed. The samples are retained in the twists of the auger bit. Prior to their collection and examination the outer surfaces should be scraped

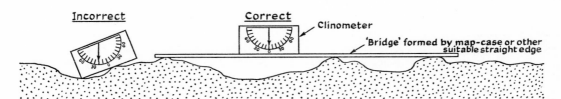

Fig. 11.3 Diagram illustrating correct and incorrect methods of obtaining dip on weathered and uneven surfaces.

to remove any material contaminated by touching the sides of the holes during the removal of the instrument.

RECORDING OF SECTIONS

The available sections may be rare or abundant according to the topography, geological history, the rock types and the extent of superficial deposits in the area to be surveyed. They may be divided into two classes: natural and artificial sections. The latter range in size from large quarries to small outcrops in cuttings, drainage ditches, foundations and sometimes even open grave shafts. As they are of a temporary nature they should always be recorded, for the benefit of future geological workers if not for the

present. The natural exposures can be prominent cliffs dominating the landscape, or small outcrops revealed in the bank of some insignificant moorland stream. During mapping, every stream however small should be traced to or from its source, for sometimes a small outcrop, only to be discovered by the conscientious worker, may be of vital importance in the proper understanding of the geology of the area. Amongst the points to be noted during the recording of a section, whether in the field or underground, the following are particularly important:

(1) The lithologies of the rocks exposed. If possible the unweathered material should be examined. Specimens of indeterminate type should be collected and examined in the laboratory.

(2) The exact position of any fossiliferous bed may be indicated on the map by an asterisk. Fossils should be carefully collected following the procedure described on page 159.

(3) The occurrence of any of the sedimentary structures described on pages 40–3. In underground observations it is essential that detailed records of such structures are made which in certain cases give an early warning of the onset of washouts and similar sedimentary discontinuities.

(4) Structural features of the outcrop including the amount and direction of dip, the nature and frequency of jointing, cleat and cleavage. The information thus obtained is shown on the map by the use of standard symbols (Fig. 11.4).

(5) The position of any boreholes, mine shafts or mine mouths, to be shown by standard symbols (Fig. 11.5).

(6) The relationship of beds to each other, i.e. faults, local unconformities, sharp, transitional and irregular contacts.

(7) The nature of the superficial deposits.

(8) The thickness of all the rock units and superficial deposits. In some cases where beds are unexposed it may be possible to excavate a shallow trench

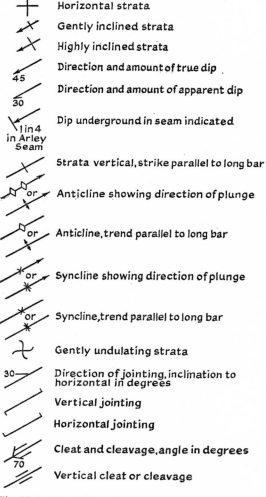

Fig. 11.4   Standard symbols for geological structures.

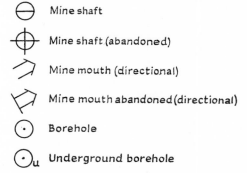

Fig. 11.5   Standard symbols for mine shafts, mine mouths and boreholes.

down to bedrock. Where a part of the sequence cannot be proved the 'thickness' of the gap should be estimated. It is important to measure the true thickness of the beds at right angles to the stratification (Fig. 11.6). The true thickness will only be in a

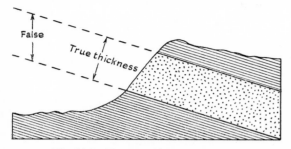

Fig. 11.6 The true thickness of a bed.

vertical plane if the beds are horizontal. Where a series of different beds occur in an exposure the section may be most clearly illustrated by means of a graphic section (Fig. 11.7) employing a series of standard symbols (Fig. 11.8).

Finally, if considered necessary, an illustration of the exposure should be made. A camera may be used for this purpose (Grice & Russell, 1952) although a rapid field sketch (Fig. 11.9) will invariably illustrate certain points more fully than an indifferent photograph. A suitable scale of measurements should be included as otherwise the illustration will be of little use for record purposes.

It is rarely possible to record all the above details on the map. Consequently the position of the exposure relative to two standard reference points, or in the case of Great Britain the Full National Grid Reference, should be obtained and a full description included in the field notebook. Alternatively the record can be made on the back of the field map by inserting a pin through the position of the exposure and writing around the pinhole.

GEOLOGICAL JUNCTIONS

The delineation of beds of differing lithologies is a major task of the geological surveyor. Thus a bed of shale is distinguished from one of sandstone and the contact or geological junction of the two beds is plotted. Faulted junctions should be distinguished and indicated on the map. Where igneous rocks occur, distinction should be made between intrusive and extrusive types and their relationships noted with adjacent sediments (pages 28–9). The actual junctions are seldom visible and their particular nature is indicated by broken lines at the inferred positions of contacts or faults, or continuous lines where the contacts are exposed.

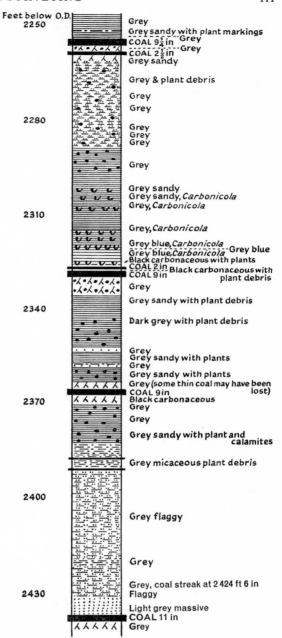

Fig. 11.7 Graphic section illustrating part of a borehole sequence.

FEATURE CHANGES

Feature changes are frequently the result of differential weathering and are accordingly of considerable use in geological mapping, apart from those

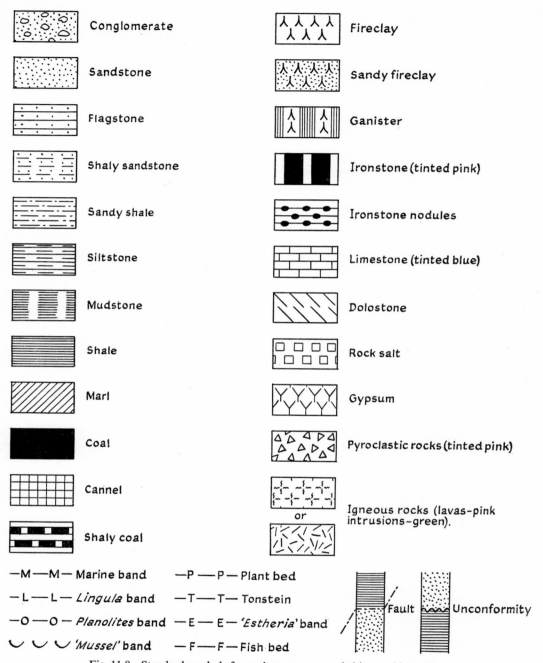

Fig. 11.8 Standard symbols for rock types as recorded in graphic sections.

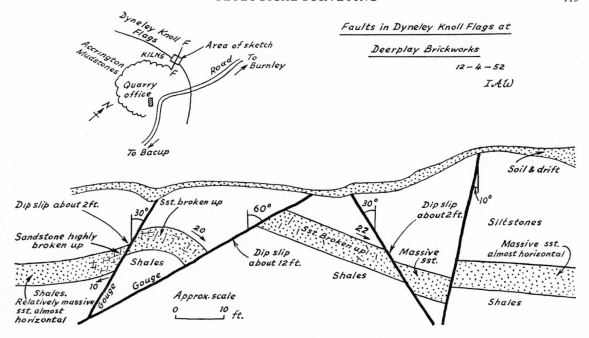

Fig. 11.9   Field sketch recording details of faulting.

areas obscured by thick superficial deposits. Except in the latter case, every natural gradient change is indicative of the underlying rock type and is accordingly shown on the field map (Fig. 11.10) by hachuring. Thus steep, often rocky slopes tend to be formed by hard beds such as sandstones, limestones and most igneous rocks, whereas softer shales, mudstones or clays usually form less steep and more vegetated features. The rocks controlling the features may be seen and proved in the occasional stream section or, if no outcrops are discovered, may sometimes be deduced from soil and vegetation changes. Where the soil and drift cover is thin, which is often the case on steep slopes, it may be possible to 'turf out' a small section to expose the bedrock.

From gradient changes alone it is rarely possible to be certain of the exact position of the junction between two beds, for the base of the steep feature is usually some distance below that of the bed primarily responsible for it. In such cases where the junctions are unexposed other evidence must be used.

SPRINGS

The positions and occurrence of springs are directly influenced by the lithologies and structures of an area, and consequently the student should be familiar with the various types (pages 101–2, Fig. 10.11). They most frequently occur along the contacts between overlying permeable and underlying impermeable beds such as sandstones and shales, and may therefore be used to locate the junctions between such beds. Apart from their occurrence along normal sedimentary junctions, springs may also be located along faults. The latter group are generally distinguished by their comparatively straight linear development as opposed to the frequently more sinuous junctions revealed by springs developed along sedimentary contacts.

On the other hand in limestone areas, sinkholes and potholes are again indicative of lithological changes and faults. Thus in the Yoredale Series of W. Yorkshire the junctions between impermeable shales and the underlying limestones are often revealed by the development of sinkholes along the contacts. Conversely the base of a limestone is often suggested by a spring-line. Also a straight linear development of sinkholes may be formed in the broken ground of a fault, although such an arrangement can also occur along a prominent joint direction. Even where a fault itself is obscured, its proximity is sometimes indicated by a zone of secondary dolomitization (page 39).

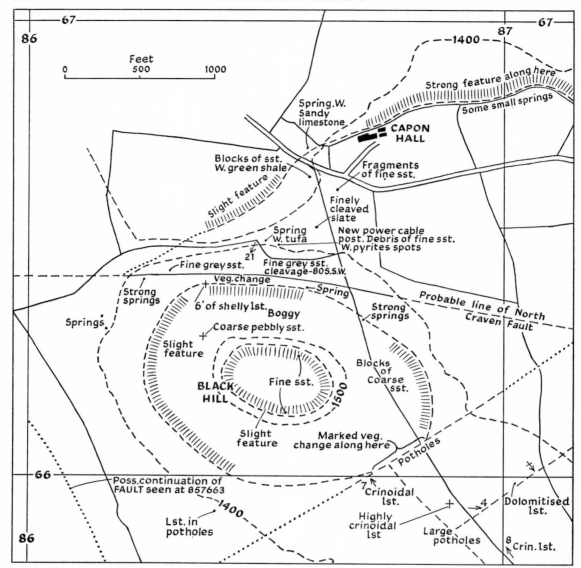

Fig. 11.10   Part of a field map of the Malham area, Yorkshire. (Note the information derived from features, springs, potholes and vegetation changes.)

SOIL CHANGES

In driftless areas the soil type is a result of the weathering of the bedrock. Besides the obvious rock fragments turned up by both man and animal from the subsoil its actual nature is often indicative of the parent rock. A few examples may be given:

Heavy sticky soils—argillaceous rocks;
Sandy soils—arenaceous rocks;
Crumbly and fairly dry soils—calcareous rocks.

Again the colours of the soils are often due to the character of the rocks from which they are derived. For example, the pink coloration of the soils of the English Midlands developed on the pinkish Keuper Marl is most noticeable and contrasts with the rather grey soils developed over Coal Measure shales or mudstones. The presence of underlying till is invariably indicated by the soil containing numbers of glacial erratics which have been wedged upwards by frost action.

Soil creep (page 95) is common on steep slopes so that their mantle, although derived from rocks in proximity, is not necessarily indicative of the character of the immediately underlying rock. Consequently when utilizing such evidence the rule should be to note the *upper limit* of a particular soil type or rock fragment. This limit should be approximately coincident with the geological junction (Fig. 11.11).

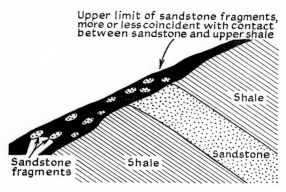

Fig. 11.11 The effect of soil-creep.

VEGETATION CHANGES

The *natural* vegetation developed in a particular area is dependent primarily upon the soil type and hence where drift deposits are thin or absent, upon the underlying rocks. Accordingly vegetation changes reflect underlying lithological changes and are to be used in geological mapping. Where undisturbed by farming the changes may be so striking as to render junction mapping a simple task. An excellent example is in the Charnwood Forest area of Leicestershire where there are large numbers of scattered inliers of Pre-Cambrian rocks surrounded by Triassic beds. The latter relatively soft rocks weather to a fertile soil whereas over the much harder Pre-Cambrian outcrops the soil is shallow and comparatively sterile. Consequently the position of the Triassic/Pre-Cambrian junction may be estimated by the very considerable vegetation changes. Again amidst the Yoredale outcrops of the West Yorkshire highlands the alternations of limestones, shales and sandstones are often clearly shown by the differing vegetation. In this district the lush green sheep pastures developed on the limestones contrast strongly with the brown, rather sour and tussocky vegetation growing upon the shales. Similarly heather and bracken may be found along the sandstone outcrops whereas such plants only rarely occur over limestone soils.

Of more specialized use are certain indicator plants, the distribution, or occurrence of certain abnormal varieties, of which is controlled by the presence in the soil of chemical elements derived from underlaying ore deposits (Hawkes & Webb, 1962, pp. 305–14). Thus in some areas of northern England ancient lead workings are often marked by a concentration of the Spring Sandwort (*Minuartia verna*), whilst copper-bearing beds in deposits of N. Wales are characterized by the luxuriant growth of the Sea-Pink (*Armeria maritima*).

THE USE OF THE AUGER

Occasionally there are no exposures of a particular bed although its presence may be indicated by one or more of the previously described effects. In some cases its nature can be determined by hand drilling. In a drift-covered area it may be possible to bore through the superficial deposits thereby revealing their thickness and sometimes the type of bedrock. Care should be taken lest false thicknesses are recorded owing to incomplete penetration resulting from the presence of large boulders in the superficial deposits. Several auger holes should always be drilled to obviate this possibility.

UNDERGROUND GEOLOGICAL SURVEYING

Wherever possible a record should be made of every new underground section since the evidence revealed is only of a temporary nature. Where several drivages or faces intersect a sequence of dipping strata a geological plan should be prepared. The procedure is that of plotting the structural and lithological features on both sides of a drivage, one's position being located by direct measurement.

Apart from the compilation of underground geological maps, the plans of any abandoned workings within the mapping area should also be consulted. Such plans may show the abandoned shaft sections and also reveal the positions, and in some cases the throws, of faults. Where a folded or inclined sequence was worked, the direction and amount of full dip may often be calculated from spot heights recorded in the workings of a particular seam.

PHOTOGEOLOGY

The stereoscopic interpretation of aerial photographs is now a widely used aid in geological mapping (Eardley, 1941; Miller & Miller, 1961). Particularly in undeveloped areas photogeological studies can save much of the laborious and comparatively unremunerative field work formerly necessary for the location of areas of possible mineral wealth. Moreover in such areas the base maps used by the field geologist will most probably have been prepared from the photogrammetric examination of aerial photographs and may indeed be a simple photographic mosaic. Aerial photographs used for photogeological analysis are principally of the *vertical* type taken when the camera is more or less pointing vertically downwards. These are most often prepared as an overlapping series with a minimum overlap of about 60 per cent between successive exposures. In the area of common overlap between two adjacent photographs it is possible, by the use of a stereoscope, to obtain a perspective image or three-dimensional 'model' of the land surface. Sometimes *oblique* photographs of a type similar to Plate 4a are used. Although these may often be most easily understood by the non-expert they are generally less useful for detailed interpretation procedures since they are difficult to view stereoscopically and so the geological features can seldom be accurately transferred on to base maps.

From the stereoscopic examination of the aerial photographs the effects of differential weathering resulting in feature changes are readily apparent. As noted previously such changes reflect similar variations in the underlying rocks. Similarly vegetation changes may be plotted and are often more noticeable upon aerial photographs than on the ground where the observer may be confused with irrelevant details. Sometimes an indication of the rock types is given by the particular drainage pattern, as for example when a spring-line is developed at the base of a limestone series. Where the rocks crop out the occurrence of different types may be suggested by tonal variations of the photograph resulting from the differing rock colours. From such effects the general geological structure of an area may be deduced (Plate 9). Thus sedimentary junctions are offset by faults, plunging folds may be recognized from the convergence of their opposite limbs, and in detailed photogeological analysis it is sometimes even possible to calculate the rate of dip and thickness of strata by photogrammetric methods.

THE REPORT

After the map is completed the final stage in the geological survey of an area is the presentation of the report. It is noticeable that many students find this task the most difficult. Accordingly the following suggestions are made with regard to the preparation of a geological report. This may concern an area actually mapped by the student, one merely visited during field studies, or be based on the laboratory analysis of a published geological map. The report should be fully intelligible to persons unacquainted with the area studied. It must therefore be clear, logical and assembled in an orderly fashion. In most cases the reports can be subdivided and headed along the following lines:

(1) *Introduction*. This should consist of a brief reference, illustrated by suitable maps, to the location, regional geological background and, where appropriate, any previous geological research in the area.

(2) *Geological succession*. A general summary of the succession should be followed by a detailed formational account including details of palaeontology. Where appropriate, measured sections may be illustrated graphically.

(3) *Geological structure*. The geological structure should be considered under the following subheadings.

(a) *Folding*—the trend, symmetry and type of folds.

(b) *Faulting*—a discussion of any faults present including details of the amount and direction of displacement, nature of the faults, hade and trend.

(c) *Unconformities*—the type of unconformity together with the field evidence for its occurrence. A brief outline of the development of the future.

The geological structure may be illustrated by photographs and a number of geological cross-sections. Where a section is not perpendicular to the strike (i.e. parallel with the stratal dip), the true dip must be corrected to the apparent dip in the direction of the section (page 68).

(4) *Igneous activity*. Give an account of the nature of igneous rocks and their relationships to the country rocks. In mining areas their actual or possible effects on the quality of the coals should be considered.

(5) *Superficial deposits*. Describe the nature and origin of any superficial deposits and note their thickness wherever possible. It is important to consider the effects that such deposits may have on the working of any comparatively shallow coal seams.

(6) *Geomorphology*. Briefly discuss the relationship of the major geomorphological features to the geology of the area.

(7) *Economic geology*. The occurrence of mineral deposits, coal seams, building and road stones, sands and gravels, etc., should be reviewed. In particular, seam sections, types of coals, their variations and the amount of proving must be recorded.

(8) *References*. Give a list of all published work consulted and quoted in the text.

Lastly, although perhaps giving some amusement to the reader, a journalistic account such as the following is irrelevant in the geological report of an area: 'The ingenuity of our party was taxed to the full when we were confronted with a river in full spate. It was finally decided that the only way to cross was to emulate the pioneers and wade! The spectacle which followed is beyond description' (from the field report of an ex-mining student).

BEHAVIOUR IN THE FIELD

As geologists and students we rely on the good nature of farmers and landowners on whose ground we work. An inconsiderate party, causing offence to such people, can effectively restrict access for future geologists. Please remember this. Accordingly the following fieldwork code is suggested.

(1) Always ask permission to examine exposures and quarry sections. If the nature of your interest is explained permission will rarely be refused.

(2) It is usual to leave all gates in the position found. In certain cases a gate may be intentionally left open to allow free movement of livestock. However should a gate be found open alongside a public road and there is any danger of livestock straying then the gate should be closed.

(3) Be particularly careful in climbing fences and stone walls. The careless removal of a topstone from one of the latter can cause a whole length of the structure to collapse. If possible climb walls at their corner junctions where they are strongest. Similarly a fence or gate is most safely climbed close to an upright post.

(4) Avoid disturbing livestock, particularly in their breeding season.

(5) Do not walk across growing crops, and remember that these include grass for hay and silage.

(6) During the collection and wrapping of specimens please remove any litter. Be particularly careful about tidying up a site where extensive hammering has taken place. Any rock chippings should be collected and preferably buried as otherwise a sharp rock fragment could seriously maim what might be a particularly valuable farm animal.

(7) Avoid unnecessary hammering as in natural outcrops this only serves to disfigure the results of many a thousand years of weathering. One well directed blow should be sufficient to detach most specimens. In some cases it will be impossible to extract a fossil visible upon a weathered rock surface. If so, please leave it intact and do not damage it in a half-hearted attempt at removal. Due to weathering, some future geologist may be fortunate enough to remove the complete specimen.

REFERENCES

EARDLEY, A. J. (1941) *Aerial Photographs. Their Use and Interpretation*, 1st ed., New York, Harper.

FORRESTER, J. D. (1946) *Principles of Field and Mining Geology*, 1st ed., New York, Wiley.

GRICE, C. S. W. & G. A. RUSSELL (1952) Still photography in coal mines, *Res. Rep. Saf. Mines Res. Bd* **53**.

HAWKES, H. E. & J. S. WEBB (1962) *Geochemistry in Mineral Exploration*, 1st ed., New York, Harper & Row.

HIMUS, G. W. & G. S. SWEETING (1955) *The Elements of Field Geology*, 2nd ed., London, University Tutorial Press.

LAHEE, F. H. (1961) *Field Geology*, 6th ed., London, McGraw-Hill.

MILLER, V. C. & C. F. MILLER (1961) *Photogeology*, 1st ed., London, McGraw-Hill.

MILNER, H. B. (1962) *Sedimentary Petrography* **1**, 4th ed., London, Allen & Unwin.

12

STRATIGRAPHY

A knowledge of coalfield stratigraphy and the utilization of stratigraphic principles is an important aspect of the education of the mining engineer. Only by the application of such knowledge can the coalfield or individual colliery be efficiently and safely worked. As well as the obvious use of correlative studies in establishing the correct horizons of seams encountered in new ground, other equally important stratigraphic studies include the accurate prediction of seam positions, water-bearing horizons and roof and floor conditions. Such information must be at hand for the successful economic and safe development of new areas. The geological survey is the first step in development work.

BASIC PRINCIPLES
SUPERPOSITION AND FAUNAL SUCCESSION

Although first suggested by Nicolaus Steno, the Danish bishop of Hamburg, in the middle seventeenth century, it was not until the early nineteenth century that the fundamental concept of *superposition* as being indicative of relative age was first successfully applied. About this time a number of European scientists were beginning to survey geologically parts of their own countries. In England, William Smith, a civil engineer primarily engaged in canal construction, noted a 'regularity in the strata' of what were later established as the Mesozoic systems. Working on the basis that the lowest strata of an area are older than the overlying beds, Smith constructed the most well-known of the early geological maps. Only in areas of severely folded and faulted rocks is this concept of superposition inapplicable, for then some of the oldest strata may be overfolded or thrust across geologically younger rocks (Fig. 12.5). In the normal unfolded or gently folded sedimentary sequence the rocks become progressively younger in an upwards direction.

Having so established the local geological sequence it is necessary to apply palaeontological methods for its extension outside that area. Very few sequences are constant in character when traced laterally, rapid facies changes (see below) occur so that a sandstone may pass laterally into a rock of very different aspect but of the same age. Since outcrops are rarely continuous, and therefore such changes can seldom be visually traced, other means must be employed to establish the relative ages of often dissimilar and therefore apparently unrelated sequences. In the late seventeenth century the naturalist Hooke hinted that strata may be arranged in order of their relative ages and correlated over wide areas by using the fossil assemblages contained in them. By their evolutionary development the many groups of fossils exhibit progressive changes when traced through the stratigraphical column (Table 19). Hence the *faunal succession* and, to a lesser extent, the *floral succession* of the fossiliferous rocks are utilized for their stratigraphic division. Smith was one of the first to apply this successfully in the construction of his geological map, and is commonly regarded as the founder of modern stratigraphy.

SUB-DIVISIONS OF GEOLOGICAL TIME

By the utilization of the principles of superposition and faunal succession the vastness of geological time has been subdivided into a large number of units just as seconds, minutes and hours may be recognized in a day. In the consideration of the sub-divisions (Dunbar & Rodgers, 1957, pp. 289–307, Størmer, 1966, pp. 5–28) a distinction is made between the time units themselves and the strata deposited at a certain time (Table 20). Thus the succession of rocks comprising the *Carboniferous system* was deposited during the 80 million years of the *Carboniferous period*.

The most comprehensive time unit is the *era*, of which three are recognized and characterized by major stages in the development of life. Each era contains a number of geological *periods*, the equivalent *systems* being defined by particular fossil assemblages. The systems themselves are further sub-divided by increasingly narrow palaeontological definition, into *series*, *stages* and *zones*. The latter, the most basic units, are recognized by the occurrence of one or a few fossil species. Such fossils may not necessarily be confined to their particular zone

TABLE 19

The Stratigraphical Range of Certa in Fossil Groups

('Pleistocene) Tertiary	MAN →
Cretaceous	AMMONITES, BIRDS
Jurassic	CERATITES, MAMMALS, REPTILES
Triassic (New Red Sandstone)	
Permian	
Carboniferous	GONIATITES
Devonian (Old Red Sandstone)	LAND PLANTS
Silurian	TRUE GRAPTOLITES, CORALS, LAMELLIBRANCHS, FISHES
Ordovician	NAUTILOIDS
Cambrian	TRILOBITES, BRACHIOPODS
Pre-Cambrian	TRACES OF SIMPLE LIFE RARE

TABLE 20

The Major Stratigraphic Units

Time units	Complementary stratigraphic units
ERA	*ERATHEM*
PERIOD	SYSTEM (e.g. Carboniferous)
EPOCH	SERIES (e.g. Namurian)
Age	Stage (e.g. Marsdenian)
Episode	*Zone (e.g. R. gracile)*

only although they will be most common in it. For example the mussel *Anthraconaia lenisulcata* gives its name to the Lenisulcata Zone of the Westphalian (Coal Measures) in which it attains its maximum population density; it does however occur in the Yeodian Stage of the underlying Namurian (Table 31). The proverb 'One swallow does not make a Summer' may for our purposes be modified to 'The discovery of one zonal fossil may not indicate that

particular zone'. It is the fossil assemblage rather than the solitary specimen which is important.

Unfortunately the tabular representation of the geological column (Table 2) with continuous lines between the various sub-divisions contributes to the common misconception that their limits are universally and accurately defined. This is not so, for the junctions between the stratigraphic divisions are more often blurred than sharp. For example, in Britain we are unsure of the exact position of the junction between the Permian and Triassic systems and therefore also of that between the Palaeozoic and Mesozoic Eras. Since about this horizon the rocks are unfossiliferous and also there is considerable lateral variation in rock types, it is impossible even to be sure that the particular horizon taken as the junction in one area is at all equivalent to that used a few miles away. Where a basal Carboniferous unconformity is developed, as over most of Britain, it is possible in such areas to demarcate the lower limit of that system. But in Devonshire the exact base is less certain, for there the Devonian-Carboniferous sequence is conformable and the junction lies at some horizon in the 'Transition Series'. Furthermore none of the sub-divisions employed, although *equivalent in stratigraphic succession*, are necessarily equivalent in age throughout the world (Hawkes, 1957, pp. 312–14). Many animal groups have slow migration rates and consequently the occurrence of a common fossil species at localities hundreds or thousands of miles apart does not indicate that the rocks containing it were deposited contemporaneously in the same year or even in some cases in the same millenium (Fig. 12.1).

FACIES

Most stratigraphic horizons when considered over a wide area exhibit lateral changes in rock types and

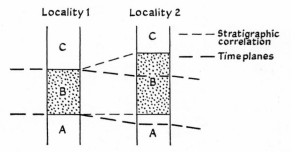

Fig. 12.1 The stratigraphical equivalence of strata does not imply their exact contemporaneity of deposition. Thus fossil B would only have appeared at locality 2 some time after first evolving at locality 1.

fossil contents. In fact vertical sections of the same horizon may appear entirely unrelated and are easily mistaken for separate horizons. The reason for such apparent anomalies is that the rock types and their contained faunas, together regarded as a particular *facies* (Dunbar & Rodgers, 1957, pp. 135–56), are determined by their depositional environments. Lateral changes of facies therefore reflect similar changes in the original sedimentary environment. Let us consider a modern coastal region and some of the sediments deposited along it. In many such areas a belt of sand-dunes forming above sea level is replaced below it by shingle, beach sands and muds. All these sediments are deposited more or less contemporaneously but if the sediment types were examined individually this would seldom be apparent. Moreover very different animals inhabit the areas above and below sea level, so that it would be difficult to prove the stratigraphic equivalence of the deposits by their faunas. There is little resemblance for instance between the contemporaneous faunas of the coastal margins and the open seas.

It is therefore not surprising that correlation between different facies types is difficult, for both the rocks and fossils are often peculiar to the individual facies. For example, within about 10 miles, four distinct facies exist in the Lower Carboniferous of N.W. Yorkshire (Fig. 12.2). In the south over 7000 ft of black bituminous limestones (Chatburn Limestone), cherty limestones (Pendleside Limestone) and shales (Worston and Lower Bowland Shales), accumulated in the muddy waters of a subsiding basin. To the north in a shallow and clear-water sea about 700 ft

of the exceptionally pure Great Scar Limestone was first deposited before the invasion of the sea by the deltaic facies of the Yoredale Series. The latter, over 1000 ft thick, are composed of limestones, shales, cross-bedded sandstones and thin coals. Intermediate between the shelf and basin, a fourth facies, the Malham Limestone, is composed of highly fossiliferous unbedded deposits formed as a barrier reef. Each particular facies may be zoned according to the various fossil types present. But, since few of the fossils are common to more than one facies, it is only by the discovery of the occasional 'strays' that the very dissimilar Pendleside, Malham and Great Scar Limestones, and at a higher level, the Bowland Shales and Yoredale Series can be correlated.

GEOSYNCLINES AND FOLD MOUNTAINS

Geosynclines (De Sitter, 1964, pp. 390–6) are rapidly subsiding elongated submarine basins in which great thicknesses of sediments accumulate and are subsequently folded. That subsidence and sedimentation occur contemporaneously is indicated by the essentially shallow-water characters of the geosynclinal sediments, which may nevertheless total over 10 miles in thickness. It must be emphasized that geosynclines did not therefore commence as oceanic deeps. Greywackes predominate amongst the sediments and are in fact regarded by many as typical of the geosynclinal facies. Along the margins a relatively thin shelf facies, composed of sandstones, shales and limestones, and deposited over a relatively stable and slowly subsiding area, is developed (Fig. 12.3a).

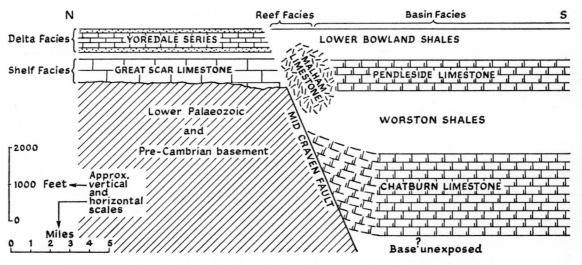

Fig. 12.2 Facies variations in the Lower Carboniferous succession in north-west Yorkshire.

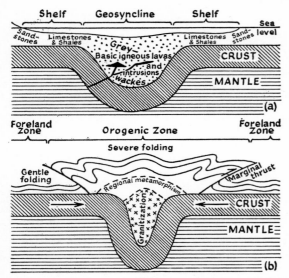

Fig. 12.3 Diagrams showing the development of a fold mountain system (b) from an initial geosyncline (a).

Ultimately as the subsidence continues the sediments in the lower levels of a geosyncline become melted and ultra-metamorphosed to granitic rocks, which form intrusions of batholithic size, (page 32) frequently occupying the cores of fold mountain systems. At higher levels the sediments may be regionally metamorphosed (pages 48–9, Fig. 6.5).

In a later stage the sediments are severely folded and faulted and may indeed be thrust over the little-affected marginal shelves or forelands (Fig. 12.3b) as were the Moine Series of N.W. Scotland (Fig. 12.5). This process of folding or *orogenesis* should not be visualized as a sudden happening occupying a relatively short length of time, but rather as an increasing number of earth-movements which together resulted in the formation of a major fold system. Subsequent to the folding the thick accumulations of geosynclinal sediments are finally uplifted to form the world's great mountain systems.

The close association between former geosynclines and the most intensely deformed parts of the Earth's crust, which form its mountainous areas, clearly points to their common origin. As to the primary mechanism there is a considerable degree of uncertainty and several theories have been proposed and successively rejected (De Sitter, 1964, pp. 485–502). At the present the most accepted theory concerns the formation of sub-crustal convection currents which are generated by temperature differences within the earth. Geosynclines may therefore form where opposing currents meet and descend, and as these increase in intensity so the area is compressed

with consequent folding of the sediments. At some later stage the currents decrease in intensity so that the area begins to rise.

BRITISH STRATIGRAPHY

Apart from the Carboniferous system described more fully in Chapter 15, it is considered unnecessary for the student to be acquainted with the detailed stratigraphy of the other systems. However, since these may be sometimes encountered either below the Carboniferous or forming cover rocks in the concealed coalfields, a brief review is given of their principal features. Should a more detailed treatment be required the student is referred to one of the more specialized textbooks (Craig, 1965; Neaverson, 1955; Stamp, 1957; Wells and Kirkaldy, 1966) or to the appropriate geological survey publications (see Appendix). Similar accounts, some of which are referred to in Chapter 13 and the Appendix exist for other countries.

PRE-CAMBRIAN ROCKS

The vast assemblage of rocks included in the Pre-Cambrian embrace over five-sixths of the Earth's history. Only rarely fossiliferous, the rocks are often highly metamorphosed and folded so that considerable difficulty is experienced in the determination of a local sequence, let alone one applicable to a region. Correlation and subdivision are similarly difficult, at present being largely restricted to lithological methods which are clearly unsatisfactory where wide facies variations are possible. The recent application of radiogeological methods of dating now enables absolute ages to be determined, and there is little doubt that in the near future the Pre-Cambrian will be divided into several distinct periods by the use of this method. Most certainly the Pre-Cambrian should not be regarded as a single period or even era when the subsequent ones are of such relatively short duration (Table 2).

Since the Pre-Cambrian rocks form the foundation upon which all succeeding systems were deposited they must necessarily be of world-wide distribution, either cropping out at the surface or occurring at depth. In Britain most of the outcrops occur in Scotland (Fig. 12.4) where four major divisions are recognized (Table 21). The Lewisian Complex includes some of the world's oldest known rocks, for parts exceed 2500 million years in age. Composed of a series of high grade schists and gneisses and intruded by doleritic dykes and larger granitic masses, the complex is situated largely to the west of the Moine Thrust. The complex is overlaid unconformably by the Torridonian (Fig. 12.5), an unmetamorphosed group of arkosic sandstones, conglomerates and shales with a predominantly red

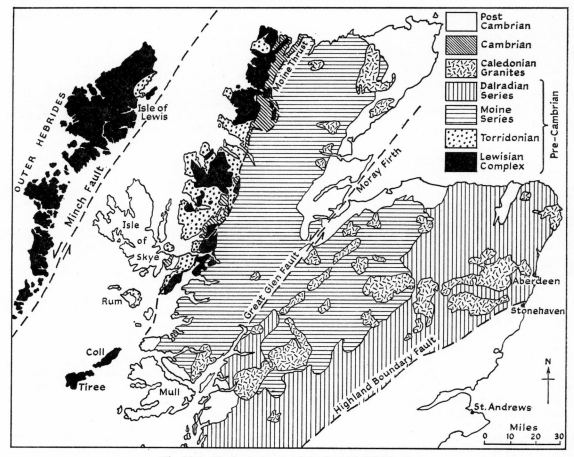

Fig. 12.4   Geological map of the Scottish Highlands.

TABLE 21

The Pre-Cambrian Rocks of Scotland
(The approximate minimum age of the divisions,
based on radiogeological dating, is given where known)

West of the Moine Thrust	*East of the Moine Thrust*
	DALRADIAN SERIES (+500 million years)
TORRIDONIAN	
	MOINE SERIES (+740 million years)
——Unconformity——	
LEWISIAN COMPLEX (+1600 million years)	

coloration. Between the Moine Thrust and Great Glen Fault the isoclinally folded Moine Series form most of this area. Initially deposited as sediments and subsequently metamorphosed during the Cale-

donian Orogeny (page 126), the series is composed of predominantly schistose rocks considerably affected by intrusions. The overlying Dalradian Series occur only to the south of the Great Glen Fault and are mostly of a sedimentary origin. They are composed of many metamorphic rock types including schists, slates, quartzites and marbles. Recumbent folding is common, and an early Caledonian age is ascribed to their metamorphism.

South of Scotland the Pre-Cambrian forms more discontinuous and smaller outcrops. In Wales the most extensive outcrops occur in Anglesey where the basal gneisses, comparable with the Lewisian Complex, are overlaid unconformably by a series of metamorphosed sedimentary and volcanic rocks. In the St David's area of S. Wales a series of Pre-Cambrian tuffs and intrusions form the core of a number of small anticlines. The major English outcrops are situated in Shropshire and Herefordshire where, be-

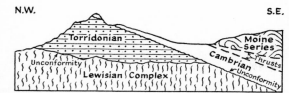

Fig. 12.5   Section across Cùl Mòr, north-west Scotland, illustrating the disposition of the Cambrian and Pre-Cambrian rocks.

ing harder and therefore more resistant to erosion than the surrounding strata, they form a picturesque group of hills. Gneisses form part of the Malvern Hills, whereas in Shropshire, the Wrekin and associated inliers are composed of the volcanic Uriconian Group. The most continuous outcrop is that of the Longmynd, composed of partly inverted arenaceous and argillaceous sediments. Lesser outcrops include those of the Lizard, Cornwall (schists and gneisses), Charnwood Forest, Leicestershire (pyroclastic material) and Ingleton, Yorkshire (greywackes and mudstones).

Economically the British Pre-Cambrian is of but minor importance. The more siliceous rocks may be locally quarried for roadstones and some of the schists and slates, notably in Argyll, are still worked for roofing materials. Various minerals have at some time been exploited though few are produced at present. It should be noted, however, that some of the world's most important ore deposits, as for example, those of the African copper belt, occur in the Pre-Cambrian.

Pre-Cambrian fossils

Fossils are extremely rare in the Pre-Cambrian (Glaessner, 1966, pp. 29–50) and many of those discovered are themselves of a problematic nature in that their zoological affinities are uncertain. Amongst the oldest traces of life on the Earth, the simple structures closely resembling primitive algae (related to the green 'scum' which forms on stagnant ponds) described from the Fig Tree Series of South Africa and over 3 000, and possibly over 3 500, million years old must take pride of place. The most fossiliferous Pre-Cambrian exposure is that in South Australia where over 1 400 specimens of jellyfish, soft corals and worms have been assiduously collected from late Pre-Cambrian rocks. In Britain, various fossils, including possible soft corals from an outcrop in Charnwood Forest and probable plant spores from the Torridonian, have been described.

It is considered that the relative scarcity of remains and traces of Pre-Cambrian life results largely from the soft-bodied nature of the animals and the consequent lack of hard parts capable of fossiliza-

tion. Moreover, the considerable degree of metamorphism which many of the rocks underwent would effectively destroy or render the discovery of any such fossils most difficult.

PALAEOZOIC ERA

The lower limit of the Palaeozoic Era is taken at the base of the Cambrian, since when present, the system is usually separated from the underlying Pre-Cambrian by a profound unconformity. Also the comparative abundance and development of many forms of Cambrian invertebrate life is in strong contrast to the extreme rarity and simplicity of fossils from the underlying rocks. The upper limit of the era, taken at the Permian-Triassic junction, is similarly placed by reason of the marked palaeontological break which occurs between the two systems. Triassic fossils have more affinities with those of the overlying systems than with Permian forms. This vast era, embracing six systems and occupying nearly 400 million years of geological time, is itself subdivided at the Silurian-Devonian junction (Fig. 12.6). At about that time the maximum phase of the Caledonian orogeny occurred so that the Upper Palaeozoic systems are often unconformable on those of the Lower Palaeozoic.

Cambrian system

Major localities. N. Wales (Harlech and Llanberis), S. Wales (St David's), Shropshire (Iron Bridge and Church Stretton), Warwickshire (Nuneaton), N.W. Highlands of Scotland (Fig. 12.4).

Series. Lower, Middle and Upper.

Lithologies. Basal conglomerates, sandstones, greywackes and slates. A middle horizon of flagstones and siltstones (*Lingulella* Flags). Upper Cambrian shales and mudstones (Tremadoc Beds). In Scotland the lower arenaceous beds are succeeded by a limestone sequence (Durness Limestone).

Palaeontology (With regard to the genera noted throughout this chapter as characteristic fossils of a particular horizon it should be realized that they are not always confined to it and may sometimes also occur at higher or lower levels). Exclusively marine faunas.

Brachiopods (marine invertebrates. The soft parts of the animal are enclosed by two shells or *valves* which are unequal in size and shape)—*Paterina* (L. Camb.), *Lingulella* (U. Camb.).

Graptolites (extinct marine invertebrates. Colonial animals which lived in cups or *thecae* arranged along branches. Of a net-like (dendroid graptolites) or miniature hacksaw-blade (true graptolites) appearance)—*Dictyonema* (U. Camb.).

Trilobites (extinct marine invertebrates. The hard parts, which were segmented, covered the back of the

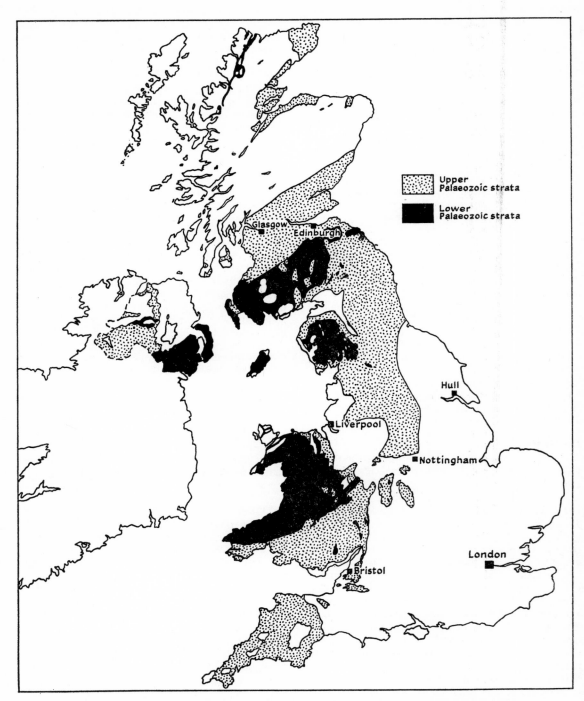

Fig. 12.6   Map showing the distribution of Lower and Upper Palaeozoic strata in Great Britain.

animal. Some resemblance to the modern wood-louse)—*Callavia* (L. Camb.), *Paradoxides* (Fig. 12.9a) (M. Camb), *Olenus*, *Angelina* (U. Camb.).

Conditions of deposition. Rudaceous and arenaceous basal beds developed as a littoral facies during a marine transgression across the Pre-Cambrian land surface: hence the basal unconformity. Geosynclinal deposition of over 12 000 ft of sediments in N. Wales. Essentially shelf deposition of about 4 000 ft of sediments in the Midlands (Fig. 12.7). The Cambrian depositional basin of N.W. Scotland was probably separated from that of England and Wales by a land mass, since the faunas of the two areas bear little resemblance to one another.

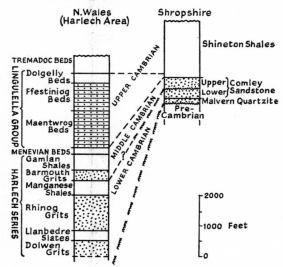

Fig. 12.7 Vertical sections illustrating the Cambrian successions in North Wales and Shropshire.

Economic geology. Over 2 000 ft of Lower Cambrian slates (Llanberis Slates) formerly extensively worked in N. Wales. Basal Stiperstones or Hartshill Quartzite (orthoquartzite) quarried in Shropshire and Warwickshire for roadstones. Dioritic intrusions in Midlands quarried for roadstones. Metallic mineral veins in North Wales formerly worked for non-ferrous metals including gold.

Ordovician system

Major localities. Scattered and extensive outcrops throughout Wales, Shropshire, Lake District, Isle of Man, Southern Uplands.

Series. Arenig, Llanvirn, Llandeilo, Caradoc and Ashgill. The last two, the highest of the system, are often grouped together as the Bala Series.

Lithologies. Vast effusions of lavas, principally of acid and intermediate types and accompanied by pyroclastic materials, occur together with marine sediments in all localities. The most intensive eruptions were those of the Lake District (Borrowdale Volcanic Series) where over 12000 ft of volcanic materials are largely of Llanvirn age. Marine sediments include a basal group of conglomerates and sandstones succeeded by shales and limestones.

Palaeontology. Exclusively marine faunas.

Brachiopods—'*Orthis*', *Sowerbyella* (Caradoc).

Graptolites—*Didymograptus* (Fig. 12.9b) (Arenig, Llanvirn), *Dicranograptus* (Caradoc), *Dicellograptus* (Ashgill).

Trilobites—*Asaphus*, *Ogygiocarella* (Llandeilo), '*Trinucleus*' (Fig. 12.9c) (Caradoc).

Conditions of deposition. Extensive pre-Arenig earth movements occurred so that the lowest Ordovician was deposited unconformably upon older rocks. Geosynclinal deposition in Wales (over 12 000 ft of non-volcanic sediments in Plynlimmon area alone), the Lake District and the Southern Uplands. Shelf deposition accompanied by a Caradoc marine transgression in Shropshire where Lower and Middle Ordovician are absent. East of here a probable land mass existed since no Ordovician rocks have been proved in the English Midlands. The volcanic eruptions, of both sub-aqueous and sub-aerial types, were accompanied by intrusions which were commonly doleritic in nature.

Economic geology. Extensive outcrops of slates are worked in the Lake District (Westmorland Green Slates) and North Wales (Maesgym Slates). Igneous rocks locally quarried for roadstones. Extensive vein mineralization in North Wales, Shropshire and the Lake District.

Silurian system

Major localities. Central Wales, Shropshire, Lake District, Southern Uplands.

Series. Llandovery, Wenlock and Ludlow.

Lithologies. Essentially a monotonous series of greywackes and mudstones forming a typical geosynclinal facies in Central Wales (16 000 ft), Lake District (13 000 ft) and Southern Uplands (8 000 ft). In Shropshire the shelf facies (6 000 ft) is composed of basal conglomerates and sandstone succeeded by shales and limestones (Fig. 12.8).

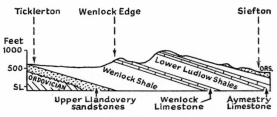

Fig. 12.8 Geological section across Wenlock Edge, Shropshire, showing the Silurian succession.

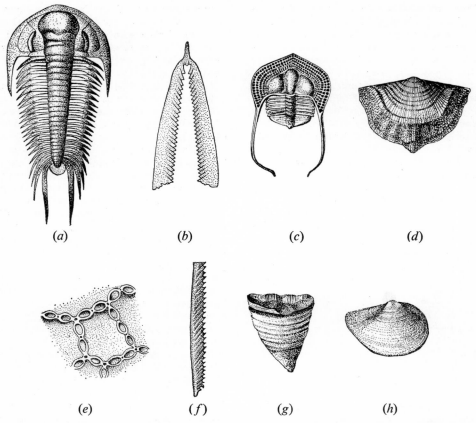

Fig. 12.9   Palaeozoic fossils: (*a*) *Paradoxides* (×¼), (*b*) *Didymograptus* (×1), (*c*) '*Trinucleus*' (×1), (*d*) *Leptaena* (×1), (*e*) *Halysites* (×2), (*f*) *Monograptus* (×2), (*g*) *Calceola* (×1), (*h*) *Schizodus* (×1).

Palaeontology. Exclusively marine faunas.

Brachiopods—*Pentamerus* (Llandov.), *Atrypa. Leptaena* (Fig. 12.9d) (Wen.), *Conchidium* (Lud.).

Corals (marine invertebrates. The soft parts of the animal, which may be either colonial or solitary, are enclosed in a cylindrical or conical external shell. Vertical internal divisions or *septae* appear in cross-section as the 'spokes' of a wheel)—*Favosites, Halysites* (Fig. 12.9e), *Heliolites* (Wen.).

Graptolites—various species of *Monograptus* (Fig. 12.9f).

Trilobites—*Phacops* (Llandov.), *Calymene, Dalmanites* (Wen.).

Conditions of deposition. Earth movements in early Silurian time, forming a temporary land mass in the Midlands, are evidenced in that area by the basal Upper Llandovery unconformity above which shallow-water shelf deposits occur. Geosynclinal deposition continued elsewhere. The two major facies are reflected in both the rock types and fossils. Grap-

tolites are the major fossils in the geosynclinal sediments whereas the thicker-shelled trilobites, brachiopods and corals occur in the limestones and shales of the Midlands. Vulcanicity, so dominant during the Ordovician, almost completely ceased towards the end of that period so that only small and isolated outbursts occurred during the Silurian.

Economic geology. Limestones, notably the Wenlock or Dudley Limestone of the Midlands, are quarried for cement manufacture, agricultural lime and metallurgical flux. Greywackes and sandstones are worked for road and building stones. Some vein mineralization in Wales and the Southern Uplands.

Caledonian orogeny

Lower Palaeozoic sedimentation was essentially of two types, geosynclinal and shelf. In the former conditions vast thicknesses of sediments, possibly totalling 40 000 ft in Wales, accumulated in rapidly subsiding troughs (Jones, 1955, pp. 424–39). Sedimentation and subsidence was comparatively slower and of a more intermittent nature over the adjacent shelves, as for instance in the English Midlands where up to about 10 000 ft of sediments occur. Throughout this time the progressive instability of the Earth's crust is indicated by the many earth-movements, evidenced by marine transgressions and unconformities, and the widespread Ordovician vulcanicity. Such movements were early phases of the Caledonian orogeny which attained maximum development in late Silurian and early Devonian time. During the orogeny the geosynclinal sediments were most intensely affected, so that a series of structures trending approximately NE–SW were formed. Of these the most notable are the complex recumbent folds and thrusts of the Scottish Highlands and the less complex folds of the Southern Uplands, the Lake District and Wales. During the main phase of the orogeny the structural developments were accompanied by the intrusion of the many granitic masses exposed at present in Scotland and the Lake District.

Devonian or Old Red Sandstone system

Major localities. S.W. England, S. Wales, Welsh Borders, Central and N.E. Scotland.

Series. Lower, Middle and Upper.

Lithologies: (1) Marine or Devonian facies—Sandstones, shales and limestones becoming predominantly arenaceous in N. Devon and Somerset. Extensive flows of basaltic lavas in Upper Devonian.

(2) Continental or Old Red Sandstone facies—a lower argillaceous group succeeded by thin concretionary limestones, shales, sandstones and conglomerates. In Scotland, the whole succession is essentially arenaceous with thick flagstone sequences and also andesitic lavas.

Palaeontology. Brachiopods—*Spirifer* (all horizons), many Silurian genera survive.

Corals—*Calceola* (Fig. 12.9g), *Heliolites*, *Thamnopora* (M. Dev.).

Goniatites (extinct marine invertebrates. The soft parts of the animal were enclosed in a planispiral shell which was internally divided by fluted partitions) —*Tornoceras* (L. Dev.), *Anarcestes* (M. Dev.), *Manticoceras* (U. Dev.).

Trilobites—*Phacops* (L. Dev.), *Proetus* (U. Dev.).

Fish—*Cephalaspis*, *Pteraspis* (L. O.R.S.), *Coccosteus* (M. O.R.S.), *Holoptychius* (U. O.R.S.).

Land plants—*Gosslingia* (L. O.R.S.), *Rhynia* (M. O.R.S.), *Cyclostigma* (U. O.R.S.).

Conditions of deposition. The Caledonian earth movements resulted in a southerly migration of the Palaeozoic shore line so that much of Britain north of the Bristol Channel was a semi-arid land mass. Consequently two major facies are recognized, a marine or Devonian facies in S.W. England and a continental or Old Red Sandstone facies over the rest of the country. The prevalent red coloration of the Old Red Sandstone is usually attributed to deposition in a warm, semi-arid environment. The arenaceous beds accumulated in intermontane lakes in the north, and upon a coastal plain in the south. During periods of drought the former evaporated causing the formation of thin limestones. Contemporary vulcanicity was prevalent in Scotland and Northumberland and was followed by an intrusive phase. Late Caledonian movements are indicated by the basal Lower Old Red Sandstone, and basal Upper Old Red Sandstone unconformities in most areas.

Economic geology. Various horizons are quarried for constructional materials, notably the Delabole Slates and Torquay Limestones of S.W. England, the Caithness Flagstones of N.E. Scotland and the many Caledonian granites such as at Aberdeen, Dalbeattie and Shap. In Scotland the sandstones are important sources of groundwater, the mineral content of which has influenced the location of the large brewing industry in the Edinburgh area.

Carboniferous system

Major localities. S.W. England, S. Wales, Central and Northern England, Central Scotland (Fig. 15.1).

Series. Dinantian ('Carboniferous Limestone'), Namurian ('Millstone Grits'), Westphalian ('Coal Measures') and Stephanian ('Barren Red Measures').

Lithologies. The Dinantian in England and Wales is chiefly composed of limestones and shales. In Scotland limestones are less abundant and sandstones, oil shales and considerable thicknesses of basaltic lavas comprise much of the succession. The Namurian principally consists of sandstone, shales and thin coal sequences. In Northern England limestones are also developed and in Scotland a more typical coal measure facies occurs. Excepting Southwestern England, where the upper Culm measures are composed of greywackes and shales, the Westphalian series is characterized by cyclothemic sequences of shales, sandstones, seat-earths and coals The Stephanian is essentially composed of reddish argillaceous beds and sandstones.

Palaeontology. Brachiopods—*Spirifer* (Fig. 15.8b), '*Productus*' (Fig. 14.2b) (Dinantian), *Lingula* (Fig. 14.2c).

Lamellibranchs (The soft parts of the animal are enclosed between two valves, each often a mirror-image of the other. By this feature they may readily be distinguished from brachiopods)—*Dunbarella* (Fig. 14.9b) (Namurian & Westphalian), *Carbonicola* (Fig. 14.12a), *Anthraconaia* (Fig. 14.12d.), *Naiadites* (Fig. 14.12g) (Westphalian).

Corals—'*Zaphrentis*' (Fig. 14.4b), *Caninia* (Fig.

14.4a), *Dibunophyllum* (Fig. 15.8c), *Lithostrotian* (Dinantian).

Goniatites—*Goniatites* (Fig. 15.8e) (Dinantian), *Homoceras* (Fig. 15.10), *Reticuloceras* (Fig. 15.10) (Namurian), *Gastrioceras* (Figs. 14.6b, 15.10) (Westphalian).

Land plants—*Lepidodendron* (Fig. 14.15a), *Sigillaria* (Fig. 14.15b), *Stigmaria* (Fig. 14.15c), *Calamites* (Fig. 14.16a), *Annularia* (Fig. 14.16b), *Alethopteris* (Fig. 14.17a), *Mariopteris* (Fig. 14.17d).

Conditions of deposition. During Dinantian time shallow-water marine sedimentation occurred around the landmass of St George's Land which extended across central England and Wales. Deltaic deposition is characteristic of the Namurian and Westphalian. Occasionally the sea transgressed across the deltaic swamps and deposited thin, but widespread, horizons of marine shale. Vulcanicity persisted throughout most of the Carboniferous in Scotland and there were lesser volcanic eruptions in central and south-western England.

Economic geology. Virtually the whole of the total annual British production of about 187 500 000 ton (1965) of bituminous coal and anthracite is deep-mined from Carboniferous seams. Of the various coalfields (Fig. 15.14) those of Yorkshire and the East Midlands are pre-eminent in having a total production reaching almost 50 per cent of the national total. With regard to the interseam rocks (Chapter 7) the shales and mudstones are major sources of brick clays whilst the fireclays and ganisters are extensively worked as sources of refractory materials. Numerous Dinantian limestones are quarried for agricultural lime and cement manufacture, concrete aggregate and roadstone. Hematite occurring in the limestones is at present mined in North Lancashire and Glamorgan.

Armorican or Hercynian orogeny

Although attaining a maximum intensity in late Carboniferous and early Permian times the Armorican or Hercynian orogeny had a gradual development at least throughout the former period. A number of movement phases are indicated by unconformities and marked lithological changes present within many Carboniferous sequences. The principle phases are as follows.

Nassauian phase. Contemporaneous earth movements are evidenced by unconformities within the Dinantian Series (Carboniferous Limestone) of S. Wales and adjacent areas.

Sudetic phase. A phase of faulting and folding in pre-Namurian time is reflected in the basal Namurian (Millstone Grit Series) unconformity in most areas.

Malvernian phase. Unconformities (Trueman, 1947, pp. lxxxiv–lxxxv) occur at or near to the base

of the Upper Westphalian (Upper Coal Measures) as, for example, at Ingleton below the Red Measures, at Coalbrookdale below the Coalport Beds (here the unconformity is the famous Symon 'Fault') and in S. Wales and the Forest of Dean at the base of the Pennant Measures (Fig. 12.10). At about this time the granite masses of Devon and Cornwall, the cupolas of a single elongated batholith, were intruded.

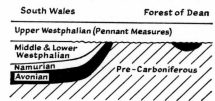

Fig. 12.10 Diagrammatic section illustrating the effects of the Malvernian phase of folding. (After A. Trueman.)

Saalic phase. The effects of the orogenic climax, in Britain during late Carboniferous and early Permian times, cannot always be distinguished from those of the preceding phases since Upper Westphalian rocks have a limited distribution. The maximum deformation occurred in Pembrokeshire (Fig. 12.11) and S.W. England, where the rocks are both overfolded and traversed by many large thrusts. Thus at Haverfordwest the Pre-Cambrian is thrust over the Carboniferous whilst in Devon and Cornwall granitic intrusions were also emplaced. Outside this main orogenic zone the structures become less complex. Clearly the easterly and south-easterly trending synclines containing the S. Wales (page 72), Somerset and E. Kent (page 91) coalfields are foreland structures produced by the northerly drive of the great Armorican fold systems of the Continent. Elsewhere the trend of the Armorican folds is more northerly as in the Warwickshire and N. Staffordshire (page 73) coalfield synclines and the Pennine anticline (pages 71–2). Renewed uplift along Caledonian and possibly earlier basement structures is suggested by the north-easterly trending folds of the Northumberland, Durham and East Midlands coalfields.

The commonest Armorican structures encountered by the mining engineer are the many faults affecting the coalfields, for within the colliery take the fold structures are seldom traversed. Principally the faulting is normal in character so that outside the S. Wales and associated coalfields, that is away from the main compression zone, reverse faults, such as that at Thringstone in Leicestershire (page 81), are relatively uncommon. Wrench faults probably of Armorican age include the Neath and Tawe valley disturbances of S. Wales (page 84).

It is not proved that the many faults affecting the

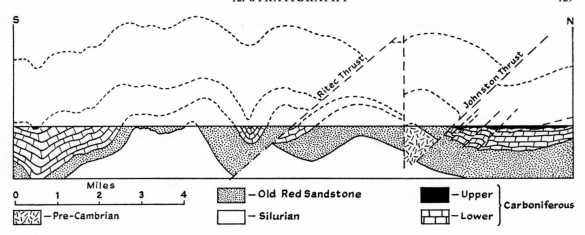

Fig. 12.11   Diagrammatic section across Pembrokeshire showing the Armorican structures. (After O. T. Jones.)

coalfields are entirely of Armorican age for later movement undoubtably occurred along those faults, which, in the concealed coalfields, extend into the cover rocks (page 75). Although such later movement phases can of course only be proved where the post-Carboniferous cover is preserved, it is probable that many coalfield faults moved during several orogenic periods and indeed some were initiated during the Alpine orogeny. In the concealed coalfields the apparent infrequency of faults in the cover may merely reflect the difficulties of proving the structures in the usually poor surface exposures.

From the disposition of the existing coalfields it is apparent that many owe their preservation to Armorican structures. The synclinal nature of most coalfields is clearly not coincidental. Orogenic effects of a deleterious nature were the considerable uplifts along anticlinal folds which resulted in the erosion of the Westphalian (Coal Measures) from these areas. Thus the Westphalian of Lancashire and Yorkshire was originally continuous until Armorican uplift along the Pennine anticline resulted in the separation of the two coalfields.

Permian system

Major localities. Ayrshire (Mauchline Basin), Dumfriesshire, Cumberland and Westmorland (Vale of Eden), Durham, Yorkshire, Nottinghamshire, S. Lancashire, E. Devon.

Series. Local subdivisions.

Lithologies. In E. England (Fig. 12.12) a basal group of aeolian sandstones and shales of variable thickness. The succeeding Magnesian Limestone is a locally fossiliferous and concretionary dolostone, attaining a maximum thickness of over 800 ft in Durham, and thinning progressively south until beyond

Nottingham the formation is absent. This is overlaid by argillaceous deposits with evaporites (page 39, Fig. 5.5).

The remaining Permian outcrops are largely composed of coarse red millet-seed sandstones of variable thickness (e.g. the Collyhurst Sandstone of S. Lancashire varies from zero to 2345 ft) and succeeded by red shales and evaporites (Fig. 12.12). In Ayrshire a lower group of basalt lavas occurs.

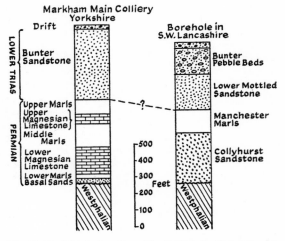

Fig. 12.12   Vertical sections illustrating the Permian and lower Triassic successions in the Yorkshire and Lancashire coalfields.

Palaeontology. The only notable fossiliferous beds are the Marl Slate (numerous fish remains) and the Magnesian Limestone (brachiopods—*'Productus'*, *Pterospirifer*, lamellibranchs—*Bakevillia*, *Mytilus*, *Schizodus*—Fig. 12.9h).

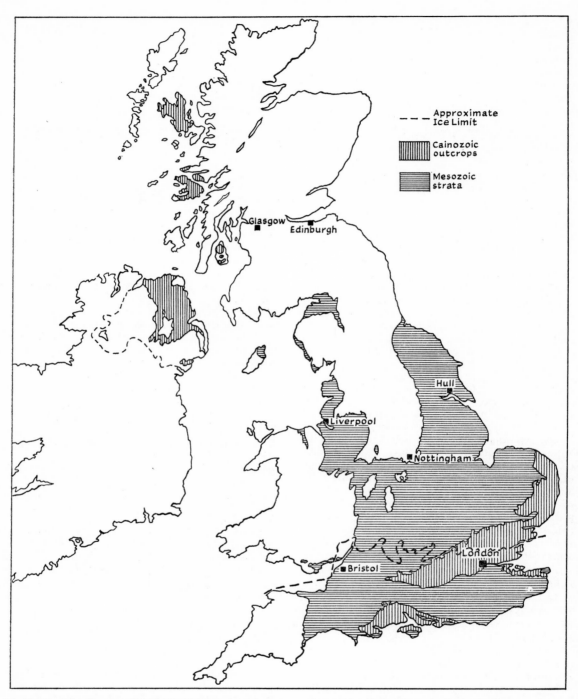

Fig. 12.13   Map showing the distribution of Mesozoic and Cainozoic strata in Great Britain together with the maximum extent of the Pleistocene ice sheets.

Conditions of deposition. Following the Armorican orogeny much of Britain was an arid or semi-arid land mass over which shifting and cross-stratified dune sands were deposited unconformably across eroded outcrops of Carboniferous strata. In N.E. England the Zechstein Sea extended at first up to the Pennines and occasionally around them into Cumberland and Lancashire. Its increasing salinity is suggested by the formation of dolostones succeeded by evaporites. Considerable vulcanicity occurred in Scotland and Devonshire.

Economic geology. Deposits of gypsum and anhydrite are worked in N.E. England (Billingham) and Westmorland (Kirkby Thore). Important beds of potash-salts have been located at depth in N.E. Yorkshire (Fig. 5.5). Sandstones, especially that at Mauchline, are quarried for building stone. The Magnesian Limestone is similarly worked and is also used in the metallurgical industry.

MESOZOIC ERA

Where the systems are fossiliferous considerable differences exist between the faunas and floras of the Permian and Triassic. At about this time a major break in the history of life occurs, for many of the Palaeozoic groups become either less important or extinct (Table 19). Consequently the Triassic is regarded as the oldest period of the Mesozoic era (Fig. 12.13). In this respect the evidence is outside Britain since, in this country, fossils are extremely rare in Upper Permian and Triassic rocks.

Triassic system

Major localities. Cheshire, Lancashire, Yorkshire, Nottinghamshire, Midland Counties, Somerset.

Series. On the Continent three series are recognized. In Britain only two, the Bunter succeeded by the Keuper, can be identified. The junction between the Permian and Triassic systems is uncertain in Britain owing to the largely unfossiliferous nature of the rocks. Consequently some authorities favour their amalgamation as either the New Red Sandstone or Permo-Triassic system.

Lithologies. The red coloration of all but the highest beds characterizes the system. A lower group of conglomerates (Bunter Pebble Beds) and sandstones up to 3 000 ft thick are succeeded by the Keuper Marls, of similar thickness and containing important evaporite horizons totalling almost 2 000 ft of saliferous beds in Cheshire.

Palaeontology. Fossils are rare, so that in Britain the system is subdivided on lithological grounds. The occasional fossils found include plant, fish and reptile remains, the latter including, at several localities, well preserved footprints.

Conditions of deposition. During the Lower Bunter the continental conditions of the Upper Permian prevailed, although the less arid nature of the climate is indicated by the sheet-flood deposits of the pebble beds which were probably the effects of torrential rainstorms. The Keuper Marls most probably represent fine wind-blown dust trapped in saline lakes or marine embayments in which the evaporites were precipitated.

Economic geology. Deposits of gypsum and anhydrite largely mined in Nottinghamshire (Gotham, Newark), Derbyshire (Chellaston) and Staffordshire (Fauld). Extensive exploitation of rock salt deposits in Cheshire mainly by brine-pumping. The Keuper Marls provide one of the major sources of brickclay. Underground water is chiefly derived from the Bunter sandstones which have exceptionally high yields; it has for instance been calculated that over 50 million gallons a day are drawn by public bodies alone from these sandstones in Lancashire and Cheshire.

Jurassic system

Major localities. A continuous arc extending through England from N.E. Yorkshire to Dorset. Outliers include those in S. Wales, the Inner Hebrides and Sutherland.

Series. Lower, Middle and Upper.

Lithologies. A lower series often over 1 000 ft thick of alternating argillaceous limestones and shales which locally contain two important ironstone beds (the Frodingham and Cleveland Ironstones). Succeeded in southern England by the Inferior and Great Oolites, composed of oolitic limestones, calcareous sandstones and ironstones (the Northampton Sand Ironstone). In northern England and Scotland a group of sandstones, argillaceous beds and occasional coal seams. The Upper Jurassic contains sandstones, limestones and two thick argillaceous horizons, the Oxford and Kimmeridge Clays, each over 600 ft thick where fully developed.

Palaeontology. Ammonites (exclusively marine invertebrates, all now extinct. They possess many similarities to the goniatites from which they may be distinguished by the highly frilled nature of their internal partitions)—*Amaltheus, Phylloceras* (Fig. 12.14a) (L. Jur.), *Parkinsonia* (M. Jur.), *Kosmoceras* (U. Jur.).

Brachiopods—*Spiriferina* (L. Jur.), *Ornithella, Rhynchonella* (Fig. 12.14b) (M. Jur.).

Corals—*Isastraea, 'Thamnastrea', Thecosmilia* (U. Jur.).

Echinoids (exclusively marine invertebrates. External skeletons composed of many perforated calcite plates forming globular, discoidal or heart-shaped bodies. Modern 'sea-urchins')—*Clypeus* (M. Jur.), *Hemicidaris* (Fig. 12.14c) (U. Jur.).

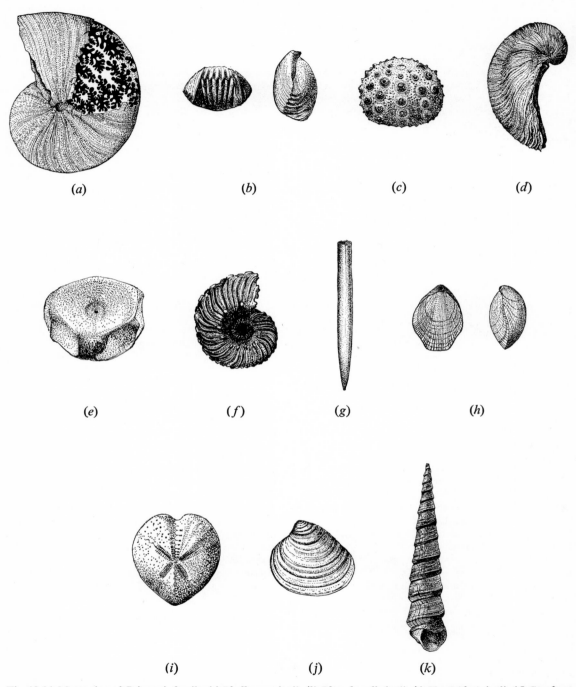

Fig. 12.14 Mesozoic and Cainozoic fossils: (a) *Phylloceras* ($\times \frac{1}{4}$), (b) *Rhynchonella* ($\times 1$), (c) *Hemicidaris* ($\times \frac{1}{2}$), (d) *Gryphaea* ($\times \frac{1}{2}$), (e) Reptile vertebra ($\times \frac{1}{2}$), (f) *Hoplites* ($\times \frac{1}{2}$), (g) *Belemnitella* ($\times \frac{1}{2}$), (h) *Terebratula* ($\times \frac{1}{2}$), (i) *Micraster* ($\times \frac{1}{2}$), (j) *Astarte* ($\times 1$), (k) *Turritella* ($\times 1$).

Lamellibranchs—*Gryphaea* (Fig. 12.14d.), *Ostrea* (L. Jur.), *Trigonia* (M. Jur.).

Reptiles (Fig. 12.14e)—*Ichthyosaurus, Plesiosaurus.*

Conditions of deposition. The basal Jurassic was deposited during a marine transgression probably affecting all but the highland areas of Scotland and Wales. Shallow-water sediments characterize the system. Deltaic deposition is indicated in the ill-named Estuarine Beds of Middle and Upper Jurassic age chiefly in northern England and Scotland. Contemporaneous earth-movements along pre-Jurassic fold axes resulted in both thinner sequences and unconformities in some areas.

Economic geology. Sedimentary ironstones, accounting for the bulk of British iron-ore production, are worked largely by open-cast methods in Yorkshire, Northamptonshire, Lincolnshire and Leicestershire (page 40). About one-third of the bricks manufactured in Britain are from the Oxford Clay chiefly in the Bedford and Peterborough areas. Most other argillaceous horizons are locally worked for brick manufacture. The Jurassic limestones form valuable building and ornamental stones such as those of Ancaster, Bath, Cheltenham and Rutland. South of Bath, a non-plastic clay, the Fuller's Earth, is mined for use in the woollen, foundry, pharmaceutical and petroleum industries. At Brora, on the Sutherland coast, the Upper Jurassic Brora Main Seam, a pyritic bituminous coal about 3 ft 6 in thick, is mined for local use (Fig. 12.15), (Read, *et al.* 1925, pp. 74–8. At Kimmeridge Bay, Dorset, a small

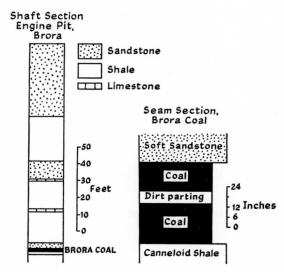

Fig. 12.15 Sections in the Brora coalfield. (Highland Colliery Ltd.)

oilfield is situated in the Oolitic Limestone along the Purbeck anticline (Brunstrom, 1963, pp. 18–20).

Cretaceous system

Major localities. A broad outcrop, to the east of that of the Jurassic, extending from N.E. Yorkshire to Dorset and with a western extension in southern England.

Series. Lower and Upper.

Lithologies. In southern England the Lower Cretaceous is composed of unconsolidated sands and clays, the latter containing clay ironstones and limestones, succeeded by glauconite sandstones (the Lower and Upper Greensand) which pass laterally into the Gault Clay. In northern England, a lower group of clays, limestones, sandstones and ironstones. The Upper Cretaceous is formed by the Chalk, a fine-grained white limestone (page 39) which, apart from the occurrence of flints as scattered nodules and in more distinct layers, is a remarkably uniform rock. It attains a maximum thickness of over 1 600 ft in the Hampshire Basin.

Palaeontology. Ammonites—*Hamites, Hoplites* (Fig. 12.14f), (L. Cret.), *Baculites, Scaphites, Schloenbachia* (U. Cret.).

Belemnites (exclusively marine. The internal skeletons of ancient cuttle-fish. The solid *guard*, most commonly found, is usually cylindrical or conical with a smooth external surface)—*Hibolites* (L. Cret.), *Belemnitella* (Fig. 12.14g), (U. Cret.).

Brachiopods—*Crania, Terebratula* (Fig. 12.14h).

Echinoids—*Cardiaster, Holaster* (L. Cret.), *Echinocorys, Marsupites, Micraster* (Fig. 12.14i), (U. Cret.).

Lamellibranchs—*Nucula, Unio, Pecten* (L. Cret.), *Inoceramus* (U. Cret.).

Conditions of deposition. A late Jurassic phase of uplift resulted in a temporary regression of the Mesozoic sea so that the basal Cretaceous is usually unconformable. In southern England the lowest Cretaceous rocks are of deltaic facies whilst those in Northern England are marine deposits. At that time the two areas were separated by a land mass. By Upper Cretaceous time this was submerged so that the Chalk is entirely a shallow-water marine deposit.

Economic geology. The various Lower Cretaceous clays are all locally used for brick manufacture in southern England. A few hard horizons of the Chalk, for example the Totternhoe Stone of Lincolnshire, are used for building stone, though the formation is mainly quarried for cement manufacture and agricultural lime. It is an important aquifer in most areas (page 102). Lower Cretaceous ironstones were formerly extensively worked in the Weald, and the Claxby Ironstone is at present mined in Lincolnshire. It is noteworthy that the oldest British mines are those of Norfolk and Sussex where Neolithic man, in about the second millenium B.C., worked the Upper Cretaceous flints from a complex series of shafts and galleries.

CAINOZOIC ERA

A marked change is at once apparent between the lithologies and fossils of the Mesozoic systems and those comprising the Cainozoic Era. The Cainozoic rocks are, in Britain, often unconsolidated or only partially consolidated deposits of gravels, sands and clays. Many of the fossil groups characteristic of the Mesozoic are absent. The ammonites for instance, so common in the Jurassic and Cretaceous systems, are not found in the succeeding systems. Moreover, it was in the Cainozoic that the mammals became common and replaced the reptiles as the dominant forms of life. Similar changes are also apparent in the floras of the two eras, so that the Cainozoic trees and other plants most clearly resemble our modern vegetation. Most certainly the era is that of 'recent life'.

As yet there is no settled opinion as to the sub-division of the era. Some authorities recognize about six distinct systems even though the whole of the era embraces only the last 70 million years of geological history. In this account only the Tertiary and Pleistocene are considered as separate systems.

Tertiary system

Major localities. East Anglia, the Hampshire and London Basins, and parts of the Inner Hebrides.

Series. Eocene, Oligocene, Miocene, Pliocene (sometimes considered as separate systems).

Lithologies. In southern England essentially sands, gravels, marls, clays and lignites. On the Inner Hebrides and parts of the adjacent mainland over 6 000 ft of basalt lavas together with associated intrusive rocks of granitic and gabbroic types.

Palaeontology. Lamellibranchs—*Corbicula*, (Eoc.), *Corbula*, *Erodona* (Olig.), *Astarte*, (Fig. 12.14j) (Plioc.).

Gasteropods (univalve shells consisting of a long tube, open at one end and usually coiled into a screw-like spiral—modern snails)—*Fusus*, *Naticina* (Eoc.), *Batillaria*, *Vivaparus* (Olig.), *Trochus*, *Turritella* (Fig. 12.14k) (Plioc.).

Echinoids—*Schizaster* (Eoc.), *Clypeaster* (Olig.), *Spatangus* (Plioc.).

Conditions of deposition. In late Mesozoic time folding and erosion occurred so that the basal Tertiary sediments are unconformable upon older strata. The period was one in which a series of marine transgressions and recessions took place so that marine, lagoonal and continental sediments form a complex interdigitation of beds. Considerable vulcanicity accompanied by an intrusive phase occurred in north-western Britain. Miocene sediments are unknown in Britain due to the effects of the Alpine orogeny (see below).

Economic geology. Over 400000 ton per annum of highly plastic clays, used in the ceramic industry (ball-clays), are both mined and quarried in Devon and Dorset (Bloore & Booth, 1961, pp. 884–96, Scott, 1929). A relatively small percentage of bricks are manufactured from Eocene clays, notably the London Clay and Reading Beds. Other products include Eocene moulding sands, and building and roadstones from the Scottish igneous rocks.

Alpine orogeny

Throughout the Cainozoic era orogenic movements occurred in most parts of the world. The high mountain ranges of the Alps, Himalayas, Rockies and Andes were formed during this orogenic period, which indeed cannot be considered as having ended yet. In Britain the maximum phase is of Miocene age and the effects are most obvious in southern England where the deformation and dislocation of lower Cainozoic sediments may be proved. Since the area was on the edge of the main Alpine orogenic zone which lay to the south, the structures developed are less complex than those of the great fold mountains. Nevertheless the easterly trending folds of the southern counties may be locally overturned and sometimes overthrust as along the Dorset coast near Lulworth. It is not considered that the orogenic effects were confined solely to the southern counties, for renewed movement along many Armorican faults and fold axes must have occurred throughout Britain. Furthermore, structures including for example, the Cheshire basin and Cleveland uplift of N. England, and involving Jurassic as well as Triassic and Permian strata, are largely of Tertiary age.

Pleistocene system

Embracing the last million years of geological history, the Pleistocene period, considered by many as extending to the present day, is the meeting point of geological, archeological and historical studies. The system is characterized by the superficial deposits discussed on pages 103–7 and the remains of man himself or his tools and weapons are amongst the criteria utilized in its sub-division. For part of the period large areas of the world (Fig. 10.7), including much of Britain (Fig. 12.13), was covered by the ice sheets and glaciers of the 'Great Ice Age'. That this was not one single event, but composed of several glacial phases separated by lengthy periods of time, is indicated by the interdigitation of glacial and inter-glacial deposits. Since the latest regression of the continental ice sheets the recent superficial deposits including the blown sands, alluvial and peat deposits have been, and are still being, formed.

REFERENCES

BLOORE, W. J. & C. L. BOOTH (1961) Potters' or ball-clay mining in south Devon, *Trans. Instn Min. Engrs* **120**, 884–96.

BRUNSTROM, R. G. W. (1963) Recently discovered oil-fields in Britain, *Proc. Sixth World Petrol. Cong.* Section 1, Paper **49**.

CRAIG, G. Y. (editor) (1965) *The Geology of Scotland*, 1st ed., Edinburgh, Oliver & Boyd.

DE SITTER, L. U. (1964) *Structural Geology*, 2nd ed., London, McGraw-Hill.

DUNBAR, C. O. & J. RODGERS (1957) *Principles of Stratigraphy*, 1st ed., New York, Wiley.

GLAESSNER, M. F. (1966) Precambrian palaeontology, *Earth-Sci. Rev.*, **1**, 29–50.

HAWKES, L. (1957) Some aspects of the progress of geology in the last fifty years, *Q. Jl geol. Soc. Lond.* **113**, 309–21.

JONES, O. T. (1955) The geological evolution of Wales and the adjacent regions, *Q. Jl geol. Soc. Lond.* **111**, 323–50.

NEAVERSON, E. (1955) *Stratigraphical Palaeontology*, 2nd ed., Oxford, Clarendon Press.

READ, H. H., G. ROSS, J. PHEMASTER & C. W. LEE (1925) Geology of the Country around Golspie, Sutherland, *Mem. geol. Surv. Scotld.*

SCOTT, A. (1929) Special Reports of the mineral resources of Great Britain, **31**, Ball Clays. *Mem. Geol. Surv.*

STAMP, L. D. (1957) *An Introduction to Stratigraphy*, 3rd ed., London, Allen and Unwin (Murby).

STØRMER, L. (1966) Concepts of stratigraphical classification and terminology, *Earth-Sci. Rev.* **1**, 5–28.

TRUEMAN, A. (1947) Stratigraphical problems in the coal-fields of Great Britain, *Q. Jl geol. Soc. Lond.* **103**, lxv–civ.

WELLS, A. K. & J. F. KIRKALDY (1966) *Outline of Historical Geology*, 5th ed., Allen & Unwin (Murby).

13

SOME MAJOR COALFIELDS

It is the author's experience that many students are entirely unfamiliar with the geological features, output and often even the location of foreign coalfields. Accordingly, the brief outlines are given of a few selected coalfields in non-European but English-speaking countries. In a review of this type it is obviously impossible to include sufficient detail for the local student. However, all the coalfields are described in the memoirs of the relevant national geological surveys, to which references are given in the text.

AUSTRALIA

Widespread *Pre-Cambrian* outcrops occur in Western and South Australia and in the Northern Territory (David, 1950) where the major occurrences are separated only by a thin cover of younger strata. The oldest parts of the sequence are formed by schists, gneisses and granitic rocks overlain by sandstones, greywackes, shales and limestones. A major orogenic phase resulted in extensive folding and metamorphism before the deposition of the Adelaide System forming the upper part of the Pre-Cambrian. This is represented by little folded and only feebly metamorphosed sandstones, shales and dolostones together with tillites, indicative of a severe glaciation, in the highest beds.

During most of the *Palaeozoic Era*, geosynclinal sedimentation affected eastern Australia. The remainder of the continent was a relatively stable area over which a basinal facies of limestones, shales and sandstones was deposited along a number of marine embayments or 'seaways' between the Pre-Cambrian land masses. In the geosyncline sedimentation was essentially of the greywacke-type punctuated intermittently by effusions of rhyolitic lavas and interrupted by orogenic phases. During the Devonian the geosynclinal sediments were intensely folded and intruded by granitic rocks after which time basinal sandstones and shales were deposited. In the early Permian a severe glaciation, as evidenced by tillites and fluvioglacial deposits, affected the continent. Marine sedimentation was confined to the present eastern seaboard and over most low-lying areas of Australia terrestial sediments accumulated.

Along the margins of the Permian sea fluviatile sedimentation accompanied the formation of Australia's principal bituminous coal deposits.

In contrast to the Palaeozoic the *Mesozoic Era* was for the most part a time of fresh-water accumulation. A series of depressions in Queensland, New South Wales, Victoria and Western Australia were infilled with fluviatile sandstones, lacustrine shales and occasional coals together with some marine shales and limestones deposited during periodic marine transgressions. Tertiary sedimentation followed a similar pattern in that a series of clays, sandstones and gravels accompanied by lignites accumulated for the most part in fresh-water swampy conditions. In the lower Tertiary of eastern Australia a considerable thickness of lavas—the Older Basalts—were erupted. Some marine sedimentation took place in western Australia.

THE SYDNEY COAL BASIN

The most important Australian coal deposits are those of Permian age occurring in the State of New South Wales. Excepting the Sydney coalfield, situated in the centre, all the coalfields are located on the north-eastern and south-western flanks of the Sydney Basin (Fig. 13.1) sometimes designated the Main Coal Province (David, 1950, pp. 425–54). Altogether the coal measures occupy about 16000 square miles (Fig. 13.2).

Succession

The Permian system is composed of two marine and two coal measure sedimentary units. The basal *Lower Marine Series* is completely developed only in the lower Hunter valley upon the north flank of the Sydney basin. The series has a maximum thickness of about 6000 ft and consists of a basal group of shales, tuffs and lavas, succeeded by conglomerates and in turn overlaid by limestones, shales and mudstones.

The succeeding *Lower* or *Greta Coal Measures* crop out along the northern flank of the Sydney basin west of Newcastle where they are exposed in a

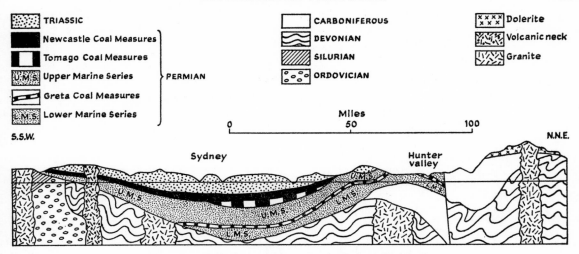

Fig. 13.1   Geological section across the Sydney Coal Basin.

series of folds of which the largest is formed by the Lochinvar dome. In the south they crop out only in the Clyde River district since they are much overstepped by the Upper Marine Series. The series, predominantly composed of conglomerates, sandstones and shales, is usually about 300 ft thick. Two important seams occur, the Top or Main Greta seam from 6 ft to 34 ft thick and the Lower or Homeville seam with a maximum thickness of 22 ft.

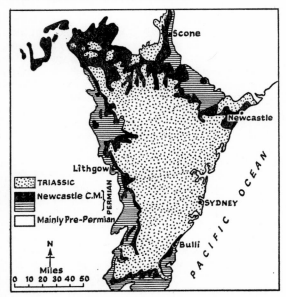

Fig. 13.2   Geological sketch map of the Sydney Coal Basin.

The *Upper Marine Series* in the lower Hunter valley consists of up to 6 000 ft of conglomerates, occasional tillites, sandstones and shales. The series thins southwards so that along the southern margin of the Sydney basin about 3 500 ft of shales, mudstones and lavas occur.

In the Hunter valley the *Upper Coal Measures* are composed of two stages, the Tomago stage confined to that valley and the overlying Newcastle Coal Measures. Elsewhere the latter either directly succeed the Upper Marine Series or, in the north-west, are unconformable upon older strata. The Tomago Stage is composed of up to 3 000 ft of mudstones, shales, sandstones and coals. Several of the coal-seams are over 4 ft. The Upper or Newcastle Coal Measures occur over almost the whole of the Sydney basin although in the central parts they lie at considerable depths and are concealed by the Mesozoic cover. Consequently, with the exception of the concealed Sydney coalfield, the principal coalfields are confined to the margins of the basin. At Newcastle fourteen seams occur in about 1 500 ft of strata (Fig. 13.3) within which a slight unconformity is developed below the Redhead conglomerate. Rapid lithological variations are a feature of this area in which the Borehole seam, about 10 ft thick, and the overlying Burwood or Victoria Tunnel seam of similar thickness are the most important seams. In the southern fields the Newcastle Coal Measures (Fig. 13.3) contain at least seven seams although only the three highest are generally worked. Of these the Bulli seam with an average thickness of about 6 ft is the most extensively worked.

Some evidence of a non-sequence occurs at the

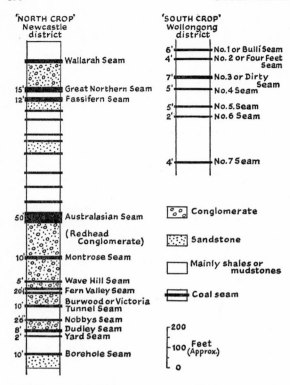

Fig. 13.3 Generalized vertical sections illustrating the productive sequence of the Newcastle Coal Measures. (After T. W. E. David.)

base of the *Triassic* cover rocks which occur in the central parts of the coal basin. A three-fold division of the system into the Wianamatta, Hawkesbury and basal Narrabeen Series, may be established on lithological grounds. The system is composed of conglomerates, sandstones and shales of fresh-water facies.

Structure

The dominant structure is the great Sydney coal basin (Fig. 13.1) trending north-north-west and truncated on the eastern margin by the sea. Superimposed on this basinal structure there are in the north a number of folds along which the principal coalfields are situated. Thus the Newcastle coalfield is contained within a southerly plunging syncline and again some other coalfields are situated on the crestal parts of anticlines where the coal measures are brought within economic depths of working. The most pronounced folding is found in the Hunter valley region. In contrast, along the southern flanks of the Sydney basin the structure is simple with gentle dips towards the centre of the basin. Both

normal and reverse faulting occurs although the latter type is apparently only developed in the northern coalfields.

A series of dolerite dykes and sills have invaded and altered the coals in places. In a few cases collieries are only concerned with mining cinder coal.

Rank and production of coals

The coals are of predominantly of high to low volatile bituminous rank. The greater part of coal production is won from the Newcastle Coal Measures. A distinct increase in coal rank occurs towards the centre and deeper parts of the coal basin. The highest rank coals are won from the concealed Sydney coalfield. As might be expected from such a wide rank variation a similarly wide range of uses is made of the coals. About 5 000 000 ton of New South Wales coal is at present exported yearly to Japan.

The bulk of Australia's bituminous coal production is derived from the Sydney basin (Australian bituminous coal production—1961—24 283 000 ton).

THE LATROBE VALLEY COALFIELD

The Latrobe Valley of Victoria contains the largest single deposit of lignite in the world. From Yallourn, situated about 80 miles east–south-east of Melbourne, the field is almost continuous in an easterly direction for about 40 miles and for much of this distance is between 5 to 10 miles wide (David, 1950, pp. 463–5; Nelson, 1963, pp. 502–8).

Succession

Resting unconformably upon a faulted sequence of mainly Jurassic strata the basal Tertiary sediments consist of about 100 ft of clays, sands, gravels and occasional lignites. They are overlain by two layers of olivine basalt separated by gravels and with a composite thickness locally reaching 500 ft.

The succeeding lignite deposits are considered to be of late Eocene—early Miocene age. There are, in the main part of the field at least three seams known respectively as the Yallourn, Morwell No. 1 and Morwell No. 2. North of Yallourn the latter two seams combine to form the Latrobe. In the Loy Yang field an additional seam, the Traralgon lies beneath the Morwell No. 2. Only very small thicknesses of strata separate the various lignite horizons which together total almost 1 000 ft of coal.

Over much of the coalfield the seams are covered by only a shallow overburden of clays, sands and gravels which average about 50 ft in the most favourable areas for lignite exploitation. Nevertheless the only surface indication of the occurrence of lignite is near Yallourn where the deposits are exposed by the Yallourn river.

Structure

The north and south margins of the coalfield appear to be bounded by early-Tertiary faults (Fig. 13.4). These resulted in the formation of the sedimentary basin in which the seams accumulated. At a later stage the lignites were themselves gently warped with a resultant slight regional dip to the north.

Rank and production of coals

All horizons may be classed as brown lignites. An analysis of the Yallourn seam is quoted in Table 45. A noticeable feature of the succession is the progressive decrease of total moisture with depth. Thus the total moisture content of the Yallourn seam is about 65–68 per cent whereas that of the Latrobe seam is about 49–53 per cent. By the application of special combustion techniques the raw lignite is effectively used for steam raising in power stations situated upon the coalfield. At present about 75 per cent of Victoria's electricity is generated from the utilization of the Latrobe deposits and by 1970 it is expected to generate 90 per cent from this source. Some lignite is briquetted for electricity generation in power stations situated some distance from the coalfield and is also used for domestic heating and the manufacture of gas.

After an unsuccessful attempt to exploit the Latrobe deposits between 1889 and 1899 the major development of the coalfield commenced in 1920. Present production is derived from two sites at Yallourn and the adjacent township of Morwell which owing to the highly favourable ratio of coal to overburden are exceptionally well suited to the opencast methods used (Plate 14). At Yallourn (*aborig:* Yalleen—brown, Lourn—fuel) only the seam of that name is worked and production in 1962 was about 13 000 000 ton. The Morwell No. 1 seam is extracted at Morwell with a production in 1962 of over 3 000 000 ton (Australian lignite production—1962— 17 080 000 ton). Total annual lignite production in the Latrobe valley is expected to exceed 25 000 000 ton by 1971.

INDIA

Over half of Peninsular India, which is that part of the sub-continent lying to the south of the Indo-Gangetic plains, is composed of *Pre-Cambrian* rocks (Krishnan, 1956; Wadia, 1953). A basal group of gneisses and schists is apparently succeeded by the Charnockite Series formed by coarse-grained, sometimes granitic rocks, probably of igneous origin, which have been highly metamorphosed. The Dharwar System, found to be over 2 200 million years old by radiogeological measurements, appears to succeed the Charnockite Series and is largely composed of schists, slates, quartzites, marbles and conglomerates. Their sedimentary origin is evidenced by the occurrence of relic structures including cross-stratification in some of the quartzites. Occurring in narrow, elongated troughs amongst the basal gneisses, the Dharwars contain important iron and manganese ore bodies in Bihar and Orissa. They are succeeded unconformably by the Cuddapah System composed of quartzites, shales, slates, conglomerates, limestones, lavas and tuffs. Unlike the older rocks those of the Cuddapah System have been subjected to only slight subsequent deformation. The overlying Vindhyan System, possibly containing some lower Cambrian sediments, has a maximum thickness of over 14 000 ft. A lower group of marine shales and limestones is succeeded by fluviatile or estuarine cross-stratified, fine-grained sandstones.

Throughout most of the Palaeozoic Era India formed part of Gondwanaland, a southern land mass which also included Australia, South Africa and South America. Consequently the stratigraphic history of these areas is closely similar. In Upper Carboniferrous to Lower Cretaceous times great thicknesses of continental sediments, represented by the *Gondwana System*, were deposited. The main outcrops in the Indian peninsula occur in three areas corresponding approximately to the present Son and Damodar valleys in the north, the Mahanadi valley and the Godavari valley in the south. In these areas the Gondwanas are preserved in a series of depres-

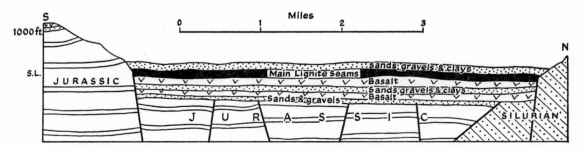

Fig. 13.4 Geological section across the Tertiary lignite field of the Latrobe valley, Victoria.

TABLE 22

Classification of the Gondwana Formations of Peninsular India

Standard scale		Series	Sub-divisions
Cretaceous	Upper Gondwanas	Jabalpur	Umia
			Jabalpur
Jurassic		Rajmahal	Kota
			Rajmahal
Triassic		Mahadeva	Maleri
			Pachmarhi
		～～～～～Unconformity～～～～	
	Lower Gondwanas	Panchet	
Permian		Damuda	Raniganj
			Barren Measures (= Ironstone Shales)
			Barakar
Carboniferous		Talchir	Talchir
			Boulder Bed

sions in the Pre-Cambrian basement. Organic re-mains are almost entirely confined to plant fossils by which the system is subdivided (Table 22). Of lacustrine and fluviatile origin, the sediments are chiefly composed of conglomerates, cross-stratified sandstones and shales, with, in the Damuda Series, the major Indian deposits of coal. At the base, the Talchir Series represents a glacial facies. For the Talchir Boulder Bed, from 50 ft to 100 ft thick, con-tains an ill-sorted mass of erratics which at Irai, Madhya Pradesh and along the Ajay River, Bihar, rest on glacially striated pavements. At these locali-ties the bed is clearly a true tillite although elsewhere it probably formed as a fluvio-glacial deposit. Since deposition the Gondwana sediments have been only slightly affected by orogenic movements and conse-quently their dip is only slight.

Towards the close of the Cretaceous period the basaltic *Deccan Traps* were erupted from a number of volcanic fissures. Great thicknesses of such lavas cover over 200 000 mile^2 of the north-western region of the peninsula.

The Tertiary system is represented by small out-crops of sands, limestones and clay-rocks in coastal areas. The most recent sediments are the alluvial deposits in the major valleys of which those of the Ganges have been proved by boring to be several thousand feet in thickness.

THE JHARIA COALFIELD

The Jharia coalfield (Fox, 1930; Mehta & Murthy, 1957; Sharma & Ram, 1966, pp. 85–91) lies about 150 miles north-west of Calcutta in the Dhanbad district of Bihar. The total area of the coalfield is about 175 mile^2 (Fig. 13.5).

Succession

The Gondwanas occur as an outlier amidst the granitoid rocks and gneisses of the Pre-Cambrian. Owing to their prevailing southerly dip the oldest Gondwana strata crop out along the northern margin and progressively younger strata crop out south-wards.

The *Talchir Series* forms a wide outcrop in the northwest from whence a narrower outcrop can be traced along the northern margin. The basal boulder bed, of apparent fluvio-glacial origin, is about 50 ft thick and is succeeded by over 700 ft of fine-grained arkosic sandstones and greenish shales.

A wide sickle-shaped outcrop covering about

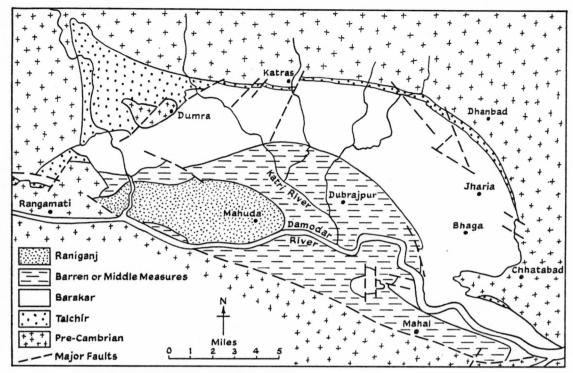

Fig. 13.5 Geological sketch map of the Jharia coalfield. (After Mehta and Murthy.)

84 mile² is formed by the overlying *Barakar Stage* of the *Damuda Series*. The Barakars are composed of over 2 000 ft of white to buff-coloured coarse- and medium-grained sandstones, conglomerates, shales and coal seams. Over twenty-five workable seams occur with a total thickness of over 250 ft (Table 23) and comprise the major coal-producing horizons of the coalfield. Four sub-stages are recognized according to the lithological features and heavy mineral contents of the sandstones.

The overlying *Barren* or *Middle Measures* are mainly exposed in the central and southern part of the coalfield. They consist of nearly 2 000 ft of fine sandstones, shales and carbonaceous shales. Unlike the equivalent Ironstone Shales of the Raniganj coalfield clay ironstones are only feebly developed.

Over 1 500 ft thick, the strata of the *Raniganj Stage* occupy an oval area in the south-western part of the coalfield. Eight workable seams occur within a sequence of fine-grained sandstones and shales.

Structure

The Jharia coalfield is situated within a faulted basin elongated along an east–west axis. The regional dip averages about 15 degrees in a southerly direction. The coalfield is much affected by faulting and the southern margin is formed by a major boundary fault with a downthrow of over 5 000 ft north-east, throwing Pre-Cambrian basement rocks against the Raniganj Stage and Barren Measures.

Intrusive rocks are of basic and ultrabasic composition. The former consist of a series of dolerite dykes occurring in the western area of the coalfield. The ultrabasic peridotites, forming both sills and dykes, are intimately associated with the coal seams and are encountered throughout the coalfield. They have adverse effects upon the seams and in their vicinity the coals are metamorphosed into a natural coke (Jhama).

Rank and production of coals

The highest rank coals are the valuable low and medium volatile bituminous coals of the Barakar Stage. In the Raniganj Stage the coals are of high volatile bituminous rank.

Coal mining at Jharia commenced in 1894 on the linking of the coalfield to the Indian railway system. In 1959 production reached 15 197 857 ton and the

TABLE 23

The Major Coal Horizons of the Baraker Stage in the Jharia Coalfield
(after Sharma & Ram)

Sub-stage	Horizon no.	Thickness (ft)	Quality
4. Bhagaband (Phularitand) 700–900 ft thick	XVIII	6–17	Mostly superior quality coking coals. Some of the best coals in India
	XVIIIA	4–8	
	XVII	4–19	
	XVIA	6–9	
	XVI	4–16	
	XVA	7	
3. Jealgora (Bariri) 250–300 ft thick	XV	9–39	Superior quality coking coals and the most valuable seams in the coalfield. Average quality better than any other Gondwana coals (except Karharbari seams of Giridih). Ash seldom over 16%, calorific value usually more than 12 000 Btu
	XIVA	6–10	
	XIV	5–35	
	XIIIB	5–13	
	XIIIA	9–12	
	XIII	3–7	
2. Gareira (Nardkarki) 300–350 ft thick	XI/XII	4–30	Seams XII, XI and XX of generally superior quality, others inferior. All fairly coking. Ash content varies from 16 to 20%
	X & IX/X	10–60	
	IX	4–38	
	IXA	5–6	
	IX SP	5–7	
	VIIIA	7–19	
	VIII	7–29	
1. Muraidih (Golakdih) 500–600 ft thick	VII/VI/V	39–74	Mainly of inferior quality although many of the seams, especially V to VIII, are coking. Ash content generally high and seldom less than 18%
	IV	7–40	
	III	7–24	
	II	7–60	
	I	7–14	

coalfield produced over 30 per cent of India's coal (Indian coal production in 1959 was 47 821 000 ton). The field is the major source of metallurgical coking coal in India.

THE RANIGANJ COALFIELD

Situated in West Bengal and Bihar, the Raniganj coalfield (Gee, 1932; Mehta, 1956; Sharma & Ram, 1966, pp. 76–84) lies about 115 miles north-west of Calcutta. Much of the coalfield lies on the northern side of the Damodar river. The total area of the coalfield so far proved is about 600 mile^2 (Fig. 13.6).

the northern border of the coalfield and is approximately 2 000 ft thick. It is composed of cross-stratified felspathic sandstones and conglomerates together with occasional shales and some workable coals. Many of the seams average over 20 ft in thickness, and the thickest, forming coal horizon II, locally termed the Kalimati Seam, is in some parts over 100 ft thick. Fireclay horizons form an important source of refractory clays.

Consisting of carbonaceous shales with clay ironstone nodules, the *Ironstone Shales* are about 1 200 ft thick and are devoid of coal seams.

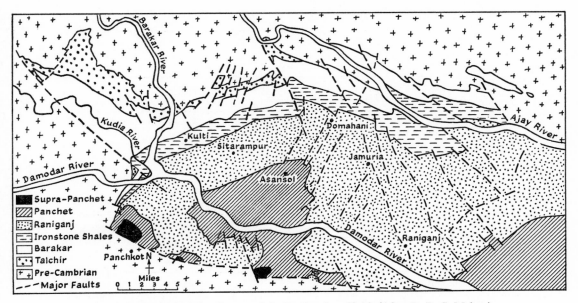

Fig. 13.6   Geological sketch map of the Raniganj coalfield. (After D. R. S. Mehta.)

Succession

Gneisses, granitic rocks and occasional quartzites of Pre-Cambrian age surround the coalfield on three sides. In the east however the productive horizons extend below a cover of laterite and alluvium so that the concealed eastern boundary of the field is as yet unproved.

Exposed along the northern and north-western border of the coalfield, the *Talchir Series* is about 900 ft thick. As in the Jharia coalfield the series consists of a fluvio-glacial boulder bed overlaid by sandstones and greenish shales which break up into prismatic fragments.

The *Damuda Series*, consisting of the Barakar, Ironstone Shale and Raniganj stages form the actual coalfield. The *Barakar Stage* crops out along

The coalfield is the type locality for the *Raniganj Stage* which attains its maximum development thereabouts and is about 3 400 ft thick. Workable seams (Table 24) are more numerous than in the Barakars and nine major horizons are recognized. Interseam strata predominantly consist of fine-grained greyish sandstones with some shales. As in the Jharia coalfield fireclays are not generally encountered in this stage.

In the central parts of the coalfield south of Asansol the Damuda Series are concealed beneath the *Panchet Series*. The latter, with a slight basal unconformity, consist of 2 000 ft of cross-stratified brown micaceous sandstones and red and greenish shales. The *Supra-Panchet Series* forms several small outliers of sandstones and conglomerates along the southern margin of the coalfield.

TABLE 24

The Major Coal Seams of the Raniganj Series in the Raniganj Coalfield
(after Sharma & Ram)

Horizon	Seam names	Thickness (ft)	Quality
IX	Gopalpur – Upper Dhadka – Satpu Khuriya – Ghusick – Siarsol – Upper Kajora – Khandra	4–19	Superior in the western part
VIII	Borachak – Nega – Jameri – Raniganj – Lower Kajora – Jambad – Bowlah – Bankola	7–25	Mixed
VII	Lower Dhadka – Narainkuri – Bansra – Sonachora – Bonbahal	5–16	Generally inferior
VI	Sripur – Toposi – Kendra – Chora – Purushottampur	7–20	Generally inferior
V	Bara Dhemo – Raghunathbati – Manohrabahal – Rana – Poriarpur – Satgram – Jotekanaki – Dobrana – Darula – Sonpur	4–9	Superior in the western and central part
IV	Dishergarh – Samla – Gobindpur – Dhasul	8–12	Mixed
III	Hatnal – Koithi	6–12	Superior
II	Sanctoria – Poniati – Bamandaband – Dahuka	4–8	Superior
I	Taltor – Gangutiya	4–6	Inferior

Structure

The general dip in the coalfield is in a southerly direction with an average inclination of about 10 degrees. In the vicinity of faults, however, notably the southern boundary faults, the dip direction is reversed and series of sharp synclinal folds are developed. Both the western and southern boundaries of the coalfield are faulted. The northern boundary appears to be an unconformity but this is itself offset by a series of north-westerly trending faults which extend across the coalfield and are associated with local folding of the coal horizons.

The coal-bearing sequences are extensively intruded by northerly trending dolerite dykes, in some cases over 100 ft thick, and also peridotite sills and dykes. The peridotite intrusions adversely affect the coals in their proximity.

Rank and production of coals

The Barakar coals are of medium volatile bituminous rank and form excellent steam and sometimes coking coals. The latter are won chiefly from the Ramnagar, Laikdih and Begunia seams. In the Raniganj Stage, from which most of the field's output is derived, the coals are of high volatile bituminous rank and are excellent gas and steam coals. Some seams produce coals which, when blended with highly caking Jharia coals, yield good metallurgical coke.

Although coal was worked in the middle eighteenth century output was negligible until the completion of the East Indian railway to Raniganj in 1855. By 1900 an annual output of over 6 million ton was achieved and in 1959 the production of 16 521 105 ton formed 34·5 per cent of India's coal output.

NEW ZEALAND

The most ancient members of the geological succession of New Zealand occur in the south-west of South Island where a Basement Complex of gneisses, schists and dioritic rocks are probably of *Pre-Cambrian* age. At the extreme north of South Island, in the Collingwood and Nelson areas, highly folded slates and quartzites are the oldest fossiliferous rocks and contain graptolites indicative of a lower *Ordovician* age. It is possible that in the same area some *Silurian* sediments also occur. At Reefton and in the Paparoa Range of South Island Lower *Devonian* shales and greywackes have yielded marine faunas. Highly folded greywackes and slates succeeding a basal volcanic group form much of the highland zone of South Island and are mainly of undifferentiated Palaeozoic, and in some parts more specifically

Permian age. *Triassic* marine sediments, consisting predominantly of shales and sandstones, occur in both South and North Islands and are succeeded conformably by *Jurassic* sandstones, conglomerates, shales and a few thin coal seams. Jurassic sedimentation was followed by strong orogenic movements which resulted in most of New Zealand being raised above sea level. Consequently *Cretaceous* and *Lower Tertiary* sediments are essentially of fluviatile and lacustrine origin and it was during this time that the major coal deposits were formed. They are succeeded by the marine deposits of a transgression which was halted in upper Tertiary time by Alpine orogenic movements. Considerable vulcanicity, particularly in North Island, occurred throughout the Tertiary and indeed persists, in the form of at least five active volcanoes, to the present-day.

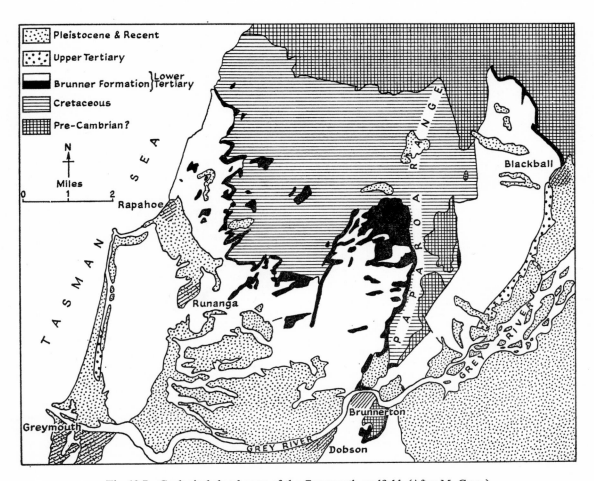

Fig. 13.7   Geological sketch map of the Greymouth coalfield. (After M. Gage.)

THE GREYMOUTH COALFIELD

Extending for about 10 miles to the north of the Grey River in South Island the Greymouth coalfield (Gage, 1952) (Fig. 13.7) yields almost two-thirds of New Zealand's total annual bituminous coal production. The main mining areas are at present to the immediate south of the Paparoa Range.

Succession

Possibly of Pre-Cambrian age, the highly folded greywackes and shales of the *Greenland Formation* crop out around the northern fringes of the coalfield and comprise the basement upon which the coal measure sequences were deposited.

Separated by a major unconformity from the Greenland formation, the *Upper Cretaceous* rocks (Table 25), of lacustrine and fluviatile origin, attain a

TABLE 25

The Geological Succession of the Greymouth Coalfield

System	Group	Formation
Tertiary	Upper Tertiary	
	～～～ Unconformity ～～～	
	Lower Tertiary	Cobden Port Elizabeth Omotumotu
		Kaiata Island Brunner
～～～～	～～～Unconformity～	
Cretaceous	Upper Paparoa	Dunollie Goldlight
	Middle Paparoa	Rewanui
	Lower Paparoa	Waiomo Morgan Ford Jay
Pre-Cambrian?		Greenland

maximum thickness in the northern and central part of the coalfield. Throughout their deposition differential warping of the basement resulted in the heaviest sedimentation along the axial part of the Paparoa Range on both sides of which a thinner sedimentary sequence occurs. The *Lower Paparoa Group* is com-

posed of basal conglomerates, the Jay formation, succeeded by the Ford formation with about 500 ft of siltstones. The Morgan formation consists of two distinct facies, a volcanic and a deltaic. A persistant coal, varying from a few inches to 30 ft in thickness, occurs near the top of the latter together with conglomerates, sandstones and shales. The overlying Waiomo formation essentially consists of a brownish mudstone up to 150 ft thick.

Important coals occur near the top and bottom of the overlying Rewanui formation which forms the sole member of the *Middle Paparoa Group*. About one-quarter of the total coal produced in the coalfield is derived from the Lower and Upper Rewanui seams.

In the *Upper Paparoa Group* the Goldlight formation, which is composed of about 500 ft of mudstone, is succeeded by the Dunollie formation which contains a similar thickness of sandstones and shales.

The uppermost set of coal measures, the *Brunner formation* is of Lower Tertiary age. An unconformity separates the formation from the Cretaceous and basement strata. Composed predominantly of sandstones and mudstones the formation is about 400 ft thick along the crest of the Paparoa Range and progressively thins to the east and west of that area. Over half the total production of the coalfield is won from the formation although in most localitites only one workable seam occurs. By mid-Eocene times regional depression of the Greymouth area brought about a marine transgression resulting in the deposition of from 2 000 ft to 9 000 ft of marine sandstones, mudstones and impure limestones of lower Tertiary age. In early Miocene time the Cretaceous and lower Tertiary sediments were deformed so that the upper Tertiary sequence of limestones, mudstones, sandstones and conglomerates were deposited unconformably upon them. The overlying Pleistocene river gravels are similarly unconformable upon earlier strata and are in turn succeeded by spreads of recent alluvium.

Structure

Four major asymmetric anticlines with severely faulted, steeply inclined and occasionally overturned eastern limbs affect the coalfield (Fig. 13.8). Of general north–south trend the folds plunge to the south so that progressively younger strata crop out in that direction. Disharmonic folding is commonly developed. Two major groups of faults occur trending between north and north–north-east, and between north-east and east. The former group are closely related to the folding and tend to be concentrated upon the anticlinical crests and the steeper limbs. Both reverse and normal faults occur.

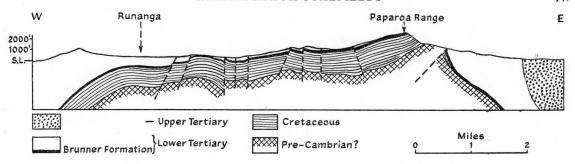

Fig. 13.8   Geological section across the Greymouth coalfield. (After M. Gage.)

Rank and production of coals

The coal rank varies from high volatile bituminous to anthracitic and is clearly influenced by the former depth of burial of the seams. The rank decreases both in eastwards and westwards directions away from the Paparoa Range in which the area the coal measures and Tertiary sediments attain their greatest thickness.

Major development of the Greymouth coalfield first commenced in 1864 and in 1964 production was 412 193 ton, (New Zealand bituminous coal production—1964—682 000 ton). The coals are mainly utilized for steam raising, gas manufacture and the production of metallurgical coke.

THE OHAI COALFIELD

Situated about 50 miles north–north-west of Invercargill the Ohai coalfield (Bowen, 1964) is a small unit of about 40 mile² situated on the edge of the Southland plains of South Island.

Succession

The productive upper Cretaceous and lower Tertiary strata (Table 26) occur as an outlier amidst Permian and Triassic basement rocks. The last two consist of a volcanic series succeeded by conglomerates, sandstones and mudstones.

The *Wairio Coal Measures* form a narrow outcrop along the north-eastern margin of the coalfield. Attaining a maximum thickness of 100 ft the formation consists of basal conglomerate, succeeded by sandstones, carbonaceous shales and mudstones together with a coal seam which locally is over 4 ft thick.

Although the overlying *New Brighton Conglomerate* is predominantly rudaceous some sandstones, carbonaceous shales and coals have also been proved. No good surface exposures occur and the formation has been only completely penetrated by one borehole when a thickness of 374 ft was recorded.

Attaining a maximum thickness of 500 ft the

Morley Coal Measures form the principal coal bearing sequence. As a result of penecontemporaneous and pre-Tertiary orogenic movements the preserved thickness of the formation is variable and indeed it may be locally overstepped by the Beaumont Coal Measures. The penecontemporaneous movements are particularly reflected in the rapid lithological changes in the interseam strata. Although sandstones are predominant, mudstones and conglomerates also occur. Six thick coal seams are recognized (Table 26) and are placed in three palaeobotanical zones based upon their spore contents. Owing to differential subsidence and compaction the seam intervals are variable, so that near the crest of the Ohai anticline the Morley No. 1 and 2 seams are separated by 225 ft of strata whereas on the flanks of the fold the seams are 275 ft apart.

Cropping out over a wide area in the centre of the coalfield the *Beaumont Coal Measures*, of Lower Tertiary age, are unconformable upon the Cretaceous formations. The formation is usually less than 500 ft thick and although sandstones occur it is essentially composed of argillaceous interseam strata containing characteristic ironstone concretions. Most of the coals are of sporadic occurrence and seldom exceed 10 ft in thickness.

The succeeding Orauea Mudstone and Pleistocene river gravels are entirely without coal seams.

Structure

The coalfield is affected by a series of south-west and south–south-west plunging folds (Fig. 13.9) so that the Ohai Group crop out only in the north-east and progressively younger strata are encountered in the direction of plunge. Since much of the folding was contemporaneous with sedimentation the structures are more marked in the older formations. Along the margins of the coalfield the Cretaceous and Tertiary formations are faulted against basement rocks. Within the coalfield, most notably in the north-eastern area, faulting is extremely complex.

TABLE 26

The Geological Succession of the Ohai Coalfield

System	Group	Formation (with maximum thickness of major coals)			Palaeobotanical zone
Lower Tertiary	Nightcaps	Orauea Mudstone			
		Beaumont Coal Measures			*Nothofagus matauraensis*
					N. flemingii
------Unconformity------					
Cretaceous		Morley Coal Measures	Major coal seams	Star (38 ft)	*Podocarpidites marwickii*
				Morley No. 1 (51 ft) Linton Main (49 ft) Morley No. 2 (54 ft)	*Dacrydiumites*
				Couper (76 ft) Morley No. 3 (51 ft)	*Podocarpidites* cf. *ellipticus*
	Ohai	New Brighton Conglomerate			*Tricolpites pachyexinus*
		Wairio Coal Measures			*Proteacidites palisadus*
------Unconformity------					
------------Permian and Triassic Basement------------					

Rank and production of coals

A progressive increase in coal rank is apparent in a south-westerly direction. The worked coals are black lignites but it is expected that high volatile bituminous coal will occur at deeper horizons in the south-west.

Systematic development of the coal resources commenced in 1879 when mining was confined to the Nightcaps district. Consequent upon the depletion of coal reserves in that area the producing area has gradually been shifted to the west and is at present confined to the Ohai district. In 1964 produc-

tion reached 329 980 ton (New Zealand black lignite production—1964—2 038 000 ton). Almost all the output is derived from the Morley Coal Measures and is utilized for steam-raising and domestic heating.

NIGERIA

Much of Nigeria is composed of the highly metamorphosed *Pre-Cambrian* basement complex of the Dahomeyan Group, which comprises four large outcrops. The group includes gneisses and migmatites which are succeeded by a series of schists and granites associated with considerable mineralization including valuable deposits of cassiterite (tin ore) and

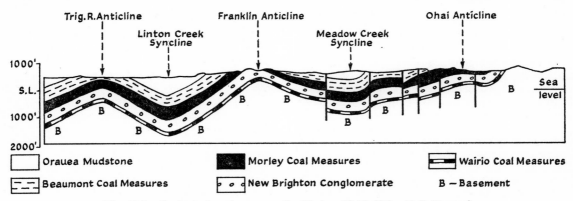

Fig. 13.9   Geological section across the Ohai coalfield. (After F. S. Bowen.)

TABLE 27

The Cretaceous Succession of South-Eastern Nigeria
(after Swardt & Casey)

Formation	Maxmum thickness (approx.) ft	Character
Lower part of the Upper Coal Measures		Predominantly sandstones, sandy shales and carbonaceous shales
False-Bedded Sandstones	1100+	Medium- to coarse-grained cross-stratified sandstones with subordinate shales
Lower Coal Measures	1300+	Fine- to medium-grained sandstones, shaley sandstones, mudstones, shales and coals
Enugu Shales, Awgu Sandstone and Nkporo Shales	2500+	Mudstones and shales with sandstone lenses and beds; or massive sandstones
——————— Unconformity ———————		
Awgu Shales	3000+	Shales with subordinate calcareous sandstones limestones
Eze-Aku Shales	2000	Flaggy calcareous shales, blue shales and mudstones and subordinate limestones and sandstones
———————Unconformity———————		
Asu River Group	6000+	Shales, micaceous sandstones and limestones

columbite (niobium ore). A profound unconformity separates the oldest sediments, of Lower Cretaceous age, from the underlying Pre-Cambrian. The *Lower Cretaceous*, consisting of a thick series of shales with subordinate sandstones and limestones, was deposited in a long marine embayment approximately following the present Benue valley. In mid-Cretaceous times an orogenic phase interrupted sedimentation so that Upper Cretaceous shales and sandstones (Table 27) overstep across the earlier sediments on to the Pre-Cambrian. During the deposition of the Enugu Shales and equivalent strata the sea retreated southwards so that the Lower Coal Measures and succeeding Cretaceous sediments were deposited in brackish-water lagoonal conditions. At about this time the vulcanicity, as for example evidenced by the basaltic rocks of southern Bornu, commenced and has persisted intermittently up to the present. *Tertiary* sediments are represented by a thick sequence of shales and sandstones, succeeded by the relatively unconsolidated Lignite Formation composed of cross-stratified sands, clays and mudstones together with some lignites. The latter at some localities in-

clude seams over 10 ft thick. The most recent sediments are the Coastal Plain Sands (Miocene or Pliocene) and the recent deltaic and alluvial deposits of the larger rivers.

THE ENUGU COALFIELD

The only exploited coalfield is that centred around Enugu in South Eastern Nigeria, and, although coals occur elsewhere, no substantial developments in other areas are envisaged.

Succession

The *Enugu Shales*, consisting mainly of argillaceous strata with some sandy shales, shelly limestones and thin ironstones, pass upward into the basal sandstones of the Lower Coal Measures. As a result of contemporaneous movement of the Okigwi anticline the shales pass laterally south of Enugu into the Awgu Sandstones and Nkporo Shale.

The *Lower Coal Measures* (Swardt & Casey, 1963, pp. 6–7) including the former 'White Sandstones' of Simpson (1954, pp. 20–1) attain a maximum thickness of over 1000 ft. They are composed of alternating fine- to medium-grained sandstones, shales, sandy shales, mudstones and coal seams. West of Enugu a persistent rhythmic sequence of sediments is well developed in which the typical cyclothem is as follows:

Shale or sandy shale;
COAL;
Carbonaceous shale passing downwards into shale;
Sandstone with a few shaley layers, or alternating sandstones and shales;
Shale or sandy shale.

The sandstones tend to be the predominant sediments and exhibit slump structures and erosional features, and are sometimes cross-stratified. At Enugu five persistent coal seams, numbered 1 to 5 upwards (Fig. 13.10) have been proved from out-

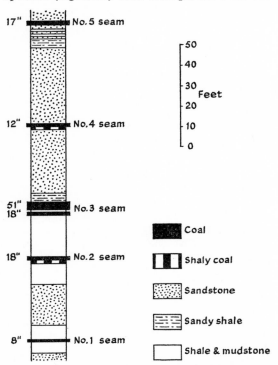

Fig. 13.10 Borehole section showing the productive sequence of the Lower Coal Measures west of Enugu.

crops and deep bores. Only the No. 3 seam (Swardt & Casey, 1963, pp. 13–14) is at present being worked. To the west and south of Enugu the seam, from 4 ft to 6 ft thick, is split by up to a foot of shale or sandy shale. Elsewhere the dirt parting locally thickens to form areas of thin coal.

The overlying *False-Bedded Sandstones* are composed largely of poorly sorted, medium- to coarse-grained, cross-stratified and unconsolidated sandstones. They form the summit of the Enugu escarpment, a prominent topographic feature rising to over 600 ft above the Enugu plain. Over most of southeastern Nigeria the *Upper Coal Measures*, with the exception of only a feeble development of thin coals, are of lithologies similar to those of the Lower Coal Measures.

As is common in the Tropics, all the rocks are extensively weathered to considerable depths—at one borehole near Enugu the weathered zone extended to over 800 ft below the surface. Such weathering has considerable economic significance, for its main effects have been the removal of coal seams so that little coal can be won by open-cast methods. Since the base of the zone of weathering is not related in depth to the present land surface or water-table it is considered that the extensive weathering may have been developed in pre-Tertiary time.

Structure

The Lower Coal Measures at Enugu dip westwards at a small angle generally of between 1 and 3 degrees (Fig. 13.11). Some minor folding of disharmonic type in the workings of the No. 3 seam is considered to be essentially a compaction effect. A series of normal faults, mostly trending north–north-west, and including the Iva Fault system (maximum downthrow 130 ft west–south-west) have been proved in the coalfield.

Rank and production of coals

The Enugu coals, occurring within groups A and B of the sub-bituminous class of the A.S.T.M. system (page 250), occur just about on the margin between black lignites and bituminous coals. An analysis of the No. 3 seam is quoted in Table 45. Their relatively high ash, low carbon and lack of coking properties compare unfavourably with British coals. Nevertheless they form acceptable boiler fuels and, owing to high tar contents, are a potential source of chemical by-products.

Coal was first discovered in 1909 and mining commenced at Enugu in 1915. From 1916, when 24 511 ton were produced, the output rose steadily to a maximum of 905 397 ton in the year 1958–9, since which time production has declined to about 550 000 ton per annum. At present the No. 3 seam is worked by drifts driven into the hillsides at the Ekulu, Iva, Obwetti, Okpara (formerly called Heyes) and Ribadu Mines. Most of the coal is supplied to the Nigerian Railway and Electricity Corporations.

SOUTH AFRICA

Outcrops of *Pre-Cambrian* rocks occur at scattered localities throughout South Africa (Du Toit,

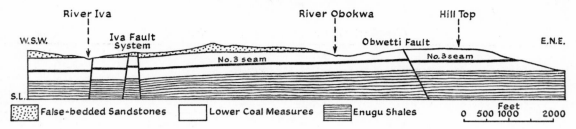

Fig. 13.11   Geological section across the Enugu coalfield.

1954; Haughton, 1963). The geologically oldest of these are the granitic rocks and metamorphosed sediments occurring in the Transvaal and locally termed the Swaziland System. Containing many valuable mineral deposits, the system was considerably affected by a major phase of granitization accompanied by the intrusion of the 'Older Granites'. In the overlying Pre-Cambrian several systems are recognized the most important of which are the Witwatersrand and the Transvaal Systems. The former, occurring largely in the Transvaal, is composed of a thick alternating succession of quartzites and slates succeeded by sandstones and conglomerates. It is the last mentioned rocks which form the famous gold- and uranium-bearing 'bankets' or 'reefs'. The overlying Transvaal System of the Transvaal and Cape Province contains limestones and dolostones succeeded by bedded ironstones with chert beds and yielding hematite, manganese and asbestos. In central Transvaal the system dips below the Bushveld Complex composed of an intrusive cluster of basic igneous and granitized cover rocks some 2 miles in thickness. At several horizons in the Pre-Cambrian of the Republic occurrences of tillites are indicative of former glacial conditions.

Of possible Cambrian age the quartzites and shales forming the Nama System occur in the western part of Cape Province. The overlying Waterberg System of the Transvaal is composed of buff and purple continental sandstones with coarse conglomerates. No fossils have as yet been reported from these beds which are everywhere unconformable upon older strata. Confined chiefly to the southern parts of the Cape Province and of late Silurian to early Carboniferous age, the strongly folded Cape System is composed essentially of sandstones, shales and an upper quartzite series. The *Karroo System*, of late Carboniferous to early Jurassic age is found over a widespread area of the Republic. The system is composed of almost entirely continental sediments which are extensively intruded by dolerite sills and dykes. Over 30 000 ft thick in the south, the system thins to the north in which area some formations are absent.

c.m.g.—11

Four series are recognized (Table 28) and it is in the Ecca Series of the Transvaal, Orange Free State and Natal that the only important South African coals are located. The basal formation of the system, the Dwyka tillite, sometimes exceeding 2 000 ft in thickness, was the product of the widespread ice age which affected the Southern hemisphere and India in Permo-Carboniferous time. Apart from in the extreme south, the system is only slightly affected by faulting and the strata are more or less horizontal.

Comparatively small outcrops of sandstones overlain by marine limestones and shales of Cretaceous age occur in the coastal parts of Natal and Cape Province. Cretaceous sedimentation was accompanied by the intrusion of the many ultrabasic kimberlite pipes which are diamondiferous in their type area. Apart from the small outcrops of marine limestones and sandstones, in the coastal areas of Cape Province, the Tertiary system is composed of fluviatile calcareous sandstones and mudstones.

THE WITBANK COALFIELD

The Witbank coalfield (Graham, 1931; Wybergh, 1922) is situated in the mid-Highveld district of the Transvaal about 80 miles east–north-east of Johannesburg and about 1 000 miles north of Capetown.

Succession

Pre-Karroo strata, occasionally encountered in mining as ridge-like projections within the coal bearing sequence and also exposed in some of the deeper valleys, are formed by the red sandstones of the Waterberg System.

The overlying *Dwyka tillite* is in the coalfield a true ground moraine and in the vicinity of some of the collieries can be seen resting on glacially striated rock surfaces. It is of irregular thickness having apparently been subjected to an erosive phase in lower Ecca time. Consequently the *Middle Ecca*, of coal measure facies, rests in places directly on the Dwyka tillite and in others on the very uneven pre-Karroo surface. Five principal seams, numbered in ascending order 1 to 5 (Fig. 13.12), occur in about 350 ft of strata.

TABLE 28

Classification of the Karroo System of South Africa

European equivalent	Series	Stage	Major lithologies	Maximum thickness (approx.) ft	
				Cape Province	Transvaal
Lower Jurassic	Stormberg	Drakensberg Volcanics	Basalts with local intercalations of pyroclasts	4 000	1 000
		Cave Sandstone	Massive fine grained sandstones with shale lenses	1 000	300
		Red Beds	Mudstones, shales and sandstones	1 600	400
Triassic		Molteno	Sandstones with shale intercalations	2 000	175
	Beaufort	Upper Beaufort	Purple mudstones and sandstones	2 000	⎫
		Middle Beaufort	Purple mudstones and sandstones	1 000	⎬ 300
		Lower Beaufort	Shales, sandstones and conglomerates	9 000	⎭
Permian	Ecca	Upper Ecca	Shales	⎫	300
		Middle Ecca	Shales, sandstones and coal seams	⎬ 10 000	400
		Lower Ecca	Shales with thin flagstones	⎭	500
Upper Carboniferous	Dwyka	Upper Shales	Shales, carbonaceous shales and flagstones	700	?
		Tillite	Tillites with thin shale and sandstone partings	2 500	30

No. 1 seam, resting directly on the tillite or separated from it by a small thickness of glaciofluvial conglomerates and shales is, owing to projections of the pre-Karroo basement, locally absent as for example under the town of Witbank. The most extensive coal is the No. 2 or Witbank Main Seam which tends to be unaffected by irregularities in the floor and, since it occurs in the lower part of the sequence, is similarly unaffected by denudation which in places has totally removed the overlying seams. True fireclays are absent and the interseam sequences are formed of shales, sandstones and conglomerates. The latter are confined to the basal measures and some, the 'resorted' or 'false Dwyka', are derived from the underlying tillite. Sandstones comprise the greater part of the interseam sequence and the rather sandy or calcareous shales are mainly developed in the higher parts of the Middle Ecca. The coals are considered (Plumstead, 1957, pp. 5–11; 1961, pp. 545–6; 1966) to have formed at several thousand feet above sea-level in a cold temperate climate. Despite their high ash contents and the absence of normal seat earths, the South African coals are most probably true autochthonous accumulations.

Structure

As in most areas of South Africa, the Middle Ecca sediments are virtually horizontal and the rare local undulations are of but minor effect. Again no faults of any magnitude occur. Owing to the absence of overlying strata and the structural simplicity, the coalfield is shallow so that the deepest mine is only 270 ft. A few dolerite dykes are encountered mainly in the southern parts of the coalfield.

Rank and production of coals

The Witbank coals are of high and medium volatile bituminous rank with high ash contents of between about 6 to 30 per cent. They form excellent steam raising coals and the No. 5 seam together with the basal part of the No. 2 seam yield metallurgical coke

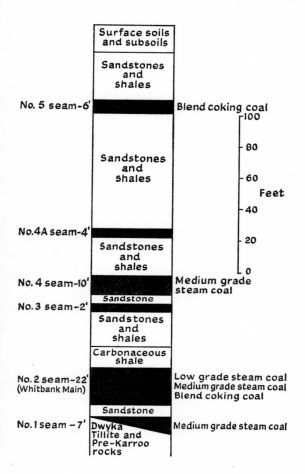

Fig. 13.12 The geological succession of the Witbank coalfield.

when blended with Natal coking coal. Most of the coal production is from the No. 2 seam.

Large scale mining around Witbank commenced in 1895 on the opening of the Pretoria railway. The coalfield is at present the principal coal producing area of the Republic yielding about half of the total South African production (South African coal production—1961—39 682 000 ton).

REFERENCES

BOWEN, F. E. (1964) Geology of Ohai coalfield, *Bull. geol. Surv. N.Z.*, **51**.

DAVID, T. W. E. (1950) *The Geology of the Commonwealth of Australia*, 1st ed., London, Arnold.

FOX, C. S. (1930) The Jharia coalfield, *Mem. geol. Surv. India* **56**.

GAGE, M. (1952) The Greymouth coalfield, *Bull. geol. Surv. N.Z.*, **45**.

GEE, E. R. (1932) The geology and coal resources of the Raniganj coalfield, *Mem. geol. Surv. India* **61**.

GRAHAM, A. C. (1931) *The Coals of the Witbank District*, Pt. 1., 1st ed., Johannesburg, Transvaal Chamber of Mines.

HAUGHTON, S. H. (1963) *The Stratigraphic History of Africa south of the Sahara*, 1st ed., Edinburgh, Oliver & Boyd.

KRISHNAN, M. S. (1956) *Geology of India and Burma*, 3rd ed., Madras, Higginbothams.

MEHTA, D. R. S. (1956) A revision of the geology and coal resources of the Raniganj coalfield, *Mem. geol. Surv. India* **84**, Pt. 1.

MEHTA, D. R. S. & B. R. N. MURTHY (1957) A revision of the geology and coal resources of the Jharia coalfield, *Mem. geol. Surv. India* **84**, Pt. 2.

NELSON, A. (1963) Mining brown coal in Australia, *Colliery Guard.*, **206**, 502–8.

PLUMSTEAD, E. P. (1957) *Coal in Southern Africa*, 1st ed., Johannesburg, Witwatersrand University Press.

PLUMSTEAD, E. P. (1961) The Permo-Carboniferous coal measures of the Transvaal, South Africa—an example of the contrasting stratigraphy in the Southern and Northern hemispheres, *C.R. 4th. Congr. Strat. Carb. Heerlen.* **2**, 545–50.

PLUMSTEAD, E. P. (1966) The story of South Africa's coal, *Optima*, **16**, 187–202.

SHARMA, N. L. & K. S. V. RAM (1966) *Introduction to the Geology of Coal and Indian Coalfields*, 2nd ed., Jaipur, Oriental.

SIMPSON, A. (1954) The Nigerian coalfield, the geology of parts of Onitsha, Owerri and Benue Provinces, *Bull. geol. Surv. Nigeria* **24**.

SWARDT, A. M. J. de & O. P. CASEY (1963) The coal resources of Nigeria, *Bull. geol. Surv. Nigeria* **28**, (with map supplement).

TOIT, A. L. Du, (1954) *The Geology of South Africa*, 3rd ed., Edinburgh, Oliver & Boyd.

WAIDA, D. N. (1953) *Geology of India*, 3rd ed., London, Macmillan.

WYBERGH, W. J. (1922) The coal resources of the Union of South Africa—the coalfields of Witbank, Springs, and Heidelberg and of the Orange Free State, *Mem. geol. Surv. S. Afr.*, **19**.

Part Two
Advanced Aspects

14

CARBONIFEROUS FOSSILS

Originally the term *fossil* was applied to any object which was discovered during excavations (*fossilis*, L.—dug up), but now the term is restricted to the remains and traces of life which existed in the geological past. Fossils are found typically in the sedimentary rocks, although distorted and indistinct forms sometimes occur in low grade metamorphic rocks and more rarely still within lavas. At some horizons fossils may be particularly common and occur in distinct bands in marked contrast to the apparently unfossiliferous surrounding strata. Strictly speaking, and especially with regard to strata younger than the Pre-Cambrian, the much-used term 'unfossiliferous' is always suspect—for who knows what an assiduous collector may discover in the future?

The stratigraphic importance of the various fossil groups will already be apparent from the preceding chapters and, in later chapters, their particular uses in Carboniferous stratigraphy and correlation will be further emphasized. Accordingly in this chapter the principal fossil groups occurring in the Carboniferous interseam strata and within the coals themselves are described.

PRESERVATION OF FOSSILS

To be preserved as fossils, animals and plants first must possess a skeleton and, secondly, at death they must be rapidly buried. In this way their disintegration and total destruction as a result of weathering agencies and the scavenging work of animals is restricted to the fleshy parts. Even so, only rarely is the entire organism preserved, as usually the soft parts are quickly destroyed by bacterial action. The almost complete remains of the Siberian mammoths are most exceptional fossils and owe their preservation to the natural refrigerating conditions of the permafrost zone.

Usually invertebrate fossils occur as three or four common forms (Moore, Lalicker & Fischer, 1952, pp. 1–5). Most shells are of a calcareous, siliceous or chitinous (chitin—a lustrous organic complex substance) nature and in some cases, as for example many brachiopods and corals, may be preserved in the *unaltered* form. In *altered* forms the original shell substance may be simply recrystallized or partially

or totally replaced by other minerals. Thus the calcareous shells of the goniatites and lamellibranchs found in some Upper Carboniferous marine bands are often replaced by pyrite. In other forms the hard parts are completely destroyed although their former shape may be determined by the trace of the fossil as a hollow *mold* or solid *cast*. Vertebrates may also be represented as *imprints* formed by the animals as they moved, so that although the Triassic dinosaurs are unrepresented in the solid form in Britain, their occurrence is indicated by the footprint beds discovered in several counties. Other rather problematical *trace fossils* (Häntzschel, 1962) include the worm burrows which are common in some Carboniferous sequences.

Plant remains have similarly varied fossil forms (Arnold, 1947, pp. 14–39). Some of the most abundant plant fossils occur as almost flat *compressions* in which the original organic substance has been converted into a thin coaly layer, as in the fossil leaves found in the roof strata of many seams. Usually corresponding *impressions* also occur. Frequently the larger roots, stems and trunks are represented by *casts* infilling cavities developed by the complete or partial decay of the plant. Such casts are most frequently developed from the soft internal parts so that their exteriors mirror the inner surfaces of the original woody bark, which may remain as a thin coaly layer. *Petrifactions* forming coal-balls and bullions have previously been described (pages 63–4) although other types include the silicified Middle Old Red Sandstone plants at Rhynie in Scotland and the petrified Triassic forests of Arizona. Finally the original waxy coatings of the minute spore cases usually occur in the unaltered form within many coal seams.

NOMENCLATURE

The multitude of names applied to the million or so fossils already described is probably the most vexing aspect of geology to the average student, particularly if he is not acquainted with the classical languages. For at first the use of such 'dead languages' may appear unnecessary and most certainly pedantic. Such a nomenclature is required however if different fossils are to be accurately defined and thereby utilized as stratigraphic guides. It is certainly of little use applying an English, Chinese or Russian name to a newly discovered fossil in one of those countries if it is untranslatable and therefore incomprehensible in any other language. At least Latin is a universally accepted language and some attempts are made to ensure that the translation is appropriate to the shape, type or original locality of the fossil.

The fundamental unit of the biological and palaeontological system of nomenclature (Davies & Stubblefield, 1961, pp. 262–77) is the *species* (Table 29). The specific name is composed of two parts. Thus *Gastrioceras listeri*, an important Upper Carboniferous species of goniatite, is composed of the *generic name, Gastrioceras*, and the *trivial name, listeri*. The generic name may be a common prefix to a number of distinct species possessing similar major and different minor characteristics, e.g. *Gastrioceras listeri, G. subcrenatum, G. cumbriense*, etc. As will be noted the generic name if used more than once in the context may be subsequently abbreviated to its initial letter, which is always printed as a capital. The trivial name is never capitalized. Also a type, commonly italic, different from the accompanying text is used for the specific name. Accordingly the student is advised to adopt this convention by always underlining, or otherwise distinguishing, such names in his written work. Other procedures often seen in palaeontological literature include the suffixing of the author's name, in ordinary type, to that of the species so that the original description can readily be found, and the use of the qualifying terms 'cf.' and 'aff'. Thus *Carbonicola* aff. *acuta* (J. Sowerby) is a related form but differing in some respects from the species described by Sowerby, and *C*. cf. *acuta*, although possibly with a greater similarity than the first form, may not necessarily be related to it. (Trueman & Weir, 1946, pp. xx–xxi).

The species, or more particularly the 'biospecies' of the biologist, is most easily defined as a member of a group of physically and anatomically similar, and freely interbreeding or potentially interbreeding animals. Therefore the cat (*Felis domesticus*) is a separate species to the dog (*Canis familiaris*) since the two cannot interbreed. The palaeontologist is however unable to apply most of these criteria and so the fossil species or 'morphospecies' is defined principally according to the shape and structure of the few hard parts which may be fossilized. Consequently although the end members of a fossil assemblage may be distinct morphological types and might therefore be considered as distinct species, the many gradations between the two may have formed part of a freely interbreeding community. The problem is where to place the division between the two species.

In palaeobotany, because of the fragmentary and disassociated nature of fossil plants, separate generic names are often assigned to particular plant parts. Leaves, stems, roots and fructifications of the same plant may therefore appear to be unrelated. For example, the generic name *Calamites* is reserved for the pith-casts of the Carboniferous horse-tails, whereas that of their leaves is *Annularia*, that of their cones, *Calamostchys* and some of their microspores are described as *Laevigatosporites*. Furthermore in any particular genus there may be included plant parts which although superficially alike may be derived from unrelated plants (Arnold, 1947, pp. 408–11; Crookall, 1929, p. 21). The fossil root *Stigmaria*, abundant in most Carboniferous seat earths, probably belonged to several distinct trees including *Lepidodendron* and *Sigillaria*. Perhaps the difficulties of the palaeobotanist may be most readily appreciated if the reader cares to relate the elements of an unknown modern flora from a sackful of separate leaves, roots and pieces of bark!

COLLECTION OF FOSSILS

In searching for fossils, certain rocks are more likely to yield well preserved specimens than others, for although occasional fossils may occur in most beds their state of preservation is often determined by the nature of the surrounding sediment. The

TABLE 29

The Divisions of the Animal Kingdom, applied to the Classification of an Extinct Carboniferous Goniatite (G. listeri), *Modern Dog* (C. familiaris) *and his Master and Companion* (H. sapiens)

Kingdom	Animalia	Animalia	Animalia
Phylum	Mollusca	Chordata	Chordata
Class	Cephalopoda	Mammalia	Mammalia
Order	Ammonoidea	Carnivora	Primate
Family	Neoicoceridae	Canidae	Hominidae
Genus	*Gastrioceras*	*Canis*	*Homo*
Species	*G. listeri*	*C. familiaris*	*H. sapiens*
		'Fido'	'Bill Sykes'

Plate 9 Vertical aerial photograph of part of Iran showing part of a plunging fold. The offsetting of some features by small faults is apparent.

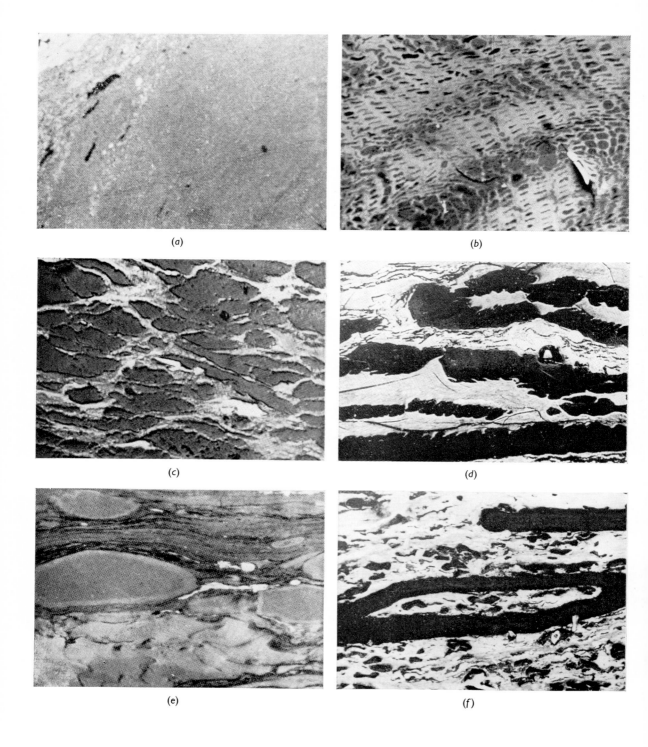

(a)

(b)

(c)

(d)

(e)

(f)

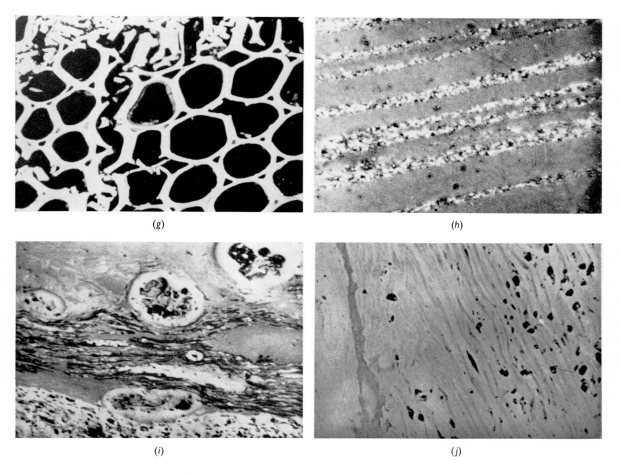

(g)

(h)

(i)

(j)

Plate 10 Microphotographs of polished sections of coal macerals.

(a) Collinite (× 400)   (b) Telinite (× 130)

(c) Alginite (× 400)   (d) Cutinite (× 100)

(e) Resinite (× 350)   (f) Sporinite (× 180)

(g) Fusinite (× 480)   (h) Micrinite (× 2 000)

(i) Sclerotinite (× 110)   (j) Semifusinite (× 250)

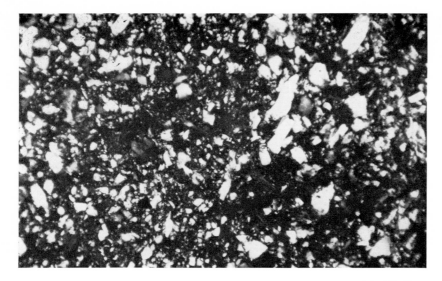

Plate 11(a) Microphotograph of a thin section of a crystal tonstein with polarized light. Contained in thin coal below the Worsley Four Foot Seam, Lancashire ($\times$ 35).

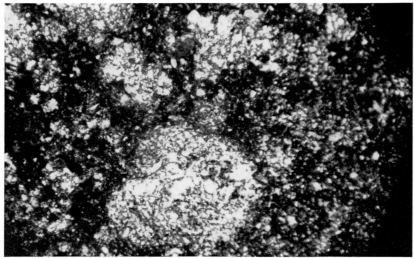

Plate 11(b) Microphotograph of a thin section of a graupen tonstein, polarized light, Tonstein Hermance, Thiers, France ($\times$ 35).

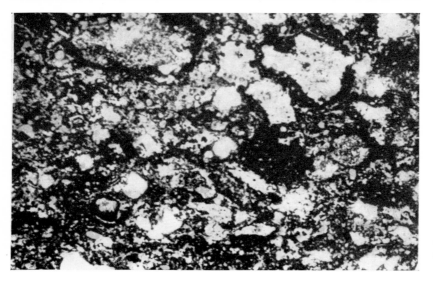

Plate 11(c) Microphotograph of a thin section of a tuffaceous siltstone above the Overton Gas Coal, Fife ($\times$ 40).

'fossil-potential' of the interseam sequence is as follows:

(1) *Conglomerates* are only exceptionally fossiliferous. Any fossils which occur are most likely to be either *derived fossils* contained in the rock fragments, or eroded prior to and partially destroyed during the deposition of the sediment.

(2) *Sandstones* sometimes contain casts of the Carboniferous trees (page 56). Delicate leaf compressions and invertebrate fossils are most often destroyed during the compaction of the sediment.

(3) *Siltstones* may contain layers rich in finely comminuted plant-debris although occasional well preserved and specifically identifiable fossils sometimes occur.

(4) *Mudstones* and *shales* form some of the most fossiliferous interseam beds. Delicately preserved plant remains are especially abundant in argillaceous roof strata. Most of the distinct bands of crushed, although specifically identifiable, marine and non-marine fossils are developed in these rocks. Occasional plant-remains and non-marine fossils may be sporadically distributed throughout the whole thickness.

(5) *Seat earths* are characterized by the large numbers of Stigmarian and smaller plant rootlets. Other macrofossils are rare.

(6) *Ironstones* may yield relatively undistorted 'solid' specimens of non-marine and occasionally marine fossils. Well preserved plant compressions also occur. Sometimes the bizarre shapes, even simulating human forms, which result from the weathering of such rocks are mistaken by the inexperienced collector for actual fossils.

(7) *Limestones* when developed in the interseam sequence may be almost entirely composed of marine or non-marine fossils.

(8) *Coal-balls* and *bullions* respectively yield the most well preserved plant and marine fossils (pages 63–4). They form however extremely rare horizons.

Excepting some of the larger plant remains which sometimes occur in their vertical growth positions, fossils are uusally orientated so that their larger dimensions are more or less parallel to the stratification. This is particularly evident in some highly fossiliferous shales when entire lamination surfaces may be completely covered with crushed fossils, so that it is virtually impossible to separate a single individual. Consequently during the palaeontological examination of a sedimentary sequence the rocks should be split along rather than across the stratification. In the case of shales, a sharp, well aimed tap as distinct from a hard blow from the hammer is usually sufficient to reveal a potential parting which may be then worked upon by gentle prizing with a thin steel blade. In this way fragmentation of the whole rock and consequent damage to any fossils is prevented. Often surface exposures of the argillaceous rocks are soft and friable so that a wet specimen may disintegrate on being rapidly dried out. This may sometimes be prevented if on collection the material is wrapped in damp newspaper and the whole mass then allowed to dry out slowly over a period of several weeks before finally unwrapping. In any case the separation and cleaning of delicate specimens should be carried out in the laboratory and not in the field or colliery.

At the time of collection the exact horizon and precise underground or surface locality from which the specimen was obtained should be noted, for without such details the fossil is stratigraphically valueless. It is insufficient to trust to the memory and the specimen should always be packed together with a brief descriptive note. One of the quickest methods is to use a book of cloakroom tickets, enclosing the 'tear-out' with the specimen and noting the horizon and locality on the remaining portion. This information can be subsequently transferred to a permanent label firmly cemented to the specimen and written with a fade-proof drawing-ink. The specimen should not be merely placed in a cardboard tray or box with the loose label underneath for it is very likely that sometime in the future the latter will be misplaced.

As to the correct identification of the fossil, a competent geological opinion should always be sought if the specific name is required. The generic name may however in many cases be readily discovered from comparison with museum material and by consulting the various descriptive papers and monographs.

MARINE FAUNA

With the exception of the Lower Carboniferous, marine strata and fossils are confined to a number of relatively thin and distinct marine bands (pages 187 and 212–4). Some of the more important Upper Carboniferous marine fossils are described below.

Brachiopods

The soft brachiopod body is enclosed within two shells which are unequal in size so that the larger *pedicle valve* is readily distinguished from the *brachial valve* (Fig. 14.1). Apart from when in the free-swimming larval stage they live more or less permanently in one place on the sea floor, to which they may be attached by cementation by a fleshy stalk called the *pedicle* or by a series of spines developed from the shell surface. Considerable variation is apparent in their shape and the cross-sectional appearance is important in classification, plano-convex forms being distinguished for instance

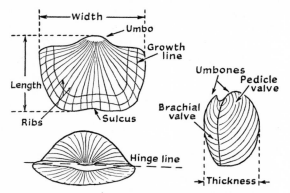

Fig. 14.1   Structural features of a brachiopod.

from concavo-convex forms. In this respect the shape of the brachial valve is always quoted before that of the pedicle valve. The phylum is subdivided into the *articulate* and *inarticulate* classes. In the latter, the valves, usually of a chitinous composition, are un-hinged and are held in place around the body of the animal by a complex series of muscles. The articulate brachiopods are distinguished by the development of a distinct *hinge line* along which the calcareous valves open and close. This is situated immediately below the curved *umbones* forming prominent apices at the posterior margin. The opposite anterior margins are usually gently rounded. External ornamentation may be parallel to the shell margins as a series of *growth lines* or coarser concentric *rugae* and also occurs as *ribs* radiating from the umbonal areas. *Spines*, or more commonly their points of attach-ment, may be seen on many forms. In some genera a prominent longitudinal depression, the *sulcus*, occurs on the pedicle valve.

Various genera have been described from the Upper Carboniferous marine bands, a few of which are briefly described below.

'*Chonetes*' (Sil.—Perm, Fig. 14.2a). Articulate brachiopods. Concavo-convex semicircular shells

often with a prominent sulcus. Hinge line straight and forming the greatest width of the shell. Radial ornament prominent. Spines developed along the hinge lines. Forms generally small in size. (Rams-bottom, 1952, p. 11–16.)

'*Productus*' (Dev.—Perm., Fig. 14.2b). Articulate brachiopods. Plano- or concavo-convex shells. Valves may be anteriorly extended as a long *trail* with little separation between the two. Pedicle valve strongly curved and often possessing a prominant sulcus. Hinge line straight and sometimes considerably extended. Radial and concentric ornament promin-ent and therefore having a net-like or *reticulate* character. Spine bases numerous. Considerable variation in size. (Muir Wood & Cooper, 1960.)

Lingula (Ord?, Sil.—Recent, Fig. 14.2c). Inar-ticulate brachiopods. Flattish but just biconvex shells. Almost equivalve. Width about half the length. Thin chitinous shells with shiny and usually dark surfaces. Extremely fine concentric growth lines developed. Carboniferous forms are mostly small and less than about 10 mm in length. Their shape and lustrous appearance is most characteristic. May occur with other marine fossils but often exclusively as '*Lingula*-bands' (page 214).

Orbiculoidea (Camb.—Tert., Fig. 14.2d). Inarticu-late brachiopods. Convexi-plane circular shells. The circular outline and conical cross-sectional appear-ance of the brachial valve is most characteristic. Chitinous and lustrous shells with fine almost cir-cular growth lines. (A well illustrated account with a comprehensive bibliography of the Carboniferous inarticulate brachiopods is that of Vangerow, 1959, pp. 36–60.)

Corals

The animal secretes a cylindrical or conical outer calcareous structure, the *corallite*, which encloses a number of important skeletal elements best seen in a horizontal section (Fig. 14.3). The *septa* form a series of vertical plates having an approximately radial arrangement around the axial area, which in some

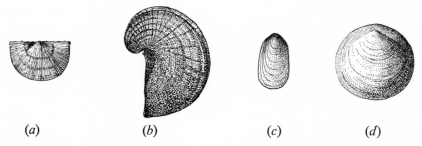

(a)   (b)   (c)   (d)

Fig. 14.2   Carboniferous brachiopods: (a) *Chonetes* ($\times 3$), (b) '*Productus*' ($\times \frac{1}{2}$), (c) *Lingula* ($\times 2$), (d) *Orbiculoidea* ($\times 2$).

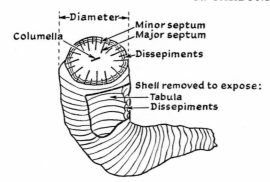

Fig. 14.3 Structural features of a simple coral.

genera contains a solid *central columella*. According to their length alternating *major* and *minor* septa may be distinguished in many forms. A *fossula* occurs where certain major septa are less prominent and shorter. *Dissepiments*, which are masses of spongy material, may sometimes form the peripheral parts of the corallite. In longitudinal section a series of floor-like partitions or *tabulae* are revealed extending across the corallite. The external surface is often irregularly wrinkled and may sometimes be coarsely fluted. Isolated *simple* corals are distinguished from *compound* forms which formed colonies.

Corals are rare in the British Upper Carboniferous but are locally plentiful in certain marine bands.

Caninia (Carb., Fig. 14.4a). Simple and often long cylindrical corals. The major septa are relatively short, often dilated, and confined to the peripheral areas. Tabulae slightly convex and bordered by a narrow zone of dissepiments. Columella absent. (Smith, 1931, pp. 6–7.)

'*Zaphrentis*' (Dev.—Carb., Fig. 14.4b). Simple, usually conical and often curved corals which there-

fore resemble miniature Saxon drinking-horns. Walls of the corallite thick. A well marked fossula imparts a bilateral septal symmetry. The major septa are relatively long and often extend to the axial area where they may appear united. Minor septa short and not always present. The tabulae are noticeably convex. Dissepiments and columella absent. (Smith, 1931, pp. 3–6.)

Goniatites

Possessing planospiral coiled external shells, the animals only inhabited a part of the outermost whorl (Fig. 14.5). The inner whorls contained a series of gas chambers termed *camerae* and sealed by *septa*, giving the animal a natural buoyancy. At the junction between a septum and the shell wall the septal *suture*, seen only on breaking back the outer whorl, is of particular importance in classification. The goniatitic suture is of essentially crenulate shape having a series of rounded *saddles* and rather angular *lobes* which are respectively convex and concave towards the aperture.

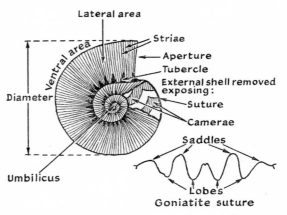

Fig. 14.5 Structural features of a goniatite.

Usually the whorls are tightly coiled so that the outer ones, partly in *involute* forms, or completely in *convolute* forms, conceal the inner whorls surrounding the *umbilicus*. On a whorl the peripheral *ventral* area may be distinguished from the *lateral* and *umbilical* areas. Goniatites possessing broad ventral areas have a globular appearance in cross-section as distinct from compressed or lenticular forms. The surface ornamentation is varied and may be an important generic or specific character. Delicate hair-like transverse *striae* often extend across the lateral and ventral surfaces. Upon the latter the striae are concave towards the aperture and on the lateral areas may swing forward from the umbilicus to form a prominent *lingua*. In some species spiral

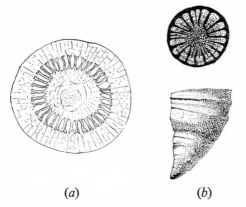

(a)   (b)

Fig. 14.4 Carboniferous corals: (a) *Caninia* (×1), (b) '*Zaphrentis*' (×2).

striae are also developed thereby forming a reticulate ornament. *Tubercles* or more extensive *ribs* may occur on particular parts of the whorls. Internal molds sometimes exhibit a series of transverse constrictions termed *varices* which are formed by localized thickenings of the shell probably deposited at the apertural margin during a pause in the growth of the animal.

Owing to their buoyancy the goniatites were floating animals and so had a widespread distribution in the Carboniferous seas. They are therefore perhaps the most important marine fossils in the Upper Carboniferous and are extensively used for both correlation and zoning. Many occur in marine shales as crushed impressions in which their surface ornamentation is often sufficiently well preserved to aid in specific recognition. The rarer solid specimens are derived from bullions and thin marine limestones.

Anthracoceras (U. Carb., typically Middle Coal Measures, Fig. 14.6a). Involute compressed shells

forms by their lesser degree of coiling. The nautiloid septum is usually a simple concavo-convex partition so that unfolded or only gently folded septal sutures are developed. All gradations exist between tapering straight forms to planospiral coils in which the whorls may be separate, only just touching (*advolute*) or developed as involute or convolute forms. Longitudinal ribs, tubercles or transverse striae form the common types of external ornamentation.

Sometimes occurring together with the goniatites, with which they may be at first sight confused, the nautiloids are of lesser importance owing to their more restricted distribution.

Cyclonautilus (U. Carb.). Planospiral highly involute forms. Whorls rounded in cross-section. Umbilicus deep and narrow. Septal sutures sinuous. External ornament of close-set fine sinuous transverse striae and occasionally also spiral striae. (Bisat, 1930, pp. 85–6, Hind, 1910, pp. 101–2.)

Ephippioceras (Carb., Fig. 14.7a). Planospiral

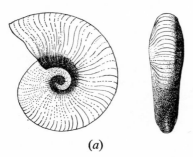 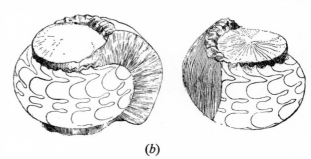

(a)   (b)

Fig. 14.6   Carboniferous goniatites: (a) *Anthracoceras* (×1) (×1), (b) *Gastrioceras* with the outer whorl removed (×½) (×½).

with narrow ventral areas. Umbilical area usually small. External ornament of very delicate transverse striae with marked linguae. Strong grooves are often present on internal surfaces and follow the general outline of the striae. (Bisat, 1930. pp. 77–9.)

Gastrioceras (U. Carb., typically Lower Coal Measures, Fig. 14.6b). Involute globular shells with broad ventral areas. Umbilical area wide. Prominent tubercles developed around the umbilical margins. Fine transverse and sometimes spiral striae developed. Occasionally very large specimens over 100 mm in diameter. (Bisat, 1926, pp. 119–22, Chalmers, 1936, pp. 153–62—a good description of *G. listeri*, but some of the other 'species' described are suspect.)

Nautiloids

The nautiloids are related to the goniatites, from which they may be distinguished by their relatively simple septal sutures and furthermore in some

highly involute forms. Distinguished from *Cyclonuatilus* by the development of a prominent saddle on the septal sutures. Surface typically smooth in most forms. (Hind, 1910, pp. 104–6.)

Metacoceras (U. Carb., Fig. 14.7b). Planospiral involute forms. Ventral area of whorls flattened. Umbilicus wide. Whorls strongly ribbed or tuberclate. In the latter case tubercles may be grouped on the umbilical and/or ventral borders. (Bisat, 1930, pp. 82–5.)

'*Orthoceras*' (Fig. 12.7c). Straight-shelled cylindrical forms usually with circular cross-sections Straight septal sutures. Surface ornament restricted to fine often sinuous striae. Several distinct genera now distinguished. (Miller, *et al.* 1933, pp. 77–111.)

Lamellibranchs

Having external biconvex skeletons composed of two calcareous valves, which except in a few genera are both of the same shape and size, the present-day

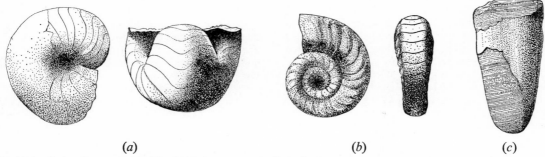

(a)   (b)   (c)

Fig. 14.7 Carboniferous nautiloids: (a) *Ephippioceras* ($\times \frac{1}{2}$) ($\times \frac{1}{2}$), (b) *Metacoceras* ($\times \frac{1}{2}$) ($\times \frac{1}{2}$), (c) '*Orthoceras*' ($\times \frac{1}{2}$).

lamellibranchs include the oysters and mussels. The valves, situated at the sides of the animal, articulate along a hinge line forming the dorsal margin (Fig. 14.8). Projecting above the hinge the *umbones* form the apical parts of the valves and commonly are inclined towards the anterior margins. Most valves are inequilateral since the umbones are rarely positioned above the centre of the hinge. Also the long

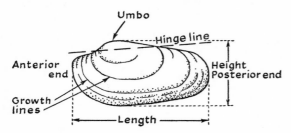

Fig. 14.8 Structural features of a lamellibranch.

axis of the lamellibranch valve is seldom at right angles to the hinge line so that most forms are oblique. In some lamellibranchs the hinge line is considerably extended as prominent *ears* which are often depressed below the level of the adjacent shell surface and are further delimited by notches in the shell margin. External ornamentation may occur as *growth lines* and coarser *wrinkles*, not always parallel

to the shell margins, *radii* extending from the umbonal areas, and in some forms *spines* and *nodes*.

Both marine and non-marine lamellibranchs occur in the Carboniferous. The former, abundant in many of the coalfield marine bands, sometimes occur in thin layers as the sole macrofossils.

Caneyella (U. Carb., Fig. 14.9a). Highly inequilateral oblique shells with relatively long straight hinge lines. Umbones not quite terminal. Surface ornamentation composed of numerous concentric wrinkles. Includes some of the species formerly described as *Posidoniella*. (Jackson, 1927, pp. 116–20.)

Dunbarella (U. Carb., Fig. 14.9b). Slightly inequilateral oblique shells with long straight hinge lines. Ears developed. Umbones small and slightly convex. Valve surfaces covered with numerous coarse radii which increase towards the ventral margin. Growth lines closely spaced and mostly fine although periodically accentuated. A pustulose ornament is developed in some species. A highly characteristic marine form originally described as *Pterinopecten*. (Jackson, 1927, pp. 96–111.)

Edmondia (Carb., Fig. 14.9c). Oblique, oval or elongated thick-shelled forms with short hinge lines. Umbones pronounced and about one third of the distance along the hinge line. Valve surfaces with strong concentric ridges and finer striae. (Hind, 1900 pp. 285–333.)

Myalina (Sil.—Perm.). Highly oblique, triangular,

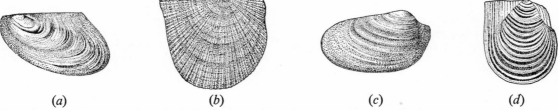

(a)   (b)   (c)   (d)

Fig. 14.9 Carboniferous marine lamellibranchs: (a) *Caneyella* ($\times 1$), (b) *Dunbarella* ($\times \frac{1}{2}$), (c) *Edmondia* ($\times \frac{1}{2}$), (d) *Poisdonia* ($\times 2$).

thick-shelled forms with long straight hinge lines. Terminal umbones at the anterior extremities. Valve surfaces ornamented by growth lines intersecting the dorsal margin at high angles. Easily confused with the non-marine lamellibranch *Naiadites*. (Hind, 1900, pp. 103–25).

Posidonia (U. Carb., Fig. 14.9d.). Inequilateral oblique forms with short straight hinge lines. Umbones situated about one third of the distance along the hinge line. Well developed ears. Surface ornament of concentric growth lines with a few conspicuous wrinkles. Formerly termed *Posidonomya* (Jackson, 1927, pp. 111–16.)

Microfossils

These minute fossils, in most cases apparent only on microscopic examination of their associated sediments, are becoming increasingly utilized for stratigraphic and correlative studies. Since they are so small the various microfossils may be obtained as complete specimens from well-cuttings whereas the larger fossils are usually fragmented, rendering even generic recognition impossible, by uncored boring procedures. Various highly specialized techniques of collection, preparation and study have been developed (Jones, 1956, pp. 7–18; Pokorny, 1963, pp. 5–36). Up to the present the marine microfossils

mum dimensions most commonly less than about 3 mm, the chitinous *carapaces* (Fig. 14.10b) are moulted several times during the life of the animal. Considerable variations exist in the types of external ornamentation, and the carapaces may be ridged, nodular, smooth or spinose. The female of the species may sometimes be distinguished by the possession of brood pouches on the carapace.

Conodonts are small tooth-like fossils less than 2 mm in maximum dimension. There is considerable uncertainty concerning their zoological affinities, for the conodonts are confined entirely to the Palaeozoic and lowest Mesozoic rocks after which time they become extinct. They form, however, excellent index fossils in many formations.

Other fossils

Other fossils occurring in the interseam marine horizons include gasteropods, trilobites, crinoids, worm borings (notably *Planolites*) and fish remains. The first-named are chiefly conispiral forms having a coiling similar to that of the common snail. Some are however almost planospiral and may therefore be mistaken at first sight for the much more important goniatites. The crinoids were fixed to the sea floor by long segmented stems and it is the latter, or isolated segments of them, which are sometimes found in

(*a*)   (*b*)

Fig. 14.10   Carboniferous microfossils: (*a*) Foraminifera (×25) (×55) (×25), (*b*) Ostracods (×22) (×22).

which have been most frequently described from their interseam strata are the foraminifera, ostracods and conodonts.

Foraminifera comprise some of the simplest members of the animal kingdom and are mostly small forms with maximum dimensions of usually less than 1 mm. The animal inhabits a chambered shell (Fig. 14.10a) of chitin, calcite or cemented arenaceous particles. The shells may be uncoiled or coiled. In the latter case, they occur as simple planospirals or more complex conical forms.

Ostracods are small bivalve crustaceans inhabiting both marine and non-marine waters. Having maxi-

some marine bands. By Upper Carboniferous times the trilobites were nearing extinction and only occasionally specimens occur.

Marine and fresh-water fish remains are common Upper Carboniferous fossils although the complete, or even partially complete specimens are extremely rare. They are most commonly found as isolated and often almost microscopic lustrous black scales, teeth and spines. Some of the more prolific horizons are the immediate shale roofs or upper canneloid parts of the coal seams. Seams such as the Better Bed of Yorkshire and Low Main of Northumberland have long been famous for their associated fish beds.

NON-MARINE FAUNA

The majority of the faunas associated with inter-seam strata are of the non-marine type. As such they are common throughout the succession occurring both as isolated individuals and in highly fossiliferous bands of sometimes considerable lateral extent and many feet in thickness. Undoubtedly the most important forms are the non-marine lamellibranchs.

Lamellibranchs

The non-marine lamellibranchs or 'mussels' are extensively utilized as zonal indices and in precise correlative studies (pages 214–5). Considerable variations in shape, size and internal structures resulting from evolutionary and environmental effects are often apparent in the shells occurring in a particular sequence. Many such variations, displayed in a continuous series around a central norm as illustrated in the *pictograph* (Fig. 14.11), have formed the subject of much detailed study in recent years (e.g. Eagar, 1953, pp. 148–73). Since the general morphological characters of the lamellibranchs have previously been described (page 163), attention will be confined to the characters of the major non-marine genera. Prior to the publication of the comprehensive monograph describing and illustrating the many different species (Trueman & Weir, 1946–56, pp. 1–272, Weir, 1960, pp. 273–320) only three genera were recognized; these are now further subdivided (Table 30) so that earlier stratigraphic accounts require some emendation.

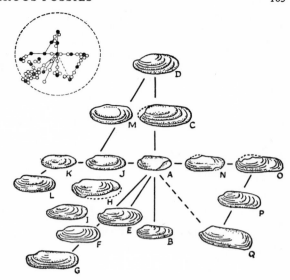

Fig. 14.11 Pictograph or variation diagram of non-marine lamellibranchs from the shell bed above the Six Inch Seam of Darwen Hill, Lancashire. (Eagar, 1952, *Liverpool and Manchester Geological Journal*, **1**, Plate XII, Fig. 2.)

Carbonicola (Fig. 14.12a). Oval or elongated, tumid and slightly oblique forms. Umbones prominent, raised above and occurring about one-third of the way along the curved hinge line. Growth lines

TABLE 30

The Classification and Stratigraphical Range of the Interseam Non-marine Lamellibranch Genera
(After Trueman & Weir, 1946, pp. XIV–XV, Fig. V, with emendation based on Weir, 1960, pp. 298–302)

Former genera	Present genera	Non-marine lamellibranch zones							
		Lenisulcata	*Communis*	*Modiolaris*	*L. Similis-Pulchra*	*U. Similis-Pulchra*	*Phillipsii*	*Tenuis*	*Prolifera*
Carbonicola	*Carbonicola*		———	———						
	Anthracosia			⊢———	———	⊣			
	Anthracosphaerium		⊢—	———	⊣				
Anthracomya	*Anthraconaia*								
	Anthraconauta						⊢———	———	⊣
	Curvirimula		————	- - - - -	- - - -	—⊣			
Naiadites	*Naiadites*						⊢		

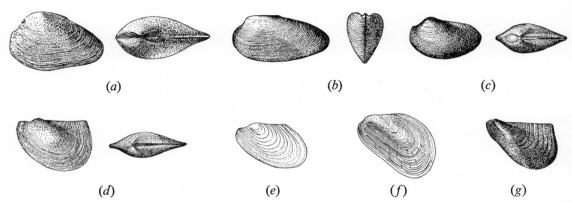

Fig. 14.12 Carboniferous non-marine lamellibranchs: (a) *Carbonicola* ($\times\frac{1}{2}$) ($\times\frac{1}{2}$), (b) *Anthracosia* ($\times\frac{1}{2}$) ($\times\frac{1}{2}$), (c) *Anthracosphaerium* ($\times\frac{1}{2}$) ($\times\frac{1}{2}$), (d) *Anthraconaia* ($\times$1) ($\times$1), (e) *Anthraconauta* ($\times$1), (f) *Curvirimula* ($\times$3), (g) *Naiadites* ($\times$1).

parallel to the ventral border and tangential to the dorsal margin. (Trueman, 1954, p. 63.)

Anthracosia (Fig. 14.12b). Elongated, compressed and slightly oblique forms. Umbones less prominent than in *Carbonicola* and do not project above the curved hinge line. Early growth lines not parallel to the ventral border. (Trueman, 1954, pp. 63–4.)

Anthracosphaerium (Fig. 14.12c). Small highly tumid and slightly oblique forms. Considerably shorter than *Carbonicola* and *Anthracosia* and seldom exceeding 1 in in length. The swollen umbones are more prominent and are raised considerably above the curved hinge line. (Trueman, 1954, pp. 65–6.)

Anthraconaia (Fig. 14.12d). Elongated and markedly oblique forms. Long straight hinge line with umbones less prominent than in the previous genera. Growth lines intersect the dorsal margin at obtuse angles. (Trueman, 1954, pp. 66–7.)

Anthraconauta (Fig. 14.12e). Highly oblique forms. Small umbones occurring at about one-fifth of the distance along the straight hinge line. Growth lines intersect dorsal margin at obtuse angles. Irregular wrinkles often developed on the shell surface. (Trueman, 1954, p. 67.)

Curvirimula (Fig. 14.12f). Oblique to semicircular small shells. Small umbones occurring at about one-fifth of the distance along the hinge line. Growth lines delicate. Curved sub-radial cracks are often developed, in which case the genus may be readily distinguished from *Anthraconauta*. (Weir, 1960, pp. 297–301.)

Naiadites (Fig. 14.12g). Highly oblique forms. Small umbones more or less terminal. Growth lines almost at right angles to the dorsal margin. The posterior margin often has a prominent embayment.

Other fossils

Apart from fish remains the remaining non-marine faunas are composed chiefly of several members of the arthropod phylum of which the present-day forms include the insects, spiders, scorpions, shrimps and lobsters. Many of the Carboniferous genera, because of their sporadic occurrence and comparative rarity, are of little use in correlative studies.

Non-marine *ostracods* (Pollard, 1966) may be abundant at specific horizons although as yet they have been little used for correlation. The *branchiopods*, represented by the modern water-fleas, may at first be mistaken for ostracods or even small lamellibranchs, since their fossilized parts consist of two thin chitinous valves up to about 5 mm in maximum dimension. Sub-concentric ridges resembling growth lines are sometimes developed. The two shells are however not united along a hinge line. Their major habitat appears to have been in fresh- or brackish-water conditions although their occurrence in some marine bands indicates their adaptive nature. Of the several Carboniferous genera, *Euestheria* (Fig. 14.13a), formerly incorrectly termed '*Estheria*' (Edwards & Stubblefield, 1947, pp. 243–4), of ap-

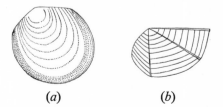

Fig. 14.13 Carboniferous brachiopods: (a) *Euestheria* ($\times$7), (b) *Leaia* ($\times$6).

Fig. 14.14   *Belinurus*, a Carboniferous arthropod (×2).

proximately circular shape and with a concentric ornament, is common at certain horizons, notably the Low and Main '*Estheria*' Beds of the Yorkshire, and the Lowton '*Estheria*' Bed of the Lancashire coalfields. Another form, *Leaia* (Fig. 14.13b) may be easily distinguished by the well developed radial ridges present on the external surface.

Insect remains, occasionally abundant in the inter-seam shales, are usually associated with plant debris. Usually only the wings, often several inches in length and possessing a delicate venation, are the only parts preserved. The blattoids or cockroaches are the most common Upper Carboniferous forms and some attempt has been made to utilize their occurrence for the correlation of the upper Westphalian (Bolton, 1930, pp. 9–48).

Other arthropod remains are notable only on account of their rarity. One particular group, represented by several genera including *Euproops* and *Belinurus* (Fig. 14.14), with wide segmented bodies and long spine-like tails, may be easily mistaken for

trilobites. The eurypterids or water-scorpions, up to several feet in length, are the rarest of all the Carboniferous arthropods although several species have been described from British localities (Moore, 1936, pp. 352–75).

Other non-marine fossils include the spirally coiled calcareous tubes secreted by the worm, *Spirorbis*. The coils are about 5 mm across and are sometimes attached to fossil plants and shells. At some horizons in the Upper Coal Measures the remains are so abundant as to form thin 'Spirorbis limestones' (page 63).

FOSSIL FLORA

Plant remains form the most abundant Upper Carboniferous fossils, occurring as fragmentary and disarticulated debris. In the following account a simple descriptive classification sufficient to determine the more common plant genera is employed.

Lycopods

The lycopods constituted a major element of the Carboniferous forests and contributed greatly to the formation of the coals. Forming the largest plants of the period, some exceeded 100 ft in height. Their simple foliage consisted of long narrow leaves forming a dense covering to the branches and stems. Reproduction was by spores (described separately) developed within cylindrical or ovoid cones. The root-like appendages are the most numerous of all the large plant fossils and in some cases, as for instance in the much-illustrated 'Fossil Grove', preserved in Kelvin Park, Glasgow, occur *in situ* spreading out from the lycopod trunks. The major genera are distinguished by the surface ornamentation of the trunks and branches.

Lepidodendron (Fig. 14.15a). Long tapering trunks,

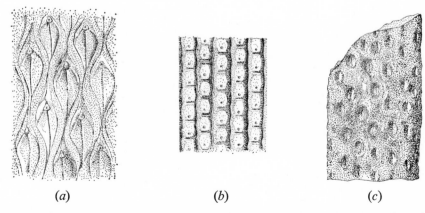

| (a) | (b) | (c) |

Fig. 14.15 Carboniferous plants—Lycopods: (*a*) *Lepidodendron* (×½), (*b*) *Sigillaria* (×½), (*c*) *Stigmaria* (×½).

unbranched in the lower parts. Characterized by the diamond-shaped leaf cushions having in each centre a rhombic leaf scar at the actual point of attachment of the leaves. The longest axes of the leaf cushions are vertical to the trunk. Upon the related and rarer genus *Lepidophloios* the longer axes of the leaf cushions are horizontal.

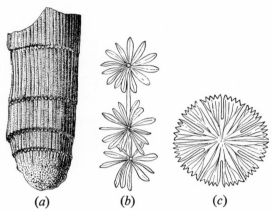

Fig. 14.16 Carboniferous jointed plants: (*a*) *Calamites* ($\times\frac{1}{2}$), (*b*) *Annularia* ($\times$1), (*c*) *Sphenophyllum* ($\times$1).

Sigillaria (Fig. 14.15b). In some species the trunks were short and thick, in others they attain a similar size to *Lepidodendron*. Bark either smooth (*Sub-Sigillaria*) or more commonly longitudinally ribbed (*Eu-Sigillaria*). Leaf cushions only rarely developed. Leaf scars arranged in vertical alternating rows and with hexagonal or more rounded outlines.

Lepidistrobus. A common fructification belonging to *Lepidodendron*, *Lepidophloios* and possibly some species of *Sigillaria*. Cylindrical cones averaging about 10 cm in length and 1·5 cm in diameter. In transverse sections the radially developed internal structures may sometimes be mistaken for the skeletal elements of a coral.

Stigmaria (Fig. 14.15c). The abundant 'roots' of the Lycopods. Smooth or wrinkled surface with small, circular, irregularly-spaced pits forming the former place of attachment of the minor lateral 'rootlets'. The latter may sometimes be seen still attached in Stigmarian specimens preserved *in situ*. The small pits forming the sole external ornament and arranged in an irregular spiral around the 'root' axis cannot be confused with the regular leaf cushions and scars of the trunks.

Jointed plants

The group are characterized by the jointed and longitudinally ribbed nature of the stems. Most often the leaves, which are born in circlets around the joints, are small in relation to the size of the stem.

Attaining heights of over 50 ft and very common as Upper Carboniferous fossils, they were the giant ancestors of the diminutive 'horse-tails' which grow at the present time in damp ground. Reproduction was by spores contained within cones.

Calamites (Fig. 14.16a). A widespread genus in which the longitudinal ribs alternate at the often constricted joints. Approximately circular leaf scars may sometimes be identified above the joints on well preserved specimens. Common as circular casts, a few inches in diameter, which may taper and curve towards their points of attachment. In the Lower Carboniferous *Asterocalamites* the longitudinal ribs are continuous across and so do not alternate at the joints.

Annularia (Fig. 14.16b). The leaf whorls of *Calamites*. Usually they occur as compressions so that the leaves and thin stems are in the same plane. The leaf bases appear to be fused and form a collar around the stem. Each leaf contains a single vein.

Sphenophyllum (Fig. 14.16c). Relatively small, jointed and longitudinally ribbed stems which seldom exceed about 1 cm in diameter. Probably many were climbing plants. The wedge-shaped leaves may be distinguished from *Annularia* by their occurrence in multiples of three, their non-fused nature and the branching venation.

Long narrow leaves

Only one Carboniferous genus of any importance is included within the group, which consisted of tall slender trees sometimes over 100 ft tall. The branches were confined to the upper parts from which a reed-like foliage was developed. The trees were seed-bearing and may have been related to the conifers.

Cordaites. Long, slender, reed- or grass-like leaves less than about 15 cm in width and sometimes exceeding 1 m in length. Owing to their great length they are seldom found complete. Numerous close-set veins, some more prominent than others, and parallel to the leaf margin.

Fern-like plants

Although superficially similar to ferns, many of the Carboniferous fern-like plants reproduced by seeds, whereas the true ferns carry spores. Consequently although the period is popularly regarded as 'the age of ferns' the term is somewhat of a misnomer for the true ferns are comparatively rare. The many plants contained in the group varied in size from small plants and climbers to the majestic 'tree-ferns' attaining heights of over 20 m and with stems sometimes exceeding 60 cm in diameter. As in the true ferns, the leaves or *fronds* are compound, being composed of rows of leaflets. The various genera may be distinguished by the leaflet shape and the nature of its venation.

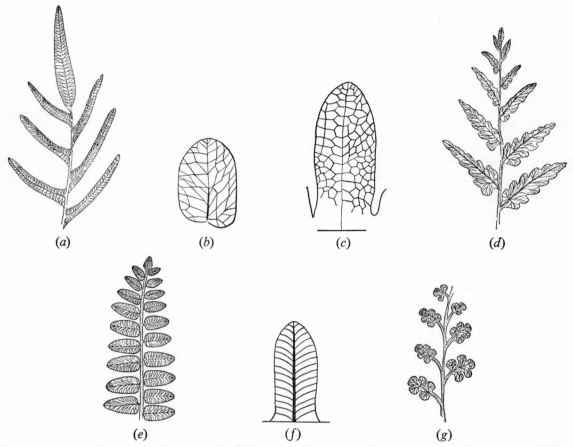

Fig. 14.17 Carboniferous fern-like plants: (*a*) *Alethopteris* (×1), (*b*) *Linopteris* (×3), (*c*) *Lonchopteris* (×2), (*d*) *Mari-opteris* (×1), (*e*) *Neuropteris* (×2), (*f*) *Pecopteris* (×5), (*g*) *Sphenopteris* (×¾).

Alethopteris (Fig. 14.17a). Large leaflets with rounded or pointed apices and almost parallel margins. Attached to the stalk along a broad base. Numerous lateral veinlets departing from a prominent medial vein at a high angle and sometimes forking several times.

Linopteris (Fig. 14.17b). Elongate-oval leaflets. Attached to the stalk at a single point. Lateral veinlets form a lace-like network. Characteristic of the Phillipsii zone.

Lonchopteris (Fig. 14.17c). Shape of leaflets similar to *Alethopteris*. The lateral veinlets however form a lace-like network. Characteristic of the lower Similis-Pulchra zone.

Mariopteris (Fig. 14.17d). Leaflets often lobed and so roughly resembling oak leaves in shape. Base of attachment commonly constricted although sometimes broad, in which case the basal parts of the individual leaflets may be in contact. Lateral veinlets

depart from a prominent medial vein at an acute angle and fork once or twice.

Neuropteris (Fig. 14.17e). Elongate-oval leaflets attached to the stalk at a single point. Medial vein forks and does not reach the apex. Lateral veinlets arched and forked. Distinguished by venation from *Linopteris*.

Pecopteris (Fig. 14.17f). Short leaflets with almost parallel margins. Base of attachment broad. The few lateral veinlets are almost at right angles to the medial vein.

Sphenopteris (Fig. 14.17g). Small and often lobed leaflets. Veins tend to radiate from the base of the leaflet.

Triganocarpus. Ovoid seeds of *Alethopteris* most often occurring as sandstone casts. Sometimes over 4 cm in length. Three longitudinal ridges are frequently present.

In a text book of this type it is neither practicable

nor necessary to include complete generic descriptions of the fossil plants. Since they are the fossils most likely to be noticed during routine colliery work it may be that more comprehensive descriptions are required by the collector. In this respect he is referred to the well illustrated account of Crookall (1929) or the more comprehensive monographs on the subject (Kidston, 1925; Crookall, 1959).

Plant spores

An important aspect of micropalaeontology is concerned with the study of plant spores contained both within the coals themselves and also in the interseam sediments. Many of the Carboniferous plants reproduced by spores, of which two major types, *miospores* (including *microspores* and *isospores*) with maximum dimensions less than about 0·2 mm, and *megaspores* which are larger forms, are recognized. The latter may be clearly seen in thin or polished coal sections as bright orange or yellow elongated compressed masses. Miospores cannot be so easily examined and have to be separated by oxidation techniques from the associated sediment or coal. In most early accounts the various spore types were identified by a code of letters and numbers which were considered suitable to express an arbitrary classification which did not imply any definite affinity between the various types (Raistrick & Simpson, 1933, pp. 226–8). Recently a binominal classification more in accordance with standard palaeontological nomenclature has been adopted. For example, spores originally named C1–C4 are regarded as belonging to the genus *Endosporites*. As with other palaeobotanical studies a degree of uncertainty exists as to the exact affinities between certain spore types. Indeed some have been shown to be merely young forms of an apparently distinct adult spore (Moore, 1946, pp. 281–8). Even so, much evidence has been accumulated in recent years about the types of spores derived from particular plant types (e.g. Smith, 1962, Table 6).

Spores are classified according to their shape, symmetry, size, internal structure and surface ornamentation. Uncompressed spores are often spherical or oval in shape and consist of two major

layers, an outer *exine* surrounding the *intine* (Fig. 14.18). The relative dimensions of the layers are important and indeed two coal types, *crassi-* and *tenui-durain*, are recognized by the predominance of miospores with relatively thick and thin exines respectively. The outer surfaces of the exines are commonly spinose, ridged, granular, nodose or pitted. Many exines separate into several layers, thereby forming bladders which in the living form may have been filled with air, so enabling the free dispersion of the spores. In many spores intines are divided by sutures forming two or three approximately equal parts in the *monolete* and *trilete* forms. *Alete* forms are those in which no suture is developed.

As it is unlikely that many students will have the opportunity to carry out practical studies of the Carboniferous spores owing to the specialized techniques involved it is not considered pertinent to include a description of the major genera. Some of the more accessible works in which these forms are illustrated and described include those of Balme (1952) and Neves (1958, pp. 4–12).

PRACTICAL WORK

Only by the examination of actual specimens in the laboratory or museum can the student acquire sufficient experience to recognize the type and therefore grasp the significance of any fossils he may discover in mining. Consequently whenever possible a limited amount of practical work should be carried out on the major types of Carboniferous fossils. It is suggested that such work should follow the following procedure:

(1) A sketch or sketches should be made of the particular fossil studied. This need not be an artistic triumph—a simple line diagram is sufficient. The approximate degree of enlargement or reduction should be given.

(2) The generic name, geological horizon and locality from which the specimen was collected should be noted.

(3) This should be followed by a short description, along the lines of the brief generic descriptions given, of the main features of the fossil together with measurements appropriate to the fossil type.

(4) Finally, the student should ascertain the stratigraphic range of the fossil.

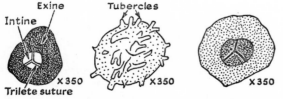

Fig. 14.18   Some Carboniferous miospores.

REFERENCES

ARNOLD, C. A. (1947) *An Introduction to Paleobotany*, 1st ed., London, McGraw-Hill.
BALME, B. E. (1952) On some spore specimens from British Upper Carboniferous coals, *Geol. Mag.* **89**, 175–84.
BISAT, W. S. (1926) The Carboniferous goniatites of the north of England and their zones, *Proc. Yorks. geol. Soc.* **20**, 40–124.
BISAT, W. S. (1930) On the goniatite and nautiloid fauna

of the Middle Coal Measures of England and Wales, *Mem. geol. Surv. Summ. Prog. G.B. for* 1929, **3**, 75–89.

BOLTON, H. (1930) On the fossil insects of the South Wales coalfield, *Q. Jl geol. Soc. Lond.* **86**, 9–48.

CHALMERS, R. M. (1936) The genus *Gastrioceras* occurring in the Lower Coal Measures of the Lancashire coalfield, *J. Manchr geol. Ass.* **1**, 147–66.

CROOKALL, R. (1929) *Coal Measure Plants*, 1st ed., London, Arnold.

CROOKALL, R. (1959) Fossil Plants of the Carboniferous Rocks of Great Britain *Mem. geol. Surv. G.B. Palaeont.* **4**, Pt. 1.

DAVIES, A. M. & C. J. STUBBLEFIELD (1961) *An Introduction to Palaeontology*, 3rd ed., London, Allen & Unwin (Murby).

EAGAR, R. M. C. (1953) Relative growth in shells of the fossil family Anthracosiidiae in Upper Carboniferous times, *Proc. Linn. Soc. Lond.* **164**, 148–73.

EDWARDS, W. & C. J. STUBBLEFIELD (1947) Marine bands and other faunal marker horizons in relation to the sedimentary cycles of the Middle Coal Measures of Nottinghamshire and Derbyshire, *Q. Jl geol. Soc. Lond.* **103**, 209–40.

HÄNTZSCHEL, W. (1962) Trace Fossils and problematica, *Treatise on Invertebrate Palaeontology, Part W, Miscellanea, W.* 177–232. *Geol. Soc. Am. & Univ. Kansas Press.*

HIND, W. (1900) A monograph of the British Carboniferous lamellibranchiata, **1**, *Palaeontogr. Soc.* [*Monogr.*].

HIND, W. (1910) On four new Carboniferous nautiloids and a goniatite new to Great Britain, *Proc. Yorks. geol. Soc.* **17**, 97–109.

JACKSON, J. W. (1927) New Carboniferous lamellibranchs and notes on other forms, *Mem. Proc. Manchr lit. phil. Soc.* **71**, 93–122.

JONES, D. J. (1956) *Introduction to Microfossils*, 1st ed., New York, Harper.

KIDSTON, R. (1923–25) Fossil Plants of the Carboniferous Rocks of Great Britain, *Mem. geol. Surv. G.B. Palaeont.* **2**.

MILLER, A. K., DUNBAR, C. O. & G. E. CONDRA (1933) The nautiloid cephalopods of the Pennsylvanian system in the mid-continent region, *Bull. geol. Surv. Neb.* **9**, 1–240.

MOORE, L. R. (1936) Some eurypterids from the English Coal Measures, *Proc. Geol. Ass., Lond.* **47**, 352–75.

MOORE, L. R. (1946) On the spores of some Carboniferous plants, their development, *Q. Jl geol. Soc. Lond.* **102**, 251–89.

MOORE, R. C., LALICKER, C. G. & A. G. FISCHER (1952) *Invertebrate Fossils*, 1st ed., London, McGraw-Hill.

MUIR-WOOD, H. & G. A. COOPER (1960) Morphology, classification and life habits of the Productoidea (brachiopoda), *Mem. geol. Soc. Am.* **81**, 1–447.

NEVES, R. (1958) Upper Carboniferous plant spore assemblages from the *Gastrioceras subcrenatum* horizon, north Staffordshire, *Geol. Mag.* **95**, 1–19.

POKORNY, V. (1963) *Principles of Zoological Micropaleontology*, **1**, 1st English ed., London, Pergamon.

POLLARD, J. E. (1966) A non-marine ostracod fauna from the Coal Measures of Durham and Northumberland, *Palaeontology, Lond.* **9**, 667–97.

RAISTRICK, A. & J. SIMPSON (1933) The microspores of some Northumberland coals and their use in the correlation of coalseams, *Trans. Instn Min. Engrs* **85**, 225–33.

RAMSBOTTOM, W. H. C. (1952) The fauna of the Cefn Coed marine band in the Coal Measures at Aberbaiden, near Tondu, Glamorgan, *Bull geol. Surv. Gt Br.* **4**, 8–30.

SMITH, A. H. V. (1962) The palaeoecology of Carboniferous peats based on the miospores and petrography of bituminous coals, *Proc. Yorks. geol. Soc.* **33**, 423–70.

SMITH, S. (1931) Some upper Carboniferous corals from South Wales, *Mem. geol. Surv. Summ. Prog. G.B.* 1930. Pt. 3, 1–13.

TRUEMAN, A. E. & J. WEIR (1946–56) A monograph of British Carboniferous non-marine lamellibranchia, Parts I, II, III, IV, V, VI, VII, VIII, IX, pp. i–xxxii, 1–272, *Palaeontogr. Soc.* [*Monogr.*]

TRUEMAN, A. E. (1954) *The Coalfields of Great Britain*, 1st ed., London, Arnold.

VANGEROW, E. F. (1959) Die fauna des West deutschen obercarbons, *Palaeontographica* **113**, Abt. A. 36–60.

WEIR, J. (1960) A monograph of British Carboniferous non-marine lamellibranchia, Part X, pp. 273–320, *Palaeontogr. Soc.* [*Monogr.*]

15

BRITISH CARBONIFEROUS STRATIGRAPHY

Since many of the world's major coalfields are of Carboniferous age a knowledge of the system is of obvious importance to most readers. As in Chapter 12, the stratigraphical details will be discussed with reference to the British outcrops (Fig. 15.1) and details of other countries may be obtained from the appropriate references of Chapter 13 and the Appendix.

CLASSIFICATION

The system was originally defined by Coneybeare and Phillips in 1822 when the Old Red Sandstone was considered as the lowest division:

Coal Measures;
Carboniferous Limestone;
Old Red Sandstone.

In 1839 the Old Red Sandstone was correctly recognized as being a facies of the Devonian and so relegated to that system. In America two separate systems, the Mississippian and overlying Pennsylvanian, separated by an unconformity, are recognized and consequently when reading American stratigraphic literature the student should be aware of the approximate equivalence (Table 31) of the two systems with the Lower and Upper Carboniferous divisions of western European workers.

Since many of the early geologists concentrated their attention on the well exposed sequences in Northern England the lithological characters of the system in that area were taken as typical and the three well known Carboniferous divisions established:

Coal Measures. So called from the occurrence throughout Britain of workable coal seams in strata of that age.
Millstone Grit Series. Named after the coarse sandstones of the Pennines which were formerly extensively quarried for building material and grinding wheels.
Carboniferous Limestone Series. In most of England the Lower Carboniferous is predominantly made up of limestones.

Although the above terminology is logically applicable in some parts of Britain, it is clearly inappropriate for many localities. For example, the lowest Carboniferous of Scotland is largely composed of sandstones and shales and it is obviously confusing to describe these rocks as the 'Carboniferous Limestone Series'. Furthermore palaeontological work has recently shown that the beds so named in Scotland are largely of Upper Carboniferous age anyway. Similarly in the same country the sandstones of the 'Millstone Grit Series', recently significantly renamed the Passage Group (Macgregor, 1960, p. 129), are clearly not equivalent to members of that series in some other parts of Britain. The lithological terminology is less confusing in the case of the Coal Measures, for at least in Britain, the name is acceptable and therefore still commonly used since the bulk of the workable coal seams occur in that division. Even so the original classification into Lower, Middle and Upper Coal Measures was inconsistent in that the divisions were not always equivalent in every coalfield. Consequently these have recently been redefined according to the occurrence of three widespread marine horizons (Table 32) common to most of the coalfields (Stubblefield & Trotter, 1957, pp. 1–5). In Scotland however, owing to the apparent absence of two of the marine bands, the Lower, Middle and Upper Coal Measures are not exactly equivalent to those of the rest of Britain (Macgregor, 1960, pp. 128–30), (Table 31).

The use of stratal names, which can be given accurate palaeontological definitions and do not imply any particular lithological characters, is clearly an acceptable alternative to the confusion possible with the original nomenclature. Accordingly, at an international congress held in Holland in 1927, the major stratal series of the Carboniferous were defined and their use recommended in place of the local lithological names (a comprehensive review of the literature is that of Trueman, 1946, pp. xlix–lii):

Stephanian Series. Composed of the highest Carboniferous rocks, the series was subsequently shown to be ill-defined and there is doubt as to the utility of its retention as a stratigraphic division.
Westphalian Series. More or less equivalent to the Coal Measures, the series was divided according to the fossil floras (the ranges of the diagnostic plants

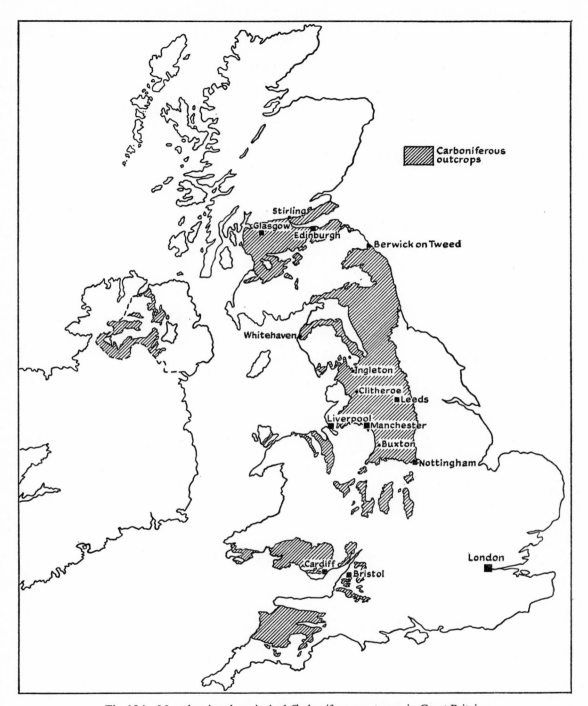

Fig. 15.1   Map showing the principal Carboniferous outcrops in Great Britain.

	USA systems	Major lithological divisions	Lithological sub-divisions					Major stratal series			Coral-brachiopod zones
			Scotland	Northumberland	Lancashire	South Wales	Devon				
UPPER CARBONIFEROUS / **PENNSYLVANIAN SYSTEM**		**COAL MEASURES**	Upper Coal Measures	Absent	Absent	Upper Coal Measures	No evidence of higher horizons	STEPHANIAN SERIES	E	MORGANIAN	
					Upper Coal Measures				D		
			Middle Coal Measures	Middle Coal Measures	Middle Coal Measures	Middle Coal Measures		WESTPHALIAN SERIES	C	AMMANIAN	
									B		
			Lower Coal Measures	Lower Coal Measures	Lower Coal Measures	Lower Coal Measures			A		
		MILLSTONE GRIT SERIES	Passage Group	'Millstone Grit Series'	Rough Rock Group	Shale Group	Upper Culm Measures	NAMURIAN SERIES	C		
					Middle Grit Group				B		
					Kinderscout Grit Group						
					Sabden Shales	Basal Grit			A		
			U. Limestone Gr.	Upper Limestone Group	U. Bowland Sh. & Pendle Grits						
			Limestone Coal Gr.								
LOWER CARBONIFEROUS / **MISSISSIPPIAN SYSTEM**		**CARBONIFEROUS LIMESTONE SERIES**	L. Limestone Gr.	Middle & Lower Limestone Groups	Middle & Lower Bowland Shales	Upper Limestone Shales	Lower Culm Measures	DINANTIAN SERIES (approximately equivalent to AVONIAN SERIES)	VISÉAN STAGE (UPPER AVONIAN)		*Dibunophyllum* Zone (D)
		Calciferous Sst. Measures: Oil Shale Group	Scremerston Coal Group	Pendleside Limestone						*Seminula* Zone (S_2)
				Worston Shales						
		Fell Sandstones			Main Limestone				Upper *Canini* Zone (C_2S_1)
		Cemenstone Group	Cemenstone Group	Chatburn Limestone Group				TOURNAISIAN STAGE (approximately equivalent to LOWER AVONIAN)		Lower *Canini* Zone (C_1)
		~?~	~?~	?						*Zaphrentis* Zone (Z)
					Lower Limestone Shales					*Cleistopora* Zone (K)

Goniatite stages	Non-marine lamellibranch zones	Floral stages	Floral zones	Miospore assemblages
	Prolifera Zone	RADSTOCKIAN STAGE	I	Assemblage of *Thymospora obscura* (XI)
arine faunas absent	Tenuis Zone		H	
	Phillipsii Zone	STAFFORDIAN STAGE	G	Assemblage of *Torispora securis* (X)
nthracoceras (A)	Upper Similis-Pulchra Zone	UPPER YORKIAN STAGE	F	Assemblage of *Vestispora magna* (IX)
	Lower Similis-Pulchra Zone		E	
				Assemblage of *Dictyotriletes bireticulatus* (VIII)
	Modiolaris Zone	LOWER YORKIAN STAGE	D	Assemblage of *Schulzospora rara* (VII)
pper *Gastrioceras* (G₂)	Communis Zone			Assemblage of *Radiizonates aligerens* (VI)
	Lenisulcata Zone		C	
:ODIAN (L. *Gastrioceras*) STAGE (G₁)		LANARKIAN STAGE		Assemblage of *Densosporites anulatus* (V)
ARSDENIAN (U. *Reticuloceras*) STAGE (R₂)			B	
NDERSCOUTIAN (L. *Reticuloceras*) STAGE (R₁)				
BDENIAN (= *Homoceras*) STAGE (H)				Assemblage of *Crassispora kosankei* (IV)
RNSBERGIAN (= *Eumorphoceras*) STAGE (E₂)			A	
ENDLEIAN (L. *Eumorphoceras*) STAGE (E₁)				Assemblage of *Rotaspora knoxi* (III)
PPER BOLLANDIAN (U. *Posidonia*) STAGE (P₂)				
OWER BOLLANDIAN (L. *Posidonia*) STAGE (P₁)				Assemblage of *Diatomozonotriletes saetosus* (II)
RACOEAN (*Beyrichoceras*) STAGE				Assemblage of *Grumosisporites verrucosus* (I)
				?

Floral zones I, H, G, F, E refer to Radstockian/Staffordian/Upper Yorkian; D refers to Lower Yorkian; C, B, A refer to Lanarkian stage.

in Britain are given in Crookall, 1955, pp. 3–5) into three zones, A, B and C. Two higher zones, Westphalian D and E, were subsequently defined, the latter as an alternative to the Stephanian. The Westphalian may be also separated into the *Morganian and Ammanian Stages* at a distinct break in the non-marine lamellibranch succession between the Upper Similis-Pulchra and Phillipsii Zones (Table 31). Corresponding to the Lower and Middle Coal Measures the upper limit of the Ammanian may be accurately defined in most coalfields as the highest Carboniferous marine band which is characterized by the goniatite *Anthracoceras cambriense.*

Namurian Series. Approximately equivalent to the Millstone Grit Series, the Namurian may be accurately defined by the utilization of the goniatite faunas.

Dinantian Series. Equated with the Lower Carboniferous, the Dinantian Series is divided into the *Viséan and Tournaisian Stages.* In Britain the series is sometimes termed the Avonian, although the two are not exactly equivalent (George, 1958, pp. 235–6).

Each series may be subdivided into a number of zones defined by the fossil content and so far the corals, brachiopods, goniatites, non-marine lamellibranchs, fossil plants and spores have been most extensively utilized:

Coral-brachiopod zones. Working in the Bristol area, Vaughan (1905, pp. 181–266) first established an acceptable zonal subdivision of the Dinantian based upon its coral-brachiopod content. The zonal names are derived from the genera of usually common members of the zones, which are nevertheless defined by particular fossil assemblages rather than by the occurrence of solitary 'index' fossils. Apart from the *Seminula Zone*, named after a brachiopod, the remaining zonal names are those of important coral genera, which, it should be noted, may range into higher zones. The coral-brachiopod faunas are most useful in those areas possessing a shelf facies. In others, where a relatively deeper-water basin facies prevailed, the goniatites have proved more reliable in zoning the Viséan.

Goniatite zones. The first successful stratigraphic utilization of the goniatites was that of Bisat (1926, pp. 40–52) who established a series of zones, relevant to the upper Viséan and the Namurian, and originally named after the dominant goniatite genera. Subsequently the scheme was extended to include the Ammanian (Bisat, 1930, pp. 75–7, Table A). Most of Bisat's original zones have since been redefined as stages (Hudson, 1945, pp. 1–9). Recently it has been proposed to erect two new stages, the Alportian (H_2) and Chokerian (H_1) in place of the Sabdenian (Hodson, 1957, pp. 6–7), and it is clear that finality has not yet been reached. The stages

themselves, characterized by a particular goniatite genus although named after a type-locality, are often indicated in the abbreviated form taken from the initial of the stage genus. Thus the Pendleian (Lower *Eumorphoceras*) Stage may also be termed E_1, and its three zones expressed as E_{1a} (lowest), E_{1b} and E_{1c} (highest).

Because of their rapid rates of evolution and their widespread distribution the goniatites have proved to be the most reliable means of subdividing the Namurian. In the Westphalian they occur at less frequent horizons and consequently can only be utilized as broad zonal indices. Nevertheless they are of considerable importance since they serve to define the marine bands taken as the boundaries of the Lower, Middle and Upper Coal Measures (Stubblefield & Trotter, 1957, pp. 2–3, Plate 1), (Table 32).

Non-marine lamellibranch zones. The non-marine lamellibranchs have so far proved to be the most useful fossils for the zoning of the British Coal Measures. Although some attempts were made in the late nineteenth century, it was not until the early 1920s that Trueman and several collaborators, by studying the progressive variations of large assemblages of non-marine lamellibranchs, established the basis of the present zones. Their original work (Davies & Trueman, 1927, pp. 210–57) was chiefly applied to the South Wales coalfield, where the following zones were identified:

Zone of *Anthraconauta tenuis*;
Zone of *Anthraconauta phillipsii*;
Zone of *Anthraconaia pulchra*;
Zone of *Anthracosia similis*;
Zone of *Anthraconaia modiolaris*;
Zone of *Carbonicola ovalis* (amended to the zone of *C. communis*).

Subsequently the zones were modified and those of *Anthraconaia lenisulcata* and *A. prolifera* added to the base and top respectively of the original sequence (Table 31). In stratigraphic accounts the generic names are omitted. In most cases the zonal boundaries are indefinite and some overlap of faunas occurs. At two horizons, coinciding with widespread marine bands occurring between the Lower and Upper Similis-Pulchra Zones, and between the latter and the succeeding Phillipsii Zone, there is a marked change in faunas (Table 30, Chapter 14) so that the zonal limits are more accurately defined.

Floral stages and zones. A major floral change occurs at about the base of the Sabdenian Stage. Above this mid-Carboniferous 'plant break' four floral stages have been designated as:

Radstockian;   Yorkian;
Staffordian;   Lanarkian.

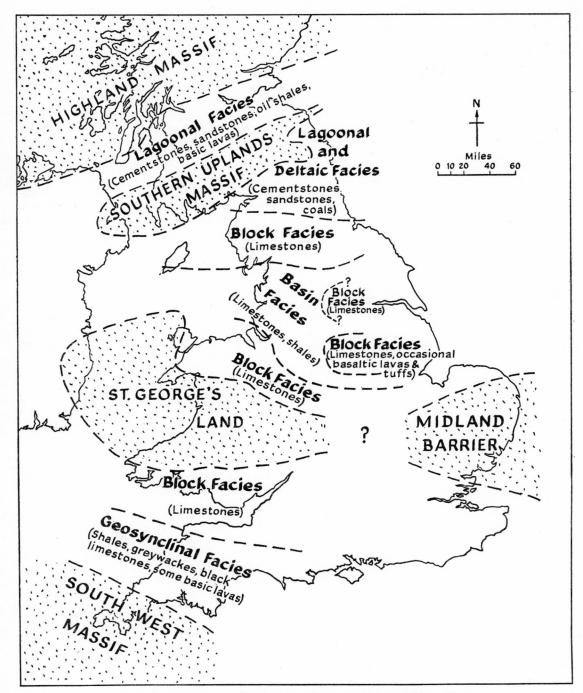

Fig. 15.2 Palaeogeographical map of Great Britain during Viséan time.

Each stage is defined by the total floral assemblage and the relative frequency of the various species. The divisions are applicable to most coalfields but since they each embrace a considerable thickness of strata have only a limited use in stratigraphic studies. Consequently a series of nine floral zones, from A to I, was proposed (Dix, 1934, pp. 794–828) for the Upper Carboniferous succession, and applied in particular to that of South Wales. Owing to the often considerable vertical range of most of the plant species as at present defined such a detailed zonation is practicable only if the very rare fossils of a limited range are employed. Consequently, the precise local boundaries of the zones are in most cases difficult if not impossible to determine.

The use of miospores for the division as distinct from the correlation of individual horizons of the Carboniferous is a relatively recent development. In the first studies three spore assemblages, termed S1, S2 and S3, were defined for the Coal Measures (Balme & Butterworth, 1952, pp. 870–9). Later work has permitted a more detailed subdivision of much of the Carboniferous. Eleven assemblages, all defined by the total spore content and relative abundance of certain species rather than by the occurrence of the isolated exotic form, are now recognized for the major coal-bearing strata of Britain (Smith & Butterworth, in press).

STRATIGRAPHICAL DETAILS

DINANTIAN SERIES

The lower limit of the Dinantian Series is well defined in most British localities where a marked basal unconformity is developed. In parts of South West England however, the base is less obvious, for here the lowest Carboniferous and highest Devonian strata are conformable and may be regarded as forming a transition series. The upper limit of the Lower Carboniferous is likewise in some areas only to be determined by detailed palaeontological work, whilst in other localities the Namurian is clearly unconformable on the underlying beds. Considerable variations of facies occur in the Dinantian and therefore several areas or *provinces* are distinguished by their different sedimentary histories.

It is in the *South-Western Province* that the most complete Dinantian succession occurs. The major outcrops are those of South Wales, Gloucester, Somerset, Devon and Cornwall. Excluding the last two counties, three main divisions are recognized, and their particular lithologies reflect a marine transgression from the south followed by a regression in upper Dinantian time. The Lower Limestone Shales, up to 800 ft in thickness, consist of a lower arenaceous group, succeeded by highly fossiliferous crinoidal limestones and shales. These are overlaid by the Main Limestone, exceeding 4 000 ft in Pembrokeshire although thinning considerably to the north, and composed of well-bedded crinoidal and oolitic limestones together with a group of dolostones. A later southerly recession of the Dinantian sea is indicated by the diachronous character of the arenaceous beds forming part of the Upper Limestone Shales. For these shore-line deposits, including the Drybrook (low S_2) and Cromhall (upper D_2) Sandstones of the Forest of Dean and Bristol areas, occur at progressively higher horizons to the south. Throughout much of the Carboniferous period sedimentation was affected by a land mass, loosely termed 'St George's Land' (Fig. 15.2), extending across central Wales and England. A northerly tilting of this area and consequent uplift in the South-Western Province during upper Dinantian time resulted in a southerly migration of the shore line in proximity to which the sandstones were deposited (Fig. 15.3).

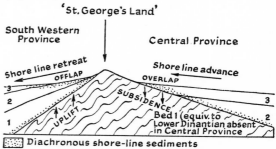

Fig. 15.3 Diagram to illustrate offlap and overlap in the South Western and Central Provinces during Dinantian time.

In marked contrast to the Carboniferous sediments of the rest of Britain, the Culm Measures of Devon and Cornwall include geosynclinal deposits developed as a facies extending across to continental Europe. Their order of succession is difficult to determine owing to the complex folding and faulting developed during the Armorican orogeny (page 128). The Lower Culm Measures of Dinantian age include shales, sandstones, black limestones and cherts together with a volcanic development of basic lavas and tuffs. The Upper Culm Measures, composed predominantly of shales and greywackes, appear to be chiefly of Namurian age although the occurrence of goniatites and non-marine lamellibranchs indicate the presence of the Lenisulcata and Communis Zone of the Westphalian in the highest beds. 'Culm' is a local name for the highly crushed powdery anthracites which sporadically occur in beds up to 14 ft in thickness. They were chiefly worked in the eighteenth century around Bideford (Ussher, 1901, pp. 382–3).

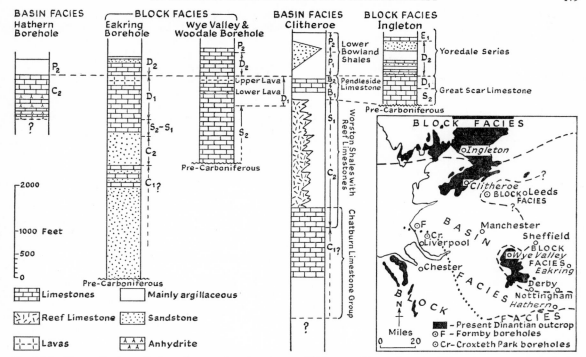

Fig. 15.4 Generalized vertical sections and palaeogeographical map illustrating the Dinantian sequences of the Central Province.

The influence of St George's Land as a northerly barrier to the Tournaisian sea is apparent from the probable absence of rocks of that age over Britain apart from in the South-Western Province. For the most complete Dinantian succession in the *Central Province*, an area defined to the south by St George's Land and to the north by the Stublick-Ninety Fathom Fault System of Northumberland, is that exposed in north-east Lancashire (Fig. 15.4) where the lowest strata exposed are only doubtfully Tournaisian in age. Similarly in a deep borehole in Derbyshire near Buxton where pre-Carboniferous rocks were penetrated, and in north-west Yorkshire where the basal Carboniferous is exposed, no strata older than Viséan occur. We may therefore infer that it was not until Viséan time that any considerable extension of the Dinantian sea affected the area to the north of St George's Land. Indeed, in the Lower Viséan, sedimentation was perhaps restricted to the basinal facies (page 120, Fig. 12.2; Fig. 15.4) exemplified by the 7 000 ft of dark bituminous limestones and shales exposed in North-east Lancashire. By Upper Viséan time the sea transgressed across the basin margins to deposit the shallow-water shelf sediments of the Great Scar and Derbyshire Limestones overlaid by the deltaic Yoredale Series. During this time con-

temporary vulcanicity is evidenced in Derbyshire by the occurrence within the limestone of agglomerate vents, basaltic lavas and tuffs.

In the *Northern England Province*, which is limited to the north by the Scottish Southern Uplands, the oldest coal seams of economic importance in Britain are developed. Essentially the sedimentary history of the province is one of open seas in the south being progressively invaded by deltaic sediments. The latter were derived from the erosion of a northern massif formed by the Southern Uplands which was only locally submerged. Consequently limestones are less common in the succession than in the previously considered provinces, and sandstones and shales predominate (Fig. 15.5). The lowest rocks, the Cementstone Group, attaining a maximum thickness of over 2 000 ft and unconformable upon the Old Red Sandstone, are composed of rhythmic alternations of shales, impure limestones, dolostones and sandstones with lenticular developments of basal conglomerates. The cementstones themselves are argillaceous, sometimes dolomitic, limestones precipitated from a highly saline lagoonal environment. Succeeding the group are the Fell Sandstones, a diachronous series up to 1 000 ft thick and composed of thickly-bedded cross-stratified deltaic sandstones.

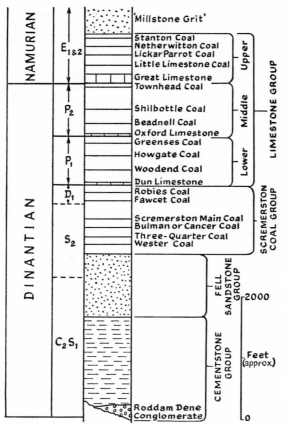

Fig. 15.5 Generalized vertical section showing the Dinantian and Namurian succession of Northumberland.

tually confined to the Midland Valley. The Cement-stone Group, forming the lowest Carboniferous strata and most probably unconformable throughout the province on pre-Carboniferous rocks, are very similar to the equivalent Northumberland beds. A maximum thickness of over 1 000 ft of alternations of thin cementstones and shales is developed in Ayrshire. The group becomes predominantly aren-aceous when traced to the east. Subdivided at the Burdiehouse Limestone, the succeeding Oil Shale Groups are over 5 000 ft thick near Edinburgh. Com-posed predominantly of ordinary shales (in Scotland termed blaes, to distinguish them from oil shales, Table 12) and cross-stratified deltaic sandstones, the groups also contain thin non-marine limestones, tuffs and sporadic coals. Consequently the true oil shales only form about 3 per cent of the total thick-ness. The oil shales themselves (Fig. 15.6), commonly between 2 ft and 5 ft thick, although occasionally up to 15 ft thick, are individually variable in thickness

Attaining a maximum thickness of 1 000 ft near Berwick-on-Tweed, the Scremerston Coal Group in that area contains ten workable seams including some over 6 ft thick (Hopkins, in Trueman, 1954, pp. 293–4). The interseam deltaic strata are chiefly com-posed of cementstones, shales, sandstones and seat earths. As the group is traced to the south and west the number of marine horizons increases until in Cumberland the equivalent Birdoswald Limestone Group contains only a few workable coals, notably the Thirwall and Chapelburn Seams. In Northum-berland the Lower and Middle Limestone Groups fall within the Dinantian where the sequences of limestones, shales, sandstones, seat earths and coals resemble the Yoredale Series of the Central Province. As the groups are traced to the north the limestone members of the cyclothems fail and the coals increase in thickness. They are however only worked on a small scale at the present.

Sedimentation in the *Scottish Province* was vir-

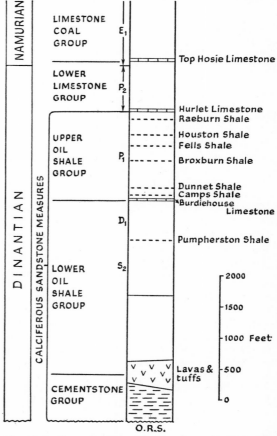

Fig. 15.6 Generalized vertical section showing the Dinantian succession of east central Scotland.

and contain numerous shale and sandstone partings. The sediments accumulated as the periodic infillings of a number of shallow lagoons, situated to the east of a major volcanic area developed at this time in West Scotland. The resinous materials concentrated in the oil shales were most probably derived from decaying plants washed into the lagoons from adjacent delta surfaces and sand banks. In Scotland the highest Dinantian strata are represented by the Lower Limestone Group, which, it should be noted, is equivalent to the Middle Limestone Group of Northumberland. A maximum thickness of over 700 ft of predominantly deltaic arenaceous strata with thin coals is developed in the eastern outcrops. Southwestwards in Ayrshire, less than 100 ft of limestones and shales were deposited in shallow shelf seas.

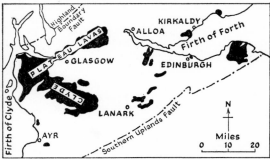

Fig. 15.7 Sketch map showing outcrops of Carboniferous volcanic rocks in central Scotland.

Contemporaneous vulcanicity occurred throughout Dinantian time in the Scottish province (Fig. 15.7). Olivine basalts form the bulk of the lavas although trachytes, andesites and rhyolites are locally common. The most extensive volcanic accumulations are the Clyde Plateau Lavas, between 2 000 ft to 3 000 ft thick, and cropping out in a wide arc to the east of Glasgow. Numerous dykes and sills were intruded during the volcanic phase, and throughout the province the denuded volcanic centres form many agglomerate- and lava-filled vents such as that of Arthur's Seat, Edinburgh.

Palaeontology

The more typical Dinantian genera include:
Brachiopods—*Composita, Dielasma* (Fig. 15.8a), *Pugnax, Spirifer* (Fig. 15.8b), '*Productus*' (Fig. 14.2b).
Corals—*Caninia* (Fig. 14.4a), *Dibunophyllum* (Fig. 15.8c), *Lithostrotian, Lonsdaleia* (Fig. 15.8d), *Palaeosmila, Zaphrentis* (Fig. 14.4b).
Goniatites—*Beyrichoceras, Goniatites* (Fig. 15.8e).
Lamellibranchs—*Caneyella* (Fig. 14.9a). *Dunbarella* (Fig. 14.9b), *Leiopteria* (Fig. 15.8f), *Posidonia* (Fig. 14.9d).

Economic geology

Although the Dinantian coal seams of the Northern England Province were much worked in the past, extraction nowadays has virtually ceased since the coals have a high volatile content and furthermore contain abundant dirt partings. The output of Scottish oil shale, from which various oils and their derivatives were manufactured by distillation, attained a maximum in 1913 when $3\frac{1}{4}$ million ton were mined chiefly in Midlothian and West Lothian. Since that time production has fallen and recently declined altogether. South of Edinburgh, at Cous-

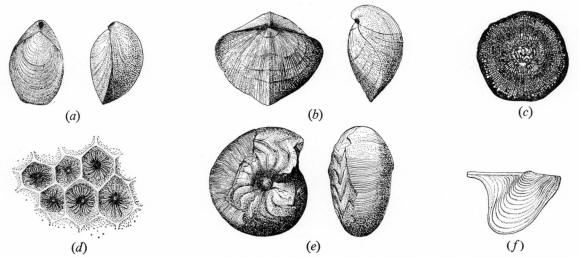

Fig. 15.8 Dinantian fossils: (a) *Dielasma* (×1) (×1), (b) *Spirifer* (×½) (×½), (c) *Dibunophyllum* (×½), (d) *Lonsdaleia* (×1), (e) *Goniatites* (×1½) (×1½), (f) *Leiopteria* (×1).

land, the Oil Shale Groups are penetrated by bore-holes which yield small quantities of gas at present supplied to the Gas Council.

The limestones, particularly in England and Wales, are extensively quarried as sources of cement, agricultural lime, metallurgical flux, roadstone and aggregate. An important dolostone sequence in the Main Limestone of S. Wales is worked for refractory purposes along the south-eastern border of the coalfield. Lead-zinc mineralization, as both fault-infillings and replacement deposits, occurs locally within the limestones, and the orefields of the Men-dips, Derbyshire hills, Halkyn area of N. Wales and the N. Pennines were highly productive in the nine-teenth century. Nowadays mining, yielding in the main barite, calcite, fluorite and witherite ($BaCO_3$), is restricted to a few localities only (see papers by various authors in *The Future of Non-Ferrous Mining in Great Britain*, the proceedings of a symposium published by the Institute of Mining and Metal-lurgy, 1959). Hematite, occurring as replacement deposits within the limestones, is at present mined in the Furness district of Lancashire and at Llanharry in Glamorgan.

Supplies of roadstone and aggregate are derived from the igneous rocks. In particular the dolerite intrusions of the Scottish province are worked chiefly for this purpose.

NAMURIAN SERIES

The base of the Namurian when conformable upon the Dinantian is defined at the first appearance of several goniatite genera including the zonal form, *Eumorphoceras*. Also at about this horizon many of the lower Carboniferous goniatites became extinct. Elsewhere the Sudetic phase of the Armorican orogeny (page 128) resulted in the folding and subsequent erosion of the Dinantian so that a basal unconformity was developed. This is particularly

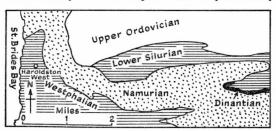

Fig. 15.9 Map showing basal Namurian overstep in Pembrokeshire, Wales.

noticeable along the northern margin of the S. Wales coalfield where a progressive Namurian over-step occurs across the Dinantian (Fig. 15.9). Thus near Blaenavon in Monmouthshire, the Viséan is

completely overstepped and only the Lower Lime-stone Shales remain. Again at Llangwm in Pem-brokeshire the entire Lower Carboniferous was eroded so that thereabouts the Namurian is uncon-formable upon the Old Red Sandstone and further west, upon Silurian and Ordovician strata.

Arenaceous sediments are common in the Namu-rian, which typically exhibits a deltaic facies. The maximum development is that of the Central Pen-nines in N. Derbyshire, Yorkshire and Lancashire where the series exceeds 6 000 ft in thickness (Fig. 15.10). Here the prominant coarse-grained, com-monly cross-stratified and sometimes arkosic sand-stones were deposited during the progressive south-westwards extension of a series of deltas across the area. Thin coal seams often occur above the sand-stones and are in turn succeeded by a variable thick-ness of argillaceous strata. In the latter, thin bands of marine shale containing rich goniatite faunas were deposited during periodic marine transgressions across the delta swamps. The series thins to the south and in parts of the English Midlands is absent alto-gether along the northern flanks of 'St George's Land' (Fig. 9.5). In N. Wales the close proximity of such a land mass to the south is reflected in the lateral passage from the marine Holywell Shales of Flintshire into essentially shallow-water sandstones and conglomerates in southern Denbighshire (Fig. 15.11).

A development of limestones occurs in the lower Namurian Upper Limestone and Hensingham Groups of Northumberland (Fig. 15.5) and Cum-berland (Fig. 15.12) respectively. Coals are present at several horizons and some, notably the Little Lime-stone Coal, are worked near Alston where the latter seam is a semi-anthracite (Trotter, in Trueman, 1954, p. 317). In Cumberland an unconformity occurs at about the horizon of the Udale Coal, for the H, R_1 and R_2 stages are absent. Similarly the Upper Limestone Group (E_1–E_2) of Northumber-land are the highest beds in that area to yield any diagnostic Namurian fossils.

In Scotland the Limestone Coal Group (E_1) is a highly important coal-bearing sequence (Mac-gregor, in Trueman, 1954, pp. 342–71). The group (Fig. 15.13) attains a maximum thickness of over 1 300 ft north-east of Glasgow and thins towards the south and east. Around Edinburgh the group was formerly termed the Edge Coals since in that area the seams crop out along the steeply inclined flanks of the Midlothian basin. A coal measure facies is typically developed so that the normal interseam sediments (Chapter 7) occur. Contemporaneous vul-canicity is evident from the frequent intercalations of agglomerates, tuffs and lavas, and in West Lothian almost the whole of the group is composed of lavas.

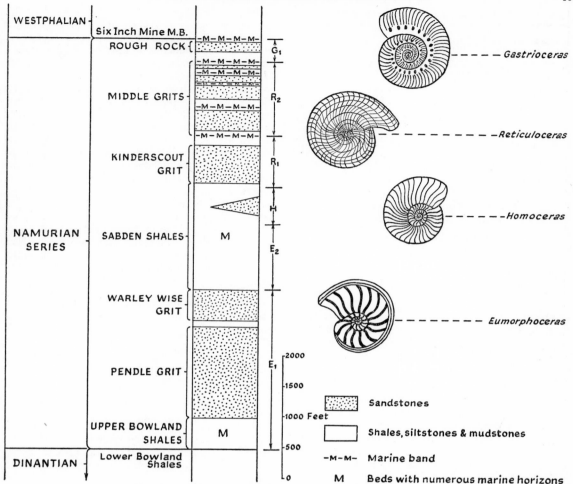

Fig. 15.10   The Namurian succession and major goniatite genera in east Lancashire.

Also, in places the coals have been affected by igneous intrusions, in some cases with beneficial effect, to form low-volatile steam coals. With the exception of the Glasgow-Stirling area considerable lateral variation of sediments, resulting from their

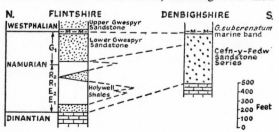

Fig. 15.11   Diagrammatic vertical sections illustrating the Namurian succession of North Wales.

restricted deposition in a series of isolated basins, renders correlation of the seams across the coalfields uncertain and consequently seam nomenclature is extremely localized. The marine band occurring within the shales termed the Black Metals and also that forming the Johnston Shell Bed form the most constant marker horizons. The succeeding Upper Limestone Group, of Arnsbergian (E_2) age and therefore only partly equivalent to the group of that name in Northumberland (Table 31), is over 1 500 ft thick in Stirlingshire and thins appreciably to the south and west. The group is predominantly arenaceous and the limestones, seldom over a few feet in thickness, tend to be argillaceous. They are nevertheless easily recognizable and together with the associated highly fossiliferous marine shales form useful marker bands. The occasional coals which

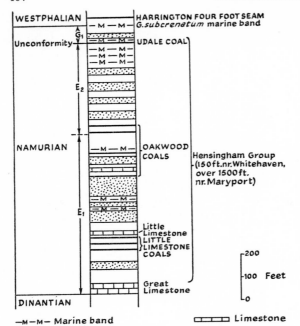

Fig. 15.12 Generalized vertical section showing the Namurian sequence of west Cumberland.

occur in the group are of an inconsistent nature and have been but little worked. Formerly called the 'Millstone Grit', the Passage Group extends into the Lower Westphalian. Having a maximum thickness of 1 000 ft in Stirlingshire, the group is largely composed of a series of massive coarse-grained sandstones overlying more argillaceous beds. Coals occur locally and sometimes attain considerable thicknesses, as for example in the Bowhill Basin of Fife where several coals and their associated dirt partings are over 30 ft thick. In the Glasgow district fireclays and siliceous seat earths occur at two horizons near the top (Bonnybridge siliceous seat earth) and base (Glenboig fireclay) of the group. In Ayrshire the group is almost entirely volcanic, with over 500 ft of basaltic lavas. The overlying Ayrshire Bauxitic Clay, occasionally up to 30 ft thick, is a product of the weathering and decomposition of the lavas in Carboniferous time. Although the base of the Passage Group just falls within the Arnsbergian (E_2) Stage there is little evidence of the occurrence of the succeeding Namurian stages which may well be absent as in northern England. It is probable that during much of Upper Namurian times Scotland and Northern England formed part of a land mass, the erosion of which yielded the deltaic sediments of the Pennine areas.

So far we have only considered the Namurian

rocks deposited to the north of 'St George's Land'. To the south of this land mass in S. Wales two major diachronous lithological divisions may be recognized. Following the Sudetic fold movements the southern margin of 'St George's Land' lay not far to the north of the present margin of the coalfield. Consequently the Lower Namurian in this area is represented by the shoreline sandstones and conglomerates of the Basal Grit, whilst in the south, where deeper-water conditions prevailed, the whole Namurian succession is essentially argillaceous. As submergence continued below the Namurian sea, shale deposition extended over the northern outcrops so that the basal sandstones are overlaid by the Shale Group. Apart from in the Forest of Dean and Bristol areas, where possibly some of the diachronous Viséan sandstones extended into the Namurian, and the geosynclinal Upper Culm Measures (page 178) there is no evidence for Namurian deposits in southern England. In the Kent coalfield the Westphalian rests unconformably on Dinantian limestones.

Palaeontology

The goniatites are undoubtedly the most useful fossils by which the Namurian may be zoned and

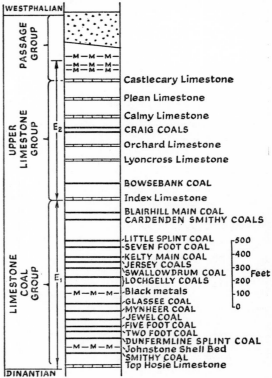

Fig. 15.13 Generalized vertical section illustrating the Namurian succession of central Fife.

correlated. Important genera include *Eumorphoceras* (Fig. 15.10), *Homoceras* (Fig. 15.10), *Reticuloceras* (Fig. 15.10) and *Gastrioceras* (Figs 14.6b; 15.10).

Brachiopods include the inarticulate genera of *Lingula* (Fig. 14.2c) and *Orbiculoidea* (Fig. 14.2d). In the Lower Namurian limestones of northern England and Scotland the genera more typical of the Dinantian also occur.

Thin-shelled lamellibranchs are found in association with goniatites in the marine bands and more common forms in the Upper Namurian are *Dunbarella* (Fig. 14.9b) and *Posidonia* (Fig. 14.9d).

Nautiloid genera include several rare although stratigraphically useful forms such as *Tylonautilus*.

Economics

In Scotland over half of the annual production of some 16.5 million ton of coal is mined from the Limestone Coal Group chiefly in the Central, Fife, Alloa and Lothian areas. Steam, coking, gas and domestic coals are produced. In the same areas high grade refractories are worked and the Bonnybridge and Glenboig seat earths (Table 15) of the Passage Group have long been exploited in the Glasgow district. The Ayrshire Bauxitic Clay is both mined and quarried for similar purposes although its initial lack of plasticity necessitates blending with other clays prior to manufacture. Fireclay horizons are mined to a limited extent in the Pennines, and in Wales some of the more highly siliceous horizons in the Basal Grits and Cefn-y-Fedw Sandstone Series are worked for the production of silica bricks.

Most of the sandstones have been quarried for constructional materials, and sandstones such as those of Darley Dale in Derbyshire, Giffnock and Bishopriggs near Glasgow are of more than local repute. Some of the more friable beds are worked for moulding sands as those of the Upper Limestone Group of Scotland. Furthermore many of the Namurian sandstones are important aquifers and considerable quantities of underground water are extracted from them by public and private undertakings. In the north Nottinghamshire and Lincolnshire oilfields a little oil production is obtained from the Upper Namurian sandstones.

WESTPHALIAN AND STEPHANIAN SERIES

It is clearly impracticable to consider the detailed stratigraphy of the individual British coalfields. Such information as may be required by the student can be readily obtained from the relevant geological survey memoirs, regional handbooks and the detailed accounts of the various coalfields in the authoritative review edited by Trueman (1954). Accordingly only the general Westphalian and Stephanian stratigraphy is described:

Apart from the Scottish coalfields, where the occurrence of the important Limestone Coal Group has already been noted, the coalfield-productive sequences are confined to the Westphalian Series. The stratigraphic positions of the sequences within the latter series do however vary so that the existing coalfields (Fig. 15.14) can be classified into three distinct sedimentary provinces, as follows.

The coalfields of the *Southern Province* are those of S. Wales, the Forest of Dean, Somerset and Kent. In this province the workable coals chiefly occur in the Communis, Modiolaris, Similis-Pulchra, Phillipsii and Tenuis Zones.

The *Midland Province* embraces the coalfields of Lancashire, N. Wales, Yorkshire, Nottinghamshire, Derbyshire, Leicestershire, Staffordshire, Shropshire and Warwickshire. They were originally part of a more or less continuous sedimentary basin separated from the Southern Province by the midland land mass of 'St George's Land'. The workable coals are largely confined to the Lenisulcata, Communis, Modiolaris and Similis-Pulchra zones.

The *Northern Province* includes the Cumberland, Durham, Northumberland and Scottish coalfields. The major coals fall almost entirely within the Communis, Modiolaris and Lower Similis-Pulchra Zones.

It is thus apparent that the duration of coal formation was more prolonged in the south, so that north of 'St George's Land' the major Westphalian coals are virtually confined to the Ammanian Stage.

Ammanian stage (Lower and Middle Coal Measures)

In many respects the Ammanian strata included within the *Lenisulcata Zone* are similar to the underlying Namurian beds, for the interseam sediments are relatively coarse-grained, sandstones tend to be predominant and, excepting the Ganister or Mountain seams of the Midland Province, coals are relatively unimportant. Similarly marine horizons are numerous so that in some coalfields as many as ten marine bands have been proved.

It is in the succeeding *Communis, Modiolaris and Lower Similis-Pulchra Zones* that most of the major coals occur. Apart from the mid-Modiolaris marine band utilized as the base of the Middle Coal Measures, and a few low horizons amidst non-productive strata in the Midland Province, marine horizons are confined to the Lower Similis-Pulchra Zone. Sandstones become less common, are usually finer-grained and tend to occur as relatively localized lenses rather than beds. The interseam sediments are typically argillaceous.

By *Upper Similis-Pulchra* time coal formation had virtually ceased in Scotland, and in other coalfields the frequency of workable seams decreases so that apart from in Lancashire, North Staffordshire and

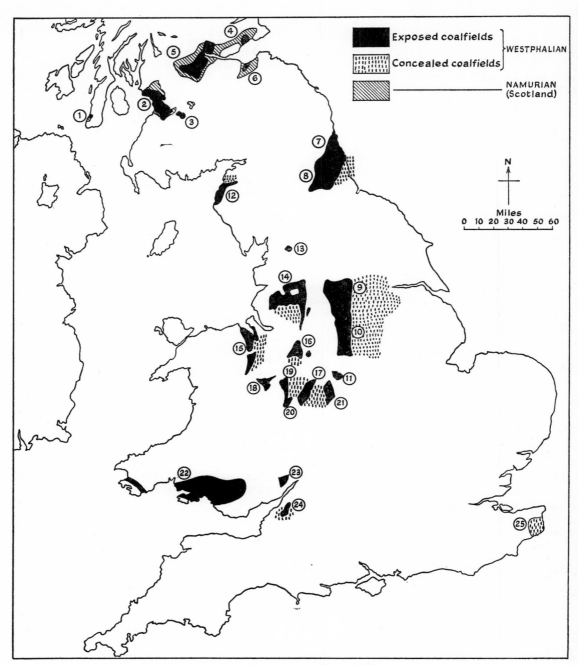

Fig. 15.14 The coalfields of Great Britain.
(National Coal Board Divisional Groupings, 1965.)

Exposed coalfields
Concealed coalfields } WESTPHALIAN

NAMURIAN (Scotland)

Scottish Division
1 Machrihanish
2 Ayrshire
3 Sanquhar
4 Fife
5 Central
6 Lothians

Northumberland Division
7 Northumberland

Durham Division
8 Durham

Yorkshire Division
9 Yorkshire

East Midlands Division
10 Derbyshire-Nottinghamshire
11 South Derbyshire-Leicestershire

North Western Division
12 Cumberland
13 Ingleton
14 Lancashire
15 North Wales

West Midlands Division
16 North Staffordshire
17 South Staffordshire
18 Shrewsbury

19 Coalbrookdale
20 Forest of Wyre
21 Warwickshire

South Western Division
22 South Wales
23 Forest of Dean
24 Somerset and Gloucestershire

South Eastern Division
25 Kent

the coalfields of the Southern Province there are few important seams above the Lower Similis-Pulchra Zone.

Essentially there is little difference between the interseam sediments (Chapter 7) of the various coalfields, and the Ammanian Stage is characierized by a continuation of the deltaic conditions of the preceding Namurian. On numerous occasions however the delta surfaces remained above water level for relatively considerable lengths of time when an extensive plant-cover developed ultimately to form the Westphalian coals. Although such phases of coal formation occurred in the Namurian they were, in England and Wales, of much shorter duration so that the coals are considerably thinner. Consequently the Namurian deltaic facies, with only thin impersistent seams, is distinguished from the Westphalian *coal measure facies* by the occurrence of widespread, thicker and therefore workable coal seams in the latter series. Occasionally coal formation was terminated by a marine transgression during which time the usually thin bands of marine shale were deposited (pages 212–4). A remarkable uniformity in the depositional levels of the various coalfield provinces is indicated by the widespread occurrence (Table 32) of the marine bands, which are confined to the Ammanian Series. From the nature of the associated sediments it is clear that the marine trans-

gressions were of a shallow-water nature so that if they had taken place across a surface of variable relief their distribution would be more restricted. Furthermore the coal swamps must initially have been situated almost at sea level for otherwise a transgression would have been accompanied by some erosion of the area with the development of a basal unconformity. In most cases, however, coal formation was terminated by submergence below nonmarine waters and the bulk of the interseam sediments accumulated in the fresh or brackish waters of lagoonal areas. The latter were possibly separated from the open sea by low sand barriers.

Comparatively little contemporaneous igneous activity occurred during the Westphalian, and even in Scotland, where the most notable development of earlier Carboniferous volcanic rocks are found, only a few beds of pyroclasts interbedded with nonvolcanic interseam sediments are restricted to the Coal Measures of Fife. In the Lower Coal Measures

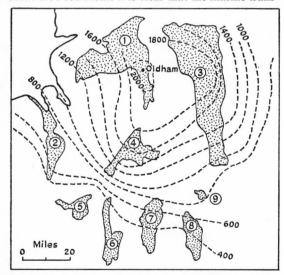

Fig. 15.15 Diagram showing the isopachytes of the Modiolaris and Lower Similis—Pulchra Zones of the Midland Province. Exposed coalfields: 1, Lancashire; 2, North Wales; 3, Yorkshire-Nottinghamshire; 4, North Staffordshire; 5, Shrewsbury; 6, Coalbrookdale and Wyre Forest; 7, South Staffordshire; 8, Warwickshire; 9, Leicestershire and South Derbyshire. (After A. E. Trueman.)

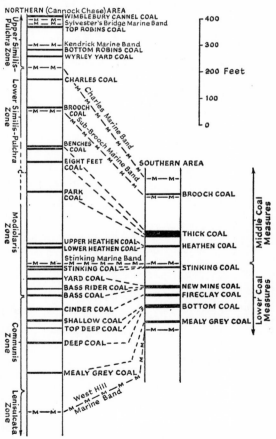

Fig. 15.16 Vertical sections showing the northward splitting of coal seams in South Staffordshire.

The Major Marine Horiz[ons

	Scotland[2]	Northum-berland and Durham (Armstrong & Price, 1954; Francis, 1965, p. 59)	Cumberland (Taylor & Calver, 1961)	Lancashire (Magraw & Calver, 1960 A)	North Wales (Magraw & Calver, 1960 B)	North Staffordshire (Earp, 1961; Eyles, 1954, pp. 33–4)	South Staffordshir[e] (Eyles, 1954 pp. 33–4; Hoare & Mitchell, 195[ ] pp. 16–8)
Middle Coal Measures	X	Down Hill	X	Prestwich Top or Upper Sankey	X	Lady or Bay	•
	Bothwell Bridge[3]	X	St Helens ?	Lower Sankey	X	Priorsfield	Sylvester's Bridge
	X	Wear Mouth ?	Risehow ?	Manchester	Ty Cerryg	Rowhurst Rider	Kendrick
	Skipseys	Ryhope or Ashington	Bolton or Brassy	Dukinfield	• ?	Gin Mine or Twist	Charles
	• ?[4]	Hylton ?	X	Moston	Warras ?	Clayton	X
	X	Kirkby's	Black Metal	Bradford	Lower Stinking	Doctor's Mine	•
	X	• ?	X	X	Gardden Lodge	Longton Hall	X
	X	High Main	Ten Quarters ?	Poynton or Ashclough	Powell	Moss Cannel	Sub-Brooc[h]
	Queenslie	Harvey	Solway	Sutton Manor	Llay	Banbury	Stinking
Lower Coal Measures[1]	X	X	X	Bullion or Upper Foot	*G. listeri*	Crabtree	Fair Oak ?
	X	*G. subcrenatum*	*G. subcrenatum*	Six Inch Mine	*G. subcrenatum*	*G. subcrenatum*	*G. subcrenat[um]*

• Located but un-named   X Not recorded to date   ? Exact correlation uncertain

[1] The complete sequence of marine horizons in the Lower Coal Measures is not shown

[2] Individual references to most horizons are given by Trotter (1960)

[3] See Anderson (1955, p. 55)

[4] See Francis and Ewing (1962, pp. 146–8)

of the Midland Province a number of basaltic lava flows and tuffs, totalling at one locality over 450 ft, have so far only been proved in deep boreholes in Nottinghamshire (Falcon & Kent, 1960, [ ] 23–5).

Although the faunas, floras and lithologies of

the British Coalfields

Warwick-shire[2]	Coalbrook-dale[2]	Yorkshire, Nottingham-shire & North Derbyshire (Edwards & Stubblefield, 1948; Goossens, 1952)	Leicestershire & South Derbyshire (Greig & Mitchell, 1955, pp. 40–3)	South Wales (Stubblefield & Trotter, 1957, Fig. 1)	Kent[2]	Continent (Bartenstein, 1950)	
X	X	Top	X	Upper Cwmgorse	X	X	C
X	X	Shafton	X	Lower Cwmgorse	X	X	
X	X	*Edmondia*	X	Five Roads	X	X	
Nuneaton	Chance – Pennystone	Mansfield	Overseal	Cefn Coed	Tilmanstone ?	Aegir or Petit Buisson or Rimbert	
X	X	Sutton	● ?	Trimsaron or Britannic	X	X	
X	X	Haughton or Swinton Pottery	● ?	Hafod Heulog or Mole ?	Snowdown ?	Lanklaar ?	
X	X	Clowne	● ?	Graigog ?	X	X	
X	Blackstone	Two Feet	X	X	X	Domina ?	
Seven Feet	Pennystone	Clay Cross	Bagworth or Molyneux	Amman	Ripple	Katarina or Quaregnon or Poissonniere	B
X	X	Alton or Hard Bed or Ganister	Alton	Cefn Cribbwr Wernffrwd or or *G. listeri*	X	Finefrau	
. subcrenatum ?	X	Pot Clay	*G. subcrenatum*	*G. subcrenatum*	X	Sarnsbank	A

A Taken as the base of the Lower Coal Measures in England and Wales and characterized by the goniatite *Gastrioceras subcrenatum.*

B Taken as the base of the Middle Coal Measures in Britain and characterized by the goniatite *Anthracoceras vanderbeckei.*

C Taken as the top of the Middle Coal Measures in England and Wales and characterized by the goniatite *Anthracoceras cambriense.*

eries are relatively similar in all the coalfields, the edimentation and subsidence rates were far from niform. Even in the same coalfield considerable thickness variations may occur between two common horizons. This is particularly evident in the Midland Province (Fig. 15.15) where a southerly

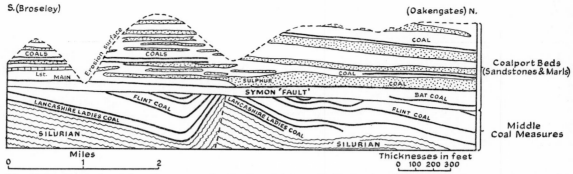

Fig. 15.17   Reconstructed section across the Coalbrookdale coalfield showing the unconformity termed the Symon 'Fault'. The Sulphur Coal has been taken as a datum line so that folds subsequent to the deposition of the Coalport Beds have been eliminated. (After T. H. Whitehead.)

thinning occurs towards 'St George's Land'. Thus the combined thickness of the Communis, Modiolaris and Lower Similis-Pulchra Zones progressively decreases to the south between S. Lancashire (*c.* 3 000 ft), N. Staffordshire (*c* 2 500 ft), Cannock Chase (*c* 1 200 ft) and S. Staffordshire (*c* 500 ft). Often the most outstanding effects of such differential subsidence are the coalescence of seams towards the margins of the depositional troughs. In the coalfields adjacent to the north border of 'St George's Land' the splitting of seams (Fig. 15.16) such as the Warwickshire and Staffordshire Thick Coals is a clear reflection of the northerly subsidence. In other cases thickness variations can be sometimes attributed to the influence of rising Amorican fold structures. For example, in the N. Staffordshire coalfield a greater thickness of strata of equivalent age occurs in the Potteries syncline than over the Western anticline (Fig. 8.11).

Morganian stage and Stephanian series (Upper Coal Measures)

By definition the Morganian stage is restricted to the Phillipsii and Tenuis Zones so that the Prolifera Zone is included in the Stephanian Series. There is however little justification in Britain for such a distinction and consequently all three zones are placed in the Upper Coal Measures. In early Morganian time sedimentation was affected by the Malvernian phase of the Armorican orogeny (page 128) and in many areas the Morganian rocks are unconformable upon the underlying beds. Thus along the eastern margin of the South Wales coalfield the Pennant Measures overstep across the Ammanian onto Namurian strata, and in the adjacent Forest of Dean coalfield they are unconformable on the Dinantian and Old Red Sandstone (Fig. 12.10). Again at Ingleton, on the northern margin of the Midland Province, an unconformity occurs at the base of the 'Red Measures', whilst in Shropshire the

Symon 'Fault' is in reality an unconformity (Fig. 15.17).

The Morganian of the *Southern Province* is a major productive sequence. In S. Wales (Fig. 15.18) the coals occur within the Pennant Measures, which are composed essentially of coarse-grained felspathic cross-stratified sandstones and conglomerates. A similar arenaceous sequence occurs at about the same horizon in the remaining southern coalfields. The several seams of the Prolifera Zone in S. Wales and Somerset are the highest British productive horizons.

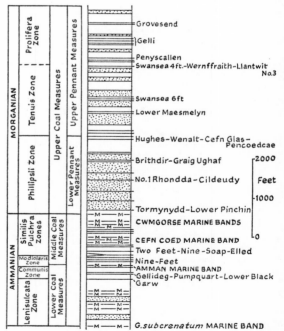

Fig. 15.18   Generalized vertical section illustrating the Coal Measure sequence in South Wales.

TABLE 33

Classification of the Morganian in the Midlands Coalfields

	Lancashire	North Wales	North Staffordshire	South Staffordshire	Shropshire	Warwickshire
	Upper Group	Erbistock Beds	Keele Group	Enville Group	Enville Group	Enville or Corley Group
Tenuis Zone	Limestone or Ardwick Group	Coed-yr-Allt Beds	Newcastle Group	Keele Group	Keele Group	Keele Group
Phillipsii Zone	Lower or Bradford Coal Group	Ruabon Marl	Etruria Marl Group	Halesowen Group	Halesowen or Highley Group	Halesowen Group
			Blackband Group	Etruria or Old Hill Marl Group	Etruria or Old Hill Marl Group	Coalport Beds	Etruria Marl Group (Much of the group may belong to the Middle Coal Measures)
		Buckley Fireclay Group	Grey ironstone Measures			

The Etruria Marl Facies is shown stippled

In the *Midland Province* (Table 33) the few workable seams, notably the Bradford Coal Group of Lancashire and the Peacock-Cannel Row Group of N. Staffordshire, are confined to the Phillipsii Zone. The most complete succession is that of the Staffordshire coalfields to the north of which the highest beds are absent. The general succession is as follows.

Enville Group. Reddish sandstones and conglomerates provisionally placed in the Carboniferous.

Keele Group. Red marls, seat-earths, sandstones, breccias and thin limestones.

Newcastle or *Halesowen Group.* Brown or grey micaceous sandstones overlaid by marls. Occasional thin coals and limestones.

Etruria Marl Group. Chiefly reddish mudstones with some lenticular sandstones and conglomerates (espleys).

Blackband Group. Shales, mudstones, ironstones, thin coals and occasional oil shales.

Grey ironstone measures. Shales, ironstones and important coals.

Owing to the scarcity of diagnostic fossils accurate inter-coalfield correlation of the groups is impossible and it appears that most have a diachronous relationship. Certainly the Etruria Marls of the several coalfields are not of identical age since in Warwickshire part of the group occurs within the Ammanian whereas in Staffordshire it is confined to the Morganian.

The reddish coloration of the Morganian sediments is most fully developed in the *Northern Province.* Both the 'Whitehaven Sandstone Series' and the 'Barren Red Measures' of Cumberland and Scotland respectively extend from the Upper Ammanian into the Morganian stages and are composed of soft reddish sandstones, marly shales, fireclays and thin worthless coals.

The development of reddish coloration in many Morganian sequences is undoubtedly a characteristic

COAL MINING GEOLOGY

192

feature of the Central and Northern Provinces. This may at first appear to indicate the onset in Upper Carboniferous time of the desert conditions of the succeeding Permian system. But it is important to distinguish the 'red beds', the coloration of which is a primary feature, from the 'reddened beds' of secondary origin (pages 64–5). The occurence of beds rich in plant remains together with thin and in some cases oxidized coals throughout most of the Morganian is clear evidence that a humid rather than arid climate prevailed. Undoubtedly much of the reddening of the Morganian sediments may be attributed to the weathering and oxidation of the land surface during early Permian time. The actual red beds of primary origin may possibly have accumulated as sediments derived from the erosion of an adjacent land surface overlaid by red volcanic soils. In this respect it is perhaps significant that in Nottinghamshire red beds equivalent to the Etruria Marls appear to pass laterally from the south, that is, away from 'St George's Land', into grey measures.

Palaeontology. See pages 159–70.

Economics. See pages 54–63.

REFERENCES

ANDERSON, F. W. (1955) in *Mem. geol. Surv. Summ. Prog.* for 1954, p. 55.

ARMSTRONG, G. & R. H. PRICE (1954) The Coal Measures of north-east Durham, *Trans. Instn Min. Engrs* 113, 973–97.

BALME, B. E. & M. A. BUTTERWORTH (1952) The stratigraphical significance of certain fossil spores in the central group of British coalfields, *Trans. Instn Min. Engrs* 111, 870–9.

BARTENSTEIN, H. (1950) Micropalaeontological research in European upper Carboniferous stratigraphy, *Geol. Mag.* 87, 253–60.

BISAT, W. S. (1926) The Carboniferous goniatites of the north of England and their zones, *Proc. Yorks. geol. Soc.* 20, 40–124.

BISAT, W. S. (1930) On the goniatite and nautiloid fauna of the Middle Coal Measures of England and Wales, *Mem. geol. Surv. Summ. Progr. geol.* for 1929, 3, 75–87.

CROOKALL, R. (1955) Fossil plants of the Carboniferous rocks of Great Britain, *Mem. G. S. Palaeont.* 4, Pt. 1, 1–84.

DAVIES, J. H. & A. E. TRUEMAN (1927) Revision of the non-marine lamellibranchs of the Coal Measures, *Q. Jl geol. Soc. Lond.* 83, 210–57.

DIX, E. (1934) The sequence of floras in the upper Carboniferous, with special reference to South Wales, *Trans. R. Soc. Edinb.* 57, 789–838.

EARP, J. R. (1961) Exploratory boreholes in the North Staffordshire coalfield, *Bull. geol. Surv. Gt Br.* 17, 153–90.

EDWARDS, W. & C. J. STUBBLEFIELD (1948) Marine bands and other faunal marker-horizons in relation to the sedimentary cycles of the Middle Coal Measures of Nottinghamshire and Derbyshire, *Q. Jl geol. Soc. Lond.* 103, 209–49.

EYLES, V. A. (1954) in *Mem. geol. Surv. Summ. Prog.* for 1953, 33–4.

FRANCIS, E. H. (1965) in *Mem. geol. Surv. Summ. Prog.* for 1964, 57–60.

FALCON, N. L. & P. E. KENT (1960) Geological results of petroleum exploration in Britain 1945–1957, *Mem. geol. Soc. Lond.* 2.

FRANCIS, E. H. & C. J. C. EWING (1962) Skipsey's marine band and red coal measures in Fife, *Geol. Mag.* 99, 145–52.

GEORGE, T. N. (1958) Lower Carboniferous palaeogeography of the British Isles, *Proc. Yorks. geol. Soc.* 31, 227–318.

GOOSENS, R. F. (1952) Marine bands proved in the new borings at Wentbridge and Darrington, Yorkshire, *Proc. Yorks. geol. Soc.* 28, 188–220.

GREIG, D. C. & G. H. MITCHELL (1955) The western extension of the Leicestershire and South Derbyshire coalfield, *Bull. geol. Surv. Gt Br.* 7, 38–67.

HOARE, R. H. & G. H. MITCHELL (1955) The geology of the Lea Hall colliery area, Rugeley, Staffordshire, *Bull. geol. Surv. Gt Br.* 7, 13–37.

HODSON, F. (1957) Marker horizons in the Namurian of Britain, Ireland, Belgium and western Germany, *Publs Ass. Étude. Paléont.* 24, 1–26.

HUDSON, R. G. S. (1945) The goniatite zones of the Namurian, *Geol. Mag.* 82, 1–9.

MACGREGOR, A. G. (1960) Division of the Carboniferous on Geological Survey Scottish maps, *Bull. geol. Surv. Gt Br.* 16, 127–30.

MAGRAW, D. & M. A. CALVER (1960A) Coal Measures proved underground in cross-measures tunnels at Bradford colliery, Manchester, *Trans. Instn Min. Engrs* 119, 475–89.

MAGRAW, D. & M. A. CALVER (1960B) Faunal marker horizons in the Middle Coal Measures of the North Wales coalfield, *Proc. Yorks. geol. Soc.* 32, 333–52.

SMITH, A. H. V. & M. A. BUTTERWORTH (in press) *Miospores in the coal seams of the Carboniferous of Great Britain,*—to be published as a monograph by the Palaeontological Association.

STUBBLEFIELD, C. J. & F. M. TROTTER (1957) Divisions of the Coal Measures on Geological Survey maps of England and Wales, *Bull. geol. Surv. Gt Br.* 13, 1–5.

TAYLOR, B. J. & M. A. CALVER (1961) The stratigraphy of exploratory boreholes in the West Cumberland coalfield, *Bull. geol. Surv. Gt Br.* 17, 1–74.

TROTTER, F. M. (1960) Lexique Stratigraphique International, 1, Europe Fasc. 3a VIII Carbonifère Supérieur (English text).

TRUEMAN, A. E. (1941) The periods of coal formation represented in the British Coal Measures, *Geol. Mag.* 78, 71–6.

TRUEMAN, A. E. (1946). Stratigraphical problems in the Coal Measures of Europe and North America, *Q. Jl geol. Soc. Lond.* 102, xlix–xciii.

TRUEMAN, A. E. (1954) *The Coalfields of Great Britain,* 1st ed., London, Arnold.

USSHER, W. A. E. (1901) The culm-measure types of Great Britain, *Trans. Instn Min. Engrs* 20, 360–87.

VAUGHAN, A. (1905). The palaeontological sequence in the Carboniferous Limestone of the Bristol area, *Q. Jl geol. Soc. Lond.* 61, 181–305.

WASHOUTS AND SPLITS IN COAL SEAMS

The discontinuities affecting coal seams may be broadly grouped into those of igneous (pages 29–31), tectonic (pages 74–84) or sedimentary origin. In the first two cases, once such structures have been encountered, their position and effect in adjacent areas may be reasonably predicted with reference to future development. Other discontinuities, mainly comprising washouts but also including particular types of seam splits, because of their erosional origin, are of more haphazard distribution. Consequently their position cannot be extrapolated for any but short distances into unproven ground.

WASHOUTS

Washouts (Raistrick & Marshall, 1939, pp. 79–101) are those areas of seams where the coal is totally or partly replaced by non-carbonaceous and often fairly coarse-grained clastic sediments. In some mining areas they are also called *dumb-faults*, *horses*, *stone dykes*, *washes* or *wants*. Of erosional origin, most washouts were formed during, or soon after, the formation of the affected seams. They may occur within any coal seam although they tend to be most commonly developed at a few particular horizons in any one coalfield. Little, if any, vertical displacements accompanied their formation so that on the total loss of a seam by a washout the coal may be encountered on the opposite side by tunnelling at the normal seam gradient.

ROLLS AND SIMPLE WASHOUTS

Roof, *rock rolls* or *nips* are particularly common where a seam is overlaid by a sandstone or conglomeratic roof. They consist of projections formed by the undersurface of the roof strata replacing the upper layers of the coal (Fig. 16.1) and consequently have deleterious effects on mechanized mining. The more elongate rolls tend to be developed in parallel swarms or *riggs*. Normally the basal surfaces of the rolls are irregular so that the coal cannot be broken cleanly from them. Occasionally however the contacts are slickensided and associated with minor compaction faults, in which case the coal may be readily separated. Some rolls pass in one direction into more typical washouts in which the whole, or

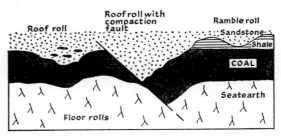

Fig. 16.1 Diagrammatic section illustrating roof and floor rolls.

greater part, of the seam is eroded. In other cases *ramble rolls* (Clarke, 1963, p. 675), which create particularly difficult roof conditions, may be separated from a seam by thin intercalations of other inter-seam strata.

Most roof rolls are simple erosional features which originated during, or soon after, peat formation. On the flooding of the peat surface local erosion occurred along minor stream channels developed in the soft upper layers of the peat. At a later stage the channels became infilled with the material forming the roll. A fairly constant current direction at the time, in some cases probably due to the initial slope of the peat surface, is indicated by the approximate parallelism of the more elongate rolls in some areas. Alternatively other rolls may have developed by loadcasting (page 43) when the overlying sediment locally sank into the mobile layers of the peat.

Distinct from the buckling of mine roadways as a result of loading due to coal extraction, irregularities may also occur in the floor of a seam affected by a rolling roof. Many such *floor rolls*, *saddles* or *horsebacks* clearly represent compaction phenomena subsequent to the deposition of the roof strata. Although the banded constituents of the seam are sometimes attenuated they are mostly continuous across the rolls. The rare case in which a seam is only partially developed over a floor roll may be considered indicative that the latter structure was in existence before the formation of the coal, and in some cases possibly originated by incipient folding.

Swilleys (Elliott, 1965) or *swalleys* (Clarke, 1963,

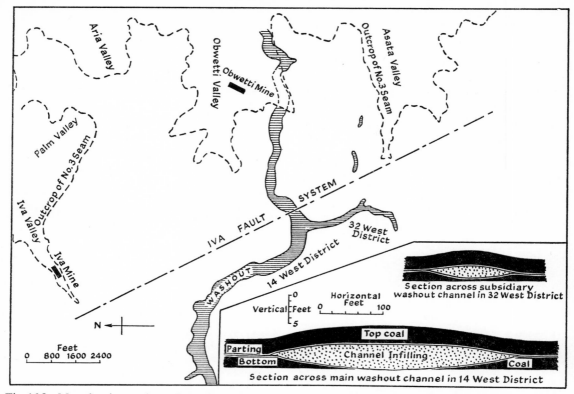

Fig. 16.2   Map showing washout channels in the Bottom Coal of the No. 3 seam, Enugu, Nigeria. (Simpson, 1954, Figs 10 and 11.)

p. 697) are elongated hollows in the topography of the base of a coal seam. Many are in effect coal filled river channels which were abandoned within the depositional phase of the seam affected. Thus, within the Top Hard seam of Nottinghamshire (Elliott, 1965) a swilley about 750 ft wide has been traced for over 22 miles. The channel consists of a hollow bordered by raised flanks along which minor faulting is commonly developed. Usually such displacements are less than the seam thickness and are of compactional origin forming during the deposition of the roof strata.

Washouts are larger features in which the coal may be totally absent and represent the channel deposits of streams and rivers flowing across the peat swamps. They are relatively narrow as compared with their often considerable lengths. In plan they resemble that of a lowland river system possessing a sinuous course and tributary offshoots, and generally taper towards their source. A good example is that described from the No. 3 seam at Enugu in Nigeria (Simpson, 1954, pp. 39–41). Here (Fig. 16.2), the principal washout composed of sandy shale and sandstone is confined to the bottom coal and has an average width of 400 ft. At one point the sinuous main washout is joined by a tributary from the south which gradually decreases in width from a maximum of 240 ft at the confluence. As is common in such tributaries the degree of incision is less than that of the main channel so that even in the axial parts of the subsidiary washout the basal layers of the bottom coal are present.

Occasionally the coal seams were eroded over widespread areas in a seemingly haphazard fashion. In some cases this resulted from the continual shifting of the river courses by the periodic silting of their channels. Other similarly barren areas of a seam sometimes represent the infillings of former lakes, in which case a partial development of cannel often occurs.

Usually the junction between a washout and the coal is highly irregular. Consequently some intimation as to the approach of a coal face towards a washout may be given by the occurrence of discontinuous, wedge-like and often arenaceous dirt partings. These become progressively persistent until they replace the whole or most of the seam at the

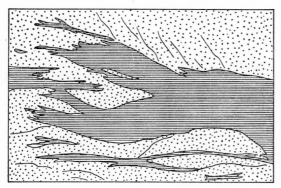

Fig. 16.3 'Fish-tail' structure at the edge of a washout (After Raistrick and Marshall.)

washout proper. Such 'fish-tails' (Raistrick & Marshall, 1939, pp. 81–3), (Fig. 16.3), indicate that the associated washout was formed after the deposition of the peat, which became undercut and splayed-out along the stratification by stream erosion. More rarely the contacts between a seam and washout are sharp and sometimes slickensided and slightly faulted from compaction effects. In such cases there may be little warning of their occurrence close to a working face. Sometimes the basal layers of a seam are continuous beneath a washout since they would be more resistant to erosion than the less consolidated surface layers of the former peat deposit. As a result of subsequent compaction effects many such attenuated seams are deflected downwards in the area local to the washout. Consequently the complete seam may be encountered more directly by a drivage at normal seam level across, and at right angles to the trend of the washout, than by following the deflected basal coal or seat earth. It is sometimes observed that a seam rapidly thickens next to a washout. Thus in several washouts in the Better Bed seam of Yorkshire the seam thickness increases from the normal 28 in to more than 6 ft (Raistrick & Marshall, 1939, pp. 84–5). The thicker coals along the margins of washouts probably resulted from the piling-up and sometimes overturning of the peat next to the stream channel by occasional flood waters.

The rocks associated with roof rolls and most washouts are predominantly sandstones, conglomerates and siltstones. The sandstones may be coarse-grained and conglomeratic, particularly in the basal parts of washouts. Quartz, ironstone and shale pebbles are the most common phenoclasts in the conglomerates, which often also include more irregular fragments and sometimes comparatively large rafts of coal. Occasionally fossil branches and trunks of the larger coal-forming trees are encountered with their longer axes more or less parallel to the trend of the

channel. Similarly the current direction, and consequently the channel trend, may sometimes be ascertained from the inclination of the cross-stratification (pages 41–2) which is particularly developed in the sandstones. Such evidence as to the washout trend is of great importance in assessing future mining development on encountering a hitherto unproved washout.

MULTISEAM WASHOUTS

Washouts affecting several seams are usually only encountered when the seams are relatively close together. Although such multiseam washouts are of erosional origin, they differ from simple roof rolls and single seam washouts in that they were produced by more powerful and deeply eroding rivers than normally occurred during the formation of the peat deposits. For the extremely gentle gradients of the latter together with their development at, or near, sea level (page 187) would effectively restrict river erosion to shallow depths. Conditions favorable to the formation of the deep channels occupied by multiseam washouts were comparatively rare, and in most cases can be attributed either to contemporaneous folding with local uplift or to differential subsidence along the edges of the sedimentary basins.

An example of the latter type is that developed in the northern part of the Warwickshire coalfield where the Two Yard Coal, between Kingsbury and Bedworth, is severely affected by washouts (Barrow *et al.*, 1919, pp. 37–8). In the Kingsbury collieries a continuous washout has been proved for over 5 miles and commonly exceeds $\frac{1}{2}$ mile in width (Fig. 16.4). Although the washout is mainly confined to the Two Yard Coal it also affects an underlying seam, separated by about 50 ft of strata, near the north-western margin of the coalfield. It is significant that hereabouts, near Dosthill, there is some evidence for the presence of a projecting mass of Cambrian rocks during the deposition of the principal coal seams (Barrow *et al.*, 1919, pp. 41–2). It is therefore probable that the washout was formed by a river flowing from this Cambrian island. The gradual decrease in erosive power as indicated by the progressive shallowing of the washout channel away from the land mass may be attributed to a similar decrease in the initial slope of the sedimentary basin towards the centre.

A remarkable series of multiseam washouts has been described from the Flintshire coalfield and is probably related to contemporaneous folding (Wedd & King, 1925, pp. 40–3). During the deposition of the Coal Measures, uplift along the Horse-shoe and Interior Anticlines accentuated the intervening Buckley Syncline. Concentrated northerly drainage along this trough resulted in the formation of a series of superimposed and occasionally multiseam wash-

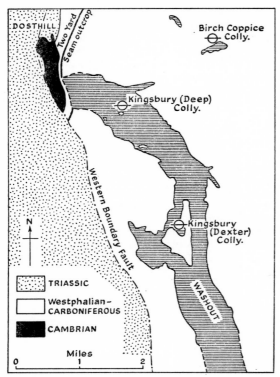

Fig. 16.4 Map showing a large washout in the Two Yard Seam in the north-western area of the Warwickshire coalfield.

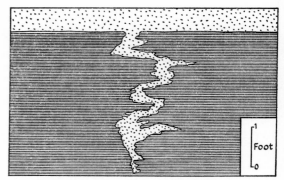

Fig. 16.5 Diagrammatic section illustrating the occurrence of a clastic dyke of sandstone within a coal seam.

outs which were located along the axial area of the syncline. At the abandoned Elm Colliery (*op. cit.*, p. 110) four superimposed and nearly coincident washouts were proved in the workings. The two highest washouts are of the multiseam type. Thus the Hollin, Bind and Massey coals are washed out by the descent of the Hollin Rock along an area over ½ mile in length. About 250 ft below the washout, the Rough and Main coals are similarly affected by the descent of the Main Rock.

SEISMIC WASHOUTS

In some coalfields one or a few seams are affected by discontinuities which, although generally less severe than the local erosional channels described above, tend to be developed on a regional scale. Such widespread disturbances were probably caused by seismic shock waves as a result of earthquakes and less severe earth-tremors during the accumulation of the coal seams (Raistrick & Marshall, 1939, pp. 92–9).

Clastic or *sandstone dykes*, *stone intrusions* or *eyes*

have been described and figured from a number of seams. They consist of irregular and frequently thin sandstone masses (Fig. 16.5) which in most cases penetrate the whole seam and are joined with an overlying sandstone. Alternatively, and less frequently, they may be connected with an underlying bed. The dykes are usually intensely crumpled and may develop wedge-like extensions along the bedding of the seam. They are sometimes accompanied by weak and fragmentary roof strata, as for example the 'clod' roof, itself attributed to seismic disturbance, above the Fox Earth coal or its equivalents in the East Pennine coalfield (Shirley, 1955, p. 273), (page 43). Although clastic dykes may form in a variety of ways (Shrock, 1948, pp. 212–20), many of those described from coal seams have been attributed to the seismic disturbance of waterlogged sediments, during which water may be expelled as a brief surface discharge. The more or less vertical ruptures so formed soon become blocked either by the injection of sedimentary material from below or by the collapse of the overlying sediments. The resulting dyke-like masses of material in the peat would subsequently be deformed during its compaction and coalification. Indeed the degree of compaction of a coal seam might be determined from the amount of crumpling which a clastic dyke contained within it has undergone. Such an estimate would be a more reliable indication of the thickness of the original peat than any so far made (page 221).

Other discontinuities attributed to seismic disturbance include some small-scale reverse faults confined to one seam and bearing no apparent relationship to the regional structure of a coalfield. Faults of this type (Fig. 16.6) may be the effect of a seismic shock causing partly consolidated sediments to move or 'lurch' a little distance forward, with a consequent slight duplication of strata. If developed on a regional scale, and overlaid by a jumbled or 'clod' roof, the seismic origin of these disturbances may be

Fig. 16.6 'Lurching' in the Haigh Moor Seam, Yorkshire. (After W. G. Fearnsides.)

accepted. However the more local occurrences having a linear distribution, as for example in the Haigh Moor seam of West Yorkshire (Fearnsides, 1916, pp. 583–608), are more probably compaction effects associated with erosional rather than seismic washouts (Edwards, 1937, pp. 111–18).

GLACIAL WASHOUTS

During the Pleistocene glaciation much of the pre-glacial topography, particularly in lowland areas, became modified and obscured by glacial deposits. Many valleys were completely blocked so that the post-glacial rivers, although often following the earlier drainage lines, may have eroded entirely new channels. Such infilled pre-glacial valleys may be encountered in shallow workings as dangerous wash-out phenomena of comparatively recent develop-ment. Furthermore since the sea level was much lower during glacial times than at present (page 104), the rock head in coastal areas below such glacial

washouts may be over 200 ft below present Ordnance Datum.

Unlike the sediments infilling the previously described washouts, those occurring in glacial wash-outs are essentially unconsolidated. In the main they are composed of till and fluvio-glacial sands and gravels (pages 105–7), although some alluvium (pages 104–5) may occur in the basal parts. All these materials are potentially mobile sediments which on penetration may form rapid influxes, as at Brance-peth Colliery (page 107, Fig. 10.15), and furthermore may release large quantities of water. Even when a stiff and apparently watertight till is encountered it must not be assumed that the material throughout the washout is of this type. Lenses of saturated fluvio-glacial deposits often occur which, if pene-trated by an exploratory drivage, may yield large inrushes of water if not themselves flowing as quicksand. Should such washouts be accidentally penetrated immediate precautions, involving the

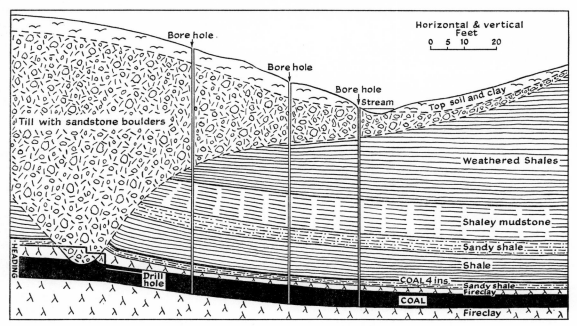

Fig. 16.7 Section illustrating a glacial washout proved in a north-east Lancashire colliery.

construction of bulkheads etc., should be taken to minimize the effects of any inrush. The state of the sediment immediately on penetration is not necessarily any indication as to its future behaviour for there may be a time lag between penetration and influx.

The possible occurrence of buried pre-glacial valleys should always be born in mind when mining at shallow depths, particularly in lowland areas. Coal seams are often terminated abruptly against the former valley sides so that there is little, if any, warning of their proximity to workings. Similarly the features may have no surface expression and even where recent erosion has followed the pre-glacial drainage lines the deepest parts of the washouts are seldom coincident with the existing valley.

One such washout was recently encountered in a small drift mine in the Lancashire coalfield (Fig. 16.7). The shale roof of a heading driven in coal changed suddenly to a wet and unconsolidated bouldery deposit which partially washed out the coal. Drivage was immediately stopped and a series of surface boreholes drilled to ascertain the nature of the trouble. These indicated that the heading had penetrated the basal and deepest parts of a glacial washout. It was fortunate that the pre-glacial stream had just eroded the upper part of the seam as otherwise, if the washout had not partly replaced the coal, there would have been no evidence of its existence

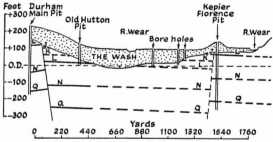

Fig. 16.8   Section across the 'Wash' in the vicinity of Durham. J, Low Main Seam, K, Brass Thill Seam, L, Hutton Seam, N, Harvey Seam, Q, Busty Seam. (After Hindson and Hopkins.)

and therefore a strong likelihood of a subsequent influx, as at Brancepeth Colliery.

A number of such glacial washouts occur in the coastal areas of the Durham coalfield. A notable example is the Team 'Wash' affecting several seams, including the Low Main and Hutton (Fig. 16.8). The washout is the infilling of the pre-glacial channel of the river Wear which was formerly a tributary of the river Tyne. The washout is proved for over 14 miles from Durham, where the meandering course of the ancient river has been extensively studied (Hindson

& Hopkins, 1948, pp. 105–16), to Gateshead in the north. At Durham the rock head is at about sea level but the floor of the washout slopes northwards, so that near Gateshead it is 188 ft below Ordnance Datum (Magraw, 1964, p. 115). Although the general line of the feature follows the Wear and Team valleys, its maximum effects are only occasionally coincident with the deepest parts of the present valleys.

SEAM SPLITS

The splitting of coal seams (Raistrick & Marshall, 1939, pp. 63–78) into two or more leaves separated by wedge-like or lenticular masses of interseam strata is a particularly common coalfield phenomenon. Indeed in some of the more intensely worked and therefore well recorded areas, as for example in the West Yorkshire coalfield (Edwards, *et al.*, 1940, p. 14), it has been stated that all the worked seams either exhibit splitting or are themselves members of a split. Unfortunately, during the initial development of a coalfield the phenomenon may remain unrecognized and, in the absence of marker horizons, result in a confusing seam nomenclature.

REGIONAL SPLITS

When splitting occurs in a seam the various leaves often retain their identities over a wide area. The splits usually result from variations in the subsidence rates of different parts of the coal-forming basins. The simplest case is that of a two-seam split which was caused by the temporary interruption of peat formation during a phase of subsidence. On the

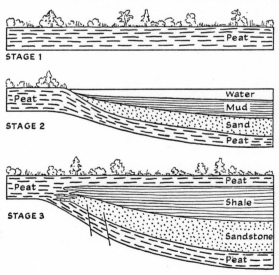

Fig. 16.9   Stages in the formation of a regional split.

Plate 12(a) Block of bituminous coal showing vitrain, durain, and clarain layers with ankerite along the cleat and pyrite along the bedding.

Plate 12(b) Fusain layer from a coal seam.

Plate 12(c) Fragment of cannel showing conchoidal fracture.

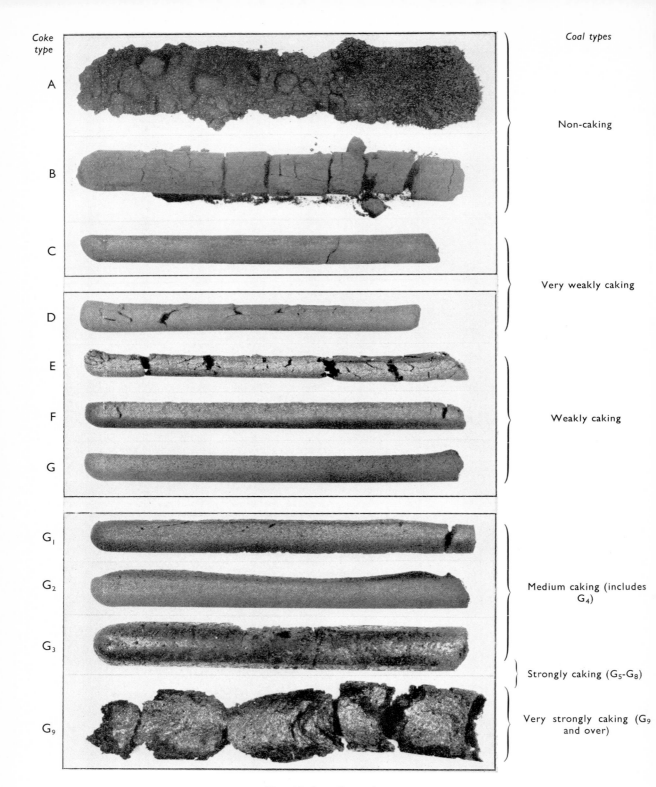

Plate 13 Gray-King coke types.
(With coke types G_1, G_2, etc., the subscript figure indicates the number of parts of electrode carbon, in 20 parts of a mixture of the coal and electrode carbon, required to give a G type (or 'standard') coke on carbonization; the cokes illustrated were made from the coal alone).

flooding of the area, interseam sediments would be deposited over the lower member of the split, whilst in an adjacent more stable area remaining above water level, peat formation would continue. Ultimately however subsidence would cease, so that peat formation would once more extend across the whole area to form the upper leaf of the split (Fig. 16.9). In the case of a multiseam split, subsidence was more intermittent so that a number of seams coalesce towards the margins of the subsiding area. Most seams exhibit splitting of this type towards the centres of the depositional basins where subsidence was at a maximum as compared with the slower rates in the marginal areas. Thus in the South Staffordshire (Fig. 15.16) and Warwickshire coalfields the famous Thick Coal, with a maximum thickness of 36 ft and 20 ft respectively, progressively splits into a number of seams in directions away from the margin of the contemporaneous 'St George's Land'.

Details of numerous splits in the British coalfields may be obtained from the relevant Geological Survey memoirs (e.g. Edwards, *et al.*, 1940, pp. 14–16) and

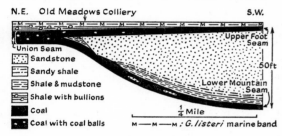

Fig. 16.10 Diagrammatic section illustrating seam splitting in the north-east Lancashire coalfield. (After W. B. Wright.)

N.C.B. Seam Folios. One of the earliest examples, which was noted over 100 years ago, occurs in the north-eastern part of the Lancashire coalfield where the Union seam, about 4 ft thick, splits into the Lower Mountain (*c*. 3 ft) and Upper Foot (*c*. 9 in) seams (Wright, *et al.*, 1927, pp. 77–8), (Fig. 16.10). The split rapidly develops in a south-westerly direction so that in less than half a mile the two members are separated by some 60 ft of predominantly arenaceous strata. Although the marginal parts of the split are sometimes occupied by badly broken ground subjected to compaction faulting, in some collieries a normal section of the Lower Mountain seam was worked to within a few feet off its coalescence with the Upper Foot seam. Locally the former seam is partially washed out by the descent of the overlying sandstone. The split has a considerable economic effect since the Lower Mountain seam, having low ash and sulphur contents, produced an excellent metallurgical coke. The overlying Upper Foot seam

C.M.G.—14

is on the other hand a highly sulphurous coal, as is also the combined Union seam (page 234).

LINEAR SPLITS

Linear splits affect relatively narrow, elongated and frequently sinuous areas of seams which occur over most of their development as single beds. Splits of this type are usually interpreted as forming by the temporary divergence of the streams which flowed across the coal-forming areas. After the deposition of the lowest coal the development of a local river channel would restrict peat formation over its length whilst peat would continue to form in the adjacent areas. On the abandonment of the channel the vegetation would encroach and gradually extend across the river deposits so that the upper coal would occur as a continuous bed. In some cases erosion of the basal peat resulted in the lower leaf of the split being washed out in the central part of the channel. When little erosion occurred the bottom coal is continuous below the channel infilling. The natures of the intervening measures between the split seams are similar to those encountered in more normal washouts, and prior warning of their occurrence may similarly be indicated by the gradual development of stone intrusions and dirt bands. Since peat is more susceptible to compaction than channel sediments, these typically possess a lenticular appearance in cross-section. The upper member of a linear split frequently rises into the roof at the channel margin and occurs some

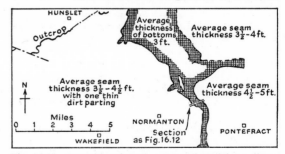

Fig. 16.11 Map showing the area effected by a linear split in the Middleton Main Seam, West Yorkshire. (After W. Edwards.)

distance above the level of the normal seam. The lower member may continue at the normal gradient or be inclined from both margins towards the axial area of the split.

A well documented example is that affecting the Middleton Main seam of the West Yorkshire coalfield (Fig. 16.11), (Edwards, *et al.*, 1940, pp. 42–6; Kendall, 1918, pp. 462–75). The complete seam consists of three distinct bands often separated by dirt partings, the Top Hards formed by interlaminated dull and bright coal, the Bottoms of softer bright

Fig. 16.12   Measured section across the linear split affecting the Middleton Main Seam at Whitwood Colliery, West Yorkshire. (After P. F. Kendall.)

coal, and an inferior basal coal. In the split area, which is occasionally over 2 miles in width, the flat-bottomed lens of intervening strata, predominantly composed of mudstone and sometimes containing a bed of cannel, attains a maximum thickness of 30 ft but is mostly about 10 ft thick. In all sinkings and borings through the split the upper leaf formed by the Hards appears to be present (Fig. 16.12). The Bottoms, forming the lower leaf and extensively worked in the affected area, is only occasionally completely washed out. A more local split in the same seam was encountered at Water Haigh colliery. The split is discoidal in plan and was probably formed by a small temporary lake in the peat bog (Kendall, 1918, pp. 473–4).

DIRT PARTINGS

The frequent occurrence of intercalations of non-carbonaceous material or 'dirt' is strong evidence of the composite nature of most seams. Since such partings are usually less than a few inches in thickness the coal seams can be worked as single units. When a parting increases in thickness to such an extent that it is impracticable to work the coals as a single bed, they are to be regarded as components of a split seam. Thus the Top and Bottom Busty seams of the Durham coalfield locally converge until they are separated by a parting which is in some localities less than 1 in thick, and are therefore worked as a composite seam. Over much of the coalfield they are worked as separate horizons and may sometimes be separated by over 20 ft of strata.

The origin of dirt partings is clearly the result of the temporary inundation of the peat surface. During the flooding of a river across a surrounding lowland area the water velocity is lowered and its transporting capacity rapidly diminishes away from the channel. Consequently only fine-grained argillaceous sediments are deposited on the floodplain, so that the partings within coal seams are usually of mud-

stone, shale or fireclay, and less commonly siltstone. Owing to the extremely slight initial slopes of the peat deposits the effects of flooding, in the form of dirt partings, are frequently widespread. In some cases a slight thickening, sometimes accompanied by an increase in grain size of the sediment, is apparent as the partings are traced towards their parent river channel, which may be represented by a washout.

NOMENCLATURE OF SPLIT SEAMS

The chaotic seam nomenclature, unfortunately still in use in some coalfields, is often due to a failure to recognize splitting when the seams were first named. Apart from a duplication of names between adjacent areas and sometimes even neighbouring collieries, an even more confusing state may be produced by the use of similar suites of seam names which are out of step between the various localities. The latter confusion may result from seam splitting remaining unrecognized and consequently misleading any attempts at sequence matching. A case in point is quoted from S. Wales where at Aberdare the next seam below the Nine Feet is the Bute, whereas in parts of the Rhondda Valley the latter name has been given to the lower member of the split Nine Feet (Adams, 1956, p. 842). Consequently the naming of seams below this horizon has been thrown out of step between the two areas. In the standard nomenclature proposed, or being proposed, for coalfields, provision is made by the use of forenames for the indication and naming of split seams. Thus in the Rhondda Valley the former Nine Feet and Bute seams are now termed the Upper and Lower Nine Feet seams respectively. Where seam index letters are employed, as in the Durham coalfield, the separate members of a split seam are denoted by the addition of subscript numerals to the common index letter. Alternatively, coalesced seams may be indicated by the combination of the respective index letters (Fig. 16.13).

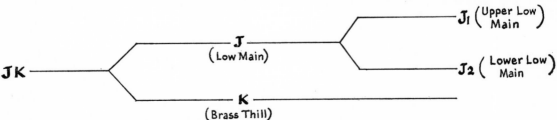

Fig. 16.13   Example of nomenclature indicating seam splits as used in the Durham coalfield.

REFERENCES

ADAMS, H. F. (1956) Seam structure and thickness in the South Wales coalfield, *Trans. Instn Min. Engrs* **115**, 839–57.

BARROW, G., GIBSON, W. CANTRILL, T. C., DIXON, E. E. L. & C. H. CUNNINGTON (1919) Geology of the country around Lichfield, *Mem. geol. Surv. Engld & Wales.*

CLARKE, A. M. (1963). A contribution to the understanding of washouts, swalleys, splits and other seam variations and the amelioration of their effects on mining in South Durham, *Trans. Instn Min. Engrs* **122**, 667–99.

EDWARDS, W. (1937) Washouts in the Haigh Moor coal of west Yorkshire, *Mem. geol. Surv. Summ. Prog. for 1935* **2**, 111–18.

EDWARDS, W., WRAY, D. W. & G. H. Mitchell (1940) Geology of the country around Wakefield, *Mem. geol. Surv. Engld & Wales.*

ELLIOTT, R. E. (1965) Swilleys in the Coal Measures of Nottinghamshire interpreted as palaeo-river courses, *Mercian Geologist*, **1**, 133–142.

FEARNSIDES, W. G. (1916) Some effects of earth-movement on the Coal Measures of the Sheffield district (south Yorkshire and the neighbouring parts of west Yorkshire, Derbyshire and Nottinghamshire), *Trans. Instn Min. Engrs* **50**, 573–608.

HINDSON, G. & W. HOPKINS (1948) The relationship of the Coal Measures to the "wash" between Shincliffe Bridge and Harbourhouse Park, Co. Durham, *Trans. Instn Min. Engrs* **107**, 105–17.

KENDALL, P. F. (1918) On the splitting of coal seams by partings of dirt. Part 1—splits that rejoin, *Trans. Instn Min. Engrs* **54**, 460–75.

MAGRAW, D. (1964) The importance of geology in the planning of undersea workings at Westoe colliery, County Durham, *Trans. Instn Min. Engrs* **123**, 101–17.

RAISTRICK, A. & C. E. MARSHALL (1939) *The Nature and Origin of Coal and Coal Seams*, 1st ed., London, E.U.P

SHIRLEY, J. (1955) The disturbed strata on the Fox Earth coal and its equivalents in the east Pennine coalfield, *Q. Jl geol. Soc. Lond.* **111**, 265–79.

SHROCK, R. S. (1948) *Sequence in Layered Rocks*, 1st ed., London, McGraw-Hill.

SIMPSON, A. (1954) The Nigerian coalfield, the geology of parts of Onitsha, Owerri and Benue Provinces, *Bull. geol. Surv. Nigeria.* **24**, 1–85.

WEDD, C. G. & W. B. R. KING (1924) The Geology of the country around Flint, Hawarden and Caergwrle, *Mem. geol. Surv. Engld & Wales.*

WRIGHT, W. B., SHERLOCK, R. L., WRAY, D. A., LLOYD, W. & L. H. TONKS (1927) Geology of the Rossendale Anticline, *Mem. geol. Surv. Engld & Wales.*

CORRELATION OF COALS AND INTERSEAM STRATA

Correlation involves the proving of the chronological equivalence of particular stratigraphic units across an area or region. In mining, correlative studies are of major importance, for without the certain identification of coal seams the geological structure, reserves and therefore economic future of a colliery or coalfield cannot be established. Many methods are employed which involve chiefly the matching of similar lithologies, sequences and faunas. Since very considerable changes of facies may often occur (pages 119–20), few methods are individually reliable and it is generally advisable to employ as many criteria as possible for the correlation of strata.

LITHOLOGICAL METHODS

Lithological methods of correlation are chiefly based on the recognition of unusual and therefore comparatively rare lithologies, distinctive mineral assemblages, the physical characters of the rocks and particular stratal sequences forming characteristic units.

COAL SEAMS

Seam lithologies

The earliest methods in which the properties of the coals themselves were utilized in seam correlation were based on the gross physical properties of the seams. Characters such as the seam thickness, the presence or absence of dirt partings, the occurrence of notable amounts of pyrite, the thickness and particular distribution of dull coal bands, the hardness and working characteristics may all be useful in correlation between closely adjacent localities. In some cases such properties may be noted subconsciously as a result of an observer's long experience in working a particular seam. Thus the opinion of a face worker whose mining lifetime may have been restricted to working one seam may still sometimes be sought for the identification of a seam perhaps encountered in development work across a fault or other discontinuity. Because of the lateral variations in lithologies and thicknesses, which are greater in some seams than others, the gross physical matching of coals should be attempted only for closely adjacent sections within, for example, an individual colliery take. If however the number of available sections is such that 'bridging' is possible it may sometimes be possible so to correlate two apparently dissimilar seams at opposite margins of a coalfield.

In the last two decades the considerable advances in coal petrology have enabled the application of correlative methods based on the identification and statistical analysis of the relative proportions of the microscopic constituents of the coals. Since the most usual methods are based on a comparison of the vertical distribution of the various lithologies present, a pillar-section of the entire thickness of the seam is first collected and a series of orientated polished surfaces prepared (Hacquebard, 1951, pp. 4–5). The microscopic examination of the polished surfaces is carried out using low- or medium-powered objectives immersed in cedar oil or methylene iodide which give a maximum contrast between the coal constituents and so facilitates their identification. The horizontal and vertical distribution of the various macerals (the basic microscopic constituents of coal, analogous to the minerals of rocks, e.g. fusinite, vitrinite, etc. (page 222) are determined at millimetre intervals throughout the seam thickness and plotted on a *coal-log* (Hacquebard, 1951, p. 11), (Fig. 17.1). A careful examination of the latter enables the subdivision of the seam into a series of petrographic units in which certain lithologies (the normal banded ingredients of coal, e.g. vitrain, clarain, etc.) predominate. Their relative proportions in each petrographic unit are calculated and illustrated as a *percentage diagram* of the whole seam (*op. cit.*, p. 20), (Fig. 17.2). For each petrographic unit the bright coal types (fusain, vitrain and clarain) are plotted on the left of the diagram and the dull coal types (durain and impure coal) plotted on the right. Since the bright and dull coals formed under relatively drier and wetter conditions respectively, a dividing line drawn between them on the percentage diagram is a reflection of the condi-

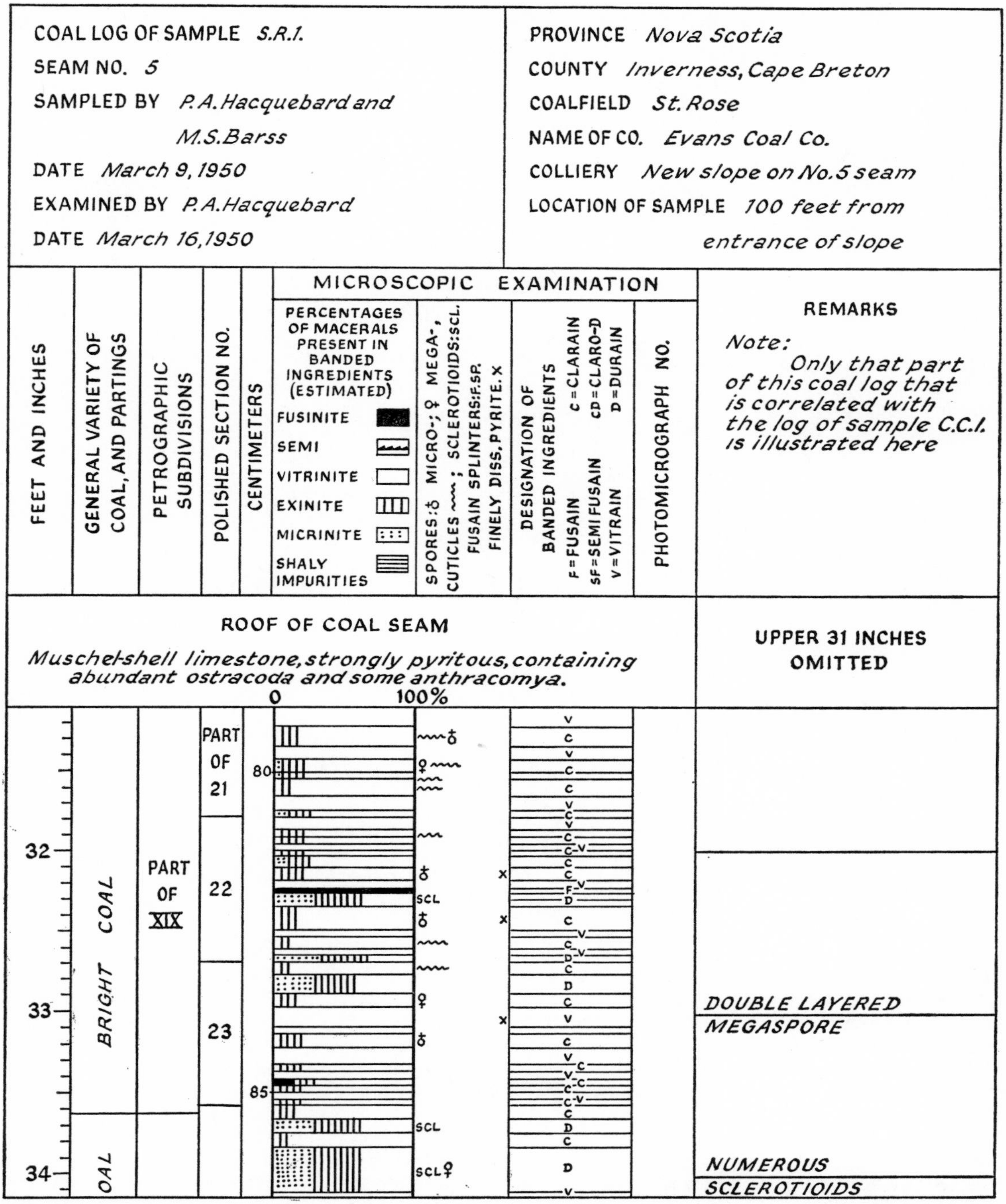

COAL LOG OF SAMPLE *S.R.1.*

SEAM NO. *5*

SAMPLED BY *P.A.Hacquebard and*
M.S.Barss

DATE *March 9,1950*

EXAMINED BY *P.A.Hacquebard*

DATE *March 16,1950*

PROVINCE *Nova Scotia*

COUNTY *Inverness, Cape Breton*

COALFIELD *St.Rose*

NAME OF CO. *Evans Coal Co.*

COLLIERY *New slope on No.5 seam*

LOCATION OF SAMPLE *100 feet from*
entrance of slope

MICROSCOPIC EXAMINATION

FEET AND INCHES	GENERAL VARIETY OF COAL, AND PARTINGS	PETROGRAPHIC SUBDIVISIONS	POLISHED SECTION NO.	CENTIMETERS	PERCENTAGES OF MACERALS PRESENT IN BANDED INGREDIENTS (ESTIMATED)	SPORES: ♂ MICRO-; ♀ MEGA-, CUTICLES ∼∼∼; SCLEROTIOIDS: SCL FUSAIN SPLINTERS: F,SF, FINELY DISS, PYRITE, X	DESIGNATION OF BANDED INGREDIENTS	PHOTOMICROGRAPH NO.

FUSINITE ■
SEMI ▬
VITRINITE □
EXINITE ▥
MICRINITE ⠿
SHALY IMPURITIES ▤

c = CLARAIN   cD = CLARO-D   D = DURAIN
F = FUSAIN   SF = SEMI FUSAIN   V = VITRAIN

REMARKS

Note:
Only that part of this coal log that is correlated with the log of sample C.C.I. is illustrated here

ROOF OF COAL SEAM

Muschel-shell limestone, strongly pyritous, containing abundant ostracoda and some anthracomya.

0   100%

UPPER 31 INCHES OMITTED

PART OF 21		80		v / c / v / c / v / c-v / c / c-v
PART OF XIX	22			c / c / F-v / D / c / c-v / D-v / c / D / c
	23	85		c / v / v-c / c-c / c-v / c / D / c / D / v

DOUBLE LAYERED MEGASPORE

NUMEROUS SCLEROTIOIDS

BRIGHT COAL

COAL

SCL

32 — 33 — 34 —

Fig. 17.1   Section of the coal log for the No. 5 Seam of the Chimney Corner Coalfield, Cape Breton Island, Nova Scotia. (Hacquebard, 1951, Fig. 3.)

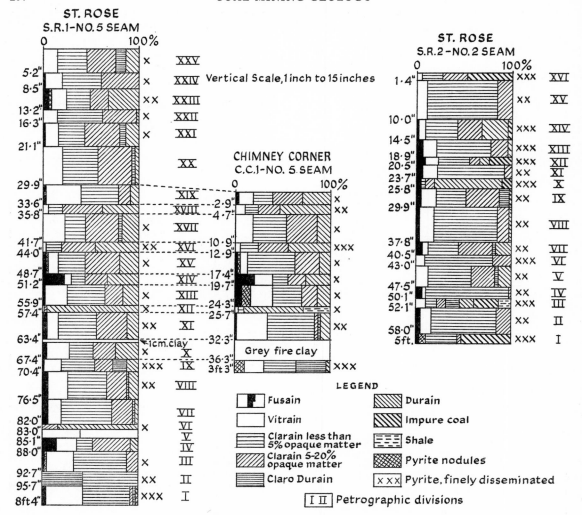

Fig. 17.2   Petrographic percentage diagrams of the Nos. 5 and 2 Seams of the St. Rose and Chimney Corner Coalfields of Cape Breton Island, Nova Scotia. (Hacquebard, 1951, Fig. 4.)

tions under which the coal formed. As these varied at different times the position of the dividing line is an important seam characteristic. It has been established in the studies so far made that the percentage diagrams of different seams in a vertical succession are dissimilar. Also, since the lateral changes in the composition of the petrographic divisions of the same seam are frequently only slight between localities up to about 3 miles apart, the technique may be used for such cases in short-range correlation (*op. cit.*, p. 20).

Sometimes however the banded constituents of the seams may be less constant and the various petrographic units rapidly lense out, in which case the correlative method previously described is clearly impracticable. Accordingly in Australia, where the Permian coals are of this nature, the *average* petrographic compositions of pillar-sections are calculated. Such compositions vary between different seams but are remarkably constant for particular seams sampled over a small area (Taylor & Warne, 1960, p. 78), (Fig. 17.3). An interesting corollary was examined by the same authors with regard to samples of run-of-mine coal. Approximately 6-in cubes from a particular seam were chosen at random and their petrographic composition determined. It was noted that the compositions differed only slightly from the composite analyses of the whole seam, so that the

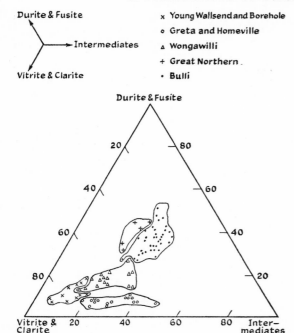

Fig. 17.3 Petrographic compositions of five Australian coal seams at various localities. The consistent separation between the various seams illustrates the possibilities of the method in correlation. (After Taylor and Warne.)

identity of some seams could possibly be obtained from a random sample (*op. cit.*, p. 78, Table 2).

A consequence of the increased emphasis placed in recent years on the microscopic examination of polished coal sections is the differentiation between the thick- and thin-walled miospores. The latter tenuispores or tenexinites (exine thickness $> 2\mu$) are apparent in cross-section as thin hair-lines, in contrast to the appreciably thicker-walled crassispores or crassexinites (exine thickness $< 2\mu$). Examination of many seams indicates that of the two types, the tenuispores are the prevalent miospores in the normal durain bands, which may therefore be termed tenuidurain. Crassidurain containing a larger portion of the thick-walled miospores is restricted to comparatively few seams. Consequently the occurrence of crassidurain is a significant diagnostic property enabling the successful correlation of the seams in which it occurs (Stach, 1955, pp. 114–16).

INTERSEAM ROCKS

Gross features

The direct visual examination of a rock sequence as exposed in a cross-measures drivage, borehole or shaft section, may reveal lithological features which by their comparative rarity may be utilized in correlation. Hence a particularly dark-coloured argillaceous horizon will contrast with the more normal greyish or bluish colours of the normal interseam shales and mudstones. Although such darker beds are sometimes important marine bands it may well be that their contained faunas are microscopic, so that the horizon may be at least initially identified by its colour alone. Alternatively, unusually light-coloured beds form readily noticeable horizons which are sometimes used as marker bands. Thus the 'Brownstone', occurring in the Woodfield and Middle Lount coal of the Leicestershire and S. Derbyshire coalfields, was a well known marker horizon even before its recognition as a tonstein (Eden, *et al.*, 1963, p. 51). Again, the 'Yellowstone', of the Limestone Coal Group of Fife, has similarly been utilized in that coalfield (Francis, 1961, p. 197). Sometimes horizons may be recognized by their relative hardness, as for example the tough, grey 'cank' of the Mansfield marine band in the Yorkshire, Derbyshire and Nottinghamshire coalfield. In other cases, shales containing numerous pyritic bodies of about pin-head size may indicate the proximity of a marine band, and, even when the latter is absent, often persist as a readily recognizable unit. Although many sandstones are notoriously variable in distribution and thickness they may nevertheless form characteristic local horizons, particularly in the Lower Coal Measures. In the Upper Coal Measures of the West Midlands the '*Spirorbis*' limestones are confined to only a few horizons in thick sequences of sandstones and shales and may therefore be traced across the coalfields by reason of their rarity in the vertical succession.

Should a microscopic examination be made, the general mineralogical features of sediments may also be utilized in correlation. Methods employing the microscopic examination of cleaned well-cuttings in reflected light proved successful during the development of the East Midlands oilfields in the wartime and immediate post-war years when coring was generally impracticable owing to the necessity for rapid drilling speeds. In the Middle and Lower Coal Measures of the region some of the more notable marker horizons included ironstones possessing oolitic textures, sandstones with bright green chamosite grains and flagstones containing brown and green micas besides the more common silvery muscovite (Falcon & Kent, 1960, pp. 50–4).

Tonstein bands

A tonstein (Williamson, 1961, pp. 9–14) is an argillaceous rock composed largely of kaolinite with smaller amounts of detrital minerals and carbonaceous materials. Tonstein bands occur both within the coals and interseam strata and their thickness mostly averages a few centimetres, although a few beds over 1 m in thickness have been recorded. They have occasionally been shown to pass laterally into shales, ironstones and sandstones. Most often the interseam tonsteins occur in association with durain or cannel coals.

In hand specimens tonsteins are fine-grained, compact and rarely laminated rocks with well developed vertical jointing. The fracture is uneven or semiconchoidal. Although they may easily be confused with ordinary interseam mudstones or shales they are frequently tougher than such sediments. Often it is difficult to isolate a tonstein from the surrounding strata although the junctions are well defined. When forming dirt bands within seams, or occurring at the base of the coal, tonsteins may be distinguished from ordinary fireclays by the regularity of their jointing as compared with the usually strong development of listric surfaces in the seat earths. Tonsteins vary in colour between black, brown, grey or white but are generally lighter than the surrounding strata. The streak is usually white or grey as a result of their high kaolinite content. Occasionally the kaolinitic masses present a speckled appearance on freshly broken surfaces. It is however only by a microscopic and sometimes X-ray examination that most specimens may be accurately determined as tonsteins. Under the microscope the kaolinite occurs either as isolated crystals or rounded crystalline aggregates set in an extremely fine-grained kaolinite ground-mass. The latter also contains variable amounts of vegetable matter, quartz, felspar and mica fragments together with rarer carbonate and other minerals. The well cleaved kaolinite crystals are particularly evident and have a yellowish, brownish or white colour in plane-polarized light. In some tonsteins the crystals occur as characteristically sinuous *vermicules* (Plate 11a).

The exact mode of origin of tonsteins is at present uncertain. Briefly the principal theories are as follows.

(1) Sedimentary: the deposition of kaolinite-rich sediments derived from the weathering of felspars occurring in granites which cropped out adjacent to the sedimentary basin.

(2) Pyroclastic: deposited as showers of kaolinite or kaolinized tuff during volcanic outbursts.

(3) Diagenetic: formed by the penecontemporaneous recrystallization of clay minerals in a markedly acid environment. Such an environment probably occurred in the coal measure basins on account of the presence of humic and sulphuric acids.

(4) Biochemical: in a comprehensive study of the Erda tonstein from Oberhäusen, West Germany, Moore (1964, pp. 235–85) attributes its formation to soil-forming processes of essentially biochemical action.

Originally a simple descriptive classification was employed, so that crystalline ('Krystall') tonsteins or granular ('Graupen') tonsteins were distinguished according to the respective occurrence of the kaolinite as either isolated crystals (Plate 11a) or rounded masses (Plate 11b). Recently (Bouroz, 1962, pp. 86–9) a classification taking consideration of both the lithological characters and possible origin of the rocks has been proposed (Table 34).

Tonsteins have in many cases a widespread distribution, and since they often possess specific characters by which particular beds may be identified are used as important marker bands. The principal macroscopic characters which are used for this purpose are the thickness, colour and geometric relations of the beds. Thus a unit formed by several relatively close bands may sometimes be identified without recourse to more tedious microscopic methods. The latter are based on the nature of the kaolinite and other components of the rocks. So far tonstein bands have been extensively used as correlative horizons in most of the continental European coalfields, and indeed some have been traced across North France through Belgium and Holland into West Germany. In Britain over forty tonstein bands occur in the Limestone Coal Group of Fife where they are associated with tuffs and lavas (Francis, 1961, pp. 195–201), and in the coalfields of the

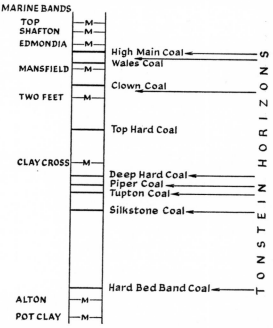

Fig. 17.4   Some tonstein horizons of the East Midlands Coal Measures.

TABLE 34

A Classification of Tonsteins (after A. BOUROZ)

Origin	Variety	Character	
Alteration of a primary deposit of tuff ORTHO-TONSTEIN	Ortho-tonstein α	Conspicuous irregular nodules containing vermicular or crystalline kaolinite	
	Ortho-tonstein β	Numerous small crystals and vermicules of kaolinite	
Redeposition and subsequent alteration of a tuff STRATO-TONSTEIN	Strato-tonstein α1	Ovoid or flattened nodules with sharp margins and crypto- or occasionally micro-crystalline kaolinite. Possessing a definite layered texture	May contain abundant detrital quartz and other sedimentary fragments
	Strato-tonstein α2	Irregular masses of crypto- or micro-crystalline kaolinite and altered felspars	
	Strato-tonstein β	Numerous small crystals or vermicules of kaolinite. (Differs from ortho-tonstein β in containing an abundance of detrital quartz and having a less homogeneous texture)	
A colloidal sedimentary deposit CRYPTO-TONSTEIN		A homogeneous and crypto-crystalline mass of kaolinite	
Probably developed from ortho-tonsteins by metamorphism META-TONSTEIN		Composed predominantly of micaceous minerals having a similar form to kaolinite	

English Midlands at least eight tonstein horizons have so far been discovered (Eden, *et al.*, 1963, pp. 47–58), (Fig. 17.4). Many similar beds undoubtedly occur in the North American, Australian and other coalfields, but up to date do not appear to have been utilized in correlation.

Tuffaceous siltstones

Sequences of tuffaceous siltstones, sometimes totalling over 20 ft in thickness, have been described from the Fife coalfields (Francis, 1961, pp. 201–10), where they may be traced for up to 10 miles in the Lower Limestone, Limestone Coal and Upper Limestone Groups. The sequences are composed of a number of units from 0·5 to 10·0 mm in thickness. Each unit is graded characteristically so that the coarsest components occur at the base, which may exhibit load casts (page 43). Tuffaceous siltstones are chiefly composed of non-igneous debris of which quartz grains up to 0·5 mm in maximum dimension are predominant (Plate 11c). Accessory minerals include felspars, white mica, green and brown pleochroic serpentine and garnet. Occasional fragments of sandstone, quartzite, mudstone and coal may also

occur. In the basal coarse layers of the graded units concentrations of glassy basaltic fragments may be altered to kaolinite or replaced by carbonate minerals.

The origin of tuffaceous siltstones is clearly related to contemporaneous vulcanicity for they occur only in or adjacent to regions, and at horizons, where more normal volcanic phenomena are in evidence. Indeed some beds pass in one direction into basaltic tuffs and in the other, away from the volcanic centres, into non-graded beds without any igneous material. There is some evidence that the associated non-graded strata accumulated in relatively shallower water conditions.

The well-graded tuffaceous siltstones are at once noticeable for the remaining interseam sequences are typically non-graded. Although they lack any individual characteristics the tuffaceous siltstones can be used in conjunction with other correlative criteria. One interesting result of their use has been the indication that various members of the sedimentary cycle were in fact contemporaneous at different localities (*op. cit.*, p. 205). It has for example been demonstrated that, over a distance of some 10 miles, an associated coal may occur either above or below the siltstone at different localities and, consequently, the seam is not exactly contemporaneous over the whole area.

Heavy mineral analysis

The principal rock-forming minerals occurring in the arenaceous and argillaceous interseam sequences possess relatively low specific gravities. On the other hand the bulk of the clastic accessory minerals which were originally derived from the erosion of igneous and metamorphic rocks have appreciably higher specific gravities. Such *heavy minerals*, arbitrarily defined as having specific gravities above 2·9 (Table 35), may vary in type and proportions between different beds and can therefore be utilized in correlation.

TABLE 35

The Specific Gravities of some Heavy Minerals

Mineral	Specific gravity
Muscovite	2·8 –3·0
Biotite	2·8 –3·2
Tourmaline	3·0 –3·2
Apatite	3·17–3·23
Augite	3·2 –3·6
Garnet	3·5 –4·3
Rutile	*c.* 4·2
Zircon	4·5 –4·7
Pyrite	4·8 –5·1
Magnetite	5·1 –5·2

The first stage in the heavy mineral analysis (Milner, 1962a, pp. 99–128) involves the careful crushing of the rock specimen. This is usually carried out by hand using a mortar and pestle. Any carbonate or other films adhering to the mineral grains are removed by gentle washing usually in dilute hydrochloric acid, after which the bulk of the lighter minerals is removed by panning. The heavy mineral fraction is concentrated in bromoform (sp. gr. = 2·87–2·90) or other liquids of high specific gravity using apparatus similar to that illustrated (Fig. 17.5). After a few minutes the heavy minerals will have accumulated at the base of the liquid, whereas quartz and other fragments of low specific gravity will form a surface crust. After washing in alcohol or benzol to extract any surplus bromoform adhering to the grains, the heavy mineral concentrate is dried by gentle heating in an oven. Sometimes the procedure may be repeated using a series of liquids of successively higher specific gravities so that the various minerals may be further subdivided as an aid to their recognition. Similarly the magnetic fraction of the heavy mineral concentrate may be isolated from the sample by using bar, horse-shoe or electro-magnets (Milner, 1962a, pp. 194–9). After

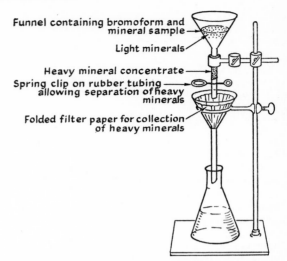

Fig. 17.5   Simple apparatus required for heavy mineral separation.

mounting in Canada balsam, the minerals are identified under the petrological microscope and the various types and relative quantities noted. The relative percentage frequencies of the heavy minerals are usually illustrated by graphical means which at the same time may illustrate vertical variations in a bed or group of beds. (Fig. 17.6).

For the correlation of a bed by such methods the relative frequencies and types of minerals in the specimens examined should be broadly similar (they

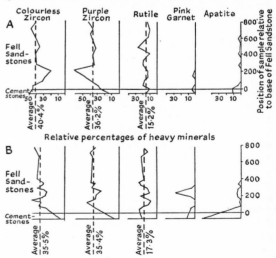

Fig. 17.6   Comparison of heavy mineral frequencies in the Fell Sandstone Group of the Harbottle (A) and Simonside (B) areas of Northumberland. (After D. A. Robson.)

will seldom, if ever, be identical). Alternatively if there is a marked difference between two samples taken from closely adjacent localities then the samples may be regarded as originating from distinct horizons. Thus in mid-Northumberland the heavy mineral content of the Fell Sandstone Group is broadly similar over an area of about 40 mile² and dissimilar to that of the underlying sandstones in the Cementstone Group (Robson, 1956, pp. 251–4).

A number of factors limit the reliability of heavy mineral analysis to essentially short-range correlation (Milner, 1962b, pp. 372–406). The heavy mineral content of a bed may exhibit considerable variations over a short distance. In some cases the variations can be ascribed to the derivation of materials from different sources. For example, consider the sediments deposited contemporaneously by two adjacent rivers eroding outcrops of acid and basic igneous rocks respectively. Around the mouth of the first river the heavy minerals will consist of the granitic subsidiary minerals such as tourmaline and zircon, whereas these will be extremely rare, if not absent, in the deposits of the second river. Consequently although the deposits are equivalent in age they will certainly not appear so by their heavy mineral content.

Cyclothem and unit matching

Considerable thicknesses of strata often occur between the more reliable marker horizons and in many cases it is necessary to correlate individual seams within such sequences. Where other methods are inapplicable correlation may be attempted by the matching of particular cyclothems (pages 44–5) as proved in several adjacent boreholes (Fig. 17.7). Great caution should be exercised in attempting such correlations, for many cyclothems are notoriously variable in their areal distribution and vertical succession, so that the straightforward matching of units is in most cases impracticable. Thus in some localities of the East Pennine coalfield only four cyclothems are present within the Upper Similis-Pulchra Zone whereas at others over twenty are developed (Duff & Walton, 1962, p. 250). Similarly the effect of differential subsidence in S. Staffordshire is reflected in the southward coalescence of seams (Fig. 15.16) and the proportionately greater number of cyclothems in the northern part of the coalfield.

Most certainly the absence of one or more beds cannot alone be used as a diagnostic character of a particular cyclothem. The abnormal rather than the 'typical' cyclothems tend to be of more significance in correlation. Sometimes a particularly thick argillaceous sequence may be a characteristic feature indicative of a certain horizon. The occurrence or absence of sandstones is on the other hand of little

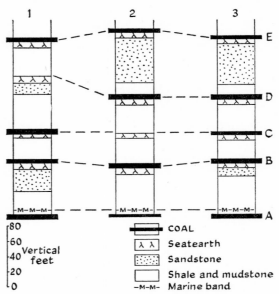

Fig. 17.7   Diagram illustrating cyclothem matching between adjacent boreholes.

significance for, apart from in the lowest Westphalian strata, such beds are extremely variable in thickness (page 54, Fig. 9.11). Seat earths are the most consistent members of the cyclothems for even when the coals were removed soon after formation the underlying fireclays by reason of their rather 'tacky' nature were in most cases only incompletely eroded. Consequently in the absence of other marker bands the seat earths may well provide key horizons enabling tentative correlations to be made.

INSTRUMENTAL BOREHOLE LOGS

During the drilling of fully cored boreholes much useful ancilliary information is obtained from the various instrumental borehole logging techniques originally developed as an aid to oilfield exploration and more recently applied to the examination of most other deep boreholes. Where percussive or mud-flush boring is practised it is even more important that the information derived from the examination of the broken rock-cuttings collected from the mud-stream is supplemented by several geophysical logging methods. These utilize the electrical and radiogeological properties of the rocks surrounding the borehole and are graphically recorded as the measuring instruments or *sondes* are lowered down the hole (Le Roy, 1950, pp. 364–436; Lynch, 1962 pp. 83–267). In some instances the actual rock types may be established by their particular geophysical properties and even if the lithologies cannot be estimated the junctions between the various beds are indicated on the instrumental graphs by sudden changes in slope. The structure of an area may therefore be interpreted by correlating the various 'highs' and 'lows' of the geophysical borehole logs (Fig. 17.8).

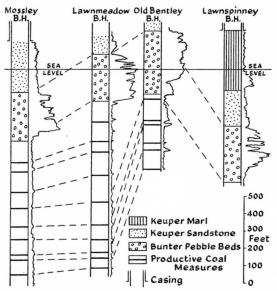

Fig. 17.8   Electrical resistivity logs for four boreholes in the South Staffordshire Coalfield. (After E. S. Polak.)

The electrical methods of borehole logging yield the most complete information. The *resistivity log* is obtained when an electric current is passed between several electrodes in the borehole and at ground

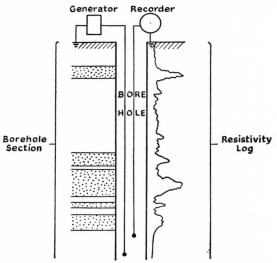

Fig. 17.9   Electrical resistivity log for a borehole penetrating a series of sandstones and shales.

level (Fig. 17.9). In such logs coals and sandstones usually show as peaks of high resistivity whilst the argillaceous interseam sediments exhibit appreciably lower resistivities. Furthermore since fresh water is an extremely poor electrical conductor many aquifers, of obvious concern to the mining engineer, possess noticeably high resistivities and may therefore be identified on the resistivity logs (Polak, 1952 pp. 499–500). No external current is applied in the production of the *spontaneous potential log* which records the self-potential of the rocks as a single electrode, connected via a sensitive recording potentiometer to one placed at the surface, is raised up the borehole. Such logs are frequently used in conjunction with resistivity studies. *Radioactivity logs*, made as Geiger or more sensitive scintillation counters are lowered down the borehole, are sometimes used to supplement the elecrical methods. In this respect some, but certainly not all, marine shales are more radioactive than non-marine shales and similarly certain tonsteins may also be revealed as unusually high peaks on such logs (Knowles, 1964, Ponsford, 1955, pp. 34–7). Alternatively and excepting extremely rare cases, coal seams are amongst the least radioactive sedimentary rocks.

Under normal drilling conditions changes in the penetration rate of the drill reflect the varying lithologies of the rocks encountered. Thus an increase in the penetration rate from about 0·3 in/min to 2·5 in/min occurs on drilling through the roof shales into a coal seam and subsequently the rate decreases again at the seat earth. By the observation of the exact drilling rate and employing relatively simple apparatus (Goosens, 1953, pp. 497–500) *penetration logs* may be constructed upon which the thickness of even thin seams and dirt bands may be accurately esti-

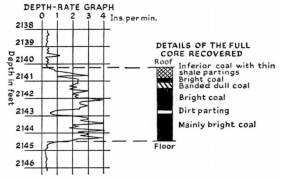

Fig. 17.10   Comparison of penetration record with the actual core recovered. (After R. F. Goosens.)

mated (Fig. 17.10). The method is however unsuitable when a weak sandstone occurs immediately above the coal, in which case the penetration rate changes little.

PALAEONTOLOGICAL METHODS

Fossil plants and animals are of common occurrence in most coalfields, and sometimes the very presence of a fossil band may serve to identify a particular part of the succession. Often however a detailed palaeontological analysis of the particular floral or faunal assemblage is necessary.

Spore analysis

Many of the coal-forming plants reproduced by spores which are abundant both within the coal seams and the interseam sediments. Because of their minute size the spores may be extracted from borehole cuttings and fragmentary cores whilst the larger fossils are often destroyed beyond recognition. Also, since they occur within the coals, suitable material for spore analysis may be collected from the coal face and does not depend on the occurrence of interseam sections which are necessary for the collection of the other fossil groups. Both the larger megaspores and the smaller miospores have been utilized in correlation, for the frequencies of the different species usually vary in a vertical sequence. Even when the total spore assemblages of two seams are similar, their vertical distribution in the seams may be significantly different. It is however evident that the spore content of a seam may change laterally especially when lithological changes occur. Consequently spore analysis is reliable only for short-range correlation up to a few miles between the sampling points.

The megaspore content of coals can be calculated from a study of thin or polished sections forming an overlapping series throughout the total seam thickness. Thus Slater (1932) and several contemporary workers determined a series of spore types, at that time numerically named, and analysed their concentration at particular horizons. Graphical representation (Fig. 17.11) of the megaspore contents of various seams clearly demonstrated the application of the method to correlation. Subsequent work supports these early conclusions (Dijkstra, 1952, pp. 163–5) although most modern workers have concentrated on the miospore contents of the coal seams.

Although the pioneer studies of miospore distribution were made by Thiessen in America much of the subsequent work has been carried out in Europe (a useful reference list is that in Balme & Butterworth, 1952, pp. 878–9). Since the miospores cannot be satisfactorily identified on polished surfaces or in thin sections it is first necessary to extract the fossils from the coal.

(1) A composite coal sample, prepared from a pillar-section through the whole section of a seam, is crushed to pass through a 30 B.S. mesh sieve.

(2) About 0·5 g of the powdered coal is treated

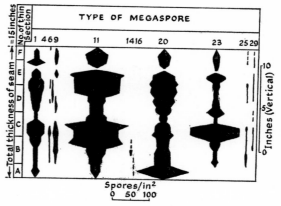

Fig. 17.11 Megaspore distribution diagram for the Better Bed Seam, Leeds, Yorkshire. (Slater, 1932, Fig. 11.)

with Schultz solution (nitric acid to which potassium chlorate has been added) for between 18 and 36 hours. The actual time taken for oxidation depends on the rank, type and, if from a surface outcrop, degree of weathering of the coal. As the reaction may proceed quite fiercely in the early stages the container should be surrounded by an ice bath and preferably placed in a fume cupboard.

(3) After washing, by decantation with water, the residue consisting of spores, plant debris and unaltered particles is treated with a 10 per cent solution of potassium hydroxide and then washed several times by decantation.

(4) A small portion of the residue is transferred to a test tube which is partly filled with water and gently shaken. After a few seconds the larger fragments will have settled so that the suspension of fine particles is composed chiefly of miospores. A drop of the suspension is placed on a microslide together with a drop of melted glycerine jelly, which forms the mount, and evaporated gently.

The miospores are identified and counted under high power magnification. Only a few species occur in most miospore assemblages and their relative frequencies, expressed as percentages of the total spore count, are plotted graphically as a histogram (Fig. 17.12). Although the actual number of miospores prepared from composite samples of a seam may differ between the various sampling points, their relative percentages are nevertheless usually similar for a local area. The utility of the method in correlation may be illustrated with reference to the loss of the Beaumont Seam across a wide front at Montagu Colliery, Northumberland (Smith, 1962, p. 37) (Fig. 17.12). On the drivage of a short heading from the Beaumont workings a thin coal was encountered which could have been the Hodge Seam some 30 ft

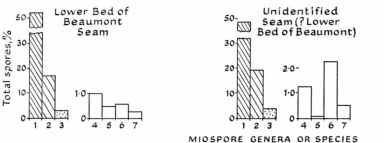

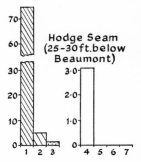

(1) *Lycospora* spp.,　　(2) *Laevigatosporites* spp.,　　(3) *Densosporites* spp.,　　(4) *Crassispora kosankei*,
(5) *Cancellatisporites tortuosus*,　　(6) *Dictyotriletes bireticulatus*,　　(7) *Schulzospora ovata*.

Fig. 17.12　Histograms of miospore frequency in coal seams at Montagu Colliery, Northumberland. Comparisons suggest that the Unidentified Seam is probably equivalent to the lower bed of the Beaumont Seam. (After A. V. H. Smith.)

below the Beaumont and faulted into juxtaposition. Miospore analysis indicated that the thin coal was equivalent to the lower part of the Beaumont Seam so that the discontinuity was a washout and not a fault.

Alternatively a series of spore profiles which illustrate the vertical distribution of the miospore species through the whole thickness of the seam may be constructed. This involves the analysis of a series of seam subsections and is considered the most reliable method of correlation (*op. cit.*, pp. 37–8).

It has recently been demonstrated (Marshall & Smith, 1965; Sullivan, 1962, pp. 362–3) that many miospores have similar ranges in the coals, associated shales and seat earths. By disintegrating such argillaceous strata with hydrofluoric acid and treating the organic residue with Schultz solution the miospores may be extracted and identified. It is thus possible to utilize the spore contents of such sediments in correlation by employing similar statistical methods as applied to those of coal seams. The method has an important potential in the correlation of anthracite seams where their high rank prevents the extraction of miospores from the coals themselves, and also in the correct identification of seat earths, when the overlying coal may be absent.

Marine bands

The marine bands which occur within some interseam sequences were mostly deposited during regional inundations of the coal-forming swamps. Since the latter were essentially low-lying and of little relief only slight subsidence of the sedimentary basins or alternatively (and more probably) a slight rise of sea-level resulted in the widespread deposition of marine sediments and fauna.

Most often the bands are only a few feet thick and in some instances are composed of less than an inch of marine strata. Even such thin bands have a wide-spread distribution and form remarkably persistent horizons. Thus the Tonge's marine band in the Lower Coal Measures of Lancashire can be correlated with the Norton marine band of the E. Pennine coalfields although its thickness rarely exceeds 3 in and at some localities it is virtually confined to a single bedding surface. On the Continent, the Plass-shofsbank is probably the same horizon (Ramsbottom & Calver, 1962, pp. 572–3), (Fig. 17.13), as is also the Fairy Mount marine band of Eire (Eagar, 1964, pp. 369–70).

The lithologies of the marine bands are predominantly argillaceous, the more typical ones being composed of intensely black and often pyritic shales. At weathered exposures they may sometimes be easily separated into paper-thin leaves often coated with secondary ferruginous minerals. Bullions (pages 63–4) containing solid fossils occur as concretions in some bands, notably that containing *G. listeri* (Table 32) in the Lower Coal Measures. In Britain, marine limestones are absent from the Westphalian, although ankeritic mudstones and siltstones may sometimes form locally persistant horizons such as the 'cank' of the Mansfield marine band. Evidently they represent the limestone phase developed during the more complete marine conditions exemplified by the cyclothems of the mid-American Coal Measures (Edwards & Stubblefield, 1947, p. 226). The highest marine bands of the British Middle Coal Measures tend to be less carbonaceous and lighter coloured so that they cannot be easily distinguished from the surrounding non-marine sediments.

Excepting those contained within bullions, the fossils (pages 159–64) are almost always decalcified and rarely retain any original carbonate shell material. They usually occur as flattened impressions sometimes coated with a thin layer of pyrite. The more resistant chitinous materials forming the hard parts

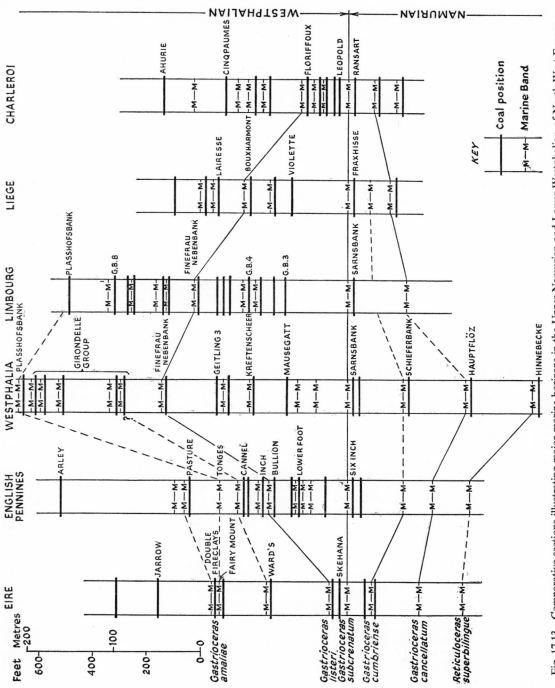

Fig. 17.13 Comparative sections illustrating major marine horizons in the Upper Namurian and Lower Westphalian of North West Europe. (After Eagar, Ramsbottom and Calver.)

TABLE 36
The Faunal Sequence of the Banbury Marine Band, Bowsey Wood, North Staffordshire
(Details of succession after J. R. Earp, 1961, p. 170)

Phase	Main genera	Thickness		'Land'	Fresh water	Brackish water	Marine
		ft	in				
Non-marine lamellibranch	*Anthracosia, Naiadites*						
Transition — — — — —	*Lingula*	10					
Marine	*Anthracoceras, Dunbarella, Lingula*	1					
— — — — —	*Lingula*		3				
Transition	Stunted *Anthracosia, Lingula*		6				
Non-marine lamellibranch	*Anthraconaia, Anthracosia, Naiadites*	3	2				
Coal							

of the inarticulate brachiopods are preserved in a virtually unaltered state and are conspicuous on account of their lustrous nature. Although the faunal assemblages of some bands may be exceptionally varied (over eighty species were recorded from the basal $5\frac{1}{2}$ in of the Cefn Coed marine band at one locality in S. Wales) most of the fossils are restricted to a few common species. The progressive development of the marine transgressions may often be demonstrated by the faunal sequences present within the bands (Table 36). Thus although *Gastrioceras* and *Anthracoceras* may occur within the same layer in some of the Lower Coal Measure bands they more often form separate layers. It is considered that the latter genus preferred the less saline and shallower waters during the early or late stages of the marine transgression (Hodson & Leckwijck, 1958, pp. 6–7). The occurrence of cf. *Anthraconaia pruvosti*, a form with distinct affinities with the non-marine lamellibranchs, in the Shafton and Lower Sankey marine bands of the E. Pennine and Lancashire coalfields is likewise suggestive of the comparatively low salinity of that particular marine incursion. Rather similar conditions are indicated by the presence of *Lingula* for, although the brachiopod may occur throughout a marine band, it is most often found in the basal and uppermost layers. Consequently *Lingula* bands, sometimes termed 'pene-

marine bands', in which the genus is often exclusively developed, are distinguished from the more normal marine bands possessing a goniatite or marine lamellibranch phase.

The various marine horizons undoubtedly form the most reliable means of correlation in the British (Table 32) and N. European coalfields. Should the faunas of several bands be indistinct or similar, the actual horizons may still be individually identified by their comparative rarity and relative positions in the non-marine lamellibranch zonal succession. For example, the marine band accepted as the base of the Middle Coal Measures can be recognized even where the diagnostic goniatite *Anthracoceras vanderbeckei* is absent, since it forms the sole marine horizon within and about the middle of the Modiolaris Zone. Some marine bands occur in the roof measures of workable coals, in which case they are of obvious use in the correlation of the underlying seams. Others, however, although forming part of non-productive sequences are nevertheless equally important since they form reliable marker horizons and datum planes for the structural interpretation of an area.

Mussel bands

The non-marine lamellibranchs most commonly occur as concentrated accumulations either directly

Plate 14 Electrically-operated bucket-wheel coal dredger at the Yallourn open-cast site, Australia. This large machine wins brown lignite at the rate of 1350 tons per hour.

Plate 15(a) Eye coal showing characteristic oval fracture surfaces. Top coal of the Brassey Seam, Lancashire ($\times \frac{3}{4}$).

Plate 15(b) Block of paper coal from near Rockville, Indiana, USA ($\times \frac{1}{2}$).

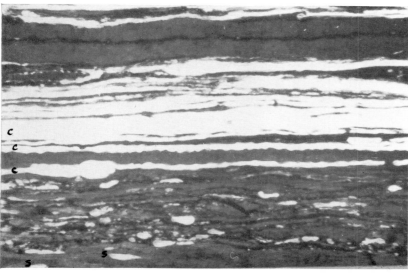

Plate 15(c) Thin section of paper coal perpendicular to bedding. C=cuticles, S=spores; remainder vitrinite ($\times 200$).

above or in close proximity to the coal seams. Recent geochemical studies (briefly reviewed by Eagar, 1960, pp. 143–6) on the boron content of the associated rocks, which in some cases appears to be proportional to the degree of salinity in which the sediments were deposited, suggest that most of the genera lived in slightly brackish, rather than fresh water, lagoons or estuaries. Such conditions were relatively localized as compared with the widespread marine transgressions. Thus many mussel bands are restricted in their development to individual, and in some cases local areas of the coalfields so that, particularly in the Middle and Upper Coal Measures, most bands are suitable only for short-range correlation. In the Lower Coal Measures a few are of more regional distribution, as for example the highly fossiliferous mussel band above the Bassy-Soft Bed seams of the Midland Province.

Most commonly the mussel bands are only a few feet thick and many of the thicker horizons are really composed of several distinct bands separated by unfossiliferous strata. Their lithologies are most frequently argillaceous, in which case the shells tend to be partly crushed and distorted. Solid specimens, often occurring as casts, are usually preserved in ironstone nodules and bands. Occasionally a band may be composed of siltstones or fine sandstones, but in such rocks the fossils are seldom sufficiently preserved to be specifically recognizable. The thick whitish or yellowish carbonate shells render many mussel bands particularly prominent. Although only seven major Westphalian genera (pages 165–6) occur, a large number of species have been described. As an individual species may range through a considerable thickness of strata and furthermore exhibit variation within a single band, a few random identifications are seldom diagnostic of a horizon. It is only by the collection of a comprehensive faunal assemblage and the employment of statistical methods of analysis that a particular mussel band can be identified. However in some cases a band may form part of a characteristic unit, in which case its occurrence alone may be sufficient to establish the correlation. Again, the constant occurrence of a sequence of markedly dissimilar forms within a band may serve to distinguish it from others without recourse to detailed palaeontological examination. In this respect the Hopkins Shell Bed, above the Harvey-Beaumont seams of Durham and Northumberland, characterized by a ostracod-rich basal assemblage and an upper layer in which *Anthracosia* is dominant, forms a major marker horizon in both coalfields.

'Estheria' bands

The chitinous valves of the small branchiopod *Euestheria* (page 166) range throughout the Coal

Measures but are most abundant in the upper part of the Communis and in the Similis-Pulchra Zones. Such '*Estheria*' or conchostracan bands can seldom be specifically identified from their contained faunas although their relationship to faunal zones or marine bands may sometimes establish their identity. In Nottinghamshire and Derbyshire the Main '*Estheria*' Band, composed of black shales up to about 4 ft thick and occurring approximately half way between the Shafton and *Edmondia* marine bands, is a recognizable marker horizon (Edwards & Stubblefield, 1947, pp. 231–2). However in the Yorkshire coalfield *Euestheria* occurs at several horizons in this part of the sequence and is consequently of lesser value. Certain bands appear to occur at similar horizons in several coalfields (Magraw, *et al.*, 1963, pp. 160, 164) and may therefore be utilized in generalized inter-coalfield correlative studies.

Fish beds

Fish remains are only rarely found as complete or partly complete fossils and usually occur as isolated shiny black scales, spines and teeth sporadically distributed in the interseam shales and mudstones. Sometimes however such finely comminuted debris is sufficiently abundant in the black shale roofs of the seams, and also within some cannel coals, as to form distinct fish beds. Such thin horizons can in some cases be traced over a wide area within a coalfield and may therefore be used as auxiliary criteria for the correlation of an underlying seam. Owing to their fragmentary nature the specific identification of the fish remains is a highly specialized task and normally impracticable. Consequently the utilization of particular fish assemblages as definitive of individual beds is hardly ever attempted. Nevertheless the possibilities of using such faunas when other correlative methods prove unsatisfactory should be considered. For example, nine horizons in the lower Coal Measures of W. Yorkshire yielded some ninety fish species, of which over half were only recorded from single horizons chiefly above the Better Bed and Adwalton Stone coals (Wray, *et al.*, 1930, pp. 158–61). Although collections above the other seams may have been incomplete, it seems likely that some fish beds may contain definitive short-ranging forms.

Plant beds

Plant remains (pages 167–70) are often abundant in the roof strata of many seams. Owing to their wide stratigraphic range the recognition of a few species is seldom sufficient to identify a particular horizon. As with the non-marine lamellibranchs the correlation of plant beds rests in most cases on a study of their total floral assemblages. Although the assemblages of some beds may be composed of similar plants they may be distinguished by differences in the relative proportions of the various species. In the collection of such assemblages great care must be taken to obtain a truly representative sample, and at each locality it is necessary to collect from as great an area as possible. Otherwise, species of some of the larger fossils may appear to be predominant due to their fragmentation into numerous individual specimens. The method is applicable to short-range correlation over a few miles. It should be regarded with caution for greater distances since particular plant assemblages may sometimes be confined to restricted areas.

In summary it will be apparent to the reader that some methods are suitable only for relatively short-range correlation within an individual colliery or group of collieries. This is particularly so with regard to the various lithological methods. Thus the reliability of correlations based on sequence matching, coal lithologies or heavy mineral analyses decreases in proportion to the distance apart of the individual sections and sampling points. So far the tonstein bands have been the only lithological criteria which have been satisfactorily employed in long-distance correlation across several coalfields. Some of the palaeontological methods are however more applicable to regional correlation. In this respect the marine bands have proved unique for the correlation of specific horizons throughout many British and other European coalfields. Again, certain of the mussel and 'Estheria' bands undoubtably extend across several coalfields. Other palaeontological methods are less reliable.

Whenever possible several independent lines of evidence should be followed in the correlation of a particular horizon. No single method is entirely infallible but if several independent lines of enquiry all point to a similar conclusion then such a correlation is indeed strong. Finally, although the ultimate responsibility for a correlation will generally rest with the geologist, it is in many cases due to the observation of the mining engineer or surveyor that a particular lithological or palaeontological marker horizon is first noticed. In development work detailed records of lithologies and the position of any fossil band, however insignificant it might seem at the time, should be made. For it may well be that on some future occasion such records will be of invaluable assistance when the original locality is inaccessible.

REFERENCES

BALME, R. E. & M. A. BUTTERWORTH (1952) The stratigraphical significance of certain fossil spores in the central group of British coalfields, *Trans. Instn Min. Engrs* 111, 870–9.

BOUROZ, A. (1962) Sur la pluralité d'origine des tonstein, *Annls Soc. géol. N.* 82, 77–94.

DIJKSTRA, S. J. (1952) The stratigraphical value of megaspores, *C.R. 3rd Congr. Strat. Carb. Heerlen* 1, 163–8.

DUFF, P. McL. D. & E. K. WALTON (1962) Statistical basis for cyclothems: a quantitative study of the sedimentary succession in the east Pennine coalfield, *Sedimentology* 1, 235–55.

EAGAR, R. M. C. (1960) A summary of the results of recent work on the palaeoecology of Carboniferous non-marine lamellibranchs, *C.R. 4th Congr. Strat. Carb. Heerlen* 1, 137–48.

EAGAR, R. M. C. (1964) The succession and correlation of the Coal Measures of South Eastern Ireland, *C.R. 5th Congr. Strat. Carb. Paris* 1, 359–74.

EARP, J. R. (1961) Exploratory boreholes in the north Staffordshire coalfield, *Bull. geol. Surv. Gt Br.* 17, 153–90.

EDEN, R. A., ELLIOT, R. W., ELLIOTT, R. E. & B. R. YOUNG (1963) Tonstein bands in the coalfields of the east Midlands, *Geol. Mag.* 100, 47–58.

EDWARDS, W. & C. J. STUBBLEFIELD (1947) Marine bands and other faunal marker horizons in relation to the sedimentary cycles of the Middle Coal Measures of Nottinghamshire and Derbyshire, *Q. Jl geol. Soc. Lond.* 103, 209–56.

FALCON, N. L. & P. E. KENT (1960) Geological results of petroleum exploration in Great Britain 1945–1957, *Mem. geol. Soc. Lond.* 2, 1–56.

FRANCIS, E. H. (1961) Thin beds of graded kaolinized tuff and tuffaceous siltstone in the Carboniferous of Fife, *Bull. geol. Surv. Gt Br.* 17, 191–215.

GOOSENS, R. F. (1953) Some methods of obtaining additional information from boreholes: Part 1—recording the rate of penetration during drilling, *Trans. Instn Min. Engrs* 112, 497–500.

HACQUEBARD, P. A. (1951) The correlation by petrographic analyses, of No. 5 seam in the St. Rose and Chimney Corner coalfields, Inverness County, Cape Breton Island, Nova Scotia, *Bull. geol. Surv. Can.* 19, 1–33.

HODSON, F. & W. V. LECKWIJCK (1958) A Namurian marker-horizon at Busbach, near Aachen, western Germany, *Publs Ass. Étude Paléont.* 35, 1–13.

KNOWLES, B. (1964) The radioactive content of the Coal Measures sediments in the Yorkshire-Derbyshire coalfield, *Proc. Yorks. geol. Soc.* 34, 413–46.

LEROY, L. W. (1950) *Subsurface Geologic Methods*, 2nd ed., Golden, Colorado School of Mines.

LYNCH, E. J. (1962) *Formation Evaluation*, 1st ed., New York, Harper & Row.

MAGRAW, D., CLARKE, A. M. & D. B. SMITH (1963) The stratigraphy and structure of part of the south-east Durham coalfield, *Proc. Yorks. geol. Soc.* 34, 153–205.

MARSHALL, A. E. & A. H. V. SMITH (1965) Assemblage of miospores from some upper Carboniferous coals and their associated sediments in the Yorkshire coalfield, *Palaeontology* 7, 656–73.

MOORE, L. R. (1964) The microbiology, mineralogy and genesis of a tonstein, *Proc. Yorks. geol. Soc.* 34, 235–85.

MILNER, H. B. (1962a, 1962b) *Sedimentary Petrography* 1 (1962a), 2 (1962b). 4th ed., London, Allen & Unwin.

POLAK, E. J. (1952) The electrical logging of boreholes drilled for coal in the West Midlands Division, National Coal Board, *C.R. 3rd Congr. Strat. Carb. Heerlen* **2**, 493–500.

PONSFORD, D. R. A. (1955) Radioactivity studies of some British sedimentary rocks, *Bull. geol. Surv. Gt Br.* **10**, 24–44.

RAMSBOTTOM, W. H. C. & M. A. CALVER (1962) Some marine horizons containing *Gastrioceras* in North West Europe, *C. R. 4th Congr. Strat. Carb. Heerlen* **3**, 571–76.

ROBSON, D. A. (1956) A sedimentary study of the Fell Sandstones of the Coquet valley, Northumberland, *Q. Jl geol. Soc. Lond.* **112**, 241–58.

SLATER, L. (1932) Microscopical study of coal seams and their correlation, *Trans. Instn Min. Engrs* **83**, 191–201.

SMITH, A. V. H. (1962) Application of fossil plant spores to coalfield geology, *Sheffld Univ. Min. Mag.*, pp. 33–9.

STACH, E. (1955) Crassidurain—A means of seam correlation in the Carboniferous coal measures of the Ruhr, *Fuel* **34**, 95–118.

SULLIVAN, H. J. (1962) Distribution of microspores through coals and shales of the Coal Measures sequence exposed in Wernddu claypit, Caerphilly (South Wales), *Q. Jl geol. Soc. Lond.* **118**, 353–69.

TAYLOR, G. H. & S. St. J. WARNE (1960) Some Australian coal petrological studies and their geological implications, *Proc. Internat. Committee Coal Petrology* **3**, 75–83.

WILLIAMSON, I. A. (1961) Tonsteins: a possible aid to coalfield correlation, *Min. Mag.* **104**, 9–14.

WRAY, D. A., STEPHENS, J. V., EDWARDS, W. N. & E. N. BROMHEAD (1930) Geology of the Country around Huddersfield and Halifax, *Mem. geol. Surv. Engld & Wales.*

18

ORIGIN AND PROPERTIES OF COAL

Coal is a combustible sedimentary rock occurring in workable quantities as distinct beds or seams mostly only a few feet thick. It is formed from accumulations of plant remains modified by chemical, biological and physical processes during and after burial. The degree of alteration which such deposits have attained determines their position or *rank* in the coalification series commencing at peat and extending through lignites to bituminous coal and finally anthracite (pages 236–9). Thus anthracite is of a higher rank than bituminous coal, having been subjected to a greater degree of alteration from the original peaty substance. Coals of similar rank may however exhibit considerable variations in their physical and chemical characters owing to initial differences in the depositional conditions and nature of the vegetation. Thus the bright and dull layers visible in most bituminous coals are formed by several distinct lithotypes which are chemically and physically dissimilar. Consequently the general characteristics of coals are determined by the variable proportions of lithotypes present. Besides such organic material, small quantities of inorganic and incombustible minerals are also present in almost all coals. These may therefore grade into carbonaceous sediments, such as oil shales, containing high proportions of inorganic minerals and not therefore included in the coalification series. Again, where the degree of compaction and alteration is relatively slight, as in peat and some brown lignites, the sediments are not regarded as true coals. Nevertheless they are the first members of the coalification series and as such require consideration in this and the next chapter. Chemically the members of the series are predominantly composed of carbon (50–98 per cent), oxygen and hydrogen, together with lesser amounts of sulphur, nitrogen and ash-forming constituents.

Although noted by the classical Greeks and probably worked by the Chinese over 2 000 years ago, it was not until the Industrial Revolution in the early nineteenth century that coal became the major source of fuel. Since then production has risen to almost 2 500 000 000 ton per annum. Most of the world's proved reserves occur in the Northern Hemisphere (Table 37). Most of the highest rank coals are of Carboniferous and Permian age but important deposits occur in all systems above the Devonian (Table 38). Although certain coal-like substances have been discovered in the Pre-Cambrian and Lower Palaeozoic systems they are of extremely localized occurrence since land plants, from which the coal resources of the world are derived, became abundant only in upper Devonian time.

TABLE 37

Coal Resources of the World
(Published by the World Power Conference, 1962)

Regions	Coal (ton × 10⁹)		Lignite (ton × 10⁹)		Peat (ton × 10⁹)
	Proved reserves	*Probable total reserves*	*Proved reserves*	*Probable total reserves*	*Probable total reserves*
Western Europe (excluding USSR)	205	415	72	87	46
North America	114	1160	22	430	13
Central and South America	1	3	—	—	—
Africa	26	76	—	—	—
Asia	6	1090	—	5	1
Oceania	2	13	40	98	—
Rest of World	219	4772	60	1401	164

TABLE 38

The Age of the Coal Resources of the World

Era	System		Age in million years	Localities
C E N O Z O I C	Pleistocene		— 1 —	Peat deposits in most areas
	T E R T I A R Y	Pliocene	—11—	Lignites in: Hungary (Zala), Indonesia (Sumatra-Lematang, E. Borneo), Italy (Tuscany), Japan, Rumania (Comanesti), USA (Alaska)
		Miocene	—25—	Lignites in: Argentina (Patagonia), Austria (Upper Austria, Styria), Canada (Columbia), Czechoslovakia (Eger Valley, Teplice), Denmark (Jutland), Germany (Cologne Cottbus), Greenland, Holland (S. Limburg), Hungary (Pásztó), Japan, New Zealand (Otago), Yugoslavia (Bosnia)
		Oligocene	—40—	Lignites in: Australia (Victoria), Canada (Columbia), Chile (Arauca), Great Britain (Devonshire), New Zealand (N. & S. Auckland, Southland), Rumania (Cluj, Petrosani), Spitzbergen, Turkey (Kutahya), Yugoslavia (Ljubljana)
		Eocene	—70—	Mainly lignites in: Canada (Saskatchewan, Vancouver), Germany (Halle, Leipzig, Magdeburg, Saxony, Thuringia), India (Assam), Indonesia (Sumatra-Umbilin), E. Java, New Guinea (Vogelkop), Japan, New Zealand (Nelson, Westland), Pakistan (W. Punjab), Spitzbergen (King's Bay), USA (Alaska, Dakota, Montana), Yugoslavia (Bosnia, Dalmatia, Istria)
M E S O Z O I C	Cretaceous		— 135 —	Lignites and bituminous coals in: Australia (Queensland), Bulgaria (Balkans), Canada (Alberta, Columbia, Saskatchewan), Columbia (Bogotá), France (Basse-Provence), Germany (Hanover), Greenland (Disko), Japan, Mexico (Barroteran, Eagle Pass, Sabinas), New Zealand (Nelson, Southland), Nigeria (Enugu), Peru (Andean Provinces), USA (Rocky Mt. states), USSR (Burega, Chita, Sakhalin, Vilui), Yugoslavia (Serbia)
	Jurassic		— 180 —	Coals in: Australia (New South Wales, Queensland), China (Szechwan), Egypt (N. Sinai), Hungary (Pécs), Iran (Demavend, Kerman), Sweden (Skåne), USSR (Fergana, Georgia, Irkutsk, Kansk)
	Triassic		— 225 —	Coals in: Australia (Tasmania), Mexico (Santa Clara), Poland (Katowice, Kielce), USA (N. Carolina, Virginia), USSR (Urals)
P A L A E O Z O I C	Permian		— 270 —	Coals in: Antarctica, Australia (New South Wales, Queensland, Tasmania), China (Honan, Hopeh, Shansi), France (Central Plateau), Germany (Saxony), India (Bengal, Bihar, Orissa, Korea (Samchok, Yongwol), Rhodesia (Wankie), USA (Maryland, Ohio, Pennsylvania), USSR (Kuzbass, Pechora), Union of S. Africa (Natal, Transvaal).
	C a r b o n i f e r o u s	Upper	— 330 —	Coals in: Algeria (Abadla, Colomb-Béchar), Belgium (Kempen, Sambre-Meuse), Brazil (Rio Bonito, Rio Grande do Sul), Canada (New Brunswick, Nova Scotia), Czechoslovakia (L. Bohemia), France (Nord, Pas de Calais), Germany (Aachen, Ruhr, Saar), Great Britain (see Fig. 15.14), Holland (Peel, S. Limburg), Morocco (Djerada), Poland (Silesia), Spain (Granada, Oviedo, Santanander), Turkey (Eregli), USA (Appalachian, Gulf and Interior States), USSR (Donbass, Karaganda)
		Lower	— 350 —	Coals in: Canada (Arctic Isles), Great Britain (Northumberland), Spitzbergen, USA (Pennsylvania), USSR (Moscow and Ural Basins)
	Devonian			Coals in: Bear Island, Canada (Arctic Isles)

ACCUMULATION OF COAL

During the last century (Moore, 1940, pp. 138–43) there was a lengthy controversy as to the actual mode of accumulation of coal deposits. On the one hand they were considered to have accumulated from peaty masses of vegetable matter which remained more or less in the place of growth as *in situ* or *autochthonous* deposits. Alternatively it was argued that much of the vegetation had been eroded and redeposited many miles from the source to form *drift* or *allochthonous* coals. The principal facts relevant to the respective theories are as follows.

(1) The occurrence below most coals of seat earths containing numerous fossil roots is regarded as strong evidence for the autochthonous origin of the seams. Seat earths are considered by most authorities to have functioned as soils during at least the initial stages in the development of the coal-forming vegetation. Similarly the absence of seat earths beneath most cannel and boghead coals, which also differ in many other respects from the normal members of the coalification series, is indicative of their allochthonous origin.

(2) The presence of erratic boulders (page 64) in certain seams has been quoted in support of the allochthonous nature of the latter. The comparative rarity of such boulders is however incompatible with the universal application of the theory. They were more probably deposited during the flooding of the land surface prior to burial beneath non-carbonaceous sediments.

(3) Fossil trunks of large trees with roots still attached are occasionally discovered in positions normal to the stratification of the seams and are often regarded as evidence of the autochthonous nature of the surrounding coal. Such stumps might however have been floated into the depositional area and settled in upright positions owing to the greater weight of their basal parts together with the stabilizing effects of their root systems.

(4) The autochthonous origin of many coals is evidenced by their low content of inorganic ash-forming minerals. Had they accumulated as drift deposits much larger quantities of sands, silts and clays would have been deposited contemporaneously and so incorporated within the seams. In this respect the inorganic mineral content of cannel and boghead coals is relatively high and it is accepted that such coals accumulated in rivers and lakes. It has been suggested that the low inorganic mineral content of the normal coals resulted from the natural sorting of water-born materials, so that the inorganic particles and vegetable debris were selectively deposited according to their differing densities and the decreasing velocities of the transporting aqueous currents. Such an argument implies an unusually high degree of aqueous sorting seldom encountered in modern sedimentary studies.

(5) Particularly with regard to the Carboniferous coals, formed from a tropical or semi-tropical vegetation (page 221), it may be argued that their distribution in high polar latitudes suggests the transportation of plant debris by oceanic currents into sedimentary basins thousands of miles away from the forest areas. An alternative and more probable explanation, supporting the autochthonous theory and advocated by many independent lines of enquiry, is that the land masses were differently positioned in the past. During the Carboniferous period many areas of the Northern Hemisphere may well have been situated nearer to the Equator and have since 'drifted' into their present positions.

It is nowadays generally accepted that the Carboniferous coals of Europe and North America are of an autochthonous nature whereas many Permian coals, such as those of India, may represent allochthonous accumulations.

THE COAL SWAMPS

With regard to the North-West European and North American Carboniferous coalfields, the sedimentary basins in which the coals and associated interseam sediments accumulated were characterized by essentially non-marine conditions. In these regions marine horizons are thin and rarely form more than about 2 per cent of the total sedimentary thickness. Throughout most of the depositional history shallow, fresh- or brackish-water conditions prevailed, as evidenced by the nature of the interseam fossils (pages 159–67) and sediments (pages 54–64). Phases of slower subsidence alternated with more rapid sinking, so that a large number of cyclothems (pages 44–5) may be identified in the local succession. During the coal-forming phases very shallow-water conditions at first prevailed so that aquatic plants (e.g. *Calamites*) grew in rather stagnant swamps. Gradually the bog surfaces became elevated above water level by the accumulation of peat derived from the decaying plants so that larger trees (e.g. *Lepidodendron*) gained a footing. At the same time meandering streams and rivers flowed through the forests to deposit as channel infillings, the conglomerates and sandstones now occurring as washouts within the seams (Chapter 16). The sedimentary basins themselves were continuous across large areas which possessed little relief and lay relatively close to sea level. Such conditions are indicated by the widespread nature of the occasional marine horizons, as in North-West Europe (page 187, Table 32), and the closely similar sedimentary histories of many coalfields now separated by post-

Carboniferous orogenic movements and subsequent erosion. Similarly in North America the distribution of coals such as the Pittsburgh seam, which may be mined throughout an area of about 10 000 mile² from Ohio to the Appalachians, indicates remarkably uniform sedimentary conditions.

In contrast the various Permian coalfields of India and Australia were isolated basins even during the formation of the coal seams. Areas of considerable relief often separated the sedimentary basins which may also have been situated well above sea level, for in these areas there is a total absence of contemporaneous marine strata. Again, the Carboniferous Saar coalfield of Germany and the Permian coalfields of Central France originated as similar small isolated land-locked or *limnic* basins in marked contrast to the much larger and low lying *paralic* basins of North-West Europe (Trueman, 1946, pp. lii–liii, lxxviii–lxxxiv).

CLIMATIC CONSIDERATIONS

At present peat is forming in a wide variety of climatic regions ranging from the muskeg of the Arctic tundras to the tropical swamps of Borneo. The essential climatic condition for peat accumulation is a high humidity. Since a warm climate is not necessary for peat formation it must therefore be emphasized that coals should not be automatically equated with their initial formation in a tropical climate. In this respect the occurrence of growth rings in fossil plants is an important criterion of the prevailing climatic conditions during the deposition of coal seams. In recent vegetation they are clearly related to phases of accelerated growth in a marked seasonal climate such as exists in the temperate rain forests. Conversely, in the equatorial forests there is little climatic difference between the seasons so that growth is more or less constant and growth rings are seldom or only feebly developed. Thus the almost total absence of growth rings in the Carboniferous plants of the Northern Hemisphere suggests that a tropical, rather than a temperate, climate without any well-marked seasonal rhythm, prevailed throughout the accumulation of the peats. Similarly the giant leaf fans and thin barks of most of the Carboniferous trees 'are all characteristics of a tropical and subtropical rain forest' (Kräusel, in Nairn, 1961, p. 249). In contrast, the Permian coals of the southern continents and India were developed from a flora markedly different from that of the Carboniferous. This, the *Gondwana Flora*, exhibits well defined tree rings indicative of sharply defined seasonal climatic variations. Such a climate was more probably temperate, and in some areas possibly glacial, rather than tropical. Certain of the coal-bearing horizons, as for example the Barakar Stage in the Jharia and

Raniganj coalfields of India (pages 140–4), occur above the tillites and fluvioglacial deposits of a Carboniferous and early Permian ice age (King, in Nairn, 1961, pp. 320–3).

THICKNESS OF THE ORIGINAL PEAT

Various attempts have been made to establish the ratios between the thickness of the peat deposits and the coal seams formed from them. Unfortunately they cannot be established with any certainty and must be regarded only as broad estimates. It is suggested that allowing for dehydration and coalification a ratio of 15 to 1 is not excessive for the relative degree of compaction from peat to coal (Raistrick & Marshall, 1939, pp. 53–4). Such an estimate does not however imply that the original peat deposits were at any stage exceptionally thick. Thus 10 ft of coal was not necessarily derived from a peat deposit 150 ft thick. Recent peat accumulations already show a considerable degree of compaction and it is estimated from the spacing of plant debris at different levels that a compaction of at least 5 to 1 has taken place in the basal parts. Consequently a seam of coal some 4 ft thick may have been formed from less than 30 ft of peat.

There is similarly no satisfactory way of calculating the rate of accumulation of ancient peat deposits as many variable factors including rates of growth and decay, types of plants and the contemporary climatic fluctuations are involved.

PETROLOGY OF COAL

Coal, although often considered as a mineral, as for example in mining legislation, should be more strictly regarded as a group of rocks with a common organic origin. Just as other rocks are composed of various minerals, so coals are also composed of a number of constituents which may only be identified by use of the microscope. Coal petrology is a rapidly expanding subject of great technological importance and with a highly specialized nomenclature (Tomkeieff, 1954) unfortunately complicated by the several systems of classification at present in use (Francis, 1961, pp. 306–37; Krevelen, 1961, pp. 58–71). Thus, different terminologies are used for the constituents as determined by the microscopic examination of thin sections of coal in transmitted light (Thiessen-Bureau of Mines System, employed in North America) and of polished coal sections as examined in reflected light (Stopes-Heerlen System, employed in Europe).

STOPES-HEERLEN SYSTEM

The terminology of the above system, at present chiefly restricted to bituminous coals, has been most recently considered, defined and illustrated by the

International Committee for Coal Petrology (*International Handbook of Coal Petrography*, 1963, Pts. 1 & 2, 2nd ed., German, English and French editions published by, and obtainable from, the Centre National de la Recherche Scientifique, 15, Quai Anatole-France, Paris 7e, France). In the classification the coal components are progressively separated into *lithotypes* (commonly with the suffix *-ain*), *microlithotypes* (with the suffix *-ite* or the prefix *micro-*), *maceral groups* (with the suffix *-nite*) and *macerals* (with the suffix *-nite*). Thus the lithotype *vitrain* occurs as extremely bright thin bands easily recognizable by the unaided eye on the coal face. Vitrain itself upon microscopic examination is revealed as being predominantly composed of the microlithotype *vitrite*, which is chiefly formed of the macerals *collinite* and *telinite* together comprising the *vitrinite* maceral group.

Macerals and maceral groups

The *macerals* are the elementary microscopic constituents of coals and as such are analogous to the minerals of other rocks. Individual macerals differ widely in chemical, physical and technological properties which themselves alter with the rank of the coal. They may be placed into three categories or *maceral groups* according to their technological properties:

Vitrinite is the primary constituent of bright coal and includes:

(1) *Collinite* (Plate 10a). Structureless.

(2) *Telinite* (Plate 10b). Possessing a well defined cellular structure. Both vary according to the coal rank from grey to yellowish white in reflected light and have a lower relief than most other macerals. In transmitted light their colour varies from orange to dark red. They originated from the woody and cortical tissues of the coal-forming trees.

On heating, vitrinite forms a fused and well swollen button as the main product. Since minute cracks are extensively developed vitrinite is easily pulverized and is consequently a major component of mine dust.

Exinite or *Liptinite* is composed of one or more of the following macerals.

(1) *Alginite* (Plate 10c). Cellular structure sometimes apparent. Very dark in reflected light. Yellow to orange in transmitted light. Composed of algal remains. The principal constituent of boghead coal.

(2) *Cutinite* (Plate 10d). Occurs as narrow bands often serrated along one edge. Dark grey to black in reflected light. Yellow to brownish red in transmitted light. Composed of waxy plant cuticles. Abundant in some clarains.

(3) *Resinite* (Plate 10e). Commonly as round, oval or rod-like masses and more rarely as thin films intruded along the cleat during coalification. Dark grey to black in reflected light. Yellow to reddish orange in transmitted light. Formed from fossil plant resins and waxes. Present in small proportions in most bituminous coals.

(4) *Sporinite* (Plate 10f). The remains of spore exines which are present as typically flattened bodies parallel to the stratification. Grey, brownish to black in reflected light. Golden, yellow to brown in transmitted light. Common in dull coals.

Exinite on heating is largely transformed into gas and tar owing to its high volatile and hydrogen content. It is a very tough constituent of coals and consequently adds to their strength and similarly restricts the formation of dust.

Inertinite is the group term for the following macerals:

(1) *Fusinite* (Plate 10g). Possesses a well defined cellular structure with round, oval or elongated cell cavities. White to yellowish in reflected light. Opaque in transmitted light. The relief is high and especially noticeable. Possibly derived from contemporary forest fires (see fusain, page 224). Widely distributed in coals as lenses, thin partings and small fragments. An extremely friable and therefore dust-forming constituent of coal.

(2) *Micrinite* (Plate 10h). Finely or coarsely granular material. Light grey to white in reflected light. Usually opaque in transmitted light. Probably derived from strongly decayed plant material. A particularly common and very strong constituent of dull coals which is associated with miospores.

(3) *Sclerotinite* (Plate 10i). Composed of rounded bodies or fine interlaced filaments. White in reflected light. Reddish brown to opaque in transmitted light. The relief is generally high. Possibly composed of the fossil remains of fungae. A minor constituent of coals, may be difficult to distinguish from other members of the inertinite group, particularly in some Australian coals, so that the retention of the term is questioned (Taylor & Cook, 1962, pp. 41–52).

(4) *Semifusinite* (Plate 10j). Possesses a cellular structure although on a smaller scale than fusinite. Light grey to white in reflected light. Orange red to opaque in transmitted light. Origin probably similar to fusinite. Widely distributed as lenses, thin partings and small fragments.

The inertinite group includes those macerals which are almost chemically inert. Thus on heating they have only low yields of by-products and will not cake. Consequently their occurrence restricts the coking abilities of coals.

Microlithotypes

Characteristic associations of macerals are termed *microlithotypes* (Table 39), the nature and relative

TABLE 39

Classification of Microlithotypes

Microlithotype	Principal maceral groups	Remarks
VITRITE	Over 95% Vitrinite	An abundant constituent of bituminous coal
LIPTITE or SPORITE	Over 95% Exinite	An important constituent of cannels and torbanites, otherwise rare in bituminous coal
FUSITE	Over 95% Inertinite (excepting micrinite)	Two varieties: (i) powdery, soft fusite (ii) consolidated, hard fusite (in which cellular cavities are infilled by inorganic minerals) Widely distributed but not abundant
MICROITE (Acceptance of the term in the Stopes-Heerlen system still under discussion)	Over 95% Inertinite (micrinite + 50%)	An important constituent of Permian coals in the Southern Hemisphere
CLARITE (Hydrite)	Over 95% Vitrinite and Exinite. (Each must exceed the proportion of inertinite)	Two varieties: (i) Clarite V – rich in vitrinite (ii) Clarite E – rich in exinite Widely distributed and particularly common in clarain
DURITE	Over 95% Inertinite and Exinite. (Each must exceed the proportion of vitrinite)	Two varieties: (i) Durite E – rich in exinite (ii) Durite I – rich in inertinite Particularly common in durain
VITRINERTITE	Over 95% Vitrinite and Interinite. (Each must exceed the proportion of exinite)	Two varieties: (i) Vitrinertite V – rich in vitrinite (ii) Vitrinertite I – rich in inertinite Generally rare in low rank coals
DUROCLARITE	Vitrinite + Exinite + Inertinite (Each must exceed 5%; the proportion of vitrinite must exceed that of inertinite)	Widely distributed as thick bands in most coals
CLARODURITE	Inertinite + Exinite + Vitrinite (Each must exceed 5%; the proportion of inertinite must exceed that of vitrinite)	

proportions of which determine the macroscopic appearance of the coal. Such microlithotypes may include up to 5 per cent of pyrite or less than 20 per cent of other non-carbonaceous minerals. If these percentages are exceeded a number of distinct microlithotypes—carbopyrite (page 234), carbarligite (page 234) and carbankerite (page 234)—are recognized. In the petrological examination of coals only those microlithotype bands or lenses over 50 μ in width, measured at right angles to the lamination, are noted.

Lithotypes

Lithotypes consist of the several macroscopically recognizable banded constituents or ingredients of coal. As such they are synonymous with the rock types of inorganic sediments and may be employed as the basis of a simple coal classification without recourse to microscopic examination (Table 40). Originally only four major lithotypes were distinguished:

TABLE 40

A Simple Petrological Classification of Bituminous Coals

Class	Sub-class	Lithotypes
Humic coal	Bright coal	Vitrain
		Clarain
		Fusain
	Dull coal	Durain
Sapropelic coal		Cannel
		Torbanite

Vitrain (Plate 12a). An ingredient of bright or soft coal, vitrain occurs as brilliant, black, non-laminated bands and lenses seldom more than 1 cm in width. It is absolutely clean to the touch, breaking in the fingers into small, sharp-edged cubic pieces across which the fracture is conchoidal. Microscopic examination shows that vitrain is predominantly composed of microlithotypes very rich in vitrinite and derived from the bark tissues of the larger coal-forming plants (Raistrick & Marshall, 1939, pp. 181–92, Figs. 51–74). Thus the coalified bark remaining as a thin film around fossil casts of the larger trees is most often composed of vitrain. It is considered to originate under fairly dry surface conditions. On burial the stagnant ground waters of the peat deposits inhibited total decay of the plants so that the woody structure was almost completely preserved.

Durain (Plate 12a). The term 'durain' is more or less synonymous with hard or dull coal. Durain appears as dark grey or black, hard, compact bands sometimes a foot or more in thickness. Occasionally very thin wisps or hair-like streaks of bright coal may be seen. The fracture, the rough surface of which has a dull or earthy lustre, is granular. Cleat fractures are only feebly developed (page 85). Under the microscope durain is seen to contain considerably more non-carbonaceous mineral matter than the bright coals. Similarly greater quantities of miospores are usually present so that two varieties— *crassidurain* and *tenuidurain*—characterized by the occurrence of thick- and thin-walled spores respectively, may sometimes be distinguished (page 205). The macroscopic equivalent of durite, durain is

considered to have formed where the peat surface was below water level. Under such conditions the plant debris became finely disintegrated and decomposed so that only the resistant exinite and inertinite components escaped total destruction. At the same time considerable proportions of inorganic sediment would also be deposited to be ultimately incorporated in the coal.

Clarain (Plate 12a). The second ingredient of bright coal, clarain possesses a silky and less brilliant lustre than vitrain. It is composed of alternating bright and dull black laminae which by definition are less than 3 mm and are commonly less than 1 mm thick. As with vitrain, cleat fractures are usually well developed. Microscopic examination reveals the composition of clarain to be variable, and all three maceral groups are present. The brightest layers are composed largely of vitrinite whereas exinite and inertinite are predominant in the duller layers. Clarain probably formed under conditions alternating between those in which vitrain and durain originated.

Fusain (Plate 12b). Fusain is a common constituent of bright coal, occurring as thin silvery-black bands most commonly a few millimetres thick. Occasionally it forms lenses up to about 8 in thick. It is typically a very soft and friable, fine, soot-like powder forming that part of the coal which is dirty to the touch. A hard variety, due to secondary mineral infiltration, does however exist and sometimes occurs in proximity to igneous intrusions. The coal often breaks along the fusain layers, in which case the lithotype appears as flattened fibrous masses with a satin-like lustre. Upon other than lamination surfaces it has a dull lustre. Microscopically it is equivalent to fusite. From its close physical and chemical similarity to wood charcoal, fusain is generally believed to have formed in forest fires, possibly sparked off by lightning, which swept across the peat deposits. Such an origin it supported by the occurrence of occasional vitrain lenticles enclosed in fusain in the same way that a partly burnt wood fragment is only charred on the outside. Alternatively it has been suggested that fusain may have originated as a result of bacterial action causing local heating, but not necessarily conflagration, in a manner somewhat analogous to spontaneous combustion in damp hay.

In addition to the above lithotypes, typical of the *humic* or *normal coals* which contain relatively small percentages of hydrogen, several varieties of the hydrogen rich *sapropelic coals* are also distinguished:

Cannel (Plate 12c). Most usually a dull coal with sometimes a waxy lustre, cannel is black in colour. It tends to have a conchoidal fracture and cleat fractures are absent. Although cannel sometimes occurs as thin beds or lenses within humic coals, it more often forms their 'tops' or 'bottoms' and as such may be left unworked. It occurs also as thin monolithic seams seldom exceeding 2 ft in thickness and usually of a limited extent. Lamination is not apparent in hand specimens although when examined microscopically an extremely small-scale form is frequently seen. The density is lower than that of normal coals and hand specimens emit a characteristic 'woody' or hollow sound when struck. Cannel is composed principally of micrinite, exinite and non-carbonaceous minerals of clastic origin. Because of its high hydrogen content, cannel burns readily with a bright smoky flame and was, in the nineteenth century, much valued for the manufacture of illuminating gas. Small splinters may sometimes be ignited simply with a match. A considerable number of vernacular terms (Tomkeieff, 1954, p. 118) including 'black-jack', 'bone-coal', 'cornish' and 'parrot-coal', have been applied to the coal in various localities.

Torbanite (Boghead coal). In many respects the physical properties of torbanites and cannels are similar. Hand specimens of the two may however be distinguished sometimes by the browner colour and rather tougher nature of torbanite. Microscopic examination reveals that torbanite is composed of alginite together with finely dispersed inertinite and vitrinite. As in cannel considerable amounts of non-carbonaceous mineral matter are also present. A continuous range of transitional varieties occurs between the two lithotypes.

The sapropelic coals accumulated in conditions different from those in which the humic coals formed. An aquatic origin is indicated by the notable quantities of non-carbonaceous sedimentary materials present, which are sometimes accompanied by fish and other aquatic fossil remains. They represent allochthonous accumulations of finely comminuted vegetable debris which were deposited in local lakes amidst the normal peat bogs. Thus the canneloid roofs of some humic coal seams were deposited during the inundation of the land surface at the close of peat formation.

THIESSEN-BUREAU OF MINES SYSTEM

An approximate correlation of the above system with the Stopes-Heerlen system is indicated in Table 41. Three major *coal components*: anthraxylon, visible as brilliant black bands and partly equivalent to vitrinite, *fusain*, and *attritus*, occurring as dull bands with a granular texture, are recognized. On thin-section examination *opaque* and *translucent attritus*, composed of various constituents, may be identified. The principal coal types are as follows:

Banded coals all containing more than 5 per cent of anthraxylon:

(1) *Bright coal*. A coal composed largely of anthraxylon and translucent attritus. Opaque attritus is limited to a maximum of 20 per cent. Bright coal is the most abundant of the banded coals and approximates to vitrain and clarain.

(2) *Splint coal*. A hard, rather blocky coal with an irregular fracture and dull lustre. Splint coal is composed predominantly of attritus and contains at least 30 per cent of the opaque constituents.

(3) *Semisplint coal*. Containing between 20 and 30 per cent of opaque attritus, the coal is intermediate between the first two types. Splint and semisplint coals are approximately equivalent to durain.

Non-banded coals all contain less than 5 per cent of anthraxylon. The two types recognized, *cannel* and *boghead* (torbanite) are equivalent approximately to the similarly named lithotypes of the Stopes-Heerlen system.

PHYSICAL PROPERTIES OF COAL

The utilization and workability of a coal is partly determined by physical properties such as strength, caking power and calorific value. Other properties, notably the optical reflectance of coals, are remarkably fine indices of rank (page 239) and are employed in coal classification. A detailed treatment of the subject is unnecessary for the mining student and accordingly only a brief review is given. Recent and comprehensive accounts of the subject include those of Brame and King (1955, pp. 104–15), Francis (1961, pp. 667–717) and Krevelen (1961, pp. 310–429).

DENSITY

The variable density of coals is an important factor in coal preparation, enabling the separation of those coals with a high 'dirt' content from other more valuable types. Variations in rank, nature and proportion of constituents, moisture content, and the actual method of measurement employed, all affect the density of the coal. In this respect liquid density determinations, using liquids such as water or alcohol, differ from measurements employing helium as the displacement medium. Thus the helium densities are less than those determined in water for the same coals if their carbon contents are below about 85 per cent. For higher ranks the aqueous are less than the helium densities. Such differing results are reflections of the porosity of the coals, for only helium is capable of more or less completely penetrating the ultra-microscopic pore spaces. Consequently the *true density* of a coal, as established using helium as the displacement medium, should be distinguished from its *apparent density* which may be calculated in

TABLE 41

An Approximate Correlation between the Petrological Terms employed in the
Stopes-Heerlen and the Thiessen-Bureau of Mines Systems
(Data from the *International Handbook of Coal Petrography*, 1963, 2nd ed.)

Reflected light		Transmitted light		
Stopes-Heerlen system		Thiessen-Bureau of Mines system		
MACERAL GROUP	Macerals	Constituents of attritus		COMPONENTS
		Translucent	Opaque	
VITRINITE	Collinite	Humic degradation matter[1]		ANTHRAXYLON[2]
	Telinite			
EXINITE	Alginite	Algae and algal matter		ATTRITUS
	Cutinite	Cuticles and cuticular matter		
	Sporinite	Spores and pollen		
	Resinite	Resins and resinous matter		
INERTINITE	Sclerotinite	Brown matter[3]	Opaque matter	FUSAIN[4]
	Micrinite			
	Semifusinite			
	Fusinite			

[1] That part of the vitrinite less than 14 microns in thickness measured perpendicular to the bedding
[2] Includes all vitrinite greater than 14 microns in thickness measured perpendicular to the bedding
[3] Also includes those parts of semifusinite that are semitranslucent
[4] Forming beds more than 37 microns thick

water and preferably employing a suitable wetting agent (Ettinger & Zhupakhina, 1960, pp. 388–90). Suitable corrections are made for the occurrence of moisture and incombustible mineral matter. Normally only the apparent densities are determined, which are sufficient for most practical purposes. In Fig. 18.1 the apparent densities are plotted for the various members of the coalification series. It will be seen that a density minimum occurs in bituminous coals with a carbon content of about 86 per cent, beyond which the density increases rapidly through the high-rank bituminous and anthracite members of the coalification series.

POROSITY

Coal is interspersed by minute pores of differing size and capillaries so that it possesses in effect an ultra-microscopic sponge-like structure. The porosity, or volume percentage occupied by such pores, may be calculated from density measurements using helium and then mercury as displacing media. Under normal pressures helium alone will penetrate and fill the pore spaces so that the difference between the two density measurements is an indication of the porosity. Alternatively water may be used in place of mercury if the coal specimen is first coated with a thin transparent impervious film (Ettinger & Zhupakhina, 1960, pp. 390–1). In the lower rank coals the porosity may exceed 20 per cent but it rapidly diminishes to a minimum at the highest rank bituminous coals (carbon content 89 per cent), above which point it increases towards the anthracites (King & Wilkins, 1944), (Fig. 18.2).

If the mercury is subjected to pressure it is possible to force some into the pore spaces, although even under high pressures not all are filled. Consequently it is believed that two pore systems occur in coal, one formed by larger pores which are penetrated by mercury under pressure and the other composed of ultra-fine pores which remain accessible only to helium.

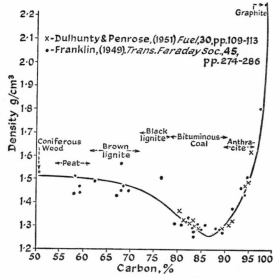

Fig. 18.1 Relationship between apparent density and the rank of coal (as indicated by the carbon content).

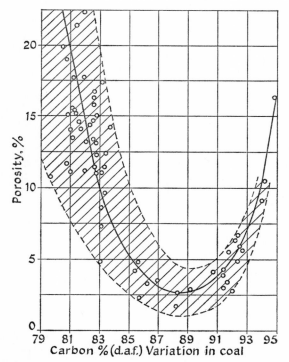

Fig. 18.2 Variation in coal porosity with rank. (After King and Wilkins.)

STRENGTH

The strength of coal is related to its hardness and friability. A standard estimate of hardness is the Vickers micro-hardness test, in which a pyramidal or spherical indenter is pressed with a specified force and for a specified time into the coal specimen. The depth and area of penetration may then be taken as a measure of the hardness. Such tests reveal a maximum hardness at coals with a carbon content around 83 per cent and a minimum at about 90 per cent carbon. Anthracites with carbon contents of over 93 per cent behave as elastic materials (Fig. 18.3).

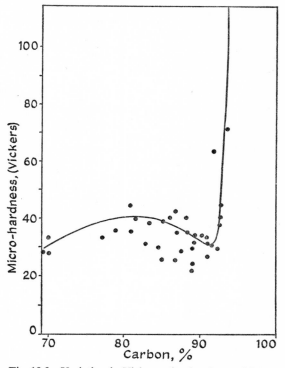

Fig. 18.3 Variation in Vickers microhardness with coal rank. (After D. W. V. Krevelen.)

However, the strengths of coal specimens as determined in the laboratory cannot yet be reliably equated with their actual *in situ* strengths which must be considered when assessing the mechanization potential of a coal face, particularly with regard to its ploughability. The *penetrometer* (Pomeroy, 1963, pp. 641–5) has therefore been developed to estimate the *in situ* strength at the coal face. With the apparatus, an indenter is driven about 4 in into the coal and the required load measured for $\frac{1}{4}$-in increments of penetration. From tests made in a number of British collieries it is shown that there is a close correlation in normally cleated coals between the haulage force required during coal ploughing and the coal strength as determined by the maximum resistance of a seam to penetration (*op. cit.*, pp. 702–3).

The friability of a coal has a considerable effect on the amount of degradation that occurs during its transportation and preparation. This can be predicted by determining the *impact strength index*. For such an estimation a steel plunger is dropped for a constant number of times onto a coal sample at the base of a steel cylinder. The percentage of coal remaining in the initial size range after the test is the impact strength index (*op. cit.*, pp. 700–4). Similarly the strength may also be assessed by its grindability, as determined by the amount of work required to grind a specified coal sample to a uniform size. Coals with a carbon content of about 90 per cent have a maximum grindability, which is in accordance with other strength determinations.

REFLECTANCE

The reflectance of a coal is the percentage of incident light reflected from a polished surface. It is determined by the microscopic examination, under oil immersion, of the vitrinite macerals in reflected light. A photocell (Broadbent & Shaw, 1955, pp. 390–5), or Berek microphotometer (Seyler & Edwards, 1949, pp. 121–7), is used as the measuring instrument. Since the reflectance increases continuously with the coal rank, its determination is a rapid method of quantitatively assessing the carbon content (Fig. 18.4) and other chemical characters of a

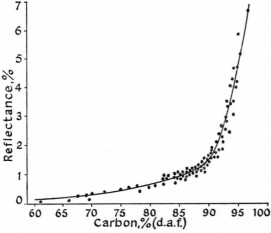

Fig. 18.4 The maximum reflectance of vitrinites in cedar oil. (After D. W. V. Krevelen.)

coal. Moreover as it is apparently unaffected by weathering, unlike other properties, the reflectance of an outcrop sample may be used as a guide to the

normal chemical and physical properties of the coal at depth (Chandra, 1962, pp. 185–93).

CAKING PROPERTIES

The caking property of a coal is determined by its power in powdered form to swell and agglutinate on heating. As such it is of primary importance in assessing a coal's technological uses. Unfortunately the terms 'caking' and 'coking', as used in the description of coals, are often mistakenly regarded by students as being synonymous. This is not so, and the term 'coking coal' should be restricted to the description of those coals which are used for the manufacture of metallurgical coke. Caking coals are not necessarily coking coals. Many are only weakly caking and therefore require blending with more strongly caking varieties before a good quality coke may be obtained from them. Several tests, each assessing slightly different characteristics and so not exactly equivalent, have been designed to record the caking properties. The swelling of coal is determined by the crucible swelling or alternatively by Arnu-Audibert's dilatometer test, and the agglutinating power by the Roga or Gray-King assays.

Crucible swelling number

For measuring the swelling properties of a coal on heating, the crucible swelling number, also called the swelling index, is determined (British Standard **1016**, Part 12, 1959, *Caking and Swelling Properties of Coal*). The coal sample is first ground to pass a 72 mesh B.S. test sieve. It is then heated rapidly in a silica crucible of specified size for one and a half minutes to 800 °C. In the next minute the temperature is raised to 820 °C and maintained at this level until the volatile matter is burnt off or for $2\frac{1}{2}$ min, whichever is the greater period of time. The crucible is cooled and if the residue is coherent the coke button is removed and compared with a standard series of numbered profiles (Fig. 18.5) to determine the crucible swelling number. If the residue is noncoherent the swelling number is zero.

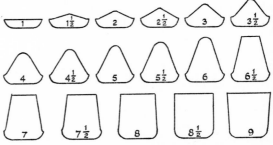

Fig. 18.5 The standard series of crucible swelling profiles. (*British Standard* 1016, Pt. 12, 1959.)

Gray-King coke type

The Gray-King coke type is used as a parameter in the N.C.B. classification of British coals (pages 250–3). After grinding the sample to pass a 72 mesh B.S. test sieve, 20 g of coal are heated under standard conditions (*op. cit.*) in a hard glass or transparent silica tube, at a uniform rate of increase from 300 °C to 600 °C for a period of 1 hour. The carbonized residue is compared with a series of standard illustrations (Plate 13) and descriptions (Table 42) and designated *A* to *G* and G_1 to G_9. With coke types G_1, G_2, G_3, etc., the subscript figures denote the number of grams of electrode carbon in a 20 g mixture of electrode carbon and coal to form a hard strong coke of type *G*. The cokes in the standard illustration were prepared from coal samples alone.

The general relationship that exists between the caking properties, as expressed by the Gray-King coke type, and ranks of coal is illustrated in Fig. 18.6. Owing to differences in the chemical composi-

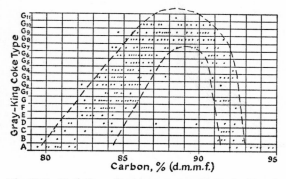

Fig. 18.6 Variation of caking power with rank. (Based on N.C.B. Scientific Department analyses.)

tion of the various macerals, wide variations in caking power exist in coals of the same rank below about 88 per cent carbon. In the higher rank coals the macerals are less differentiated so that smaller variations in caking power occur in coals of similar rank and consequently the band is narrower.

CALORIFIC VALUE

In English-speaking countries the standard unit of measurement for assessing the calorific value of a fuel is the British Thermal Unit (Btu). The latter is defined as the quantity of heat required to raise the temperature of one pound of water through 1 °F. Determinations are made by means of the bomb calorimeter, which consists essentially of a closed vessel (the bomb) immersed in water in a calorimeter. On igniting the coal sample in oxygen maintained

under pressure in the bomb, the temperature rise of the water is measured under standard conditions and the calorific value calculated (British Standard **1016**, Part 5, 1957, *Gross Calorific Value of Coal and Coke*). Alternatively it may be approximately determined from the elemental chemical composition of a coal (Brame & King, 1955, pp. 30–32, 496–8; Francis, 1961, pp. 371–2).

The calorific values of coals with carbon contents below about 92 per cent exhibit a marked relationship to their rank (Fig. 18.7). A slight decrease in calorific

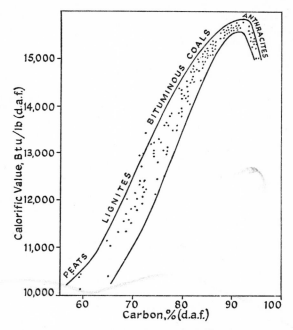

Fig. 18.7 Variation of calorific value with rank. (Based on U.S. Bureau of Mines analyses.)

value occurs in the anthracites. In coals of similar rank, notably those with carbon contents less than about 85 per cent, wide variations in calorific values may be attributed partly to their differing maceral and lithotype compositions. Thus the values are highest in exinites and lowest in micrinites, whilst those of vitrinites are intermediate. Consequently a seam composed predominantly of lithotypes such as vitrain and clarain, which contain relatively small quantities of micrinite, will have normally a higher calorific value than another coal of the same rank but composed chiefly of micrinite-rich components. As it is a basic technological property of obvious value in assessing the merits of coal as a fuel, the calorific value is utilized as a parameter in several coal classification systems (pages 247–54).

TABLE 42

Description of Gray-King Coke Type with their Coking Properties, N.C.B.
Coal Classes and approximate equivalence of Crucible Swelling Numbers

Coke type	Description	Coking properties	N.C.B. coal types	Crucible swelling number
A	Non-coherent – usually in powder form but may contain some pieces which however, cannot be handled; retains original volume	None	100 (A) 201a	0–½
B	Barely coherent – some loose powder; pieces can be picked up but break into powder on handling; retains original volume	Poor Only to be used as a diluent to coals with excessive coking properties	303 901 902	0–½
C	Coherent but very friable – usually one piece but easily broken; retains original volume		202	
D	Shrunken, moderately hard – may be fissured; can be scratched with the finger nail; stains the fingers on rubbing vigorously; usually dull and black; fritted rather than fused		303 801 802	
E	Shrunken, fissured and hard – usually very fissured with moderate metallic ring; does not stain the fingers on rubbing; grey or black with slight lustre	Weak Only to be used as an addition to coals with good coking properties	202 203	1–4
F	Slightly shrunken, hard and strong – may be fissured; moderate metallic ring; cross-section well fused and greyish		303 (E–F) 701 702	
G	Hard and strong, occupying same volume as original coal (= 'standard coke') – well fused with a good metallic ring			
G₁	Slightly swollen, hard	Moderate Preferably to be blended	203 204 302 601 602	4½–6
G₂	Moderately swollen, hard			
G₃	Highly swollen; fills tube without increase in length			
G₄	Very highly swollen types		203 204 301 601 602	
G₅		Good Prime coking coals	204	6½–8
G₆			301	
G₇			501	
G₈			502	
G₉ and over		Excessive Must be blended with a diluent	301 401 402	8½–9

CHEMICAL PROPERTIES OF COAL

The broad chemical properties of coals as illustrated by their proximate and ultimate analyses are briefly discussed below. For detailed and authoritative accounts of these and other aspects of coal chemistry the reader is referred to one of the several recent textbooks on the subject (Francis, 1961; Kreulen, 1948; Krevelen, 1961).

PROXIMATE ANALYSIS

A proximate analysis (British Standard **1016**, Part 3, 1957, *Proximate Analysis of Coal*) is the simplest and most rapid method of illustrating the general characteristics of a coal. Such analyses are commonly used for the commercial assessment of coals and involve the determination of the relative percentages of moisture, volatile matter, ash and fixed carbon present. Often the sulphur content and calorific value are also estimated.

Moisture content. This is calculated from the loss of weight which occurs when a coal is oven-dried at about 105 °C. A knowledge of the moisture content is important for commercial purposes since heat is lost on its evaporation and thus the efficiency as a fuel is lowered. In the classification of low rank coals (page 254) the moisture content is an important parameter.

Volatile content. For the determination of the volatile content, one gram of the coal is heated for 7 min at 925 °C out of contact with the air. The loss in weight, less that already calculated for the moisture, is expressed as a percentage of the initial weight of the sample. The volatile content indicates the gas and tar yields and also certain combustion characteristics of a coal. Normally for gas production it should be greater than about 30 per cent, although the quality of the coke produced may well render gasification economic at lower values. For ordinary household fuels burnt on open fires high volatile percentages were formerly preferred since such coals burn with a pleasing luminous flame. In certain classifications of high rank coals (pages 247–54) the volatile content is used as a parameter.

Ash content. The ash content is represented by the incombustible residue remaining after a coal has been incinerated to a constant weight. Clearly it is a deleterious constituent having adverse effects upon the fuel values and combustion characteristics of coals.

Fixed carbon content. The fixed carbon content is calculated by subtracting the moisture, volatile and ash percentages from 100. Since the percentage of fixed carbon increases with the quality and rank of a coal, it forms the basis of several classifications, as for example the A.S.T.M. system (page 250). However, since fixed carbon, as determined in a proximate

analysis, also includes small amounts of oxygen, nitrogen and sulphur, it does not accurately express the percentage of true combustible carbon in a coal.

ULIMATE ANALYSIS

The ultimate analysis (British Standard **1016**, Part 6, 1958, *Ultimate analysis of Coal*) is a much more specialized procedure involving the determination of the relative percentages of the carbon, oxygen, hydrogen, nitrogen and sulphur present in the pure coal substance. Suitable corrections are made to exclude those elements such as carbon within the carbonate minerals (page 232) which do not contribute to the fuel value. Other elements only present in minute quantities are not quoted in the actual ultimate analysis. They may however be determined separately and recorded, particularly if their occurrence, as for example chlorine, phosphorous and arsenic, has adverse effects upon the utlization of the fuel.

CORRECTIONS FOR MOISTURE, ASH AND INCOMBUSTIBLE MINERAL MATTER

Analytical results are often corrected to exclude the moisture and incombustible constituents in order to illustrate the chemical composition of the pure coal substance (Table 43). Otherwise, small changes in the coal substance, of particular significance in coal classification, would tend to be obscured because of the sometimes relatively high proportions of other constituents. On the other hand for industrial purposes uncorrected or only partly corrected analyses representing the quality of the coal as supplied to the consumer may be more suitable.

Corrections for moisture

Coal as mined or supplied to the consumer contains both *free water* and *inherent moisture*. Uncorrected analyses of coal at this stage are quoted on an *as-received* basis. The free water occurring within cleat fractures and adhering to the coal surface is readily lost on drying in air. Consequently analyses quoted as *air-dried* reveal the proportion of inherent moisture present within the intermolecular spaces and fine pores of the coals. The moisture determinations during proximate analysis are usually made on an air-dried basis. When the moisture content is known the analysis may then be corrected to a *dry* basis:

Example. In a proximate analysis quoted on an as-received basis, the moisture and volatile matter contents were 5·1 and 18·1 per cent respectively. The volatile matter content adjusted to a dry basis may be calculated by:

TABLE 43

A Coal Analysis Reported on Various Bases
(N.C.B. Scientific Department)

Property	As received basis	Air-dried basis	Dry basis	Dry, Ash-free basis	Dry, mineral matter-free basis
Proximate analysis—					
Moisture	13·0*	9·1	—	—	—
Volatile matter	32·8	34·3	37·7	41·6	40·3
Fixed Carbon	46·1	48·1	52·9	58·4	59·7
Ash	8·1	8·5	9·4	—	—
Mineral matter	9·8	10·2	11·2	—	—
Calorific value (Btu/lb)	11 300	11 810	12 990	14 330	14 580
Sulphur (total)	1·69	1·77	1·95	—	—
Sulphate sulphur	0·08	0·08	0·09	—	—
Pyritic sulphur	0·77	0·80	0·88	—	—
Organic sulphur	0·84	0·89	0·98	—	1·10
Sulphur in ash (as sulphur in coal)	0·25	0·26	0·29	—	—
Carbon dioxide	0·47	0·49	0·54	—	—
Chlorine	0·58	0·61	0·67	—	0·19†
Phosphorus	0·035	0·037	0·041	—	—
Ultimate analysis—					
Moisture	13·0	9·1	—	—	—
Ash	8·1	8·5	9·4	—	—
Carbon	63·4	66·3	72·9	80·5	82·0
Hydrogen	4·3	4·5	5·0	5·5	5·5
Nitrogen	1·3	1·4	1·5	1·7	1·7
Sulphur (combustible)	1·4	1·5	1·7	1·8	1·1‡
Difference (oxygen, etc.)	8·5	8·7	9·5	10·5	9·7

Results are expressed as percentages unless otherwise indicated
* Free moisture 4·3, inherent moisture 8·7
† Assumed organic chlorine
‡ Organic sulphur

Volatile matter (dry)

$$= \text{Volatile matter} \times \frac{100}{100 - \text{moisture}} = \frac{1810}{94.9}$$

$$= 19.1\%$$

Fixed carbon (d.a.f.)

$$= \text{Fixed carbon} \times \frac{100}{100 - \text{moisture} - \text{ash}}$$

$$= \frac{6340}{89.3} = 71.1 \text{ per cent.}$$

Corrections for incombustible constituents

The bulk of the incombustible constituents (pages 233–5) remain as residual ash after combustion of the coal during analysis. Usually corrections are made to a *dry, ash-free basis (d.a.f.)*:

Example. In a proximate analysis quoted on an as-received basis, the moisture, fixed carbon and ash contents were 3·8, 63·4 and 6·9 respectively. The fixed carbon content adjusted to the dry, ash-free coal may be calculated by:

However, corrections to a dry, ash-free basis provide only an approximation as to the composition of the pure coal. During analysis such constituents undergo compositional changes so that the parent materials may be over 10 per cent heavier than the ash. Consequently analyses, particularly of those coals with more than about 5 per cent ash, should be corrected to a dry, *mineral-matter-free basis (d.m.m.f.)* which gives the most accurate representation of the properties of the coal substance (British Standard **1016**, Part 16, 1961, *Reporting of Results*, pp. 11–14). A simplified formula for the estimation of the mineral matter present is that derived by the British Coal Utilization Research Association:

Mineral matter
$$= 1 \cdot 10 \text{ ash} + 0 \cdot 53 \text{ S}_{total} + 0 \cdot 74 \text{ CO}_2 - 0 \cdot 32$$

INCOMBUSTIBLE CONSTITUENTS OF COAL

The incombustible constituents occurring as adulterants in all coals are also referred to as *ash-forming* (Brame & King, 1955, pp. 82–6) or *inorganic constituents* (Francis, 1961, pp. 635–66) and *mineral matter* (Raistrick & Marshall, 1939, pp. 197–9) or *mineral inclusions* (*International Handbook of Coal Petrography*, 1963, 2nd ed.). Besides their more obvious correlation with the type and amount of ash or clinker which remains after the combustion of a fuel, the presence of some constituents, particularly the volatile chlorides, may result in the corrosion of furnace linings and the deposition of troublesome deposits in boiler tubes. From a com-

mercial viewpoint two major groups, one of which is capable of separation from the coal, may be recognized (Table 44). The principal constituents are as follows:

Clay minerals

Most of the clay minerals, chiefly of illitic or kaolinitic type, occur as microscopic intermixtures with the coal macerals. They were principally deposited as clastic material during the formation of the peat and as such may be associated with minor amounts of mica, quartz and other rarer mineral grains. Apart from the occasional occurrence of rounded, and therefore possibly aeolian, detrital grains, most of the minerals appear to have been deposited during the periodic flooding of the bog surfaces. Since the bright coals most probably formed in relatively dry conditions, it is not surprising that clay minerals are less abundant in such lithotypes than in durains and sapropelic coals of aquatic origin. Less common occurrences, which appear to have been deposited from a solution or a colloidal form, are those infilling plant cells, as noted in some Australian coals (Taylor & Warne, 1960, pp. 80–1).

TABLE 44

Classification of Incombustible Constituents of Coal

MICROSCOPIC GROUP	Inherent inorganic matter
Composed of finely disseminated constituents which since they are so intimately mixed with the coal are impossible to separate in coal preparation. They therefore form the principal source of ash in washed coals. Their presence adds to the strength of coal. Most abundant in durain, fusain and cannel.	(a) Composed of inorganic constituents absorbed by the coal-forming plants from the underlying soils and ground waters during growth (*Primary Mineral Matter*) (b) Composed of inorganic constituents infilling the plant cells and deposited from solutions during (*Primary Mineral Matter*) or subsequent to (*Secondary Mineral Matter*) peat formation
	Intermixed clastic matter Composed of clastic debris incorporated within the peat as a result of aqueous or aeolian deposition (*Primary Mineral Matter*); abundant in durains and cannels of aquatic origin
MACROSCOPIC GROUP	Bedding deposits
Composed of macroscopic aggregations of mineral matter coarsely mixed with the coal and occurring as lenses, nodules, beds and cleat infillings. Most of the constituents may be extracted during coal preparation	(a) Composed of layers and lenses of aqueous or aeolian clastic sediments deposited during the peat formation (*Primary Mineral Matter*) (b) Composed of lenses and concretions of carbonate and sulphide minerals deposited during and immediately subsequent to peat formation (*Primary Mineral Matter*) or subsequent to coalification (*Secondary Mineral Matter*)
	Cleat deposits Chiefly carbonate and pyritic minerals deposited from solutions percolating along cleat fractures subsequent to coalification (*Secondary mineral matter*)

Carbargilite, composed of various coal micro-lithotypes intimately mixed with between 20 and 60 per cent by volume of clay minerals, is microscopically equivalent to carbonaceous shale. More concentrated accumulations of clay minerals form the macroscopically recognizable 'dirt bands', mudstones and similar argillaceous partings within the seams.

Carbonate minerals

The carbonates of calcium, iron, magnesium and manganese are some of the most obvious of the incombustible constituents since they occur as the common cleat infillings of coal seams. Although of variable composition, the carbonates are often loosely regarded as being synonymous with ankerite $(Ca_2MgFe(CO_3)_4)$. Usually less than 1 mm thick, such cleat infillings are whitish in freshly mined coal but the ferruginous varieties rapidly become reddish brown on exposure to air. Since the bright coals possess a high cleat frequency (page 85) the carbonate minerals form a considerable proportion of the incombustible mineral matter of these coals. Clearly they are of secondary origin, having been deposited by percolating solutions at some time after the cleat formation. Carbonate concretions, present as coal-balls in some seams immediately overlaid by marine bands, have already been discussed (pages 63–4).

The above carbonate deposits may be largely removed during coal preparation. In addition to such macroscopic occurrences, they also form intimate intermixtures with the coal and occur for example within the former cell cavities of the hard variety of fusite. *Carbankerite* is a microlithotype composed of between 20 to 60 per cent by volume of carbonate minerals.

Sulphide minerals

Pyrite is the commonest of the sulphide minerals occurring in coal seams and as such is the parent material of most of the sulphur recorded in coal analyses. It occurs as microscopic concretions and globules, macroscopic beds, lenses and nodules, cleat infillings and also in the microlithotype carbopyrite. Microscopic pyrite is intimately associated with certain coals, particularly those overlaid by marine strata (Wandless, 1959). High sulphur concentrations are therefore characteristic of such seams and may also be developed in closely underlying coals as a result of the precipitation of pyrite from descending solutions. For example, in S. Wales the Rider Coal, beneath the Amman marine band, has a sulphur content of over 3 per cent, whilst that of the Meadow Seam 10 ft below is less than about 1 per cent. Where the two seams converge the sulphur content of the Meadow Seam rises to over 2 per cent

(Fenton, *et al.*, 1962, p. 462, Plate 10, Fig. 5b). Similarly in north-east Lancashire the Lower Mountain Seam, with usually less than 0·7 per cent sulphur, forms a high grade coking coal. Conversely the overlying Upper Foot Seam with a marine roof is unsuitable for coke production owing to its high sulphur content. In the area where the two seams coalesce the sulphur content throughout the combined Union Seam is over 5 per cent. It is probable that at least some of the pyrite occurring in coals beneath marine strata is of organic origin and was precipitated by bacterial action (Thiessen, 1920, pp. 924–5).

Carbopyrite is a microlithotype containing between 5 and 20 per cent by volume of finely disseminated pyrite.

Macroscopic pyrite, variously termed *brasses*, *brazils*, *sulphur balls*, etc., may occur in beds up to several inches in thickness or as lenses or nodules which are sometimes connected by thin stringers. Certain seams, such as the aptly named Brass Vein in the Swansea area of South Wales, may be characterized by unusually high concentrations of pyrite. In such cases the pyritic layers and segregations are possibly of biochemical origin. The pyrite occurring as a cleat infilling in association with carbonates and more rarely other sulphides including galena and sphalerite, is clearly of secondary origin and was precipitated from percolating ferruginous solutions. During weathering the pyrite may be decomposed to jarosite $(KFe_3(SO_4)_2(OH)_6)$, a soft, powdery, yellow mineral which, when occurring with coal, is sometimes loosely regarded as 'sulphur'. Such occurrences of macroscopic pyrite can usually be removed during coal preparation and may be utilized for the manufacture of sulphuric acid.

Rare elements

Abnormal concentrations of rare elements have been reported from various seams and coal ashes (Abernethy & Gibson, 1963; Bethell, 1963, pp. 478–92). In normal analytical procedure such elements as beryllium, boron, germanium, arsenic, molybdenum, gold, uranium, etc., are seldom specifically recorded and if determined at all are usually grouped together as 'trace elements'. From studies of modern forest conditions it is generally believed that many rare elements were abstracted in solution from the weathered bedrock by deep-rooting plants and concentrated in the top soil and coal-forming vegetation. In other cases the coal seams may have become enriched after coalification by absorption from circulating ground waters.

Apart from germanium, used in the manufacture of transistors, the commercial extraction of such elements in uneconomic. However their occurrence in some coals and consequent enrichment in coal ash and flue dust may produce troublesome conditions because of their toxic qualities. Thus in 1900 an outbreak of arsenic poisoning in Lancashire was traced to the contamination of beer. Although most of the arsenic was attributed to the use of impure sugars, traces were nevertheless introduced from the kiln-drying of hops which had been heated over coal containing extremely minute quantities of the poison.

REFERENCES

ABERNETHY, R. F. & F. H. GIBSON (1963) Rare elements in coal, *Inf. Circ. U.S. Bur. Mines* **8163**.

BETHELL, F. V. (1963) The distribution and origin of minor elements in coal, *J. Inst. Fuel.* **36**, 478–92.

BRAME, J. S. S. & J. G. KING (1955) *Fuel, Solid, Liquid and Gaseous*, 5th ed., London, Arnold.

BROADBENT, S. R. & A. J. SHAW (1955) Reflectance of coal, *Fuel* **34**, 385–403.

CHANDRA, D. (1962) Reflectance and microstructure of weathered coal, *Fuel* **41**, 185–93.

ETTINGER, L. & E. S. ZHUPAKHINA (1960) Method of determining porosity of mineral coals, *Fuel* **39**, 387–92.

FENTON, G. W., ADAMS, H. F. & P. L. RUMSBY (1962) The mapping and appraisal of the characteristics of British coal seams, *Trans. Instn Min. Engrs* **121**, 454–64.

FRANCIS, W. (1961) *Coal*, 2nd ed., London, Arnold.

KING, J. G. & E. T. WILKINS (1944) The internal structure of coal, *Proc. Conf. Ultra-fine Struct. of Coals and Cokes. B.C.U.R.A.* pp. 46–56.

KREULEN, D. J. W. (1948) *Elements of Coal Chemistry*, 1st ed., Rotterdam, Nijgh & van Ditmar.

KREVELEN, D. W. VAN (1961) *Coal*, 1st ed., Amsterdam, Elsevier.

MOORE, E. S. (1940) *Coal*, 2nd ed., New York, Wiley.

NAIRN, A. E. M. (editor) (1961) *Descriptive Palaeoclimatology*, 1st ed., New York, Interscience.

POMEROY, C. D. (1963) Routine strength tests on coal, *Steel & Coal* **187**, 640–5, 698–704.

RAISTRICK, A. & C. E. MARSHALL (1939) *The Nature and Origin of Coal and Coal Seams*, 1st ed., London, E.U.P.

SEYLER, C. A. & W. J. EDWARDS (1949) Technique of coal petrography, *Fuel* **28**, 121–7.

TAYLOR, G. H. & A. C. COOK (1962) Sclerlotinite in coal—its petrology and classification, *Geol Mag.* **99**, 41–52.

TAYLOR, G. H. & S. St. J. WARNE (1960) Some Australian coal petrological studies and their geological implications, *Proc. Internat. Committee Coal Petrology* **3**, 75–82.

THIESSEN, R. (1920) Occurrence and origin of finely disseminated sulphur compounds in coal, *Trans. Am. Inst. Min. & mettal. Engrs* **63**, 913–26.

TOMKEIEFF, S. I. (1954) *Coals and Bitumens, Nomenclature and Classification*, 1st ed., London, Pergamon.

TRUEMAN, A. E. (1946) Stratigraphical problems in the Coal Measures of Europe and North America, *Q. Jl geol. Soc. Lond.* **102**, xlix–xciii.

WANDLESS, A. M. (1959) The occurrence of sulphur in British coals, *J. Inst. Fuel* **32**, 258–66.

RANK AND CLASSIFICATION OF CARBONACEOUS DEPOSITS

RANK OF COAL

The *rank* of a solid fuel is defined as its position in the *coalification* or *carbonification series* extending from peat at the lowest rank, through lignite and bituminous coal to anthracite which forms the highest rank. Essentially the rank of a fuel, as defined by its physical and chemical characters (Tables 45 & 46), is determined by the degree of metamorphism to which it has been subjected (pages 240–7). The principal members of the coalification series are as follows.

PEAT

Of Pleistocene and recent age, peat occurs as a soft unconsolidated deposit at, or near, the surface in beds seldom more than about 30 ft thick. Most deposits are waterlogged and one of the most notable characteristics of the material is its high moisture content, which in undrained deposits is between 90 and 95 per cent of the total weight. This may be reduced by air-drying techniques to about 35 per cent. In colour peat varies from brown to black with darker varieties occurring in the basal layers of the deposit. Similarly, although the upper layers are of a fibrous nature and include recognizable plant stems, leaves, tree roots etc., the basal parts become more compact and homogeneous. Consequently in some of the thicker peat bogs several distinct layers can be identified. Thus in the north of England (Trotter, 1952, pp. 130–3) the immature, light brown, fibrous *top peat* is seldom more than 3 ft thick and is worthless as a fuel. It is separated by about 6 ft of dark brown to black *breast peat*, with a partial fibrous structure, from the jet black and appreciably denser *bottom* or *pot peat*.

Although the calorific value of peat when calculated on a dry basis is about 9 500 Btu/lb, the value of air-dried peat is only about 6 000 Btu/lb. This low value, as compared for example with that of bituminous coal (Table 45), together with a low bulk density and consequent higher transportation and storage costs, restricts the utilization of peat to those countries, such as Eire, where coal deposits are scarce. In such countries, apart from being a cheap domestic fuel, considerable quantities of peat are now being worked for the generation of electric power by using specially designed boiler plants and furnaces. Other uses include the production of sound-insulating boards and peat moss, the latter being used extensively in horticulture (Brame & King, 1955, pp. 47–9; Miller in Meenan & Webb, 1957, pp. 130–47). Much is still won by hand cutting; the peat is cut into thin slabs or brick-shaped *turves* and air-dried by assembling it in honeycomb stacks. Mechanized harvesting methods including the milled and hydro-peat processes have been developed by the industrial consumers for large scale production.

LIGNITE

With the notable exception of the Lower Carboniferous seams of the Moscow basin, most lignites are of late Cretaceous or Tertiary age. Individual seams are commonly tens of feet in thickness and many occur within relatively unconsolidated sands and clays at shallow depths below the surface. More rarely lignites may exceed 100 ft as in Victoria, Australia, where the thickest continuous seam in the world was proved in a borehole at Loy Yang to be 757 ft thick and to occur beneath only about 90 ft of overburden. Unfortunately the term 'lignite' is differently defined in various countries (Table 47). In Britain for example the terms 'brown coal' and 'lignite' are usually regarded as synonymous, whereas in Germany the latter term is restricted to distinct fragments of wood enclosed in brown coal. Again in North America 'brown coal' is an unconsolidated deposit whereas 'lignite' is consolidated, and much of the 'brown coal' of Germany would be classed as sub-bituminous. In this account two groups, composed of brown and the higher rank black lignites, are recognized as being intermediate in rank between peat and bituminous coal.

The *brown lignites* vary from yellowish to dark brown in colour and possess a predominantly dull or

TABLE 45

Chemical Analyses of the Coalification Series

Locality	Horizon	Proximate per cent (air-dried basis)				Ultimate per cent (dry, ash-free basis)					Calorific value, Btu/lb (dry ash-free basis)	Rank
		Moisture	Volatile matter	Fixed carbon	Ash	Sulphur	Hydrogen	Carbon	Nitrogen	Oxygen		
[1]Eire [average analysis]	Recent		67·0	30·6	2·4	0·3	6·0	57·0	1·3	33·0	9 500	Peat
New Zealand, South Canterbury	(Tertiary)	30·4	35·0	27·8	6·8	0·5	5·0	67·6	0·8	26·1	11 194	Brown Lignite
Australia, Victoria	Yallourn Seam (Tertiary)	13·0	44·7	40·2	2·0	0·3	4·7	68·2	0·5	26·2	11 455	Brown Lignite
New Zealand, Waikato	(Tertiary)	11·5	42·2	44·4	1·9	1·2	5·5	74·9	1·1	17·3	13 279	Black Lignite
Nigeria, Enugu	No. 3 Seam (Cretaceous)	10·1	38·3	44·5	7·1	0·5	5·3	82·2	2·2	9·8	13 700	'Black Lignite'
Great Britain, Derbyshire, Denby	Deep Hard Seam (Carboniferous)	7·8	35·3	52·5	4·4	1·03	5·2	81·2	1·43	11·1	14 330	Bituminous (High Volatile Coal)
Great Britain, Lancashire, Dunnockshaw	Lower Mountain Seam (Carboniferous)	2·0	27·8	68·5	3·7	0·3	4·5	86·8	1·9	6·2	15 000	Bituminous (Coking Coal)
[2]Great Britain, Glamorgan, Penrikyber	Nine Feet Seam (Carboniferous)	0·6	13·3	83·1	3·0	0·7	4·3	92·6	1·5	0·9	15 670	Bituminous (Low Volatile Steam Coal)
[2]Great Britain, Glamorgan, Resolven	Nine Feet Seam (Carboniferous)	1·8	7·6	85·4	5·2	1·0	3·4	93·4	1·4	0·8	15 540	Anthracite
[2]Great Britain, Carmarthen, Pen-y-moor	Nine Feet Seam (Carboniferous)	1·4	5·3	90·6	2·7	0·7	3·0	94·5	1·0	0·8	15 320	Anthracite

[1] Proximate analysis on a dry basis   [2] Ultimate analyses on a dry, mineral-matter-free basis

earthy lustre. Many are banded, the layering being caused by concentrations of particular plant constituents including yellowish, felted masses of leaves or brownish lenses and bands of resinous materials. Thin and rather lustrous films of black lignite and fusain may be visible in hand specimens. Some varieties are relatively soft and can easily be powdered in the hand whilst those of a slightly higher rank are harder and more consolidated. Many of the lighter-coloured lignites display a fibrous structure and occasional tree stumps and roots, sometimes in their growth positions, may still retain their woody nature, showing that such deposits are but little removed from peat. In the darker varieties, which grade into black lignites, a more uniform texture is developed and recognizable plant components become rarer.

Black lignites, also called sub-bituminous coals as in North America, are dark brown to black in colour. Their lustre is often silky and may sometimes be indistinguishable from that of the bituminous coals. The fibrous structure of the brown lignites is lost and most black lignites are distinctly laminated with dull and bright bands as in the bituminous coals. They are considerably harder than brown lignites and on weathering tend to separate along surfaces approximately parallel to the bedding into thin friable slabs. *Jet* is a hard, compact variety usually found in lenticular masses as in the Jurassic of Yorkshire. Since it can be turned on a lathe and polished it is sometimes used for making ornaments and beads.

Formerly, lignite production was confined to those countries where higher rank fuels were scarce or absent. In recent years however the situation has been somewhat changed by the development of more efficient preparation processes and boiler-house plant so that lignites now form over 30 per cent of the world's total annual coal production. Many deposits, particularly in the case of brown lignites, are worked by opencast methods (Plate 14), a mode of extraction favoured by the great thickness of some seams and the thin cover of overburden. One of the world's largest such enterprises is that in Victoria, Australia, where in 1962 approximately 13 million ton of lignite were produced from a single seam over 200 ft thick at Yallourn (Nelson, 1963, pp. 502–8). Owing to a loss of moisture, lignites rapidly disintegrate on exposure to air so that lengthy storage and long-distance transportation of the raw fuel is impracticable. Consequently they are consumed, or processed into more transportable briquettes, near the place of extraction. Particularly in Eastern Europe, the U.S.S.R. and Australia, lignites are extensively utilized for electricity production in power stations constructed adjacent to the opencast or mine workings. After briquetting, when the moisture content is reduced to about 15 per cent, they are less liable to slacking and spontaneous combustion and consequently may be economically transported for use as domestic and industrial fuels in areas some distance from the production sites. Many lignites are rich in tars from which valuable chemical by-products are obtained, others may be utilized for gas production, and recently excellent metallurgical coke has been produced from some of the Victorian seams (Brame & King, 1955, pp. 118–20).

BITUMINOUS COAL

The bituminous coals, mostly of Upper Palaeozoic age, are harder and more coherent than lignites. They are typically banded and the principal macroscopic types are the bright, dull and cannel coals (pages 223–5, Plates 12a, b, & c). Other less common varieties include the following.

Peacock coal sometimes occurs in bituminous and anthracite seams. The name is derived from the iridescent colours, similar to those of oil slicks observed on water, which are strikingly displayed on fracture surfaces of the coal. Although such coloration may occasionally be due to thin oil films, in most cases it appears to be caused by a thin film of iron hydroxide deposited by percolating surface waters (Moore, 1940, p. 106).

Eye, birdseye, eenie, pisolitic or *ring-fractured coal* (Plate 15a) is occasionally observed in black lignites, bright bituminous coals, anthracites and more rarely cannels. It is characterized by numerous lustrous and circular or oval fracture surfaces which in some cases exceed 3 inches in diameter. The fracture surfaces or 'eyes' are developed as closely set partings which are usually parallel to the cleat. They are sometimes covered by hair-like lines radiating from the centre and also similar fine concentric lines

parallel to the margin. Eyed coal is probably a pressure phenomena and may be likened to the percussion fractures produced when a fine piece of glass is struck with a sharp steel point (Clough & Kirkpatrick, 1909 pp. 2–11, Gage & Bartrum, 1942, pp. 86b–98b). Most instances observed by the writer occurred in proximity to faults or in thin coal lenses.

Paper coal (Plate 15b, c) is so named from its superficial resemblance to loosely packed sheets of coarse brown paper. Originally discovered in the lignites of the Moscow basin, where deposits sometimes over a metre in thickness cover many square miles, paper coals have recently been described from the Indiana coalfield. The papery texture is most apparent in the extremely friable weathered material which has a general appearance similar to leaf-mould. It is due to an abundance of waxy leaf cuticles, so that the coal may be composed of over 20 per cent cutinite. Unweathered coals are comparatively solid, in which case the typical texture is indistinct (Francis, 1961, pp. 141–5; Naevel & Guennel, 1960, pp. 241–8).

Because of their wide range of properties, the bituminous coals are suitable for almost all technological purposes (Brame & King, 1955, pp. 122–4, 180–2, 211–47, 268–72). Apart from highly caking varieties most bituminous coals can be used for *steam raising* as in electrical power stations, industrial and marine boiler plants. The most valuable include the high rank steam coals with low volatile contents and high calorific values. Finely ground pulverized fuel is becoming increasingly used in electrical power stations and for this purpose the less valuable high volatile and low caking coals are ideally suitable. For *gas manufacture* high volatile coals with a moderately high caking power are required. Domestic coke and smokeless fuels are manufactured as part of the process, although the most important by-products which render gasification economic are those derived from coal-tar. These include fuel oil, benzole, creosote oil and phenol from which a multitude of products, ranging from saccharine to explosives and perfumes to disinfectants, are manufactured. For the production of *metallurgical coke* those coals with a high caking power are required and are most often blended to produce a required coke quality. Such coals should have a volatile content below 30 per cent together with low ash, sulphur and phosphorous contents. Important by-products include tar, benzol and gas. Unlike that used primarily for gas manufacture, sized coal is not essential and slack may be used. *Domestic* fuel requirements are less stringent, although an increasing awareness of the adverse effects of smoke pollution is necessitating the development of processed smokeless fuels for the domestic market in most industrial areas.

ANTHRACITE

Comprising the most valuable and least common solid fuels, anthracites may be broadly defined as those coals with a volatile content below about 10 per cent (d.m.m.f.). Further subdivision on the macroscopic basis is impracticable. Anthracites are black and possess a brilliant or sub-metallic lustre. Their fracture is markedly conchoidal and, unlike the bituminous coals there is little, if any, tendency to break along the bedding. They are hard, brittle coals breaking often into knife-sharp fragments and are absolutely clean to the touch. Laminae in the highest ranks are rarely apparent owing to the lack of contrast between the constituents. Nevertheless slight traces of layering may be developed on weathered or abraded specimens by selective erosion.

The high carbon, low ash and low volatile contents coupled with their high calorific values render anthracites eminently suitable for steam raising and heat generation. They are particularly valuable for such purposes where bulk storage space is limited, as in marine installations, and when a smokeless fuel is required.

INDICES OF RANK

The principal physical and chemical characters which exhibit variation in the coalification series (Table 46) are summarized below.

(1) *Colour*. A general darkening of the colour is characteristic of the progressive increase in rank from peat to black lignite.

(2) *Lustre*. The lustre of peat and brown lignite is dull and earthy whilst the bright components of black lignite and bituminous coal exhibit a progressively brighter lustre until the uniformly brilliant appearance of anthracite is reached.

Similarly the reflectance of polished coal samples increases uniformly with the rank (Fig. 18.4). The property is especially useful in that the rank may be determined rapidly and accurately without recourse to more tedious analytical methods. Furthermore, unlike other rank indices, the reflectance of a sample exhibits little variation with the degree of weathering and so may be used in estimating the rank of weathered outcrop samples.

(3) *Constituent contrasts*. In peat and some brown lignites unaltered vegetable debris can easily be dis-

TABLE 46

Some Important Physical and Chemical Criteria of Rank

Character	Coalification series				
	Peat	Brown lignite	Black lignite	Bituminous coal	Anthracite
Darkening of colour	——————————→				
Lustre and reflectance[1]	————————————————————→				
Constituent contrasts	←———————————— – – – –				
Opacity	————————————————————→				
Calorific Value[2]	——————————————→| ← – – –				
Solubility	←—————				
Volatile Content	← – – – – – – – – – – – —————				
Moisture Content	←——————————— – – –|– – —→				
Carbon Content[3]	————————————————————→				
Oxygen Content[3]	←————————————————				
Hydrogen Content	– – – – – – – – – →|←———				

[1] See Fig. 18.4   [2] See Fig. 18.7   [3] See Fig. 19.1

cerned in the hand specimen. Similarly, lithotype bands may be distinguished in most black lignites and low to medium rank bituminous coals. However in the higher rank coals such constituent contrasts diminish so that anthracites appear to be amorphous.

(4) *Opacity*. The various members of the coalification series became increasingly opaque until it is almost impossible to prepare a transparent microscope slide of anthracite.

(5) *Calorific value*. A progressive increase in the calorific value is characteristic of the coalification series up to, and including, the highest rank bituminous coals (15 900 Btu/lb). A slight decrease in value to about 15 200 Btu/lb occurs in normal anthracites and exceptionally the calorific value falls to below 15 000 Btu/lb in the case of some anthracites formed by contact metamorphism (Fig. 18.7, Table 45).

(6) *Solubility*. The solubility of the coal components diminishes as their rank increases. Thus peat and brown lignites are readily dissolved in sodium or potassium hydroxide solutions. Black lignites and bituminous coals however require oxidation in nitric acid before the bulk of their constituents become soluble in alkalis.

(7) *Volatile content*. Although an average fall in volatile content is apparent throughout the coalification series, the wide range in values, due to compositional differences in the original vegetation, of the low rank coals is such that the volatile content as revealed in an isolated analysis cannot be used as an effective rank criterion (Trotter, 1952). For example, the volatile content of peat may vary between 94 and 38 per cent and that of lignites may vary by as much as 20 per cent. However in the high rank bituminous coals and anthracites it is an important criterion as a progressive drop from about 30 to below 2 per cent (d.a.f.) volatiles occurs (Table 45).

(8) *Moisture content*. The moisture content shows a trend opposite to that of the calorific value. A general decrease (Table 45) occurs from peat, through brown and black lignites to the lower rank bituminous coals. A slight rise occurs from the high rank bituminous coals, with moisture contents below about 1·5 per cent, to the anthracites which may contain about 3 per cent moisture.

(9) *Carbon content*. The contents of fixed and total carbon increases with the rank.

(10) *Oxygen content*. Conversely as the carbon content increases towards the highest rank coals, their oxygen contents decrease from almost 30 to below 1 per cent (Hickling, 1927, p. 266, Plate VI), (Fig. 19.1).

(11) *Hydrogen content*. In the low rank coals the hydrogen contents rise slightly from about 4·5 per cent in lignites to about 6 per cent in high volatile

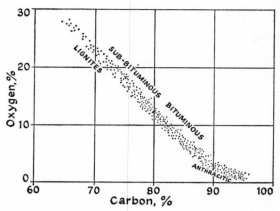

Fig. 19.1 The distribution in carbon and oxygen in about 1 200 coals. (Hickling, 1927, Plate VI.)

bituminous coals. A progressive decrease occurs in the anthracites to a minimum below 3 per cent.

The characteristics most used for determining coal rank are the carbon, volatile (suitable for high rank coals), moisture (suitable for low rank coals) and hydrogen (suitable for subdivision of anthracites) contents, together with the calorific values and reflectances. In order that accurate comparisons of lignites and bituminous coals be made, it is necessary to determine and define their ranks by noting the properties of a particular maceral, which is usually vitrinite. Otherwise the wide variations that exist in the chemical and physical natures of different macerals (pages 221–2) may obscure, or alternatively grossly exaggerate, what may be in effect only slight rank differences. The anthracites are regarded as homogenous for purposes of rank analysis because their constituents are less differentiated and can seldom be distinguished.

THE ORIGIN OF COALIFICATION

It is apparent from the progressive variation of their physical and chemical properties that the members of the coalification series are alteration products of a continuous process which commences on the death of the parent plants. Such alteration is essentially the result of biochemical and geological processes.

Biochemical alteration

Coalification starts with the biochemical alteration of the vegetation to form peat. Carbonaceous materials seldom accumulate in nature for they are normally rapidly and almost completely decomposed by fungal and bacterial action. However, during the formation of peat the total decomposition of the vegetation is arrested by the marked acidity and low oxygenation of the bog environment. Under such conditions, which are progressively more marked at depth, the micro-organisms become less active so that accumulation as peat of the partly altered plant remains exceeds the rate of total decomposition. It is generally considered that the biochemical stage of coalification terminates at the formation of peat. Nevertheless there is evidence that bacteria can occur in and attack lignites and higher rank coals (Rogoff, et al., 1962, pp. 2–13). Accordingly it was suggested, largely by Fuchs and McKenzie Taylor (summarized in Francis, 1961, pp. 191–3), that bacterial action may play a significant role throughout coalification and even determine the actual rank attained.

Effect of time

The effect of time is sometimes considered to be an important factor in coalification. Generally the older coals tend to be of a higher rank than their geologically younger counterparts. Thus many anthracites and high rank bituminous coals are of Palaeozoic age whereas most low rank bituminous coals and lignites are restricted to the Mesozoic and Cainozoic Eras respectively (Table 38). Such a relationship between geological age and rank is however superficial. The high ranks of most of the Palaeozoic coals are the result of their greater depths of burial and orogenic disturbance as compared with the relatively shallow and little-folded younger and lower rank coals. In those regions where the latter coals have been subjected to severe folding and deep burial their rank is similarly high and clearly bears no relationship to their geological age. For example in the gently folded Moscow basin, lignites and low rank bituminous coals of Lower Carboniferous age occur whilst Cretaceous, and even Tertiary, anthracites are associated with intensely folded strata in some of the western states of North America. Furthermore, it is apparent that coalification is a relatively rapid process since rounded and well worn coal pebbles are sometimes found in interseam sandstones and conglomerates. Such pebbles clearly represent material which had already attained a considerable degree of coalification prior to erosion, as otherwise deformation and shrinkage would have occurred during their subsequent redeposition and burial.

Hilt's Rule and depth of burial

In 1873 Professor Carl Hilt observed in several continental coalfields that a general relationship existed between the chemical properties of coals and their stratigraphic positions at a given locality. He demonstrated that a general decrease in the oxygen content of seams occurs with depth and also that the ratio of fixed carbon to volatile matter similarly in-

creased with depth. Such characteristics are definitive of coal rank and accordingly his observations have since formed the basis of Hilt's Rule, which may be stated as follows.

In a vertical sequence, at any one locality in a coalfield, the rank of the coal seams rises with increasing depth.

It should be emphasized that the various sampling points must be vertically one above another as in a shaft or borehole section, since otherwise lateral variations in rank may obscure any vertical differences. Furthermore, since there are exceptions to the statement it is only to be regarded as a rule and not as a law. The general validity of Hilt's Rule has been accepted, but it has been questioned in many instances:

(1) *Relationship between depth and carbon content.* One of the most comprehensive accounts, supported by a wealth of analytical data, is that of Millot, Cope & Berry (1946). In this the rank-depth relationship was considered for forty-two coals encountered in over 3 500 ft of strata penetrated by the Pie Rough borehole in the North Staffordshire coalfield. It was shown that the average and regular increase in carbon content (d.m.m.f.) per 100-ft increment of depth was 0·23 per cent (Fig. 19.2). A considerably higher rate is exhibited by the lignites of Victoria,

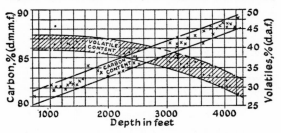

Fig. 19.2 Variation of carbon and volatile contents with seam depths, Pie Rough Borehole, Staffordshire. (After J. O'. N. Millot.)

Australia. In a series of boreholes at Maryvale through 1 200 ft of coal the carbon content (d.a.f.) increased at the rate of 0·5 per cent per 100 ft (Edwards, 1945). For sub-bituminous coals a rate of carbon increase of 0·37 per cent per 100 ft is quoted for a 550-ft sequence in the Ohai coalfield of New Zealand (Suggate, 1959, p. 84). The latter coals are intermediate in rank between the Australian lignites and the English bituminous coals so that it appears that the carbon increase rate throughout the coalification series is not linear and slows down towards the highest rank coals.

(2) *Relationship between moisture content and depth.* A progressive loss of moisture occurs in the

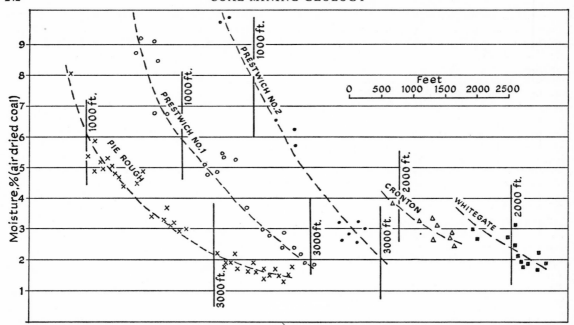

Fig. 19.3   Variation of moisture content with depth as illustrated by coal analyses from five boreholes in Great Britain. (Data from Millot, *et. al.*, 1946, Tables II–VIII; and Trotter, 1952, Tables VIII, XII, 1954, Tables II, III.)

coalification series up to and including the lower rank bituminous coals and for such coals is closely related to the depth of burial of the seams (Trotter, 1952, pp. 155–9; 1954, pp. 279–81). The actual rate of decrease itself decreases with depth, that is, with increasing rank, so that the moisture contents of a sequence of coals plot as a parabolic curve (Fig. 19.3).

(3) *Relationship between volatile content and depth.* As previously noted, the volatile contents of low rank coals of similar rank may exhibit considerable variation. Consequently any decrease as a result of increasing depth may be obscured by the more prominent variations due to the coal type. Even where a decrease in volatile content is apparent in such coals it is moreover slight. In the high rank coals such compositional differences are less well defined and marked decreases with depth occur. Consequently any considerations of depth-volatile relationships should be confined to those coals with volatile contents less than about 42 per cent (Suggate, 1956, p. 203).

In the high rank coals the rate of decrease itself increases to about 23 per cent volatiles, but in the highest ranks the rate decreases (*op. cit.*, pp. 209–13), (Fig. 19.2). At Pie Rough for example the rate of change for the low rank coals (average volatile contents—42 per cent d.a.f.) at 1 000 ft was only 0·035 per cent per 100 ft. At greater depths the rate increased progressively from 0·21 per cent per 100 ft at 2 000 ft, to 0·60 per cent per 100 ft in coals (average

volatile contents—32 per cent d.a.f.) at 4 000 ft. The latter rate agrees fairly closely with those of 0·69 per cent per 100 ft quoted for high rank coals in the Appalachian coalfields, and an average of 0·61 per cent per 100 ft suggested for similar coals in South Wales, Kent, Holland and Westphalia (Reeves, 1928, pp. 800–2).

(4) *Relationship between calorific value and depth.* Up to the highest rank bituminous coals the calorific values increase with depth. Thus at Pie Rough (Fig. 19.4) the values show a constant increase at an aver-

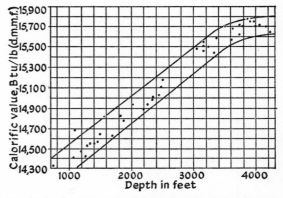

Fig. 19.4   Calorific values plotted against seam depths, Pie Rough Borehole, Staffordshire. (After J. O'. N. Millot.)

age rate of 50 Btu per 100 ft up to 15 600 Btu at about 3 500 ft. At greater depths the rate falls markedly as the maximum calorific value of coals is approached.

Hilt's Rule is undoubtedly applicable in many coalfields and some of the more common objections may well be a result of structural disturbances together with compositional abnormalities in the coals:

(1) *Occurrence of abnormal coals.* Departures from the rule are sometimes due to the occurrence of sapropelic and other coals with similarly high exinite contents, the analyses of which exhibit much higher volatile and hydrogen percentages than those of other more normal coals. For example, in a borehole sequence a seam of cannel in the strata between two humic bright coals would on analysis obscure any general volatile decrease. If the sapropelic nature of the coal was ignored the analyses might therefore be quoted as evidence against Hilt's Rule. In this respect it would be worthwhile if the rank variations with depth were examined for a particular maceral such as vitrinite rather than for average seam sections or sub-sections.

(2) *Comparison of closely adjacent seam analyses.* Normal variations in chemical composition as a result of compositional differences in the original vegetation may obscure only slight percentage changes with depth. In this respect an early consideration of adjacent seams in various collieries of the S. Wales coalfield indicated that only about half the cases clearly supported Hilt's Rule. When the data were subsequently re-examined it was demonstrated that there were remarkably few exceptions to the rule if comparisons were restricted to analyses of coals which were more than 100 yd vertically apart (Hickling, 1932, pp. 323–4).

(3) *Misleading indices of rank.* It is particularly unfortunate that the rule is often loosely regarded as expressing a depth-volatile relationship for all coals irrespective of their ranks. If considered in this way the rule may well appear unjustified in the case of low rank coal sequences. Conversely, although the depth-moisture relationship is in accordance with the rule up to and including the low rank bituminous coals, the moisture content is clearly an unsuitable criterion when below about 2·5 per cent, as in high rank bituminous coals and anthracites. Below the latter percentage the decrease is only extremely slight and may indeed change to a slight increase.

(4) *Structural disturbance of the seams.* Hilt's Rule is most often questioned in heavily folded and overthrust fields. Apart from the obvious anomalies created by inversion of strata, the general increase of rank with depth may be modified by other coalification factors (pages 244–5).

(5) *Lateral variations in rank.* Sometimes where actual vertical sections are lacking the rank variations in a stratigraphic sequence are compared with coal samples collected from localities which may be considerable lateral distances apart. In such cases lateral variations in rank may totally obscure any true relationship between depth and rank.

So far our attention has been confined to the relationship between the rank of coals and their present depths at particular localities. It is, however, apparent that their depths during coalification have little relevance to the present-day depths of the coals since they were originally buried beneath considerable accumulations of other sediments. Various attempts have been made to determine the actual depths at which coals attained their particular ranks. In the case of the high rank Palaeozoic coals, calculations based on the possible thickness of a former cover are clearly subject to considerable degrees of uncertainty. In the more recent coalfields the former depths of burial may be determined more accurately since most of the overlying sequence may be preserved. Also, even if much erosion has taken place, almost complete sequences of cover rocks sometimes occur at the edges of the coalfields so that estimations as to the original depths of the seams may be made with reasonable confidence. If the thickness of the former cover and actual rank of a coal is known it is then possible to postulate the depth of burial of other ranks. This may be calculated from the rates of increase or decrease with depth established for the various chemical properties of the coals. Accordingly, from data principally based on the Cretaceous and Lower Tertiary Greymouth coalfield of New Zealand, it is suggested that anthracites may form at depths below 20 000 ft and lignites at less than about 9 000 ft (Suggate, 1959, pp. 88–91), (Fig. 19.5).

The primary cause of rank increase with depth cannot be considered to be the static pressure exerted by the former thickness of overburden. From thermodynamic principles this cannot affect the chemical properties of the coals (Krevelen, 1961, p. 47). The only effect such pressure would have would be to reduce the porosity and hence influence to some degree the moisture content of the coals. Accordingly it is suggested that the depth-rank relationship is most probably related to the geothermal gradient, which in most areas at present is about 1 °C per 100 ft. This may however have been very different in the past and is at present considerably greater in areas of igneous activity. In Japan for example the rate of increase is locally over 5 °C per 100 ft in areas adjacent to volcanic centres. Consequently local or regional variations in the rate of rank increase may reflect similar variations in the contemporary geothermal gradients.

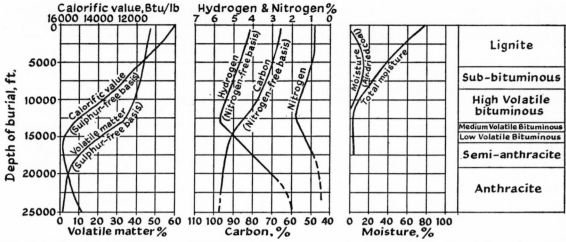

Fig. 19.5   Changes of calorific value, volatile matter, carbon, hydrogen, nitrogen and moisture with depth of burial—
average type coals. (Suggate, 1959, Fig. 40.)

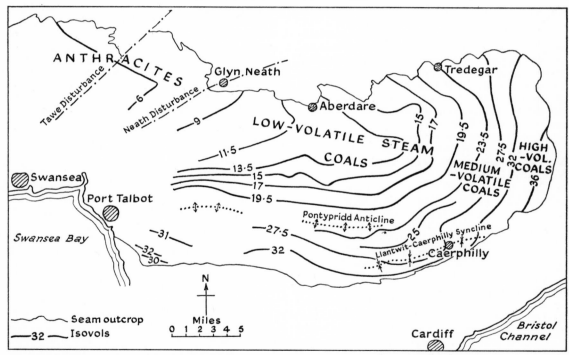

Fig. 19.6   Isovol map illustrating lateral variation in rank of the Nine Feet Seam, South Wales. (*Nine Feet Seam Folio*,
Fig. 14, N.C.B. Scientific Department.)

Orogenic effects and the Roberts-White Law

Excepting the local developments which sometimes occur in the vicinity of igneous intrusions (pages 49–52), the anthracites and the highest rank bituminous coals are confined to those coalfield areas which have been most severely affected by orogenic forces and are consequently highly folded and overthrust. When traced towards such regions the seams exhibit a gradual increase in their ranks. Such lateral variations are clearly revealed on plotting upon a map the coal analyses for a particular seam and joining the points of equal carbon, volatile or calorific values as *iso-carbs, iso-vols* or *iso-cals* respectively.

Thus in South Wales (Fig. 19.6) there is a general increase in rank in a south–north direction in the western part of the coalfield and a general increase towards the north-west in the eastern half. Consequently the various iso-lines are approximately parallel to the southern and eastern margins of the coalfield. They are however abruptly truncated along the northern margin and although exhibiting a very broad relationship to the general synclinal structure (page 72) show no relationship to the present-day depth of burial of the seams (Fig. 19.7). From the irregular spacing of the iso-characters, such as the carbon content plotted at unit intervals, it is apparent that the rate of lateral variation is irregular and varies in different parts of the coalfield. The coals (cf. National Coal Board, Scientific Department, Coal Survey, 1959, *Seam Folio of the Nine Feet Seam*) exhibit a progressive change from high volatile bituminous types, through medium and low volatile coking and steam coals, to high grade anthracites. The latter are confined to the north-western part of the coalfield. It is considered significant that the latter area is characterized by the development of small-scale, but nevertheless severe, fold structures associated with reverse and wrench faults. Although Hilt's Rule is generally applicable the depth effects are relatively small as compared with the marked lateral variations.

A similar lateral variation occurs in the North American Appalachian coalfields where the coals exhibit a progressive easterly increase in rank. Thus

only gently folded low rank bituminous coals with fixed carbon contents of less than 60 per cent in Ohio pass through successively higher ranks into anthracites with fixed carbon contents of over 95 per cent in the highly folded and overthrust sequences of north-eastern Pennsylvania (White, 1925, pp. 256–8), (Fig. 19.8). In a detailed study of over 2000 analyses of the Lower Kittanning seam of south-western Pennsylvania, Stadnichenko (1934, pp. 513–28) demonstrated that even in only slightly folded rocks the fixed carbon content increased by over 25 per cent in some 50 miles between Kittanning and Windbar.

Since the high rank coals, with the exception of some contact-metamorphosed varieties, are confined to those areas most affected by orogenic movements, it appears therefore that such movements have had at least some influence upon the formation of the highest rank coals. From a review of lateral variations in rank in the North American coalfields, White (1925, pp. 264–72) considered that the progressive coalification was due to regional pressure-metamorphism. He demonstrated that anthracites are associated with reverse faulting and overthrusting and suggested that the strong directional pressures involved in the development of such structures were primarily responsible for the high degree of coalification. The theory was later modified by Roberts (1950, pp. 325–9) who believes that the effects of differential pressure are subordinate to the frictional heat developed during overthrusting and severe folding. Accordingly he proposed the Roberts-White Law:

The rank of a coal is determined by, and increases with, the intensity of the orogenic or tectonic forces, and the natural heat-treatment, to which the coal has been subjected.

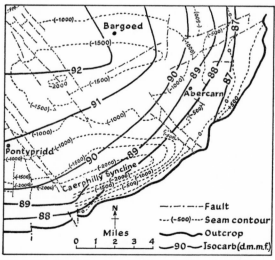

Fig. 19.7 Seam contours and isocarbs for the Nine Feet Seam, South Wales. (*Nine Feet Seam Folio*, N.C.B. Scientific Department.)

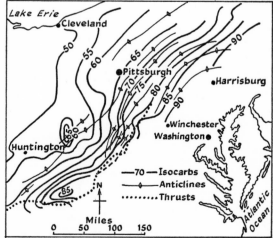

Fig. 19.8 Lateral rank variations in the North Appalachian coalfield, U.S.A.

TABLE 47

Approximate Correlations of some Coal Classification Systems

Percentage moisture (ash-free)	Volatile percentage (dry ash-free)	Calorific value Btu/lb (Moist ash-free)	E.C.E. International class number	USA A.S.T.M. coal groups	Great Britain (N.C.B. coal groups)	Germany	France
	3·0—			Meta-anthracite	Anthracite (100)	Anthrazitkohle	Anthracite
	6·5—		1A	Anthracite			
	10·0—		1B				
			2	Semi-anthracite	Low-volatile steam coals (200)	Magerkohle	Charbon maigre
	14·0—		3	Low-volatile bituminous coal (approx. equivalent to semi- or super-bituminous coal)		Esskohle	Charbon quart-gras
	20·0—						Charbon demi-gras
			4		Medium-volatile coals (300)	Fettkohle	Charbon gras à court flamme
	28·0—		5	Medium-volatile bituminous coal			
	33·0— c. 33·0 41·0	13950—	6	High-volatile A bituminous coal	High volatile coals (400–900)	Gaskohle	Charbon gras proprement dits
	c. 33·0 44·0	12960—	7	High volatile B bituminous coal		Flammkohle	Charbon flambant gras
	c. 35·0 50·0	10980—	8	High volatile C bituminous coal and Sub-bituminous A coal		Glanzbraun-kohle (Bright brown coal)	Charbon flambant secs
	c. 42·0 50·0	10260—	9		Black lignite		
			10	Sub-bituminous B coal			
20·0—			11			(Dull brown coal)	
30·0—			12	Sub-bituminous C coal		Mattbraun-kohle	
40·0—			13	Lignite (consolidated material) and Brown coal (unconsolidated material)	Brown lignite	Weichbraun-kohle (Soft brown coal)	
50·0—			14				
60·0—			15				
70·0—							

Hartbraunkohle (Hard Brown Coal)

Contact metamorphism

The fact that coals in certain cases may exhibit an increase in rank adjacent to dykes and sills has already been noted (pages 49–52). Such contact-metamorphic effects are however extremely localized. The occurrence of anthracites adjacent to minor intrusions, in for example the Scottish and Natal coalfields, is not to be compared with the more widespread developments previously described. In none of the major fields containing high rank coals is there any evidence for the occurrence of large intrusive bodies which may have caused their high degree of coalification.

In summary it may be noted that although there is more or less general agreement that coalification beyond the peat stage is a result of metamorphism due to heat or pressure, there is still much speculation and controversy as to the exact nature of the processes involved. On the one hand it appears that the coalification of the lignites and low rank bituminous coals is related to their former depths of burial. In such cases the particular rank of the coals may be determined primarily by the effects of the geothermal gradient. Although the latter may have had some effect in controlling the degree of coalification of the highest rank bituminous and anthracitic coals, its influence was probably only subsidiary to that of more pronounced heating associated with orogenic movement. It may therefore be that there is one 'law' for the lignites and low rank bituminous coals as expressed by Hilt's Rule and the depth-of-burial theory, and another, the Roberts-White Law, for the higher members of the coalification series.

CLASSIFICATION OF COALS

Numerous systems of coal classification have been proposed and are in current use (Brame & King, 1955, pp. 90–103; Francis, 1961, pp. 361–435; Kreulen, 1948, pp. 23–8; Krevelen, 1961, pp. 10–34). Apart from a simple macroscopic classification involving the recognition of the major members of the coalification series (pages 236–9) and their lithotypes (pages 223–5, Table 40), the systems are based on the chemical and technological properties of the coals. Many national classifications have been developed for commercial requirements and are accordingly designed to embrace the particular range of coals produced in the various countries. Consequently different parameters are often used so that correlation of the various systems employed can only be made on a general basis (Table 47).

Seyler's classification

This classification, established for the bituminous coals and anthracites, and one of the most compre-

hensive both from scientific and technological viewpoints, was originally proposed in 1899 and progressively extended and refined (Seyler, 1948, pp. 213–36). It is essentially based on the ultimate analyses, calculated to a dry, mineral-matter-free basis, and technological properties of coals. In its simple tabular form (Table 48) the carbon and hydrogen percentages are used as parameters. Thus four principal groups or 'species' are defined according to the carbon content.

Anthracitic group—including those coals with over 93·3 per cent carbon (d.m.m.f.).
Carbonaceous group—including those coals with between 93·3 and 91·2 per cent carbon (d.m.m.f.).
Bituminous group—including those coals with between 91·2 and 84·0 per cent carbon (d.m.m.f.).
Lignitous group—including those coals with between 84·0 and 75·0 per cent carbon (d.m.m.f.).
The group terms may be prefixed as *ortho-*, *meta-* or *para-* if the carbon contents are respectively considered as being normal, unusually high or low. According to their hydrogen contents the groups are subdivided into a number of varieties or 'genera'.
Anthracitic variety—with a hydrogen content less than 4·0 per cent (d.m.m.f.).
Carbonaceous variety—with a hydrogen content between 4·0 and 4·5 per cent (d.m.m.f.).
Semi-bituminous variety—with a hydrogen content between 4·5 and 5·0 per cent (d.m.m.f.).
Bituminous variety—with a hydrogen content between 5·0 and 5·8 per cent (d.m.m.f.).
Per-bituminous variety—with a hydrogen content greater than 5·8 per cent (d.m.m.f.).

Those coals such as the sapropelic types with abnormally high hydrogen percentages are indicated by the prefix *per-*, and varieties with low hydrogen contents are indicated by the prefix *sub-*. Thus a coal with carbon and hydrogen contents of respectively 88·0 and 4·8 per cent would be classed as a sub-ortho-bituminous coal.

The system is most fully expressed graphically in Seyler's celebrated coal chart (Fig. 19.9). In this chart the carbon and hydrogen axes form the major rectangular co-ordinates. If these values are known then the technological properties of a coal, as expressed by the volatile and oxygen contents, calorific values and B.S. swelling numbers, may be predicted from subsidiary oblique co-ordinates. The chart is particularly applicable to the bright coals although it is slightly less reliable for assessing the properties of the dull coals (Francis, 1961, pp. 367–71).

A.S.T.M. classification

The above system (American Society for Testing Materials, *Standard Specification for Classification of*

TABLE 48

Seyler's Coal Classification

(Dry, mineral-matter-free basis)

'Genera'	'Species'						
	Anthracitic	Carbonaceous	Bituminous			Lignitous	
			Meta-	Ortho-	Para-	Meta-	Ortho-
	Carbon over 93·3%	Carbon 93·3–91·2%	Carbon 91·2–89·0%	Carbon 89·0–87·0%	Carbon 87·0–84·0%	Carbon 84·0–80·0%	Carbon 80·0–75·0%
Per-bituminous genus (Hydrogen over 5·8%)	—	—	Per-bituminous (per-meta-bituminous)	Per-bituminous (per-ortho-bituminous)	Per-bituminous (per-para-bituminous)	Per-lignitous	Per-lignitous
Bituminous genus (Hydrogen 5·0–5·8%)	—	Pseudo-bituminous species	Meta-bituminous	Ortho-bituminous	Para-bituminous	Lignitous Meta-	Lignitous Ortho-
Semi-bituminous genus (Hydrogen 4·5–5·0%)	—	Semi-bituminous species (ortho-semi-bituminous)	Sub-bituminous (sub-meta-bituminous)	Sub-bituminous (sub-ortho-bituminous)	Sub-bituminous	Sub-lignitous Meta-	
Carbonaceous genus (Hydrogen 4·0–4·5%)	Semi-anthracitic species Dry steam coal	Carbonaceous species (ortho-carbonaceous)	Pseudo-carbonaceous (sub-meta-bituminous)	Pseudo-carbonaceous (sub-ortho-bituminous)	Pseudo-carbonaceous (sub-para-bituminous)		
Anthracitic genus (Hydrogen less than 4·0%)	Ortho-anthracite True anthracite	Pseudo-anthracite (sub-carbonaceous)	Pseudo-anthracite (sub-meta-bituminous)	Pseudo-anthracite (sub-ortho-bituminous)	Pseudo-anthracite (sub-para-bituminous)		

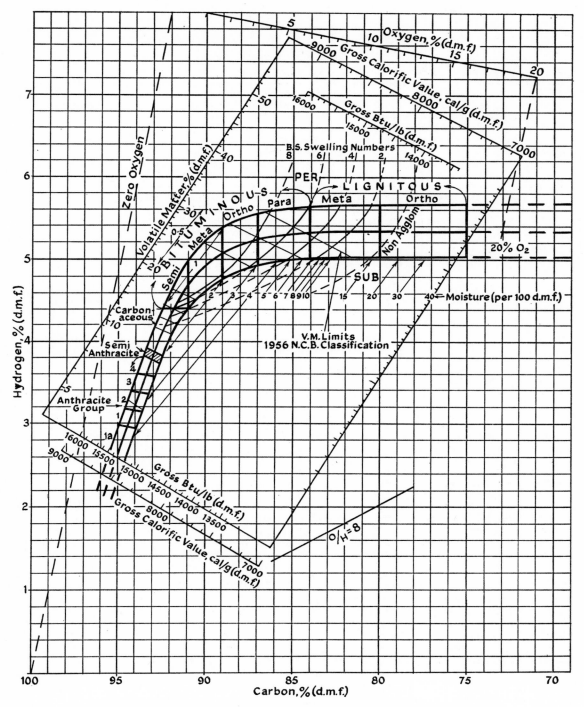

Fig. 19.9 Seyler's Coal Chart No. 47B. (British Coal Utilisation Research Association.)

TABLE 49

A.S.T.M. Classification of Coals[1]

F.C. = Fixed Carbon   V.M. = Volatile Matter   Btu = British thermal unit

Class	Group	Limits of fixed carbon or Btu mineral-matter-free basis	Requisite physical properties
Anthracitic	1. Meta-anthracite 2. Anthracite 3. Semi-anthracite	Dry F.C., 98% or more (Dry V.M., 2% or less) Dry F.C., 92% or more and less than 98% (Dry V.M., 8% or less and more than 2%) Dry F.C., 86% or more and less than 92% (Dry V.M., 14% or less and more than 8%)	Nonagglomerating[2]
Bituminous[3]	1. Low volatile bituminous coal 2. Medium volatile bituminous coal 3. High volatile A bituminous coal 4. High volatile B bituminous coal 5. High volatile C bituminous coal	Dry F.C., 78% or more and less than 86% (Dry V.M., 22% or less and more than 14%) Dry F.C., 69% or more and less than 78% (Dry V.M., 31% or less and more than 22%) Dry F.C., less than 69% (Dry V.M., more than 31%); and moist[4] Btu, 14000[5] or more Moist[4] Btu, 13000 or more and less than 14000[5] Moist Btu, 11000 or more and less than 13000[5]	Either agglomerating or nonweathering[6]
Sub-bituminous	1. Sub-bituminous A coal 2. Sub-bituminous B coal 3. Sub-bituminous C coal	Moist Btu, 11000 or more and less than 13000[5] Moist Btu, 9500 or more and less than 11000[5] Moist Btu, 8300 or more and less than 9500[5]	Both weathering and nonagglomerating
Lignitic	1. Lignite 2. Brown coal	Moist Btu, less than 8300 Moist Btu, less than 8300	Consolidated Unconsolidated

[1] This classification does not include a few coals which have unusual physical and chemical properties and which come within the limits of fixed carbon or Btu of the high-volatile bituminous and sub-bituminous ranks. All of these coals either contain less than 48 per cent dry, mineral-matter-free fixed carbon or have more than 15500 moist, mineral-matter-free Btu

[2] If agglomerating, classify in low-volatile group of the bituminous class

[3] It is recognized that there may be non-caking varieties in each group of the bituminous class

[4] Moist Btu refers to coal containing its natural bed moisture but not including visible water on the surface of the coal

[5] Coals having 69 per cent or more fixed carbon on the dry, mineral-matter-free basis shall be classified according to fixed carbon, regardless of Btu

[6] There are three varieties of coal in the high-volatile C bituminous coal group, namely, Variety 1, agglomerating and non-weathering; Variety 2, agglomerating and weathering; Variety 3, non-agglomerating and non-weathering

Coals by Rank, A.S.T.M. Designation: D 388–38: A.S.T.M. Standards 1958, Pt. 8, pp. 1078–83), widely used in North America, is suitable for the classification of coals from lignitic to anthracitic ranks (Table 49). High rank coals are classified according to their fixed carbon or volatile contents calculated on a dry, mineral-matter-free basis. Low rank coals with carbon contents less than 69 per cent (d.m.m.f.) are classified according to their calorific values calculated on a *moist*, mineral-matter-free basis. Since there are a large number of North American coals of this type the calorific values determined on a dry, mineral-matter-free basis would allow little differ-

entiation to be made. Accordingly, greater distinctions are apparent if the natural bed moisture of the coals is also considered. Caking (agglomerating), consolidation and weathering characteristics are used to differentiate between some groups.

N.C.B. coal classification

The above classification employed in Britain (*The Coal Classification System used by the National Coal Board*, 1964, N.C.B. Scientific Dept., Coal Survey) illustrates the rank of bituminous coals and anthracites and enables grouping according to their utilization (Table 50). The two parameters used for

Table 50

The Coal Classification System used by the National Coal Board
(Revision of 1964. Reproduced by permission of the N.C.B.)

Coals with ash of over 10 per cent must be cleaned before analysis for classification to give a maximum yield of coal with ash of 10 per cent or less.

Coal rank code			Volatile matter (d.m.m.f.) (per cent)	Gray-King coke type*	General description
Main class(es)	Class	Sub-class			
100			Under 9·1	A	*Anthracites*
	101†		Under 6·1	} A	
	102†		6·1–9·0		
200			9·1–19·5	A–G8	*Low-volatile steam coals*
	201		9·1–13·5	A–C	Dry steam coals
		201a	9·1–11·5	A–B	
		201b	11·6–13·5	B–C	
	202		13·6–15·0	B–G	Coking steam coals
	203		15·1–17·0	E–G4	
	204		17·1–19·5	G1–G8	
300			19·6–32·0	A–G9 and over	*Medium-volatile coals*
	301		19·6–32·0	G4 and over	Prime coking coals
		301a	19·6–27·5	} G4 and over	
		301b	27·6–32·0		
	302		19·6–32·0	G–G3	Medium volatile, medium-caking or weakly caking coals
	303		19·6–32·0	A–F	Medium-volatile, weakly caking to non-caking coals
400 to 900:			Over 32·0	A–G9 and over	*High-volatile coals*
400			Over 32·0	G9 and over	High-volatile, very strongly caking coals
	401		32·1–36·0	} G9 and over	
	402		Over 36·0		
500			Over 32·0	G5–G8	High-volatile, strongly caking coals
	501		32·1–36·0	} G5–G8	
	502		Over 36·0		
600			Over 32·0	G1–G4	High-volatile, medium-caking coals
	601		32·1–36·0	} G1–G4	
	602		Over 36·0		
700			Over 32·0	E–G	High-volatile, weakly caking coals
	701		32·1–36·0	} E–G	
	702		Over 36·0		
800			Over 32·0	C–D	High-volatile, very weakly caking coals
	801		32·1–36·0	} C–D	
	802		Over 36·0		
900			Over 32·0	A–B	High-volatile, non-caking coals
	901		32·1–36·0	} A–B	
	902		Over 36·0		

* Coals with volatile matter of under 19·6 per cent are classified by using the parameter of volatile matter alone; the Gray-King coke types quoted for these coals indicate the general ranges found in practice, and are not criteria for classification

† In order to divide anthracites into two classes, it is sometimes convenient to use a hydrogen content of 3·35 per cent (d.m.m.f.) instead of a volatile matter of 6·0 per cent as the limiting criterion. In the original Coal Survey rank coding system the anthracites were divided into four classes then designated 101, 102, 103 and 104. Although the present division into two classes satisfies most requirements it may sometimes be necessary to recognize more than two classes

NOTES

[1] Coals that have been affected by igneous intrusions ('heat-altered' coals) occur mainly in classes 100, 200 and 300, and when recognized should be distinguished by adding the suffix H to the coal rank code, e.g. 102H, 201bH

[2] Coals that have been oxidized by weathering may occur in any class, and when recognized should be distinguished by adding the suffix W to the coal rank code, e.g. 801W

Table 51

International Classification of Hard Coals

The first figure of the code number indicates the class of the coal, determined by volatile-matter content up to 33% V.M. and by calorific parameter above 33% V.M.
The second figure indicates the group of coal, determined by coking properties.
The third figure indicates the subgroup, determined by coking properties.

Group number	Groups (determined by coking properties) — Free-swelling index (crucible-swelling number)	Roga index		Subgroup number	Subgroups (determined by coking properties) — Dilatometer	Gray-King
3	>4	>45		5	>140	>G$_8$
				4	>50–140	G$_5$–G$_8$
				3	>0–50	G$_1$–G$_4$
				2	≧0	E–G
2	2½–4	>20–45		3	>0–50	G$_1$–G$_4$
				2	≧0	E–G
				1	Contraction only	B–D
1	1–2	>5–20		2	≧0	E–G
				1	Contraction only	B–D
0	0–½	0–5		0	Non-softening	A

Code numbers (columns = Class 0 to 9):

Group / Subgroup	0	1	2	3	4	5	6	7	8	9
3 / 5					435	535	635			
3 / 4				334	434	534	634			
3 / 3				333	433	533	633	733		
3 / 2				332a / 332b	432	532	632	732	832	
2 / 3				323	423	523	623	723	823	
2 / 2			212	322	422	522	622	722	822	
2 / 1			211	321	421	521	621	721	821	
1 / 2				312	412	512	612	712	812	
1 / 1		100	200	311	411	511	611	711	811	
0 / 0				300	400	500	600	700	800	900

Class indicators: V$_C$, V$_B$, V$_A$, V$_D$, VI$_A$, VI$_B$, VII, VI, III, II, I(A,B)

CLASSES

CLASS PARAMETERS		0	1	2	3	4	5	6	7	8	9
CLASS NUMBER →		0	1	2	3	4	5	6	7	8	9
Volatile matter (dry, ash-free) →		0–3	>3–10 (>3–6·5 / >6·5–10)	>10–14	>14–20 (>14–16 / >16–20)	>20–28	>28–33	>33	>33	>33	>33
Calorific parameter^a →		—	—	—	—	—	—	>13950	>12960–13950	>10980–12960	>10260–10980

(Determined by volatile matter up to 33% V.M. and by calorific parameter above 33% V.M.)

As an indication, the following classes have an approximate volatile-matter content of:
Class 6 33–41% volatile matter
7 33–44%   "   "   "
8 35–50%   "   "   "
9 42–50%   "   "   "

Note: (i) Where the ash content of coal is too high to allow classification according to the present systems, it must be reduced by laboratory float-and-sink method (or any other appropriate means). The specific gravity selected for flotation should allow a maximum yield of coal with 5 to 10 per cent of ash.
(ii) 332a . . . >14–16% V.M.
332b . . . >16–20% V.M.

^{a} Gross calorific value on moist, ash-free basis (30 °C, 96% relative humidity) Btu/lb.

classifying coals by this system are the volatile matter of the dry, mineral-matter-free coal and its caking properties as determined by the Gray-King coke type. The maximum ash content permitted for coal analysed for classification is 10 per cent. Coals with ash in excess of this limit should be cleaned before analysis. The classification is expressed numerically by three-figure code numbers known as coal rank codes. Using the criteria of volatile content four broad divisions may be recognized:

Anthracite group – main class number 100 – under 9·1 per cent volatile matter (d.m.m.f.);
Low volatile group – main class number 200 – volatile content between 9·1 and 19·5 per cent (d.m.m.f.);
Medium volatile group – main class number 300 – volatile content between 19·6 and 32·0 per cent (d.m.m.f.);
High volatile group – main class numbers 400–900 – with volatile contents more than 32·0 per cent (d.m.m.f.).

Subdivision into classes and sub-classes is made on the basis of the Gray-King coke type and narrower ranges of volatile matter. Classes are indicated numerically, from 1 to 4, as the third digit of the code, and sub-classes by the suffix 'a' or 'b'.

For example if a coal were reported as having a volatile content of 37·7 per cent (d.m.m.f.) and a Gray-King coke type E, then the N.C.B. coal rank code would be 702. Another coal with a similar coke type but a volatile content of 35·1 per cent (d.m.m.f.) would be placed in class 701.

E.C.E. international classification

After the Second World the United Nations Economic Commission for Europe appointed a committee to establish an international coal classification to enable the accurate evaluation of coals produced in different countries for purposes of international trade. Two classification systems have been proposed for hard and soft coals with calorific values respectively above and below 10 260 Btu calculated on a moist, ash-free basis. Both systems employ numerical codes of three digits.

Hard coal classification. In the classification (Table 51), (U.N.E.C.E., *International Classification of Hard Coals by Type*, E/ECE/247, E/ECE/COAL/110: Pub. Sales No. 1956, 11E.4, 1956), the major classes of coal, approximating to the rank, are indicated by the first digit. The classes are calculated according to the volatile matter content on a dry, ash-free basis or, when this exceeds 33 per cent, according to the calorific value on a moist, ash-free basis. Subdivision into groups (second digit) and sub-groups (third digit) is based respectively on the crucible swelling numbers and Gray-King coke types. The complete system also embraces a more simple classification in

TABLE 52

International Classification of Soft Coals
(Gross Calorific Values below 10260 Btu[1])

Group number	Group parameter tar yield % (d.a.f.)	Code number					
40	25	1040	1140	1240	1340	1440	1540
30	20–25	1030	1130	1230	1330	1430	1530
20	15–20	1020	1120	1220	1320	1420	1520
10	10–15	1010	1110	1210	1310	1410	1510
00	10 and less	1000	1100	1200	1300	1400	1500
	Class Number	10	11	12	13	.14	15
Class Parameter	Total Moisture % (a.f.)	20 and less	>20 −30	>30 −40	>40 −50	>50 −60	>60 −70

NOTES

The total moisture content refers to freshly mined coal

For internal purposes, coals with a gross calorific value over 10 260 Btu, considered in the country of origin as brown coals but classified as hard coals for international purposes, may be classified under this system, to ascertain, in particular, their suitability for processing

When the total moisture content is over 30 per cent, the gross calorific value is always below 10 260 Btu.

[1] Moist, ash-free basis (30 °C/96 per cent relative humidity)

which a number of statistical divisions, designated by Roman numerals, have been arranged broadly to relate coals having the same general characteristics.

Soft coal classification. The classification (Table 52), (U.N.E.C.E., *Mining and Upgrading of Brown Coal in Europe – Developments and Prospects*, pp. 14–15, E/ECE/297, E/ECE/COAL/124: Pub. Sales No. 1957, 11.E/Mim. 20, 1957) covers those coals with calorific values of less than 10 260 Btu moist and ash-free. Classification is expressed numerically in a four figure code. The classes of coals, approximating to their ranks and indicated by the first two digits of the code number, are calculated according to the total moisture contents of ash-free coals. Total moisture is defined as that present in freshly mined coal. Sub-division into groups as indicated by the last two digits of the code number is made according to the yield of tar in low temperature carbonization.

Indian coal classification

The coal classification (Table 53) adopted in India (Indian Standards Institute, New Delhi) consists of the subdivision of anthracites, bituminous coals and lignites into groups. The latter are based on the volatile contents and calorific values, which are both assessed on a unit coal, that is, on a dry, mineral-matter-free basis, together with the moisture content and caking nature of the coals. Thus the bituminous coals are divided into six groups designated B_1 to B_6. Coals of group B_6 are comparatively rare and are considered as sub-bituminous since they form a transitional group approaching lignites. Further work is being carried out to evolve a coal rank code.

A less refined classification (Table 54), (*Coal Board Manual*, Calcutta, 1962, pp. 86–7) is adopted by the Indian Coal Board solely for commercial purposes. The coals are classified into grades with reference to their purity as assessed from their ash and moisture contents.

REFERENCES

BRAME, J. S. S. & J. G. KING (1955) *Fuel, Solid, Liquid and Gaseous*, 5th ed., London, Arnold.

TABLE 53

General Classification of Indian Coals
(Indian Standards Institute)

Type	Sub-division or group		Range of volatiles, percentage at 900° ± 15°C (Unit coal basis)	Range of gross calorific value, kcal/kg (Btu/lb) (unit coal basis)	Range of Moisture percentage (mineral-free coal basis)		Chief uses
	Name	Group symbol			Near-saturation at 96 per cent RH at 40° C	Air-dried at 60 per cent RH at 40° C	
(1)	(2)	(3)	(4)	(5)	(6)	(7)	(8)
Anthracites	Anthracite	A_1	3 to 10	8 330 to 8 670 (15 000 to 15 600)	2 to 4	1 to 3	Gasification, producers, domestic stoves, and where intense local heat and no smoke are required
	Semi-anthracite	A_2	10 to 15	8 440 to 8 780 (15 200 to 15 800)	1·5 to 3	1 to 2	
Bituminous coals (caking strength increasing from B_5 to B_2)	Low volatile (caking)	B_1	15 to 20	8 670 to 8 890 (15 600 to 16 000)	1·5 to 2·5	0·5 to 1·5	Carbonization for metallurgical coke; typical coking coals
	Medium volatile	B_2	20 to 32	8 440 to 8 780 (15 200 to 15 800)	1·5 to 2·5	0·5 to 2	
	High volatile (caking)	B_3	32+	8 280 to 8 610 (14 900 to 15 500)	2 to 5	1 to 3	Coking coals, gas coals gasification
	High volatile (semi-caking)	B_4	32+	8 060 to 8 440 (14 500 to 15 200)	5 to 10	3 to 7	Gas coals, gasification, long flame heating
	High volatile (non-caking)	B_5	32+	7 500 to 8 060 (13 500 to 14 500)	10 to 20	7 to 14	Steam-raising, gasification, long flame heating
Sub-bituminous coals	Non-caking: slacking on weathering	B_6	32+	6 940 to 7 500 (12 500 to 13 500)	20 to 30	10 to 20	Steam-raising and gasification
Lignites or brown coals	Normal lignite	L_1	45 to 55	6 110 to 6 940 (11 000 to 12 500)	30 to 70	10 to 25	Steam-raising, briquetting, gasification, distillation
	Canneloid lignite	L_2	55 to 65	6 940 to 7 500 (12 500 to 13 500)	30 to 70	10 to 25	

TABLE 54

Indian Coal Grade Classification

Region	Horizon	Coking properties	Percentage moisture and ash[1]	Percentage ash[1]	Grade
Collieries situated within the states of West Bengal and Bihar	Raniganj Series		−17·5	—	Selected Grade A
			17·5–19·0	—	Selected Grade B
			19·0–24·0	—	Grade I
			24·0–28·0	—	Grade II
	Horizons other than Raniganj Series	Coking Coal		−13·0	Grade A
				13·0–14·0	Grade B
				14·0–15·0	Grade C
				15·0–16·0	Grade D
				16·0–17·0	Grade E
				17·0–18·0	Grade F
				18·0–19·0	Grade G
				19·0–20·0	Grade H
				20·0–21·0	Grade HH
				21·0–22·0	Grade J
				22·0–23·0	Grade K
				23·0–24·0	Grade L
		Non-coking Coal		−15·0	Selected Grade A
				15·0–17·0	Selected Grade B
				17·0–20·0	Grade I
				20·0–24·0	Grade II
				24·0–28·0	Grade III-A
				28·0–35·0	Grade III-B
Collieries situated within the states of Madhya Pradesh, Orissa, Maharashtra and Gujarat			−19·0	—	Selected Grade
			19·0–24·0		Grade I
			24·0–28·0		Grade II
			28·0–35·0		Grade III

[1] Mineral having ash and moisture content in excess of 35 per cent shall not be vendible as coal

REFERENCES

CLOUGH, C. T. & J. KIRKPATRICK (1909) Scottish 'eenie' coal, *Trans. Instn Min. Engrs* **37**, 2–11.

EDWARDS, A. B. (1945) The composition of Victorian brown coals, *Proc. Australas. Inst. Min. Engrs* **140**, 205–80.

FRANCIS, W. (1961) *Coal*, 2nd ed., London, Arnold.

GAGE, M. & J. A. BARTRUM (1942) Cone-in-cone and ring-fracture in coal from Greymouth, New Zealand, *N.Z. Jl Sci. Technol.* **24**, 86b–98b.

HICKLING, G. (1927) The chemical relations of the principal varieties of coal, *Trans. Instn Min. Engrs* **72**, 261–76.

HICKLING, G. (1932) The properties of coals as determined by their mode of origin, *J. Inst. Fuel* **5**, 318–28.

KREULEN, D. J. W. (1948) *Elements of Coal Chemistry*, 1st ed., Rotterdam, Nijgh & van Ditmar.

KREVELEN, D. W. Van (1961) *Coal*, 1st ed., Amsterdam, Elsevier.

MEENEN, J. & D. A. WEBB (editors) (1957) *A View of Ireland*, Dublin, British Association for the Advancement of Science.

MILLOT, J. O'N., F. W. COPE & H. BERRY (1946) The seams encountered in a deep boring at Pie Rough, near Keele, North Staffordshire, *Trans. Instn Min. Engrs* **105**, 528–70.

MOORE, E. S. (1940) *Coal*, 2nd ed., New York, Wiley.

NEAVEL, R. C. & G. K. GUENNEL (1960) Indiana paper coal: composition and deposition, *J. sedim. Petrol.* **30**, 241–8.

NELSON, A. (1963) Mining brown coal in Australia, *Colliery Guard.* **206**, 502–8.

REEVES, F. (1928) The carbon-ratio theory in the light of Hilt's law, *Bull. Am. Ass. Petrol. Geol.* **12**, 795–823.

ROBERTS, J. (1950) The thermo-dynamics of Hilt's 'law', *Colliery Guard.* **180**, 325–9.

ROGOFF, M. H., I. WENDER & R. B. ANDERSON (1962) Microbiology of coal, *Inf. Circ. U.S. Bur. Mines.* 8075.

SEYLER, C. A. (1948) The past and future of coal—the contribution of petrology, *Proc. S. Wales Inst. Engrs* **63**, 213–36.

STADNICHENKO, T. (1934) Progressive regional metamorphism of the lower Kittanning coal bed of western Pennsylvania, *Econ. Geol.* **29**, 511–43.

SUGGATE, R. P. (1956) Depth—volatile relations in coalfields, *Geol. Mag.* **93**, 201–17.

SUGGATE, R. P. (1959) New Zealand coals, their geological setting and its influence on their properties, *N.Z. Dep. sci. indstr. Res. Bull.* **134**.

TROTTER, F. M. (1952) The genesis of a fuel series of rising rank: top peat to fat bituminous coal, *Proc. Yorks. geol. Soc.* **28**, 125–63.

TROTTER, F. M. (1954) The genesis of the high rank coals, *Proc. Yorks. geol. Soc.* **29**, 267–303.

WHITE, D. (1925) Progressive regional carbonization of coals. *Trans. Am. Inst. Min. mettal. Engrs* **71**, 253–79.

Appendix
Sources of Geological Information

APPENDIX
SOURCES OF GEOLOGICAL INFORMATION

The larger mining organizations employ their own specialist geologists who are available for consultation with regard to specific geological problems encountered during mining. In the case of smaller concerns advice may usually be obtained from the various national or provincial geological surveys. Otherwise, information is available in a voluminous literature which, owing to the diverse nature of the subject, involving both regional and general studies, is scattered throughout many official publications and scientific journals. The student should at least be aware of the major publications relevant to the stratigraphy and structure of his area, and accordingly a brief synopsis is given of this aspect. An invaluable comprehensive review of the subject is that of Mason (1953). In addition, references to most stratigraphic divisions can be obtained from the *International Stratigraphic Lexicon*, a major reference work on world stratigraphy published by the Centre National de la Recherche Scientifique, 13 quai Anatole-France, Paris 7e, for the International Geological Congress. The following example from Volume 3, Part 8, concerned with India, Pakistan and adjacent areas is illustrative of the information given:

IRON – STONE SHALES   .   .   . Permian
(India)

Name given by W. T. Blanford (*Mem. Geol. Surv. Ind.*, vol. 3, p. 28, 1861) to a series of carbonaceous shales with ironstones lying between the Raniganj stage above, and the Barakar stage below in the Raniganj coalfield. These are also known as Barren Measures. The thickness is given by Blanford as 1400 ft but reduced to 1200 ft by C. S. Fox (*Mem. Geol. Surv. Ind.* **58**, p. 111, 1931) by transfer of the basal beds to the Barakars. The flora is scanty (*Glossopteris*, *Gangamopteris*, and *Noeggerathiopsis*). The age is probably Middle Permian.

(T. H. Holland, 1926; M. S. Krishnan and K. Jacob.)

GREAT BRITAIN

A considerable number of geological and mining societies publish information of importance to the coal mining industry. The major sources of information are the Geological Survey and the National Coal Board.

GEOLOGICAL SURVEY

(*Headquarters*—Exhibition Road, South Kensington, London S.W.7, and 19, Grange Terrace, Edinburgh, 9.)

Publications

(1) *Maps.* All the coalfields have been geologically surveyed and for many areas published maps, on the scales of 6 in to 1 mile and 1 in to 1 mile, are available. *Solid* and *Drift Editions* of each sheet are published where the superficial deposits are considerable. Occasionally the two are combined as a *Solid with Drift Edition*. Geological Survey maps may be purchased from Messrs. E. Stanford, Ltd., 12–14 Long Acre, London W.C.2., from whom a list of such maps in print may be obtained, or from any authorized agent.

(2) *Memoirs.* The *One-Inch Sheet Memoirs* are the 'standard' survey publications describing the geology of the relevant 1 in to 1 mile geological maps. Several editions of the memoirs describing coalfield areas may have been produced and for most purposes the latest edition should be consulted. The recently published third edition of the memoir describing the one-inch Geological Survey Sheet No. 248, England and Wales (Woodland & Evans, 1964, *The Country around Pontypridd and Maesteg*) may be taken as illustrative of the wealth of detail recorded. In this memoir, describing some 216 mile^2 of the S. Wales coalfield, the chapter headings and relevant number of pages are:

Introduction—5 pages;
Millstone Grit Series and earlier Carboniferous beds—13 pages;
Coal Measures: General—58 pages;
Lower Coal Measures: Details—30 pages;
Middle Coal Measures: Details—69 pages;
Pennant Measures: Details—62 pages;
Mesozoic—6 pages;
Structure—38 pages;
Pleistocene and Recent—19 pages;
Economic Geology—8 pages.

This detailed account may be further supplemented by consulting the many references given at the end of each chapter.

A series of *Economic Memoirs* are also published which include comprehensive accounts of coalfields and other regions of economic importance. They embrace several One-Inch sheets.

(3) *Regional Handbooks.* Eighteen handbooks are published as a general account of the geology of Great Britain. Although these are less detailed than the memoirs they provide useful introductions to the major stratigraphical and structural features of the various coalfields.

(4) *Bulletins.* Over twenty bulletins have now been

published and each contain about five papers on a variety of topics. A number of these describe recent advances in the detailed stratigraphy of several British coalfields. In such cases they may be used to supplement information contained in the previously published memoirs.

The above publications may be purchased direct from any of H.M. Stationary Offices (London office—York House, Kingsway, W.C.2). A sectional list is also available of those publications which are in print.

NATIONAL COAL BOARD

Until 1947 a systematic physical and chemical survey of British coal resources was carried out by the Fuel Research Board of the Department of Scientific and Industrial Research. Much of this information was published in over fifty *Fuel Research Papers*. Many of these, which are all out of print but obtainable from most large libraries, supplied descriptions and analyses of the principal seams and sometimes also dealt with specific points of correlation. Since the nationalization of the major part of the British coal industry the work has been taken over by the Coal Survey, a branch of the Scientific Department of the National Coal Board. An ambitious programme is being followed in the publication of a series of *Seam Folios*, consisting of maps, diagrams, tables and text summarizing the results of current research (Fenton, *et al.*, 1962). The folios present an invaluable summary of British coal resources and assess the geological features and technological properties of the major coal seams. For each coalfield a geological map, a transparent Ordnance Survey topographical map of the area on the same scale, and representative vertical sections showing the seam sequences have been prepared. Each important seam is illustrated by a series of maps giving the following information:

Physical structure;
Seam thickness;
Presence and thickness of dirt partings;
Ash content;
Sulphur content.

Additional maps provided for many seams summarize the following:

Depth relative to Ordnance Datum;
Coal rank;
Volatile matter content;
Calorific value;
Moisture content;
Carbon content;
Chlorine content;
Phosphorus content;
Sampling points;
Areas of working (shown as transparent overlays on the same scale as all the previous maps).

According to the nature of the coalfield the maps are constructed on the scales of 2 in, 1 in or $\frac{1}{2}$ in to 1 mile. The maps for each seam are all of the same scale so that they may be readily compared and are supplemented by descriptive texts and abundant analyses. Copies of the maps illustrative at least of his particular coalfield should be examined by the advanced mining student. The following seam folios are at present in print and available for purchase from the Scientific Department of the N.C.B. at Queensborough House, 12–18, Albert Embankment, London, S.E.1.

Scottish Coalfields
Wilsontown Main Seam
Fifteen Foot Seam
Bannockburn Upper Main Seam
Bannockburn Main Seam
Meiklehill Main Seam

Northumberland Coalfield
Beaumont Seam
Top Busty Seam
Bottom Busty Seam

Durham Coalfield
Busty (Top Busty and Bottom Busty) Seams
Hutton Seams

Yorkshire Coalfield
Fenton (Top Fenton and Low Fenton) Seams
Parkgate Seam

Lancashire Coalfield
Crombouke Seam
Rams Seam
Trencherbone and Peacock Seams

N. Staffordshire Coalfield
Banbury Seam
Bowling Alley Seam
Moss Seam

Coalbrookdale Coalfield
Top Coal

Leicestershire Coalfield
Middle Lount Seam
Yard Seam

Warwickshire Coalfield
Two Yard and Thin Rider Seams
Seven Feet and Thin Seams
Bench Group of Seams

Nottinghamshire and North Derbyshire Coalfield
Threequarters Seam

S. Wales Coalfield
Five Feet and Gellideg Seams
Nine Feet Seam

Kent Coalfield
Milyard Seam

Several series of abstracts are also published by the National Coal Board. Of these, *Abstracts C: Coal and Mining Geology*, published periodically by the Intelligence Group, provide most useful summaries of current world literature on the subject.

MINING AND GEOLOGICAL SOCIETIES

The premier mining publication is the *Transactions of the Institute of Mining Engineers* (*Trans. Instn Min. Engrs*) published by that institute and incorporating papers delivered at meetings of federated institutes and societies. The Transactions contain numerous papers concerned with the stratigraphy and structure of the British coalfields. A number of geological papers of relevance to the coalfield are also published in the *Proceedings of the South Wales Institute of Engineers* (*Proc. S. Wales Inst. Engrs*).

The Quarterly Journal of the Geological Society of London (*Quart. Jl geol. Soc. Lond.*) is the main publication of the principal geological society. Although most of the stratigraphic papers published in recent years are of a more fundamental and regional, rather than local, character, they are occasionally concerned with the British coalfields. There are a number of provincial geological societies which deal mostly with items of local interest. Their publications, which are sometimes of relevance to the coal mining industry, include the *Geological Journal* (*Geol. J.*) continuing the *Liverpool and Manchester Geological Journal* (*L'pool. Manchr geol. J.*), the *Proceedings of the Yorkshire Geological Society* (*Proc. Yorks. geol. Soc.*) and the *Transactions of the Geological Society of Glasgow* (*Trans. geol. Soc. Glasg.*).

OTHER SOURCES

The most recent review of the geology of the British coalfields is that of Trueman (1954), which lists also a comprehensive series of references to detailed accounts published up to that date. More general discussions of British stratigraphy are those of Craig (1965) and Wells and Kirkaldy (1966).

OTHER COUNTRIES

The following selected publications of the major coal-producing and English-speaking foreign and Commonwealth countries are given as a brief guide to the literature:

AUSTRALIA

Apart from the Bureau of Mineral Resources (*Bulletins, Summary Reports, Reports* and *Quarterly Review*), official sources of information are the various State surveys. Geological Survey publications of the individual States relevant to the stratigraphy of the major coal deposits are as follows:

New South Wales—*Bulletins* and *memoirs;*
Queensland—*Queensland Government Mining Journal;*
Tasmania—*Bulletins,* notably No. 44—*Geology and Mineral Resources of Tasmania; Reports* and *Records;*
Victoria – *Mining and Geological Journal,* published by the Department of Mines.

A comprehensive account of the geology of Australia is that of David (1950). The relevant chapters on the Australian coal deposits are followed by extensive reference lists.

CANADA

The Geological Survey of Canada issue *Memoirs, Bulletins, Papers* and an Economic Geology series which contain details and references to the geology of the various coalfields. Publications of the geological surveys of the individual Canadian provinces should also be consulted. A general account of the geology of Canada with references to more detailed publications concerning the coal deposits, is that of Reed (1949, pp. 294–409).

INDIA

Publications of the Geological Survey of India include *Memoirs,* (Volume 77 of the *Memoirs* published in 1946 is a catalogue of survey publications and an index of geological maps up to March 1946), *Records* and *Bulletins.* Society journals containing relevant information include the *Quarterly Journal of the Geological, Mining and Metallurgical Society of India* (*Quart. J. geol. Soc. India*) and the *Transactions of the Mining, Geological and Metallurgical Institute of India* (*Trans. Min. geol. metall. Inst. India*). General accounts of Indian geology, accompanied by some references to coalfield literature, are those of Krishnan (1956) and Wadia (1953). A more comprehensive treatment of the Indian coalfields including up-to-date references is given by Sharma & Ram (1966, 2nd ed.).

NEW ZEALAND

Some coalfields are covered by the *Bulletins* of the New Zealand Geological Survey and a useful review is that of Willet (in Williams, 1965, pp. 279–329). Other coalfields are described in various volumes of the *New Zealand Journal of Science and Technology* (*N.Z. Jl Sci. Technol.*). General accounts of the geology of the country are given by Reed (1949, pp. 632–66) and Williams (1965, pp. 1–5).

NIGERIA

The principal publications of the Geological Survey of Nigeria which include accounts of the coalfields are the *Bulletins* and *Annual Reports.* A comprehensive account of the coal resources was published recently (Swardt & Casey, 1963). A general account of the geology of the country is given by Reed (1949, pp. 198–207).

SOUTH AFRICA

The publications of the Geological Survey of South Africa include a number of *Memoirs* and *Bulletins* relative to the coal deposits. A further series of miscellaneous unnumbered bulletins and maps include *The Mineral Resources of the Union of South Africa* (1940, 3rd ed.) which contains an account of the coal deposits. The *Transactions and Proceedings of the Geological Society of South Africa* (*Trans. geol. Soc. S. Afr.*) contain several useful papers of relevance to the subject. Brief accounts, together with references, of southern and central African coalfields are given by Pelletier (1964). General accounts of the geology of the country together with adjacent areas are those of Du Toit (1954) and Haughton (1963).

USA

The *Bulletins* and *Professional Papers* of the United States Geological Survey include descriptions of the major coalfields. Individual State geological survey publications should also be consulted as well as the numerous publications of the Bureau of Mines which contain much of significance to the coal-mining geologist. The very extensive American geological literature is listed by Mason (1953, pp. 39–61). General textbooks, mainly concerned with North American stratigraphy, include those of Dunbar (1960), Eardley (1962), Kay & Colbert (1965) and Moore (1949).

REFERENCES

CRAIG, G. Y. (Editor) (1965) *The Geology of Scotland*, 1st ed., Edinburgh, Oliver & Boyd.

DAVID, T. W. E. (1950) *The Geology of the Commonwealth of Australia*, 1st ed., London, Arnold.

DUNBAR, C. O. (1960) *Historical Geology*, 2nd ed., New York, Wiley.

EARDLEY, A. J. (1962) *Structural Geology of North America*, 2nd ed., New York, Harper.

FENTON, G. W., ADAMS, H. F. & P. L. RUMSBY (1962) The mapping and appraisal of the characteristics of British coal seams, *Trans. Instn Min. Engrs* 121, 454–64.

HAUGHTON, S. H. (1963) *The Stratigraphic History of Africa south of the Sahara*, 1st ed., Edinburgh, Oliver & Boyd.

KAY, M. & E. H. COLBERT (1965) *Stratigraphy and Life History*, 1st ed., New York, Wiley.

KRISHNAN, M. S. (1956) *Geology of India and Burma*, 3rd ed., Madras, Higginbothams.

MASON, B. (1953) *The Literature of Geology*, 1st ed., New York, American Museum of Natural History.

MOORE, R. C. (1958) *Introduction to Historical Geology*, 2nd ed. London, McGraw-Hill.

PELLETIER, R. A. (1964) *Mineral Resources of South-Central Africa*, 1st ed., Capetown, O.U.P.

REED, R. R. C. (1949) *The Geology of the British Empire*, 2nd ed., London, Arnold.

SHARMA, N. L. & K. S. V. RAM (1966). *Introduction to the Geology of Coal and Indian Coalfields*, 2nd ed., Jaipur, Oriental.

SWARDT, A. M. J. DE & O. P. CASEY (1963) The coal resources of Nigeria, *Bull. geol. Surv. Nigeria* 28.

TOIT, A. L. DU, (1954) *The Geology of South Africa*, 3rd ed., Edinburgh, Oliver & Boyd.

TRUEMAN, A. E. (1954) *The Coalfields of Great Britain*, 1st ed., London, Arnold.

WADIA, D. N. (1953) *Geology of India*, 3rd ed., London, Macmillan.

WELLS, A. K. & J. W. KIRKALDY (1966) *Outline of Historical Geology*, 5th ed., London, Allen & Unwin (Murby).

WILLIAMS, G. J. (1965) *Economic Geology of New Zealand*, 8th Commonwealth Min. Met. Congr., 4.

INDEX